A GUIDE TO GRAPHIC PRINT PRODUCTION

»But I, on the other hand, could perhaps measure the color as well: I might guess it had a wavelength of five hundred forty millionths of a millimeter; and then this green would apparently be captured and nailed to a specific point! But then it gets away from me again, because this ground color also has something material about it that can't be expressed in words of color at all, since it's different from the same green in silk or wool. And now we're back at the profound discovery that green grass is just grass green!«

Robert Musil in <u>The Man Without Qualities</u>

Musil, Robert, Transl. Sophie Wilkins and Burton Pike. The Man Without Qualities, Volume II "From the Posthumous Papers" Part 1, Chapter 46, p. 1185. First Vintage International Edition, 1996, New York.

JOHN WILEY & SONS, INC.

A GUIDE TO GRAPHIC PRINT PRODUCTION

This book is printed on acid-free paper.

Published by John Wiley & Sons, Inc. Hoboken, New Jersey.

English language edition distributed exclusively throughout the World by John Wiley & Sons.

Published simultaneously in Canada.

This publication is designed to provide accurate and authoritative information in regard to the subject matter covered. It is sold with the understanding that the publisher is not engaged in rendering professional services. If professional advice or other expert assistance is required, the services of a competent professional person should be sought.

Wiley also publishes its books in a variety of electronic formats. Some content that appears in print may not be available in electronic books. For more information about Wiley products, visit our web site at www.wiley.com.

Text	Kaj Johansson, Peter Lundberg, Robert Ryberg. www.kapero.com
	Eva Anderson, Frank J. Martinez
Design	Robert Ryberg
Illustrations	Robert Ryberg
Photography	Albert Håkansson, Ballaleica – food, Tomas Ek, Fälth & Hässler – technique
	Joanna Hornatowska, STFI – close-ups, Johanna Löwenhamn – portraits
	Chapter opener images for chapters 2, 3, 8, 9, 11, 16 and 17 © FoodPix
Translations	Johanna Ekberg
Editorial Consultants	Ken Eklund, Elizabeth Levy, Rick Tharp, Randy West
Headings	DIN Engschrift
Main typeface	Janson Text
Paper	MultiArt Silk 130 g/m^2
Printing	Fälth & Hässler, Värnamo, Sweden, 2002. www.falthohassler.se
Image scanning	IGP and Colorcraft, Stockholm – food
	Pre Press Center, Lund – technique

ISBN-0-471-27347-3

Printed in Sweden

10 9 8 7 6 5 4 3 2 1

PREFACE

All steps in the graphic print process affect each other and involve many different people. Thus successful graphic print production is mainly about communication and cooperation. And communication is easier if you have mutual references.

This book helps you to understand the whole process and what to accomplish with your tools. And it gives you the general overview you need to communicate accurately with all people involved.

The book is the ultimate guide for printers, prepress experts, publishers and designers as well as print buyers and marketing and communication departments. It is also a perfect textbook and teaching aid for universities and courses in graphic print production.

We are very happy that this book is now published in the US and the UK. German, Spanish and Portugese editions will follow.

Good luck with your communication!

STOCKHOLM OCTOBER 2002

Kaj Johansson
Peter Lundberg
Robert Ryberg

Please contact us with thoughts, ideas and suggestions at
http://www.kapero.com

▶ **WHERE IN THE PRODUCTION?**
Each chapter is introduced with a page outlining which steps in the graphic production process that particular chapter touches upon.

▶ **PAGE REFERENCES AND THUMB INDEX**
On the first page of each chapter, there are page references to the different headings within the chapter. You will also find a thumb index to make the book easier to use.

HOW TO USE THIS BOOK

This book is written so that the content of the chapters approximates the steps in the graphic production cycle. Each chapter begins with a page listing all the different steps of graphic production, and the steps that a particular chapter focuses on are highlighted. The book is written so that you can read straight through from beginning to end or skip around to find just the specific information you need. As you get further into the book, however, it is assumed that you know about the stages of graphic production covered in preceding chapters.

We use references in the text when a field is brought up that is covered in another part of the book. A reference looks like this: [see Chapter title Subchapter number], for example [see Printing 13.2]. If a reference directs you within the same chapter, we have removed the chapter title in the reference, for example: [see 10.3.2].

When we point out specific commands or menus in software or operating systems, they are set with the typeface American Typewriter. For example, it can look like this: When you are ready to print select File -> Print. The arrow means that Print is a menu found under File.

Enjoy reading and good luck with your graphic productions.

CONTENT

1
2
3
4
5
6
7
8
9
10
11
12
13
14
15
16
17
18

INTRODUCTION

CHAPTER 1 INTRODUCTION THIS IS A BOOK ABOUT GRAPHIC PRODUCTION. GRAPHIC PRODUCTION, SIMPLY PUT, IS A SERIES OF STEPS FOR CREATING A PRINTED PRODUCT, FROM THE CONCEPTION AND EXECUTION OF A DESIGN THROUGH EDITING AND PRODUCTION OF THE FINISHED PRODUCT. IN MANY CASES, EACH STEP OF THE GRAPHIC PRODUCTION PROCESS IS PERFORMED BY A DIFFERENT PROFESSIONAL. TO ACHIEVE THE BEST PRODUCT POSSIBLE, EVERYONE CONTRIBUTING TO THE PROCESS HAS TO BE ABLE TO COMMUNICATE EFFECTIVELY WITH ONE ANOTHER.

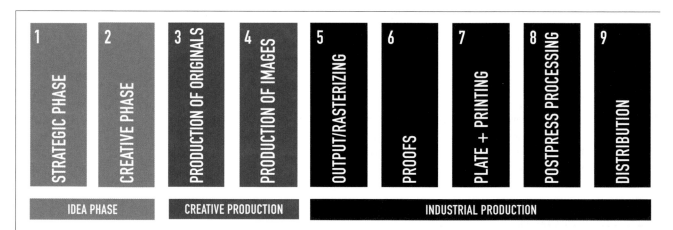

▶ THE NINE PHASES OF GRAPHIC PRODUCTION

Graphic production can be divided into nine phases. The first two phases involve the development of the creative concept. The next two focus on the implementation and further modification of this concept. The last five steps are more technical in nature and are determined by decisions made in the preceding phases.

No matter what particular aspect of graphic production you are engaged in, it's important to understand all of the steps involved. In this chapter, we will walk through each step, or phase, of graphic production.

Graphic production can be divided into nine phases. The first two phases involve the development of the creative concept. The next two focus on the implementation and further modification of this concept. The last five steps are more industrial in nature. A fundamental truth of graphic production is that in order to make the best design and material choices in the initial phases, you must understand the options available to you in all subsequent phases of production. This means thinking about the project "in reverse". For example, the type of off press processing [postpress] you'll be doing in phase eight might determine what paper you need to use in the original design concept; your choice of paper and printing method might, in turn, determine how images should be scanned and color separated in the image production phase, etc.

THE GRAPHIC PRODUCTION FLOW 1.1

To simplify the discussion about graphic production, we have chosen to divide the process into nine phases, listed here and described below:

1. *Strategic phase*
2. *Creative phase*
3. *Production of artwork*
4. *Production of images*
5. *Output/rasterizing*
6. *Proofs*
7. *Printing plates and printing*
8. *Postpress processing*
9. *Distribution*

STRATEGIC PHASE 1.1.1

Now is the time to consider the project as a whole and determine if a printed product is what is really needed [see Graphic Production 16.1]. Ask questions that will help define the product you want to create more clearly: What are the goals of this project? For whom is this product intended? What will this product be used for?

CREATIVE PHASE 1.1.2

The creative phase is about developing the design, determining the message of the work and how best to communicate with the audience for whom that message is intended. More questions bring the project into focus: What type of printed product should be created? What should this product say? How should it say it? What should this product look like?

PRODUCTION OF ORIGINAL ARTWORK 1.1.3

This phase involves writing the necessary text copy, producing original artwork, and designing page layouts. Photography is ordered and images are scanned. This phase often runs parallel with the image production in phase four. When the image production is

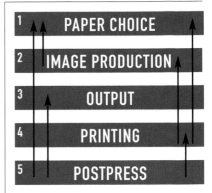

1	PAPER CHOICE
2	IMAGE PRODUCTION
3	OUTPUT
4	PRINTING
5	POSTPRESS

▶ CHOICES ARE MADE IN "REVERSE" ORDER
Common for all production steps is that you need to know what the subsequent step involves and adjust your work accordingly. The off press processes may determine your choice of paper and printing method which, in turn, determine how the images should be scanned and color separated.

▶ PARTICIPANTS – STRATEGIC PHASE
- Marketing departments
- Communication departments
- Advertising agencies
- Media advisors

▶ PARTICIPANTS – CREATIVE PHASE
- Marketing and communications departments
- Advertising and PR agencies
- Design bureaus

▶ PARTICIPANTS – PRODUCTION OF ORIGINAL ARTWORK
- Advertising agencies
- Design bureaus
- Production companies
- Prepress providers

▶ **PARTICIPANTS – IMAGE PRODUCTION**

- Photographers
- Photo labs
- Production companies
- Prepress bureaus
- Printers with own prepress
- Image bureaus

▶ **PARTICIPANTS – OUTPUT**

- Prepress bureaus
- Copiers
- Printers with own prepress
- Production companies

▶ **PARTICIPANTS – PROOFS**

- Prepress bureaus
- Printers with own prepress

▶ **PARTICIPANTS – PRINTING PLATES AND PRINTING**

- Prepress bureaus
- Printers

▶ **PARTICIPANTS – POSTPRESS PROCESSING**

- Printers
- Bookbinders

▶ **PARTICIPANTS – DISTRIBUTION**

- Printers
- Bookbinders
- Distributors

finished, digital images are installed in the original, completing this process. It is often necessary at this stage to send one or more proofs to interested parties (i.e., clients) for review and approval before moving on to step five, output/rasterizing.

PRODUCTION OF IMAGES 1.1.4

In this phase, images are photographed and developed, then scanned into the computer for further editing. The images are cropped, converted into CMYK, and adjusted as appropriate for the printing process to be used. Other types of image editing, including masks, retouches and color corrections, are also done in this phase. As with the production of original artwork, one or more proofs are usually sent out for approval before moving on to the next step.

OUTPUT/RASTERIZING 1.1.5

Text, images and original artwork are now ready to be output on film or paper. This output can take the form of color printouts, transparencies, graphic films or paper originals. Laser printers, ink-jet printers and imagesetters are a few of the types of peripheral printing units commonly employed in this phase.

PROOFS 1.1.6

To get a sense of what the final print will look like, a proof is made. It is an important step in the process, as it is the last opportunity to check the material and make any necessary changes. The proof also serves to show the printing house how the final print is supposed to look. The proof can be analog or digital. A digital proof is made using high-quality color printers, which means the proof can be made before producing the films and plates. An analog proof is made based on the films used to make the printing plates.

PRINTING PLATES AND PRINTING 1.1.7

Once the proofs are approved, it's time to make the printing plate that will be used to strike the actual prints. This plate is often made using graphic film. There are a number of different printing methods. Offset printing is probably the most widely used. Other methods include gravure printing, flexography, screen printing and digital printing. The printing method used depends upon the product desired. Paper, of course, is the material most commonly used for printing, but you can also print on materials like plastic or fabric.

POSTPRESS PROCESSING 1.1.8

After printing, the raw prints still need to be turned into a finished product. For example, prints might be cut to size, folded, glued or stitched into books or booklets, laminated or lacquered, depending on the finished product desired.

DISTRIBUTION 1.1.9

Distribution is the last phase of graphic production. The printed, finished product is now distributed to the end user.

THE COMPUTER

2

CHAPTER 2 THE COMPUTER TODAY ALL GRAPHIC PRODUC-TION IS BASED ON COMPUTERS AND SOFTWARE APPLICA-TIONS. THE COMPUTER IS THE MOST IMPORTANT COMPONENT IN THE GRAPHIC PRODUCTION PROCESS. THAT'S WHY YOU SHOULD HAVE BASIC KNOWLEDGE OF THE COMPUTER AND ITS FUNCTIONS.

▶ A COMPUTER
Essentially all production of graphic originals are done on this type of computer. The Macintosh computer is most commonly used by the graphic industry.

The computer is the foundation for all graphic production. It is used to create text, edit images, and design a layout, then merge all of these elements into a finished document. Large amounts of material can be archived and stored on a computer. Computers also run printing presses, as well as other peripheral equipment essential to graphic production, like scanners and Raster Image Processors (RIPs). In this chapter, we will cover the basic components of the computer and its functions.

Generally speaking, a computer system consists of two main components, software and hardware. Hardware refers to the physical apparatus of the computer. Items such as the hard disk, the processor, random access memory (or RAM, as it is commonly known), and the network interface card make up some of the basic elements of a computer's hardware. Additional hardware includes accessories like the monitor, keyboard, mouse, modem, printer and scanner, to name just a few. Software refers to the programs run by the computer. Basic computer software includes an operating system, utility software, drivers, applications and plug-ins.

SOFTWARE 2.1

We will start by looking at computer software. In this section, we will cover the general definition of operating systems, utility software, drivers, applications and plug-ins, as well as some software specific to graphic production. This graphic production software includes software for word processing, image editing, illustration, page layout, imposition, databases, and some additional specialized software.

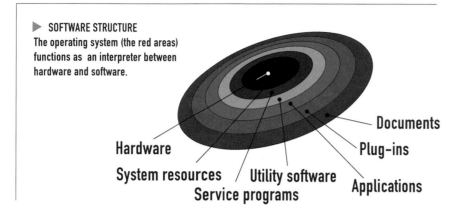

Documents

Plug-ins

Hardware

System resources / Utility software Applications
Service programs

OPERATING SYSTEMS 2.1.1

The operating system is a computer's most fundamental software. Without it, the computer wouldn't even be able to start. The operating system runs all of the basic computer functions: displaying the user interface, receiving and translating signals from the computer keyboard, saving files to the hard disk, etc. It also facilitates communication between any additional programs you are using and the computer's hardware. Examples of operating systems include Mac OS, Unix, Windows XP, LINUX and DOS.

UTILITY SOFTWARE 2.1.2

Utility software works with the operating system to provide additional operating functions above and beyond the basic set-up. An example of utility software that is used in graphic production is Adobe Type Manager (ATM), which improves the basic system's typeface management capabilities [see Typeface 3.5.2]. Screen savers and anti-virus software are other examples of utility programs.

DRIVERS 2.1.3

Drivers are software that allow the computer to work with "peripheral" hardware, like printers and scanners. Peripheral devices almost always come packaged with their own driver software, which needs to be installed on the computer's hard drive in order for the device to work.

APPLICATIONS 2.1.4

An application is software that performs a comprehensive set of functions in a specific area, such as word processing or image editing.

With regard to graphic production, there are six main software categories: word processing, image editing, illustration, page layout, imposition, and database software. In addition, there are many specialized software programs for particular graphic production needs. These include OPI software, trapping software, preflight software and software that controls RIPs, imagesetters and printing presses. In addition, administration soft-

WORD PROCESSING SOFTWARE
You write and edit texts in word processing applications.

PAGE LAYOUT SOFTWARE
In the page layout software you compose and create pages by merging text and image.

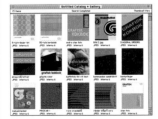

IMPOSITION SOFTWARE
In the imposition application, you "place" the pages into a digital imposition that can be output to a large film.

ILLUSTRATION SOFTWARE
You create object-based graphics in the illustration application.

IMAGE EDITING SOFTWARE
You create and manipulate pixel-based images in the image editing application.

ware is also commonly used, to handle orders and invoicing, for example. We will look more closely at the most important of these specialized applications in later chapters.

Word processing applications allow you to efficiently write and edit text in a simple format, prior to applying design elements. These applications are not meant to handle advanced design, typography or four-color processes, and therefore are not used directly in the production of original artwork. Some commonly used word processing programs are Microsoft Word and Word Perfect.

Image editing applications are tools for graphically manipulating images intended for printing. One of the most popular image editing programs is Adobe Photoshop.

Illustration applications allow you to "draw" or create original images with the help of the computer. Commonly used programs are Adobe Illustrator and Macromedia Freehand. There are separate applications for "3-D" illustration; 3D Studio and Strata Studio are two such programs.

Page layout software merges text and images into complete, laid-out pages. These applications allow you to output for professional graphic production.

The most frequently used page layout applications are QuarkXPress, Adobe InDesign and Adobe PageMaker.

Imposition applications enable you to place several pages on the same film for a complete film assembly, rather than mounting several individual films (one for each page). Examples of imposition programs include Preps, Ultimate Impostrip, Imation Presswise and Quark Imposition [see Output 9.5].

Database applications are primarily used to archive and index production items, including text files, image files and page files. Phrasea by BaseView, Extensis Portfolio (formerly Fetch), Cumulus by Canto and Imations Media Manager are some common database programs [see Storing and Archiving 7.8.1].

PLUG-INS 2.1.5

Plug-ins are also called add-in programs or extensions. They are small programs that enhance existing application software with additional functions. Sometimes plug-ins can cause problems when handing off documents from one computer to another. You may need the plug-in that was used to create a particular file on another computer in order to open it on yours.

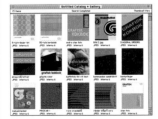

DATABASE SOFTWARE
An archive program is one of the database applications - you use it to keep documents organized. You can also categorize the documents and run searches.

HARDWARE[2.2]

Hardware refers to all the physical components of a computer—the things that you can touch. There are many different brands of computer hardware on the market today. In the graphic production industry however, Macintosh is the most commonly used, so we will focus our discussion on the hardware particular to this brand of computer. The hardware for a PC is fundamentally the same, however.

THE PROCESSOR [2.2.1]

The heart—or rather, the brain—of the computer is the central processing unit, or CPU. It performs all calculations—in other words, it does all the thinking—for the computer. The CPU executes all functions requested by the operating system and other software, and controls the operations of the rest of the computer's hardware. Examples of central processing units in Macintosh computers are G3 and G4. An equivalent example for Windows – Compatible computers would be the Intel Pentium processor.

DATA BUS [2.2.2]

The data bus handles the flow of information through the computer's hardware components. It transports data between different areas of the computer, like the random access memory, the video card and the hard disk. The data bus is connected directly to the CPU, and the capacity, or "speed", of the data bus determines how fast information can be sent through the computer and at what speed it operates.

▶ COMPUTER CABLES FOR A MACINTOSH
The ports for a Macintosh computer are designed so that you can't plug a cable into the wrong port.

RAM – RANDOM ACCESS MEMORY 2.2.3

Random Access Memory is high-speed memory that is emptied each time you turn off your computer. Say, for example, you wanted to edit an image using Photoshop. The information necessary to execute this particular function—in this case, the actual Photoshop program, as well as the image—is transferred from the hard disk, via the data bus, into RAM so that you can use it efficiently. Remember to save your document on the hard drive because it will be lost once you turn off the computer.

ROM – READ ONLY MEMORY 2.2.4

Some components of a computer's operating system are installed and stored in the ROM – Read Only Memory. They are the most fundamental elements of the operating system, including the information that the computer needs to start up, and to search for the rest of the operating system on the hard disk.

INTEGRATED CIRCUITS – IC 2.2.5

The CPU, RAM and ROM consist of so-called "integrated circuits", otherwise known as computer chips. These chips are mounted on a large circuit board called the "motherboard". All of the integrated circuits are connected to one another on the motherboard.

THE HARD DISK – DISK MEMORY 2.2.6

The hard disk is a storage medium where information, such as files or programs, is saved. When you open these saved items, they are retrieved from the hard disk. This type of information can also be stored and retrieved from external media such as floppy disks, CD-ROMs or other peripheral storage devices [see Storing and Archiving 7.2].

VIDEO CARD 2.2.7

A video card controls the display you see on your monitor. A good video card will allow for a wide range of colors, high resolution and high refresh rate, provided that you have a monitor compatible with these capabilities.

NETWORK INTERFACE CARD 2.2.8

To make communication between multiple computers and peripherals in a network possible, the computer is equipped with a network interface card. For example, the network interface card allows such functions as printing and sending and receiving email within a network configuration [See Network and Communication 8]. The network interface card has built-in connectors so that a network cable can physically connect it to printers and/or other units in the same network.

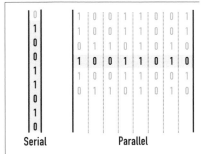

Serial   Parallel

▶ SERIAL vs PARALLEL
In a serial port all the bits (ones and zeros) follow each other. In a parallel port, all bits are transmitted in parallel along different paths.

SERIAL AND PARALLEL PORTS 2.2.9

A serial port is used to connect the keyboard, mouse, and other control devices, such as joysticks and track balls, to the computer. It is called a serial port because the signals (ones and zeros) are transmitted serially on the same circuit.

Parallel ports are those where the signals are sent simultaneously on many parallel circuits.

USB 2.2.10

USB, or Universal Serial Bus, is a new kind of serial port. It makes it very easy to connect accessories like the mouse and keyboard to the computer. The computer can "feel" what kind of unit has been plugged in and devices can be connected while the computer is on, with no need for re-booting.

The USB is also fast enough (up to 12MB/sec) to serve as a connection for monitors, CD players, printers, simple scanners, etc. A USB can also provide a power supply for low-power equipment and up to 127 devices can be connected. A new version of USB (version 2.0) has been developed, with a transfer rate of 480 MB/sec—powerful enough for video connections and other demanding transmissions. The USB version 2.0 is compatible with equipment based on today's USB version 1.1.

SOUND INPUT PORT 2.2.11

Most computers have a connection for a microphone or other sound input devices, and one for sound output devices like speakers and headphones. If your computer has a sound board, you can also route the sound input/output of your computer through a sound mixer or similar device. The quality of the sound board determines the quality of sound recording and playback on your computer.

VIDEO INPUT 2.2.12

Some computers have a connection for receiving or playing video. It requires special hardware called a video card. Many computers now have a built in video card.

SCSI 2.2.13

The SCSI device is an important feature of the Macintosh computer. SCSI (pronounced "scuzzy") stands for Small Computer System Interface. It is a high-speed interface that connects directly to the data bus and can transport huge quantities of data. Using the SCSI interface, you can connect the computer to external hard disks, scanners and other devices that handle large amounts of information.

A SCSI chain can connect up to eight units altogether. The CPU and the hard disk both count as one unit each, which means that you can connect six additional external units. Each external unit must have a unique SCSI number. Most computers have software that identify the SCSI numbers of the different units (one such software for the Macintosh is SCSI-Probe). Each external device usually has two identical connectors that allow it to form a link in the chain. The chain is finished with a terminator in the last empty connection; today, most units are self-terminating.

SCSI technology can also be used inside the computer to send data between elements like the hard disk, a CD and the RAM. This internal SCSI device is called a SCSI-bus.

IEEE 1394 FIREWIRE 2.2.14

A new, very powerful standard for data transfer is IEEE 1394, commonly known as FireWire. The transfer rate of this device is as high as 400 MB/sec, which makes it appropriate for use with high-resolution video data. With such blazing speed, FireWire may begin to replace the SCSI connector, although USB 2.0, with a transfer rate of up to 480 MB/sec, could also give FireWire a run for its money.

▶ SCSI-CHAIN
You can connect a maximum of six external units to a SCSI chain.

▶ WARNING!

If you are connecting a unit to the SCSI port, it is important to do it when the unit and the computer are turned off. Otherwise you run the risk of damaging the equipment.

▶ MONITORS
Displayed here are two types of monitors. On top is a CRT monitor and on the bottom a LCD monitor.

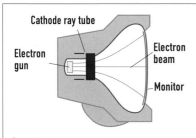

▶ CRT – AT A GLANCE
The electron gun fires electrons controlled by the cathode ray tube. When the electrons hit the monitor they illuminate the phosphor in the pixels.

▶ THE CRT SWEEP
A beam of electrons sweeps across the screen surface, pixel by pixel, row by row, until all the pixels are illuminated. In order to maintain an image on the screen, the pixels must be constantly re-lit.

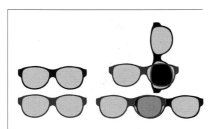

▶ LCD – HOW IT WORKS
By rotating each crystal in the LCD monitor 90 degrees, no light is let through. It works exactly like in the example of the polaroid glasses above.

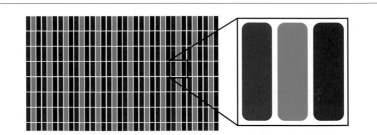

▶ WHAT A SCREEN CONSISTS OF
A screen consists of many rows with small pixels. The pixels have light sources divided into three sections, one red, one green and one blue. Depending on the strength of the light, the three light sources can create all the colors that the monitor can display.

POWER SUPPLY 2.2.15

Last, but not least, there is the power supply. Although it does not really contribute to the computer's functions, it is the largest component in the computer. The power supply transforms the 110 or 220 volts of the outlet to line voltage, the voltage the computer is working with.

THE SCREEN 2.2.16

Two kinds of screens are widely in use today, Cathode Ray Tube (CRT) screens and Liquid Crystal Display (LCD) screens. CRT is the large, fixed monitor that you usually see with desktop computers, and LCD is the flat-screen format used in laptop models, although LCD is becoming an increasingly popular option for desktops as well.

Regardless of the type of monitor, the images you see are the result of the illumination of thousands of tiny light sources. In color screens, the light sources are divided into three sections, one red, one green and one blue [see Chromatics 4.4]. If you look very closely at an active computer monitor or television screen, preferably with a magnifying glass, you will see these three distinct colors of light arranged in tiny groups all across the screen. Each group is called a "pixel" – the word is derived from the phrase "picture element." Pixels are packed tightly in uniform rows across the screen.

Each light source in the pixel can vary in strength. If you juxtapose the three colors (R, G, and B) in different intensities, the brain will perceive a specific color. The exact color perceived depends on the relative intensities of the three colored light sources. Essentially, all colors can be created on the color screen [See Chromatics 4.4.1]. In the black and white screen, the pixel consists solely of a white source of light that can assume all the shades of gray from black to white.

CRT SCREENS 2.2.17

The Cathode Ray Tube, or CRT, monitor has a screen that looks and functions like a television screen, with a higher resolution – i.e., the screen has more pixels and can therefore show more detailed images. The pixels are phosphorescent, and light up when bombarded with electrons. These electrons are generated by an electron gun. A cathode and a ray tube control the stream of electrons so that they hit the right pixels at exactly the right time, in order to produce the desired image. CRT monitors emit magnetic radiation, and their safety has been called into question as a result. This, along with the bulky size and weight of the CRT screen has encouraged a move towards the use of LCD screens with desktop computers.

LCD SCREENS 2.2.18

Liquid Crystal Display (LCD) is a flat, low-power type of screen. This technology is based on polarized liquid crystals that are illuminated from behind. Because they are polarized, the liquid crystals can be "opened" or "closed" to the background light. It works exactly like two polarized lenses being rotated at 90 degrees to each other. At the start, no light is let through. By the time the 90-degree rotation has been achieved, all the light is let through. The LCD technique is used in black and white as well as color screens.

REFRESH RATE 2.2.19

The phosphorescent pixels in CRT screens only glow for a short while after being hit by an electron. In order to maintain an image on the screen, the pixels must remain illuminated. Therefore, the pixels must constantly be re-lit. In the CRT screen, a beam of electrons sweeps across the screen surface, pixel by pixel, row by row, until all the pixels are illuminated. Then this process immediately starts over with the first pixel. The screen of a CRT screen stays constantly illuminated as long as the electron gun has time to hit all the pixels on the screen before the first pixel it hit goes dim. The speed of the beam of electrons moving across the monitor limits how fast the screen image can be changed. The faster the beam moves, the steadier the image. The speed at which all the pixels are re-lit is measured in Hertz (number of screen changes/per second). To avoid a flickering image, the beam of electrons has to sweep across the screen at least 50 times per second, or 50Hz. Today, monitors often have a speed of 70Hz or more.

In LCD screens, the nature of the liquid crystals can restrict the image. When images change rapidly, the crystals cannot always open and close fast enough to control the luminous flux accordingly. As a result, LCD screens are not necessarily the best choice for displaying moving images. Sometimes moving images leave "tails," or the entire image is distorted.

SCREEN SIZE 2.2.20

Screen size is measured in two ways. The first measurement is the same as for televisions: the length of the diagonal of the screen, stated in inches. The second measurement is the number of pixels the screen holds, width by height. The smallest standard screens made today are 14 inches with 1021 × 768 pixels. The largest are 21 inches, and hold a maximum of 1600 × 1200 pixels. The density of the pixels determines the screen resolution. The higher resolution, the smaller pixels and the greater detail. The resolution is not only determined by the screen size, but also by the video card.

WHAT MAKES A COMPUTER FAST? 2.3

When you talk about how "fast" a computer is, what you are usually talking about is the "clock speed" of its processor – i.e., something like 1000 MHz. Clock speed is a mea-

▶ SCREEN SIZE
The screen size is measured diagonally across the screen and is stated in inches (for example 17 inches as above). Although not visible on the exterior of the monitor, the entire screen is measured. The screen resolution is stated in pixels, width x height (for example 1024 × 768 as above).

▶ ASSIGNING MEMORY
If a program is operating remarkably slow, it might be because it has been assigned too little RAM.

In Adobe Photoshop for example, the recommended RAM assignment is at least five times larger than the image you are working with.

Binary number		Position value		Decimal number
1	×	2^7 (=128)	=	128
				+
0	×	2^6 (=64)	=	0
				+
1	×	2^5 (=32)	=	32
				+
0	×	2^4 (=16)	=	0
				+
0	×	2^3 (=8)	=	0
				+
0	×	2^2 (=4)	=	0
				+
1	×	2^1 (=2)	=	2
				+
1	×	2^0 (=1)	=	1
				=
				163

▶ **HOW IS A BINARY NUMBER CALCULATED?**
Displayed here is how to calculate the binary number 1010 0011's decimal equivalent, 163.

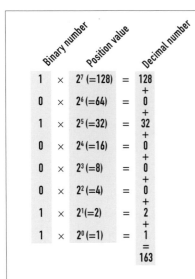

▶ **FILES vs DOCUMENTS**
Digital blocks of data are called files. A file can, for example, be a program, a system file or a driver (red). One type of file is called documents. Those are files that you have created in your own computer (green).

surement of how many calculations the processor can make per second. But there are other things that help determine the computer's speed. For example, the transfer rate of the data bus plays a major role. The faster it can send the information, the faster the computer. The computer also has something called a cache memory. Cache memory stores frequently accessed data for fast retrieval. The larger the cache, the more room for storing quickly accessible information. The size of the RAM is also important, particularly if you work with large image files. The more RAM a computer has, the less information it needs to store on the considerably slower hard disk. Working with moving or large images also requires that the video card has a relatively large RAM – also called video RAM or VRAM.

SAVING FILES THE SMART WAY 2.3.1
To work efficiently, it is important to know exactly where the files you work with are saved. Try to save your work locally on your own hard disk as much as possible – not on another computer or server in the network (see Network and Communication 8.4.1). A computer's internal hard disk is also generally faster than Zip and Jaz-disks [see Storing and Archiving 7.2].

ASSIGNING MEMORY TO SOFTWARE 2.3.2
When working with software in the computer, you have to assign it RAM. It is usually done automatically when the software is installed. When working with large images and documents however, you may need to manually increase the amount of RAM. On Macintosh systems, this is done by clicking on the program symbol, selecting the command "Get Info" under "File" and assigning the necessary amount of memory to the program. The dialogue box will display a recommended value. If you know that you work with very large documents in a certain application, you should go ahead and assign that software additional RAM. In Adobe Photoshop for example, the recommended RAM assignment is at least five times larger than the image you are working with. If the computer has less memory available than the minimum recommendation, it will not be able to start the software. The computer will usually recommend that you make more RAM available by closing other applications.

BINARY NUMBERS 2.4

Most people know that computers speak a digital language comprised entirely of ones and zeros. But what does that actually mean? Simply put, every memory unit in the computer can only save a one or a zero. So every piece of information you want to save must be translated into a series of ones and zeros.

For example, say you are trying to save a number on a computer. The computer cannot use the decimal system that we ordinarily use, in which every digit in a number can assume one of ten different values, zero to nine. Instead, the computer works with a binary notation where every digit in a number must be expressed using 0 and 1. A binary digit is called a bit. Every new bit in a number has double the value of the previous bit, and is added to the number. The first bit in a number can assume the value $1 \times 2^0 = 2^0$ or $0 \times 2^0 = 0$, the next bit $1 \times 2^1 = 2$ or $0 \times 2^1 = 0$ and the next $1 \times 2^2 = 4$ or $0 \times 2^2 = 0$ and so on.

This means a bit can only have $2^1=2$ values, 0 and 1. Three bits can represent $2 \times 2 \times 2^3=2=8$ values, 000–111, or the equivalent of 0–7 in the decimal system.

With the binary system, it is common to work in groups of eight bits, known as bytes. This system provides $2^8=256$ levels of value, 0000 0000–1111 1111, the equivalent of 0–255 in the decimal system. For example, the red, green and blue sources of light in the pixels have 256 distinct colors each in a computer running with eight bits.

FILES AND DOCUMENTS 2.5

A file is a digital object, simply consisting of ones and zeros. A file can, for example, be a program, program component or a font file. Programs can also create individual files, like images, text, or complete pages. These files are referred to as documents.

DIFFERENT TYPES OF DOCUMENTS 2.5.1

Three main types of documents are used in graphic production: text, image and page documents. They are saved in different file formats, generally corresponding to the programs they were created in. For example, files created in QuarkXPress are saved in the QuarkXPress file format. Some types of documents, like images, can be saved in several file formats. Different file formats have different features [see Images 5.3]. Files from different versions of the same software also have different features. For example, the file format for Microsoft Word 5.0 differs from that of Microsoft Word 6.0. Files from updated versions of a software generally cannot be opened in the previous version of the same software.

TEXT FILES 2.5.2

Text files are saved in two main format types: the "open format", which makes it possible to move the file to other software and platforms, or in a specific software format, like Microsoft Word. Typical open formats are the ASCII format and the RTF format. Text files saved in these formats are relatively independent from the computer platform, Windows or Macintosh, they were created or used in. Program-specific text files can sometimes run into problems if they are transferred to a different platform or software. Therefore, the open formats are most appropriate for text that needs to be imported into and edited in a page layout application.

ASCII 2.5.3

American Standard Code for Information Interchange, or ASCII, is a standard format for digital information, primarily text. There are two versions. One is based on a 7-bit coding scheme and can have up to 128 different characters. The other version is based on an 8-bit coding scheme and can have up to 256 characters. A set with 128 characters does not include all digits, letters and special characters necessary in a text, which is why this version can sometimes cause problems. ASCII is often called "a raw text file" because it does not include information about the text's design or typography. The ASCII format is readable by most programs that handle text.

▶ BINARY AND DECIMAL

Binary		Decimal
0000	=	0
0001	=	1
0010	=	2
0011	=	3
0100	=	4
0101	=	5
0110	=	6
0111	=	7
1000	=	8
1001	=	9
1010	=	10
1011	=	11
1100	=	12
1101	=	13
1110	=	14
1111	=	15

$2^4 = 16$ different values, 0 – 15

RTF ^{2.5.4}

RTF, or Rich Text Format, is an open text format that also contains codes for specific typefaces and simple typography. RTF was created to make it easy to transfer text files between different text programs while preserving the typographic information.

IMAGE FILES ^{2.5.5}

There are two main types of image files, pixel graphics and object graphics [see Images 5.1 and 5.2]. Object graphics can be saved in the generating program's own file type or as an attachable EPS file in programs like Adobe Illustrator and Macromedia Freehand. Pixel-based images are often created in scanning programs or in Adobe Photoshop. These images can be saved in Photoshop's own format, or they can be saved in standard formats such as TIFF or EPS files, which can be transferred into QuarkXPress, Adobe InDesign or Adobe PageMaker. Image files can also be compressed. This is generally done with a JPEG- or LZW-compression [see Images 5.8].

PAGE FILES ^{2.5.6}

The main page layout applications used in the graphic production industry are Quark-XPress, Adobe InDesign and Adobe PageMaker. These applications are used to merge text and image files and to design page layouts. They can import most text and image formats used in graphic production; they cannot edit images but can modify their size and orientation. Adobe InDesign can handle some editing on artwork created in Adobe Illustrator. In page layout software, only the text is saved directly in the page file. Images and font files are saved outside of the page file and are merged into the page file at printout. The image files must be attached to the page when going to print. The applications are often used for high-quality printouts on film or paper. Software like Macromedia Freehand and Adobe Illustrator are also used to design individual pages [see Document 6.1].

Page layout application use their own program-specific file formats, but they can save pages in EPS or PostScript format. Transferring files between QuarkXPress, Adobe InDesign and Adobe PageMaker is possible, but relatively problematic. Moving files within the same file format between different computer platforms is usually easier.

TYPE AND FONTS

3

CHAPTER 3   TYPE AND FONTS   WHEN WORKING WITH FONTS ON A COMPUTER, YOU MUST KNOW WHICH FONT FILES TO USE AND HOW TO GET THE OUTPUT TO LOOK LIKE WHAT YOU CREATED ON THE SCREEN. IT IS ALSO IMPORTANT TO KNOW HOW TO MANAGE FONTS. AND WHAT, FOR EXAMPLE, IS THE DIFFERENCE BETWEEN TYPEFACE AND FONT?

In this book, we will not address typography from an aesthetic point of view. However, it is helpful to familiarize yourself with certain typographic terms. To that end, this chapter will cover working with typefaces and fonts, as well as font structure. We will also look at different types of font files and utility software for typeface management.

TYPE AND FONT 3.1

To begin with, it's important to understand the difference between a typeface and a font. Typeface is the term for the design of a set of characters. Typefaces can come in a number of typestyles, such as bold, narrow, or light. Font refers to the character set in its physical form – metal type, or digital type files, for example. On your computer, a font consists of a set of typeface in a particular typestyle stored in a file. There are numerous different file types for fonts, including TrueType and PostScript Type 1, which we will touch on later in this chapter.

DIFFERENT TYPEFACES WITH THE SAME NAME 3.1.1

Some typefaces exist in a number of variations because the design differs slightly from one provider to the next. For example, the look of the Garamond typeface offered by one company may not necessarily be identical to the Garamond from a different source. This is an important distinction when, for example, you want you replace a missing font in a document. You could get some unwanted differences if the replacement font is not from the exact same source used when the document was created, even if the font names are the same.

> ▶ TYPEFACE AND FONT
>
> Typeface = The distinctive design of a set of type, distinguished from its weight (such as bold), posture (such as italic) and type size (according to Webster's Dictionary of Computer Terms).
>
> Typestyle = The weight or posture of a font, distinguished from a font's typeface design and type size.
>
> Font = One complete collection of letters, punctuation marks, numbers, and special characters with a consistent and identifiable typeface, weight (roman or bold), posture (upright or italic), and type size.
>
> Font file = Computer file containing a particular typestyle, for example Helvetica bold.

PRINT PRODUCTION TYPE AND FONTS

CHARACTERS IN A FONT 3.1.2

There are no rules for what characters should be included in a font's character set. For example, all sets do not necessarily include both capital and lowercase letters. Some fonts are collections of symbols that don't have anything to do with letters at all. In this case, each keyboard key represents a symbol, rather than a letter. When working with symbol fonts on a Macintosh computer, you can use the `keyboard` function, located in the apple menu, to determine which symbols correspond to which keys on the keyboard.

SCREEN FONTS AND PRINTER FONTS 3.1.3

Typefaces often have both screen fonts and printer fonts. The distinction is fairly self-explanatory – screen fonts are what you see and work with on your computer screen, printer fonts are those used when generating printouts. Screen fonts and printer fonts of the same typeface are stored as files. Some fonts do use the same font file for both screen and printout.

TYPEFACE AND FONT MANAGEMENT 3.2

Managing fonts on a Macintosh is relatively simple, but as there are a large number of fonts to work with, it is helpful to have utility software to keep them organized.

WHERE DO YOU GET THE FONTS? 3.2.1

There are thousands of fonts in existence today, and new ones are constantly being created. The main suppliers of fonts are Adobe, Agfa, Letraset and Monotype. The cost of fonts can vary widely. Some fonts can be downloaded for free from the Internet, but most cost anywhere from around $30 to hundreds of dollars each. Typefaces can be purchased individually or as a part of a collection of typefaces, usually stored on CD-ROM.

CAN YOU COPY FONTS? 3.2.2

It is easy to copy fonts because they don't require registration numbers or passwords when they are installed. Although the copying of fonts is fairly widespread these days, there can be legal consequences if copyright laws are violated. That said, many companies make the screen versions of their fonts readily accessible. However, anyone who wants to output to a printer or imagesetter must have the printer version of these fonts, and designers also need the printer fonts in order to scale letters or do precision kerning (changing the spacing between individual characters). Ultimately, this means you need to purchase the printer version in order to get the full functionality of the font—as well as the best possible design results.

TO MODIFY OR CREATE YOUR OWN TYPEFACES 3.2.3

It is also possible to create your own typefaces or modify the ones you already have. Macromedia Fontographer is one of many programs that provide the capability to design your own typeface. These programs can also be used to convert fonts from one computer platform to another (Macintosh to Windows, for example).

If you occasionally want to modify a typeface or create a logotype based on a typeface, you can take advantage of the fact that printer fonts are created from "bezier curves".

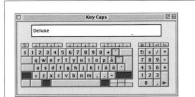

▶ **FINDING THE RIGHT KEY**
By using the `Keyboard` function located beneath the apple menu, you can quickly view a font and find out which key combinations (`alt. shift` etc.) you use to display a particular character.

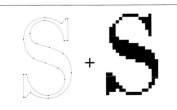

▶ **PRINTER FONT + SCREEN FONT**
Typefaces often have both screen and printer fonts. Screen fonts are what you see and work with on your computer screen. Printer fonts are those used when generating printouts.

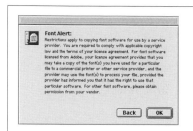

▶ HAND OFF WITH FONTS?
Displayed above is one Adobe tool for letting
you know whether fonts can be included when
handing off material.

▶ OBJECT-BASED FONTS
Object-based fonts let you adjust characters
in width and height, warp them, color them
and add effects.

▶ FONTS WITH BEZIER CONTOURS
Printer fonts are based on bezier curves. It
makes it easy to change the shape of the font
(by modifying the bezier curves) while maintaining the quality.

In both Adobe Illustrator and Macromedia Freehand, it is possible to convert the contours of the characters to bezier curves, although this technique does require that you
have a software called ATM installed (discussed later in this chapter). You can then modify them like you would an illustration. The modified characters can be saved and
imported into a font application and, if desired, they can be included in a particular font.
The modified fonts can be assigned a color in a page layout application but not a pattern
or a shade. You can also adjust characters in width, height and even warp them [see Legal
17.3.5].

HOW TO CHOOSE FONTS? 3.2.4

When selecting fonts, the simplest way is to choose from printed examples, called type
specimens. You can order catalogues with type specimens from most manufacturers. If
you do not have a catalogue, you can either select fonts directly from the screen or print
out your own type specimens.

To view the fonts installed on your computer, you can use one of a number of utilities.
Adobe Type Manager Deluxe (ATM Deluxe), for example, has a function for previewing
fonts of different sizes. Typebook is another program for viewing fonts, but only at printout. Some of these programs can be downloaded for free from the Internet, but most cost
around $20 and there are a number of options to choose from. There are utilities that
display font names in their own fonts in the font menu of the application. This simplifies
the choice but the preview takes more time. The utility software Adobe Type Reunion is
one such program.

You can always preview a screen font by double clicking on the font file. Unfortunately,
PostScript Type 1 fonts are only displayed in the screen font size and are often too small
to allow for an accurate assessment. TrueType fonts, on the other hand, are displayed in
several sizes. In a fully installed system on the Macintosh, you can use the `keyboard`
function under the apple menu to preview fonts on the screen.

HOW TO INSTALL FONTS 3.2.5

When installing new fonts on your computer, you need to make sure to store them in the
font folder within your System Folder. Screen fonts should be kept in "typeface suit-

▶ CATALOGUE WITH TYPEFACE SPECIMENS
Catalogues with typeface specimens are very
useful and are released by most font manufacturers.

▶ PRINT YOUR FONTS
Typebook is a Macintosh program for printing
sample pages of installed fonts. ATM Deluxe
can also do this.

PREVIEW IN ATM DELUXE
In ATM Deluxe you can preview fonts in different sizes and print out type specimens.

ORGANIZING FONTS IN GROUPS
In Adobe Type Reunion the fonts are organized based on typeface family. The fonts can also be viewed in their own font.

CLICK ON THE SCREEN FONT
If you double click on a screen font, it is displayed in its natural size in a separate window. Unfortunately, it is usually too small to be of any help.

KEEP IN MIND

If you don't have all printer fonts installed and you are using the command bold in the program menu, the bold version might not appear in the printout. The same applies to similar menu commands, such as italic. To avoid this problem select the bold version of the font directly from the typeface family.

cases" stored within the typeface folder, to simplify their administration (more on typeface suitcases later in this chapter).

If you are not using ATM, you will often need to access many different screen font sizes. Things can quickly become confusing when working with a number of screen font files in every typeface variation. To simplify the process, you can collect the screen font files of a particular typeface in a single typeface suitcase. The printer font files should not and, in most cases, cannot be placed in suitcases. One exception is TrueType, which allows both printer font files and screen font files to be placed in the suitcase.

If you are using ATM 4.0, more recent versions of ATM 4.0 or Suitcase, you do not need to place the fonts in the font folder. You can store them anywhere on the computer, or within the local network and activate them when necessary. ATM and Suitcase help the system locate the right font file when it is needed.

Certain software requires that fonts be stored in the font folder in the System Folder or that they are activated by a utility like Suitcase when the program is started. With some software, like QuarkXPress, you can activate or add a new font while the software is running, and it can be used right away, with no need to restart the software.

HOW MUCH MEMORY DO FONTS NEED? 3.2.6
A printer font usually uses around 32 to 64 kb of memory and a screen font between 5 and 15 kb. The smaller the screen font, the less memory required. In a typeface suitcase, however, there are usually many screen fonts in many sizes. Installed fonts also require some allocated memory on the hard disk. ATM generally recommends 100 kb of allocated memory per active font. If you are using the utility software ATM on a Macintosh, you only need one size of each screen font, which saves memory.

HOW TO CREATE ORDER AMONG FONTS 3.2.7
When you are working with many different fonts at once, it's important to note that all active fonts are taking up their share of your computer's valuable allocated RAM. A good way to make sure that you are not activating more fonts than you need at any given time

TYPEFACE SUITCASES
Screen fonts or TrueType fonts can be organized into groups in a special type of folder: a typeface suitcase. It functions as a regular folder but can only hold this type of files.

is to use a utility like ATM Deluxe or Suitcase. These utilities can activate the fonts you need while you are working without requiring you to restart the software or keep the fonts in the System Folder. You can also organize groups of fonts for specific projects, which allows you to activate all the fonts associated with that project at once.

When using utility software, you can sort your fonts in a variety of ways, depending on what makes the most sense for you. If you remember fonts by name, sort them alphabetically. You can also sort fonts by appearance. Sorting by typeface family—roman types, grotesque types, script types, etc.—is one example. You might also choose to sort your fonts by manufacturer: Adobe fonts, Agfa fonts, etc.

If you are working on a network and many people are using the same fonts, you can store them on a server that everybody has access to. By using ATM 4.0 or more recent versions or Suitcase, you can use, activate and deactivate the fonts directly from the server. Of course, this requires constant access to the server.

▶ **ORGANIZING FONTS IN GROUPS**
In ATM Deluxe and Suitcase you can organize fonts into project - specific groups and install all of them at once.

THE STRUCTURE OF FONTS 3.3

The structure of a font determines to a large extent how it can be used. Fonts can also be saved in many different types of files with different functions.

BEZIER CURVES 3.3.1

All characters in printer fonts are created using bezier curves. As a result, printer fonts are not dependent upon the resolution of the printer, and can be enlarged without taking on a jagged appearance. Printer fonts are not stored in any fixed size (10 point, 12 point, etc.) and can be scaled up or down as necessary [see Images 5.1].

HINTS FOR BETTER PRINTOUTS 3.3.2

When printing small characters on a printer with a low resolution, such as a laser printer, the thinnest parts of certain characters can be difficult to print. The number of dots per inch (dpi) is the measurement of a printer's resolution. Some characters have features that are only 1.5 dots wide [see Output 9.1.1]. The printer cannot print half a dot, so the question becomes, should the printer then adjust the line to one or two dots wide when printing this character? The result will be 50% thinner or bolder. To help the RIP choose the best course of action, there is a set of "suggestions" within the font itself, called a hint. All PostScript Type 1 fonts are hinted.

FONT IDENTIFICATION NUMBERS 3.3.3

All font files are assigned a unique identification number called a font ID. This number makes it easier for the computer to distinguish among the installed fonts. Unfortunately, there are rare instances in which two fonts have been assigned the same ID number. Problems occur if they are active at the same time. This can cause typeface collisions or font ID conflicts. The utility software Suitcase solves this automatically. It can also be solved manually by deactivating one of the fonts, or opening one of the fonts in typeface design software and assigning it a different ID number.

FONT TYPES 3.4

There are several font types: TrueType, PostScript Type 1, Multiple Master and Open Type are a few examples. The most widely used and the safest for rasterizing is PostScript Type 1.

POSTSCRIPT TYPE 1 3.4.1

PostScript Type 1 font for Macintosh actually consists of two fonts: a screen font and a printer font. The screen font is used when the typeface is displayed on the screen and the printer font when the typeface is printed. Screen fonts are not necessary when working in Windows because the printer font is used for both screen and printing.

The screen font is a set of characters saved as bit-mapped fonts: small, pixel-based images used to display the typeface on the screen. The screen font also contains information needed to link it to the printer font for printing. In other words, if you choose a bold font from the screen font menu in a program, it will link to a bold printer font when printing. This also means that if you do not have the bold version of that printer font installed, you will get an undesired result at printout – the thin version of the font you selected will most likely be used instead.

Screen fonts are usually stored in a few smaller sizes (10, 12, 14, 16, 18 and 24 points, for example). If you enlarge these pixel-based characters to a bigger size than any of the stored screen fonts, the edges will appear jagged. This can be avoided by using the ATM utility [see 3.5.2]. The printer fonts are structured with bezier curves and consist of Post-Script information [see Output 9.3].

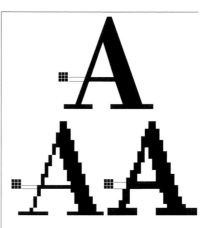

▶ HINTING
Displayed above is a letter. The thin line of the letter is 1.5 dots wide. A "hint" determines if one dot (see letter to the left) or two dots (see letter to the right) should be used for the best possible result.

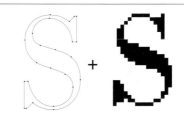

▶ POSTSCRIPT TYPE 1 FONTS
PostScript Type 1 fonts consist of two parts, one object-based printer font and a second pixel-based screen font. By using ATM, you can use the printer font as a screen font.

TRUETYPE 3.4.2

TrueType fonts consist of one single font file completely based on bezier curves. True-Type does not have separate screen fonts like PostScript Type 1. This type of font is supported by the Macintosh graphic system Quickdraw and a part of the operating system. Therefore, ATM is not required to create characters on the screen. Unfortunately, True-Type tends to cause problems when rasterizing. As a result, PostScript Type 1 fonts are primarily used in graphic production. TrueType fonts are most commonly used in Windows.

MULTIPLE MASTER 3.4.3

Multiple Master, or MM, is a development of the PostScript Type 1 format launched by Adobe. The advantage of Multiple Master fonts is that every font can assume different shapes, giving you an enormous number of styles based on the same font – from ultra-thin to extra bold and everything in between. These styles are not just typographical optical distortion (which is what happens when you select 'bold' from the font style menu in a software, for example). Instead, they are actual modifications prepared by the creator of the typeface. Multiple Master fonts only work if you have installed ATM.

If you want you can create your own typeface variations of the Multiple Master font with their own width and weight. Most programs today support the possibility to seamlessly create your own typeface variations from an MM typeface. If a program does not support that function, you can install ATM Deluxe to get the same advantages. If you have ATM, you can still use MM fonts but only a few pre-selected basic typeface variations selected by the creator of the typeface. Based on these basic typeface variations, you can interpolate your own variations.

OPEN TYPE 3.4.4

Open Type is a new font file format developed in a collaboration between Adobe and Microsoft. The format has many advantages—perhaps the most important being that the same font file can be used for both Macintosh and Windows. Furthermore, the font only consists of one file, not two like a font in PostScript Type 1-format for example. The same Open Type-file can be used both for screen display and printing.

There are two versions of Open Type-fonts. They are either based on TrueType- or PostScript-technique. For print production stick to the PostScript-version as usual in order to avoid problems when ripping. Open Type-fonts in PostScript-format also works in older PostScript-based RIPs.

▶ SUPPORT FOR OPENTYPE
Adobe InDesign has full support for all Open Types' functions (see image). QuarkXPress 5 can use Open Type-fonts, but lacks support for most functions Open Type normally would permit.

In traditional PostScript Type 1-fonts, each character corresponds to 8 bits and a font can consist of maximum 256 different characters. This means that it's necessary to create different font files for bold, narrow or capital versions of the same typeface. Open Type-fonts on the other hand are based on a standard called Unicode, corresponding to 16 bits per character and 65,000 different characters per font [see The Computer 2.4]. As a result, all typeface versions and characters imaginable can be stored in the same font file. Open Type is therefore particularly suitable for texts produced in different language versions because the same font can be used for all languages. If such production is done with a PostScript Type 1-font, it would usually require several fonts to manage languages with special characters.

It's up to the font manufacturer to determine which special characters and language versions should be included in an Open Type-font, and most fonts only contain one language.

Open Type-fonts also make advanced typography possible because the font can contain several versions of the same character—for example different character versions for the beginning or the end of a word or versions adjusted according to the character's size. Because Open Type-fonts have large character sets, you also gain access to several different ligatures.

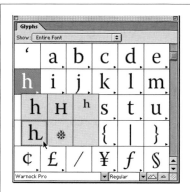

▶ CHOOSE CHARACTER VERSION
Open Type permits several versions of each character. In Indesign you can easily choose which version you'd like using the floating palette.

UTILITY SOFTWARE 3.5

Earlier in this chapter, we talked a lot about utility software for typeface management. The most common utilities in OS9 or earlier are Suitcase, ATM, ATM Deluxe and Type Reunion. These applications facilitate designing with fonts, performing functions that help to display and organize fonts on a project-specific basis.

SUITCASE 3.5.1

Suitcase is a utility that allows you to use fonts without having to install them in the system folder. The software lets you determine which typefaces should automatically be activate when the computer is turned on. You can also choose to activate a typeface temporarily. A temporarily installed typeface will deactivate when the computer is turned off or rebooted. With Suitcase, fonts can be stored in different folders or on other storage media such as hard disks, CDs or network servers. Suitcase also allows you to compile groups of typefaces that can be activate all at once. This is practical if you work with recurring projects that use the same several typefaces over and over. With Suitcase, you can also open new typefaces in an application without having to restart it.

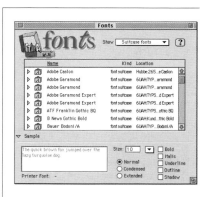

▶ SORT WITH SUITCASE
Suitcase lets you activate fonts when the computer is on without having to install them in the system folder.

It makes it possible to sort the fonts in an accessible way and to use them from a server.

ATM 3.5.2

Adobe Type Manager, or ATM, is a utility from Adobe used primarily to improve the screen display of large letters. It also facilitates the printout of PostScript typefaces on non-PostScript based printing units. ATM is more or less a requirement for doing graphic production work on Macintosh systems. ATM enables a user to use PostScript Type 1 printer fonts as screen fonts on a Macintosh, which means that characters on the screen maintain their correct appearance even when greatly enlarged. ATM also makes it possible to convert characters to character outlines which can be modified in PostScript-

▶ ATM

Adobe Type Manager enables the computer to use the size-independent printer fonts on the screen. ATM Deluxe has, in addition, a number of useful funtions, including anti-aliasing and functions similar to those in Suitcase.

▶ ANTI-ALIASING WITH ATM

ATM can anti-alias the screen font. Disable the anti-aliasing."smoothing" in ATM, when using small fonts because small, anti-aliased fonts can be difficult to read.

nnee
iilltt

▶ RANDOM SHAPES

The PostScript code allows each font to be rendered differently each time it's printed. Shown here is a typeface utilizing this function. "FF Beowulf" is an example of a Post-Script Type 1 font that can vary in shape.

based programs like Adobe Illustrator and Macromedia Freehand. Even with ATM installed, however, you will need to use screen fonts. For example, without screen fonts, the computer cannot locate the corresponding printer fonts. In addition, bit-mapped characters generated by screen font files look better on the screen in smaller sizes than the corresponding characters generated by ATM.

ATM DELUXE 3.5.3

More recent versions of Adobe Type Manager (ATM) have been supplemented with a font database. This database contains information about font styles, set-widths and weights. Among other things, this enables ATM Deluxe to replace a missing font in a document with a similar one, without changing the line arrangement (for the replacement to work, you must have Multiple Master fonts installed). When ATM discovers that a font is missing, the program creates a replacement font based on either Adobe Sans or Adobe Serif Multiple Master fonts. Based on the information about the original font stored in its font database, ATM selects the Multiple Master font that is most appropriate and scales it to the correct weight and set-width. In this way, the line arrangement and appearance of the page is maintained.

OTHER USEFUL OPTIONS WITH ATM DELUXE

Anti-aliasing

ATM Deluxe allows the screen appearance of a font's contour lines to be "softened" with tones of gray. The low resolution of the screen relative to the printed product is "hidden" by the softened contour line of the characters, and as a result, the characters on screen look more like the characters in the actual printout. Since this function may blur smaller characters, it is possible to turn off anti-aliasing for small font sizes.

Organizing Fonts in Groups

ATM allows you to organize fonts in groups. These grouped fonts can then be activated and deactivated all together. This is useful when working with projects involving a number of fonts, since you don't have to install the fonts one by one.

Searching for Fonts

ATM Deluxe can search for any font stored on the hard disk and/or storage media like CDs, disks, external hard drives, etc. For the search function to work, all screen fonts must be activated via ATM Deluxe and stored in typeface suitcases, not in the system folder's font folder.

Displaying and Printing Type Specimens

ATM can display type specimens on the screen or in printouts.

TYPE REUNION 3.5.4

Type Reunion is a useful utility from Adobe. Reunion groups all fonts by family, making it easy to select type styles for a document. For example, all fonts in the Garamond family are collected in one menu, rather than being interspersed among all other fonts in an alphabetized menu. In more recent versions of Type Reunion, the name of a particular font appears on the menu in that font style. ■

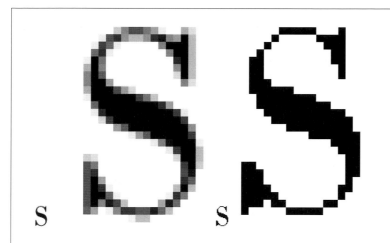

▶ ANTI-ALIASING - HOW IT WORKS

Anti-aliasing allows the fonts to be better reproduced on the screen. A font's contour lines are softened with tones of the color used. If your character looks like the one on the right (a non-antialiased character), you are probably missing the screen font and you will need ATM.

aaaaaaaa
aaaaa

▶ MULTIPLE MASTER

A font in the Multiple Master format can be assigned different weight (boldness) and set-widths almost seamlessly. The fonts are designed so it can be done in a typographically correct way.

CHROMATICS

4

CHAPTER 4 CHROMATICS THE FIELD OF CHROMATICS CONCERNS HOW THE HUMAN EYE PERCEIVES COLORS, AND HOW WE DESCRIBE AND MANAGE THOSE COLORS ON THE MONITOR AND IN PRINT. CHROMATICS IMPACTS ALL AREAS OF GRAPHIC PRODUCTION—PHOTOGRAPHY, SCANNING, SCREEN DISPLAY, PROOFING, PRINTING.

In this chapter we will cover the basic terminology of chromatics, and look at how the human eye perceives color. We will review the most common color models and discuss color mixing. We will look at color reproduction, how to get the colors you want in your printed product, and what you should think about when working with color and light in graphic production. Finally, we will review how different software manage colors.

WHAT IS A COLOR? 4.1

Color is really just a product of our minds. Our brains see different colors when our eye perceives light of different frequencies. Light is a type of electromagnetic radiation, just like radio waves, but with much higher frequencies and shorter wavelengths. The human eye is only built to perceive a limited range of these frequencies, which is called the visible light spectrum. The visible light spectrum encompasses red hues at around 705 nanometers (nm) through blue/violet hues at around 385 nm, and all the colors in between. The wavelengths just outside of the red end of the spectrum are known as infrared waves, which we perceive as heat energy. Above the violet end of the visible light spectrum, we find what we call ultraviolet light, which has so much energy that it can tan our skin!

When light containing the same amount of each and every wavelength in the visible part of the spectrum hits our eyes, we perceive it as white light. Daylight, for example, contains all wavelengths and is perceived as "white".

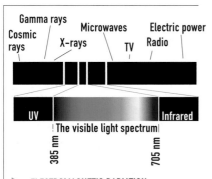

▶ ELECTROMAGNETIC RADIATION
The eye can only perceive a limited range of all electromagnetic raditation frequencies. This portion is known as the visible light spectrum.

Color perception varies from individual to individual. Some people have more difficulty perceiving colors than others. This is often referred to as color blindness, more commonly occuring in men than in women. There are different degrees of color blindness. People with color blindness may not be able to distinguish between shades of red and green, for instance.

THE COLOR OF SURFACES 4.2

When white light falls on a surface, some of the visible spectrum is absorbed by the surface and some is reflected. The color you see is the result of the reflected wavelengths of light. You could say that light is "filtered" by the surface on which it falls. For example, your lawn looks green in daylight because the surface of the grass reflects the green portion of the visual spectrum and absorbs the rest.

THE EYE AND COLOR 4.3

The retina of the eye is covered with light-sensitive receptors called rods and cones. Rods are sensitive to light, but not to color. We use the rods to see in low light—which is why everything appears almost black and white when it's dark. Cones are less sensitive to light, but they can perceive color. There are three types of cones, each sensitive to a different part of the visible spectrum: one type sees red light, one green and one blue. This combination allows us to see all colors in the visible spectrum—almost ten million shades —many more than we can create in a four-color print!

The eye also perceives tonal progression. If you were to divide the tones between black and white into 65 equal steps, the eye can perceive a maximum of 65 gray hues. If the eye were equally sensitive to changing tonalities within each of the 65 steps, it would mean that the eye's perception of gray hues follows a linear function. In reality, the eye is differently sensitive within different areas of the gray scale—its perception of tonalities is logarithmic in nature.

The eye is more sensitive to tonal variations in light areas than in dark. We can thus distinguish more distinct tonal steps in the light end of the gray scale than the dark end —in reality, the eye can distinguish over 100 distinct steps. However, if the gray scale was divided into more 100 steps, the eye would not perceive the transitions between the steps; rather, the gray scale would look to be one stepless, progressive gray scale. This is important to keep in mind in halftone screening, the technique used to print gray scales [see Output 9.1].

MIXING COLORS 4.4

A color photograph usually consists of thousands of different colors. When printing a color photograph, you cannot use thousands of different-colored inks to match these colors exactly, nor can you display such an image on a monitor using thousands of different light sources. Instead, you need to try to approximate the thousands of colors in the photo by mixing together the three primary colors. In print, these colors are cyan, magenta and yellow. On screen, the three primary colors are red, green and blue.

▶ **THE COLOR OF A SURFACE**
Incoming light is filtered when it is reflected by a surface. The composition of the reflected light gives the surface its color.

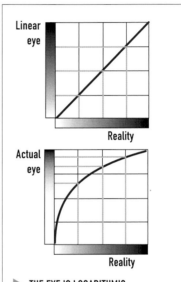

▶ **THE EYE IS LOGARITHMIC**
A linear eye would mean that we are equally sensitive to tonal differences in the entire gray scale (the upper diagram). But the eye is logarithmic and much more sensitive in the lighter gray scale (lower diagram).

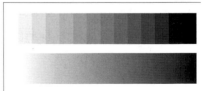

▶ **FOOLING THE BRAIN**
A gray scale is divided into rough sections, which are perceived as distinct steps by the brain. If smaller increments are used, the brain cannot perceive the differences between the transitions and instead views it as a continuous tone.

▶ THE ADDITION TABLE
Here we can see how different light sources can be combined to generate the colors yellow, cyan and magenta.

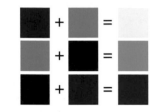

▶ SUBTRACTIVE COLOR MIXING
Different surfaces filter (subtract) different wavelengths of light. The first surface filters out the red light component. Only the green and blue component are left, which, according to the table above, generates the color cyan. The other surfaces are perceived as magenta and yellow thanks to the wavelengths of light their surfaces filter.

On monitors, three light sources – red, blue and green light – are mixed together to produce all other colors. Mixing different colored lights is called additive color mixing. This method is used in all devices that create colors with light sources—monitors, televisions, etc. In print, three different colored inks, cyan, magenta and yellow, plus black, are mixed to create all other colors. This process of mixing inks is known as subtractive color mixing.

ADDITIVE COLOR MIXING 4.4.1

"Additive color mixing" refers to the fact that you are adding some amount of red, green and blue (RGB) light to a mix in order to create new colors. If you mix together all three colored light sources at their full intensities, the eye will perceive the result as the color white. At a lower intensity, an equal mix of all three primary colors would appear to the eye as a neutral gray. If all the lights are turned off, the eye will see black. If you mix two colors at their highest intensities, without the third, you will get the following results: red + green = yellow, blue + green = cyan, and red + blue = magenta. By mixing two or more of the three primary colored light sources in different combinations at different intensities, your monitor is able to recreate the vast majority of colors that can be perceived by the human eye.

Additive color mixing is used in computer monitors, TV monitors, and video projectors. A monitor screen consists of a number of pixels. Each pixel contains three small light sources, one each of red, green and blue. The mixing of the colors of these three light sources gives the pixel its color [See The Computer 2.2.14].

SUBTRACTIVE COLOR MIXING 4.4.2

In printing, colors are created by mixing the three primary-colored printing inks, cyan, magenta and yellow (CMY). This method is referred to as "subtractive color mixing" because the ink filters the white light that falls on its surface, "subtracting" or absorbing all the colors of the spectrum except for the tone it was mixed to reflect.

An unprinted surface reflects its own color – white, if the surface is a white piece of paper, for example. In theory, mixing an equal amount of cyan, magenta and yellow ink should create black – with the inks absorbing all visible wavelengths of light. Unfortunately, the inks used for printing cannot completely filter light. Instead, when these three inks are mixed equally, the eye perceives a dark, brownish color. Because of this, a fourth ink – black (K) – is also used in printing.

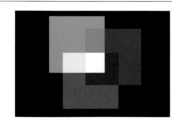

▶ ADDITIVE PRIMARY COLORS
The additive color model's primary colors and their combinations.

▶ SUBTRACTIVE PRIMARY COLORS
The subtractive color system's primary colors and their combinations.

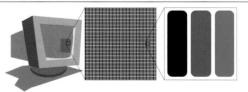

▶ THE PIXEL IN THE MONITOR
Monitors are constructed of a square pattern of pixels. Each pixel has a red, green and blue light source that can be altered in intensity. The somewhat grayish-blue color is created by a dimly lit red light source, mixing together with the green and blue light source.

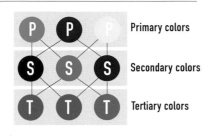

▶ PRIMARY, SECONDARY AND TERTIARY COLORS
Cyan, magenta and yellow are the primary colors of the subtractive color system. If you mix two primary colors, you get what are known as secondary colors. In this image, blue, green and red are secondary colors. If you mix all three primary colors, you get tertiary colors.

P Primary colors
S Secondary colors
T Tertiary colors

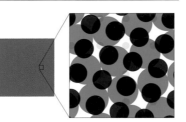

▶ A PRINTED COLOR
In prints, colors are created by mixing halftone dots of cyan, magenta and yellow in different sizes.

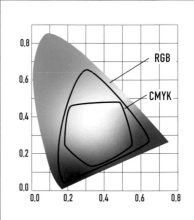

C+M+Y   C+M+Y+K

▶ BLACK IN THEORY AND IN PRACTICE
If you printed cyan, magenta and yellow on top of each other the result should be black. In practice, it turns out to be a dark brownish gray. That's why a black printing ink is added to this color model. There is some disagreement as to whether the K in CMYK comes from "Key color" or from the K in "black".

▶ COLOR GAMUTS

The color gamut is the range of colors that can theoretically be created within a particular color model. Different color models have different color gamuts. The wider the color gamut, the more colors you can create with a color model.

The three colors cyan, magenta and yellow are called primary colors. If you mix them two and two you generate secondary colors: red, green and blue/violet. In turn, if you mix the secondary colors you will get tertiary colors. Tertiary colors consist of all the three primary colors. Most visible colors can be reproduced in print by blending the primary-colored inks in different amounts. This is actually done by mixing primary-colored halftone dots of different sizes. The size of the halftone dots varies, depending on the desired shade.

COLOR MODELS 4.5

To help maintain color consistency over the course of a project, or when communicating with different vendors and graphics professionals, there are a number of standard color models you can use as a basis for describing your colors. Some of these models are used more widely than others, but they each have their advantages and disadvantages. Different models have different uses. Some models are based on how printing inks are mixed, others on precise physical descriptions of the different colors. In some models the color names are "made up", while other models define colors based on how they are perceived by the eye.

Color models have different color gamuts, which determine the extent to which colors can theoretically be created within a particular color model. The larger the color gamut a color model has, the more colors can be created within that system. There is no color model with a color gamut that corresponds to the entire visible light spectrum. Following is a short review of the most common color models: RGB, CMYK, CMYK conversions, NMI, PANTONE, CIE and NCS.

RGB 4.5.1

RGB – Red, Green, Blue – is an additive color model used for digital images or for color monitor displays. Colors are clearly defined by values indicating the combination of the three primary colors. For example, a rich, warm red is defined as R-255, G-0 and B-0.

▶ RGB HAS A WIDER GAMUT THAN CMYK
The RGB model has a wider color gamut than the CMYK model. This diagram as a whole represents the sensitive fields of the eye. The three corners represent the eye's cone cells, which are sensitive to red, green and blue. NOTE: This illustration is only schematic because it is printed in four colors, and cannot, as a result, reproduce the entire spectrum.

▶ RGB
RGB is the additive color model that is primarily used for digital images and for color monitor displays.

▶ CMY
CMY (with black included) is the subtractive color model used for creating four-color prints.

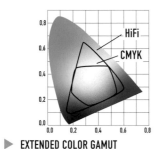

▶ EXTENDED COLOR GAMUT
High fidelity color printing will give you a wider color gamut than CMYK.

However, this really says nothing about how the eye perceives the color. In addition, the actual appearance of a certain color value is determined by the monitor or scanner that is being used. Thus, a particular color value will not necessarily look the same on different machines.

CMYK 4.5.2

CMYK stands for the colors Cyan, Magenta, Yellow and blacK, and is a subtractive color model. When you want to take a digital image and create a four-color print, you have to convert digital RGB colors into CMYK colors [see Images 5.7]. The resultant colors are defined by the percentages of CMYK inks in the combination. For example, a warm red color might be C=0%, M=100%, Y=100%, K=0%. As with the RGB model, however, this description says nothing about how the eye perceives the colors. A specific CMYK combination can also have a varied appearance, depending on the printing ink, paper stock and printing press used. CMYK color gamut is much smaller than RGB color gamut.

MULTI-COLOR CONVERSIONS 4.5.3

In the same way a digital RGB image is converted into CMYK, you can convert images into more than the four primary colors to get a wider color gamut. There are color models with six to eight printing inks. Printing with these models is sometimes called "high fidelity color printing", because you can achieve higher fidelity to the original images. The most common multi-color conversions are six-color conversions in which a green and an orange color are used in addition to CMYK. Six-color productions are hard to justify because they are difficult to proof, require experience to print and the added color range may be relatively insignificant.

HUE, SATURATION, VALUE – HSV 4.5.4

Hue, Saturation, Value, or HSV, is a color model that resembles the eye's way of perceiving colors. The model makes it easy to work with colors on the computer. There are several versions of this model, including HLS (Hue, Luminance, Saturation) and HSB (Hue, Saturation, Brightness), but value, luminance and brightness all refer to the same thing: light.

The HSV model is based on placing all the colors of the spectrum into a cylindrical configuration. The color value (i.e., brightness or luminance) is stated along the central axis of the cylinder. The distance from the center determines the color saturation, while along the periphery you can find the color hue. This model is a simple way to work with colors on a computer – you can only change the color with respect to one of the variables value, saturation or hue.

PANTONE 4.5.5

Pantone is a useful but somewhat inaccurate way of describing colors. The model is based on the combination of nine different colors selected based on their utility. The colors are divided according to a number system that makes it easy to select. The Pantone model is primarily used for printing spot colors.

A color model like the Pantone model, which uses unique pigment combinations for each different color, has a greater ability to depict saturated colors. For example, a light yellow color in a Pantone model actually is a light yellow pigment—you don't have to fool the eye with screen percent values like the CMYK model. This means that the Pantone model has a much wider color gamut than the CMYK model. When converting from Pantone to CMYK, be aware that you cannot recreate all the colors from the Pantone model.

CIE ^{4.5.6}

Comission Internationale d'Eclairage, or CIE, is a color model created by the International Commission on Illumination. The model is based on the results of extensive experiments studying the human perception of color, conducted in the early 1930s. Because each human's sensitivity to color differs, a standard colorimetric observer was created based on the average of the subjects' color perception. It was concluded that human color perception can be described according to three sensitivity curves called tri-stimulus values. These values, combined with the characteristics of the light falling on a surface and the colors in the light that the illuminated surface can reflect, can be used to very precisely define the color of the surface.

CIELAB and CIEXYZ are versions of the CIE model. CIELAB is a development of CIEXYZ and the system is based on human color perception. Because CIE is based on three different values, you could say that it is three-dimensional, and that it therefore constitutes a certain space—color space. Colors defined in the CIELAB model are assigned values for L, A and B and in the CIEXYZ model, X, Y and Z, respectively. In the CIELAB system, a movement, or change, in the color space (expressed in CIELAB values) is relative to the change in color (expressed in wavelength) wherever in the color space the movement occurs. For example, if you move between two places, or two colors, within the blue spectrum of the color space, the perceived change in color would be identical if the same movement was conducted elsewhere in the spectrum. Regardless of where a value change takes place in the CIELAB model, the eye will perceive it as equivalent because the model is based on the eye's perception.

The visual difference between two colors is expressed as ΔE (pronounced delta E). A color change within the color space based on wavelength, or distance, does not necessarily result in the same ΔE value, because the eye differs in its sensibility depending on the area of the color space. If ΔE is smaller than 1, the eye can't perceive a difference between

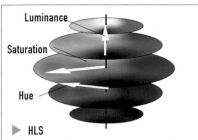

▶ HLS
Where a color is located vertically in the HLS model determines its luminance (also called brightness). The horizontal distance from the central axis determines how saturated a color is, while the hue is located along the periphery.

▶ PANTONE-GUIDE
To pick the right Pantone color, printed Pantone guides are used.

▶ CONVERTING PANTONE COLORS
Pantone colors that are converted to CMYK often come out as completely different colors. There are special color guides to facilitate this kind of conversion.

▶ RED STRAWBERRIES
Using the HLS model and moving along the hue arrow, the red strawberries get younger by changing color and turning green.

▶ GREEN STRAWBERRIES
By moving all red hues approximately a third of a turn in the color circle into the green area, all reds in the image change into green.

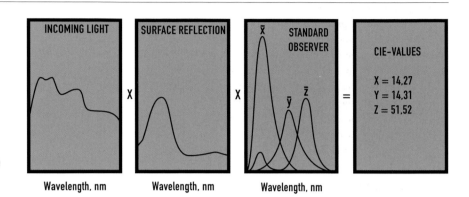

► LIGHT× SURFACE× TRISTIMULUS = CIE

Normal incoming light is composed of certain wavelengths.

The colored surface reflects some wavelengths better than others.

The eye is differently sensitive to different wavelengths as expressed by the tristimulus curves $\bar{x}$, $\bar{y}$ and $\bar{z}$. These correspond to the sensitivity in each of the three cones in the eye of a standard observer.

Multiplying $\bar{x}$, $\bar{y}$ and $\bar{z}$ respectively with the two other curves will give you three values: X, Y, and Z, also known as CIE values.

colors. CIELAB is the model primarily used in the graphic industry when a "device independent" color model is desired, because its definitions of color are based on the eye's perception of colors and the exact physical expression of that.

NCS [4.5.7]

Natural Color System, or NCS, is a Swedish color model. It is based on blackness (brightness), hue (color) and color density (saturation) and can be visualized with a double-cone diagram. Colors are divided into steps based on how the eye perceives them. NCS is primarily used in the textile and paint industries.

WHAT AFFECTS COLOR REPRODUCTION? [4.6]

Color reproduction refers to the way in which colors are reproduced on a monitor or in a particular print, etc. The two factors that have the greatest effect on how colors are reproduced are tonal range and color range. Tonal range refers to the range of colors that can be created with a specific component color from a particular color model, using a

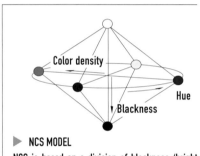

► NCS MODEL

NCS is based on a division of blackness (brightness) color density (saturation) and hue (color), which can be visualized as a double-cone diagram.

► DIFFERENT COLOR MODELS

COLOR MODEL	RGB	CMYK	MULTI-COLOR SEPARATION
PURPOSE	Red Green Blue	Cyan, Magenta, Yellow and Black	CMYK+ for ex. green, purple or orange
UTILITY	Scanning, image editing, storing	Four-color printing	Prints with stronger colors in images
FUNCTION	Additive model, wider color gamut than CMYK	Subtractive model, color gamut determined by the printing process	Subtractive model, wider color gamut than CMYK
COLOR MODEL	HSV	Pantone	CIE
PURPOSE	Hue, Saturation, Value	Pantone Matching System	Commission Internationale d 'Eclairage
UTILITY	Used on the computer	Spot colors in print	Exact physical expression, visually determined
FUNCTION	Used for color modifications on the computer	Pre-defined color samples, wider color gamut than CMYK	Device-independent storage

specific process – for example, the range of colors possible when using the cyan ink in a CMYK color model, printing on coated paper in an offset printing press. Color range is the entire range of colors that can be created with a particular color model using a specific process, as in the range of colors possible when using a CMYK color model, printing on coated paper in an offset printing press.

Thus, in terms of printing, color reproduction is primarily affected by the color model, the paper, the printing process and the inks you print with. When you create an artwork that you want to reproduce as a printed image, it is important to take these factors into consideration and make any necessary adjustments in order to achieve optimal color consistency between the artwork and the prints [see Images 5.7].

COLOR MODELS AND COLOR REPRODUCTION 4.6.1
The color model you use has an effect on color reproduction because a particular color model can only produce colors within its color gamut. Different color models have different-sized color gamuts. For example, if you are printing with Hi-Fi color (six-color printing) you will get a considerably wider color gamut than with regular CMYK, because the additional printing inks used in Hi-Fi printing expand its color gamut. This means that you can reproduce a wider range of hues and better approximate the original image.

PRINTING PROCESSES AND COLOR REPRODUCTION 4.6.2
The printing method can affect color reproduction in several ways. Different printing processes require different types of ink, for example. Each printing method also differs in how thickly inks can be layered on the printed surface. The thickness of the ink helps to determine the tonal range possible in the print. The more ink you can put on the paper, the wider the tonal range and better the color reproduction.

Another example of how a printing method can affect color reproduction can be seen with offset printing. The inks used in this process cannot bond to each other completely, because multiple colors are printed on top of each other before they dry—a technique known as wet-on-wet printing. Because of this, it is not possible to reproduce all the colors you (theoretically) should be able to based on the component color's tonal range [see Printing 13.4.4].

PAPER AND COLOR REPRODUCTION 4.6.3
The characteristics of the paper you use (color, surface, structure, print characteristics etc.) greatly affect the fidelity of the color reproduction. Few paper stocks are completely

▷ **TONAL RANGE IN PRINT**
The tonal range in print is the range of colors that can be created with a particular printing ink, taking paper and printing method into consideration. One example is the range of colors possible when printing cyan ink (from a CMYK model) on coated paper in an offset printing press.

▷ **COLOR RANGE IN PRINT**
Color range in print is the entire range of colors that can be created with a particular color model using a specific process, as in the range of colors possible when using a CMYK color model, printing on coated paper in an offset printing press.

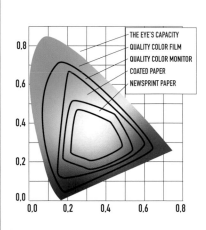

THE EYE'S CAPACITY
QUALITY COLOR FILM
QUALITY COLOR MONITOR
COATED PAPER
NEWSPRINT PAPER

▷ **DIFFERENT COLOR GAMUTS**
The diagram shows what size color gamut you can obtain with various media.

▷ **COLOR REPRODUCTION**
The way a color is reproduced in a particular print or on a monitor is called color reproduction.

▷ **COLOR CONSISTENCY**
Color consistency refers to the continuity of color between different steps in the production process, such as between the original artwork and the print.

white. Most papers have a slight hint of color, and some, like the pink paper in the Financial Times of London or the New York Observer, have a very rich hue. It is difficult to adjust color reproduction for these variations in paper color, and the appearance of a print can change greatly when printed on different paper stocks as a result [see Paper 12.5.4].

The glossiness of paper stocks varies, depending on how much light a particular paper's structure and surface treatment is designed to reflect. For example, fine art prints use paper that reflects more light than newsprint paper. The more light a paper can reflect, the greater the possible tonal range, and therefore, the better the color reproduction. Other print materials, like fabric or plastic, also have special characteristics that influence the quality of color reproduction. In order to ensure the best possible results, you can make adjustments in the color reproduction process to compensate for the shortcomings of certain print materials [see Images 5.7].

PRINTING INKS AND COLOR REPRODUCTION 4.6.4

A subtractive color model like the CMYK model is based on precise theoretical color values. In reality, the color pigments can never reproduce these colors exactly. The closer the pigments are to the theoretical values, the better the color consistency. Different printing processes require completely different types of ink, making it difficult to compare the end results.

GETTING THE RIGHT COLORS IN PRINT 4.7

To find out what the colors you created on your computer will look like in the final print, you should start by calibrating your computer system. You should then evaluate the characteristics of the printing process you have chosen. This is known as forming a characterization of the print. When you have done this, you can adjust all of your other equipment and materials (monitors, printers, proofs, etc.) to conform as closely as possible to those characteristics and simulate the print. If you do a thorough job of this, you can achieve reasonable consistency among the monitor display, color printouts, proofs and the final print. This process is fairly simple if you always produce the same product with the same equipment—as with printing a daily newspaper, for example.

It is more difficult if you are producing different products on a range of equipment. In this situation, one solution is to use a Color Management System, or CMS, which takes into account the characteristics of scanners, monitors, printers, proofs, etc.

CHOOSING A COLOR 4.7.1

We don't recommend selecting colors based on what you see on your monitor, because it's too difficult to achieve color consistency between the monitor and the final print. Instead, use color guides with examples of printed surfaces in predefined colors. General color guides can be purchased on a variety of paper stocks, but printing houses sometimes supply their own color guides. Color guides define colors in CMYK values. If you are selecting a four-color hue you can use a general color guide, but because the printing conditions vary (paper, printing press, inks, etc.) the result may not always be an exact match. If you want to be absolutely certain about the color, you should try to work with a color guide specific to the printing house that is printing your product.

If you want a very saturated or unusual color (like metallic gold or silver), you might have to choose spot colors. The most common color model for spot colors is the Pantone model. You can purchase a color guide for the Pantone model, but it is relatively expensive.

STABILIZATION AND CALIBRATION 4.7.2

Stabilization involves making sure that all printing units consistently provide the same results. Inconsistencies can occur because of mechanical errors or fluctuating environmental conditions, like humidity and temperature. Calibration involves adjusting the equipment to predetermined values so that all devices are coordinated – for example, if you set a value of 40% cyan hue in the computer, the value for cyan will also be set to 40% on the printer, in the proof or the imagesetter. The various units often come with calibration software.

SIMULATION 4.7.3

You can also calibrate your system based on experiences with similar prints. Such "simulation" is, of course, not an exact procedure, but it is fairly simple and it works relatively well.

One way to calibrate using the simulation method is to print out and view on the monitor a document that has already been through the printing process, and set your units according to its appearance. The idea is to adjust software and monitors so that the screen display is as consistent to the printed product as possible. In the same way, the color printer and proof can be adjusted to simulate the final print result. A more precise method is to take a final print and adjust the units to the corresponding values.

COLOR MANAGEMENT SYSTEMS 4.7.4

A color management system allows you to maintain control over the colors in your project throughout the production process. It allows you to view the correct colors on the screen and can make sure that outputs and proofs are similar to the printed result. Colors are always affected by the devices that display, scan or print them. By recording the various color deviations, you can create profiles that ensure those deviations are compensated for during printing. This way, the final product will correspond to the original regardless of the devices used. A color management system must define colors and remain consistent regardless of how the colors are displayed at any particular moment in the process. RGB and CMYK are "device dependent" color models because the colors will look different depending on the device used. For example, if you go into an electronics store you will find that the same image displayed on the various televisions will differ, although they all transmit the same image containing the same color values.

Because these models don't allow for consistency among different monitors, prints or processes, they are not appropriatefor color management systems.

Thus, a color management system independent of the device the color is displayed on is necessary. Such system is called "device independent" because it is not affected by the technical devices used in production. The CIELAB model is such a system. In CIELAB, the colors are defined based on the viewer's color perception. Once the colors you want to work with are associated with device independent color values, you need to adjust all your technical devices accordingly. Each apparatus in the production line has its strengths and weaknesses when it comes to color, which are evaluated and stored in device profiles. The color management system utilizes the profiles to perform such tasks as adjusting a screen's RGB signals. If the televisions from the example had used a color management system, each television would have been based on CIELAB colors and these would have been converted into RGB signals unique for each television. These values would also have been adjusted according to the device profiles and, as a result, the colors would look identical on all the television monitors in the store. In printing presses, color adjustments need to be made because of dot gain, primary colors, dampening solution, paper, etc.

Software and hardware manufacturers in the graphic production industry have partnered to work towards a standard for color management systems. The group is called International Color Consortium, or ICC, which is also the name of the new standard. So far, ICC is a specification of how the color management system should work and a standard for how color profiles should be designed.

WHAT'S INCLUDED IN THE ICC SYSTEM? 4.7.5

The ICC system can be divided into three main components:
• The device-independent color space, CIELAB, also called Reference Color Space (RCS) or Profile Connection Space (PCS) [see 4.5.6].
• ICC profiles for the various devices, for example: monitor profiles, scanner profiles, printer profiles and print profiles. The profiles describe the color characteristics of each device.
• Color Management Module, or CMM, which calculates color conversions across the different devices, based on the profile values.

When working with a color management system, all three components affect the final result. When, for example, you scan an image, the Color Management Module uses the ICC profile to compensate for the variables of the scanner by calculating the values the scanned colors should have in the device-independent color space, CIELAB.

ICC PROFILES 4.7.6

A profile describes the color space, the strengths and weaknesses of a device. The profile compares how a device reproduces colors in comparison to a preprinted color chart—reference values (based on CIELAB) that tell you what the color values should be. The dif-

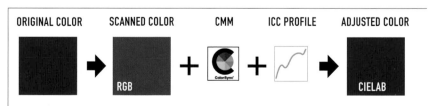

▶ ICC CORRECTION OF SCANNED COLOR
When you scan an image, the Color Management Module, CMM, corrects each scanned color by using an ICC profile taking the weaknesses of the particular scanner into consideration. It calculates which value the scanned colors should have in the device-independent color space in order to adjust the colors to correspond to the original artwork.

PRINT PRODUCTION CHROMATICS

ference between the two values is the basis for the profile and allows you to generate information regarding color compensation, i.e., how to reach the same value as the reference value on the color chart. Colors whose reference values are not included on the color chart are calculated and interpolated by the Color Management Module using two or more reference colors closely resembling the one in question.

Some manufacturers deliver profiles with products like scanners and printers. These are general profiles for the particular product model and do not take the strengths and weaknesses of the individual product into account and can provide varying results. Because of this, it's better to work with profiles created for a specific device in a specific environment. For example, even if a company only has monitors of the same make and model, you should still generate profiles for each monitor in order to achieve the best possible results.

There are several programs on the market for creating device-specific profiles, including Logo Profilemaker Pro, Agfa Colortune, Heidelberg Printopen and Scanopen. Some products have their own systems for creating profiles, including Barco and Radius.

To create profiles, you need the software and a standardized color chart with different color reference fields. The program that creates the profile has precisely defined reference values in CIELAB for each color on the chart. The color chart is printed, displayed or scanned on a particular unit and the result is compared to the reference values. For example, to create a profile for a scanner, you scan a color chart on photo paper or transparent film, and the scanned digital color chart is compared field by field to the respective reference values. The differences between the scanned values and the reference values form the basis of the profile. Profiles for output devices are generated by outputting or printing a color chart. The results are measured with a spectrophotometer, and these measurements are compared to the color reference values. A spectrophotometer is used to measure color values directly off a monitor screen, which are then, in turn, used to generate a profile.

The appearance of the color charts is defined in the ISO standard IT8. Most manufacturers of profiling software have their own charts based on IT8. There are color charts for both reflective and transparent film from leading film manufacturers such as Agfa, Kodak and Fuji. They use varying emulsions in their films and papers, which produce different results when scanned. For example, when you scan images photographed with transparent film by Fuji, you have to use a profile developed with color charts on transparent film from Fuji in order to accurately determine the correct compensation value.

Color charts consist of up to 300 color reference fields with primary, secondary, tertiary colors as well as gray tones. The color charts of the different manufacturers differ because they use their own color fields in addition to those defined in IT8. This helps manufacturers to better characterize the weaknesses of their particular devices.

COLOR MANAGEMENT MODULE (CMM) 4.7.7

The Color Management Module is a utility software that calculates the color conversion between different devices using the ICC profiles. Apple ColorSync is the most common Color Management Module and is always delivered with Apple's operating system. Many manufacturers like Kodak, Heidelberg and AGFA have their own Color Management Modules. All software that needs to convert or edit colors use a Color Management Module for color conversions. For example, scanner software uses a CMM when scan-

▶ SPECTROPHOTOMETER
A spectrophotometer measures the spectral composition of a particular color in printer outputs, proofs, prints, and on the monitor display.

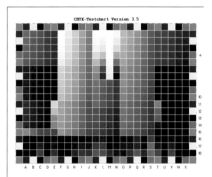

▶ IT8—COLOR TEST CHART
The appearance of the color test charts is defined in the ISO standard IT8. Most manufacturers of profile software have their own color test charts based on IT8. The color chart displayed above comes with Logo Profilemaker Pro.

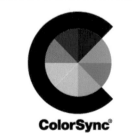

▶ COLORSYNC
Apple ColorSync is the most common Color Management Module and is always delivered with Apple's operating system.

ning an image, and image-editing software uses a CMM when converting the colors into CMYK.

When the various manufacturers decide how their particular CMM should manage conversions, they all base their decisions on the following:
• All neutral (gray) colors should be maintained when converting
• The contrast should be as high as possible after the conversion
• When converting, all devices should be able to represent all the colors. In other words, all the colors should be within the possible color space of the device

Some parts of the color space are difficult to convert and can cause problems.
For example:
• Light colors can be "flattened", or blended together, when the Color Management Module tries to create the highest possible tonal range. The same problem occurs with very dark tones.
• Saturated colors cause problems when they are outside a device's color space. They have to be translated into the device's color space in order to be reproduced. That process always changes the color in question and, in addition, may change other colors within the color space.
• Colors bordering the device's color space and covering large areas can lose nuances when they are converted.

There are four different ways for Color Management Modules to handle colors. The main difference among them is the way they manage translating colors into a device's color space. The four means of conversion are the following:
• Perceptual conversion
• Absolute conversion
• Relative conversion
• Saturated conversion

PERCEPTUAL CONVERSION [4.7.8]

The perceptual method of converting colors is mainly used when converting photographic images. When an image is converted, the relative distance in the color space, DE, is maintained. Colors outside of a device's color space are moved into the range of the device, but those colors already within the space are moved as well, in order to maintain the relative differences among all the colors. The human eye is more sensitive to differences in colors when they are viewed together than when viewed individually. For example, we can easily detect fine differences between colors when they are placed next to each other whereas when they are viewed separately we have a hard time knowing if it's the same color or not. Perceptual conversion maintains slight differences in color and is therefore the recommended method for separating photographs. The word perceptual refers to how the brain and the eye work together to perceive colors.

ABSOLUTE CONVERSION [4.7.9]

The absolute color conversion method is primarily used when simulating prints with a proof print system. The colors outside of the proof print system's possible color space are moved inside it, while those already within are not changed. Tonal differences between the colors within the possible color space and those on the border will then disappear. The method is appropriate in situations when it's important to reproduce colors as precisely as possible, as with a proof print system. To avoid the problem of losing tonal differences, you should strive for a color space in the proof system that is greater than the one for the print.

RELATIVE CONVERSION 4.7.10

Sometimes a perceptual conversion can cause images to lose contrast and saturation. In those cases, a relative conversion may provide a better result. The relative distance, DE, among colors outside of a device's possible color space is maintained after they have been moved inside. The colors within the color space maintain their values. The colors that are moved are converted into a color as close as possible to the original color by maintaining their brightness. The relative distance between two colors in the periphery of the color space changes and the two colors can now provide essentially the same value.

SATURATED CONVERSION 4.7.11

When working with object-based images, the preferred method of conversion is saturated conversion. The method strives to provide a conversion with as high a color saturation as possible. The relative distance between colors, DE, is changed, while the saturation is maintained. This allows each pixel to maintain its saturation value regardless of whether it is within or outside of the possible color space of a particular device.

DIFFERENT PARTS OF THE COLOR MANAGEMENT MODULE 4.7.12

When previewing a print on the monitor, you must take into consideration the monitor's way of displaying the image—i.e., you must make certain adjustments based on the mon-

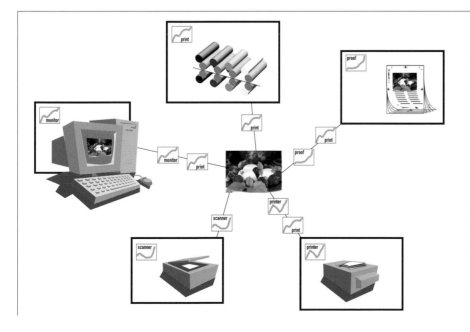

▶ COLOR MANAGEMENT SYSTEMS
Each device used in the production process has its strengths and weaknesses when it comes to color. These characteristics can be measured and stored in ICC profiles.

To simulate a print on a computer monitor you take into consideration the monitor's way of displaying colors, using information contained in the monitor profile, along with the characteristics of the print, using information contained in the output profile. You don't want to display colors on the monitor that cannot be reproduced in print. By combining the information in the two profiles you will be able to achieve a good simulation of the final print on the monitor.

If you want to simulate the printed result in a color printer output, you combine the printer profile and the output profile instead.

itor profile. This is done so the strengths and weaknesses of the monitor will be compensated for and the image will be displayed properly. You also take the color space of the print into consideration by using the print profile. You don't want to display colors on the monitor that can't be reproduced in the print. When you combine the two profiles you will get a good simulation of the final print result on the monitor. If you would like to view the result in a color printout instead, you would combine the print profile with the printer profile, etc.

IMAGES IN RGB OR CMYK 4.7.13

Today, most people still work with images in RGB or CMYK, even when using ICC systems. Which one you use depends on whether the RIP or OPI server is able to receive and separate images in RGB mode when they are being rasterized and output on film and plates [see Output 9.3.4]. If you have a workflow that supports RGB mode, you can either work with RGB images or have the images CMYK converted. The disadvantage of converting images into CMYK is that this process must be based on the specifications of a particular printing method (often before a decision has been made about how the actual product will be printed). With RGB however, images are not adjusted until the printing process has been decided upon. This also means that the images can be used for different things.

RGB FLOW 4.7.14

When working with images in RGB mode, you are using RGB color spaces predefined in CIELAB. When the image is scanned, the scanner's RGB values are compensated for and converted by using the scanner profile and the Color Management Module for CIELAB values. These can then be translated into RGB values in the CIELAB defined color space you have chosen to work with. The various RGB color spaces have different characteristics, which determine the color space you should work with. In Adobe Photoshop, you set the RGB color space under File –> Color Settings –> RGB Setup. In Adobe Photoshop 5 and more recent versions, information about the image's RGB color space is included in the file when the image is saved. This setting can be changed under File –> Color Settings –> Profile Setup, where you can also set how the program should react when opening an image that does not include information about the RGB color space.

The RGB color spaces included in Adobe Photoshop are different standards for how RGB is defined for print, video, film, TV, the Web, etc.

ColorMatch RGB is based on the RGB color space of a Radius PressView. Radius monitors are commonly used in professional graphic production and have a wide color space, suitable for graphic production purposes.

Adobe RGB has a wider color space than ColorMatch RGB. However, this also means that it contains more colors inside a CMYK color space, which can cause problems when converting from RGB into CMYK. This color space was previously called SMPTE-240M. If you come across images defined in SMPTE-240M, you should use Adobe RGB.

sRGB is a standard supported by Hewlett-Packard and Microsoft and is based on the HDTV standard. Hewlett-Packard and Microsoft use sRGB as a standard for non-PostScript-based flows and for web browsers.

sRGB is based on the color space an ordinary PC monitor can display, which has its limitations. The color space is much smaller than the other common RGB color spaces and is not appropriate for printing images because large parts of the CMYK color space are outside of its range.

Apple RGB was previously used as the standard RGB color space for Adobe Photoshop and Adobe Illustrator. Its color space is not that much larger than that of sRGB and it is therefore not suitable for graphic production.

Wide Gamut RGB has such a large color space that most definable colors can be displayed on a regular monitor or reproduced in print. As with Adobe RGB, it can cause problems when converting from RGB to CMYK because it contains so many colors.

Monitor RGB/Simplified Monitor RGB is a method that uses the monitor settings to define RGB color space and is primarily used when you don't work with ICC flows.

CIE RGB is an old RGB color space that is hardly used anymore. It is still available in Adobe Photoshop, in case you need to open an old image defined in CIE RGB.

NTSC is an old RGB color space used for video. It is available in Adobe Photoshop in case you need to open an old image defined in NTSC. NTSC is the North American standard for TV transmissions.

PAL/SECAM is a standard RGB color space used for TV transmissions in Europe.

CMYK FLOWS 4.7.15

When you work with a CMYK flow you need to make a CIELAB conversion when you want to do things like print an image on a proof print system. In other words, in a CMYK flow, the image is already adjusted and separated for the print, but it has to be converted from the print-adjusted CMYK-mode into CIELAB, and then converted to the proof adjusted CMYK-mode.

PROBLEMS WITH THE ICC STANDARD 4.7.16

Although ICC is a standard, the different programs used to develop profiles, like Logo Profilemaker Pro, Agfa Colortune or Heidelberg Printopen and Scanopen, provide different results despite following the same ICC specifications. Color Management Modules have the same problem, and can provide different results despite using identical profiles.

These problems are a result of the fact that the ICC standard's specifications are not precise enough. Because the standard was developed by many different partners from various fields, it has not been tightly monitored. Instead, there has been room for different companies to adjust the standards in order to get optimal results with their particular products.

The standard only defines how the profiles should be structured, not how the Color Management Modules should use them. All colors not included as reference values are interpolated by the Color Management Module using values from two or more colors that closely resemble the original color. How that is calculated in the Color Management Module and how the program differentiates among manufacturers is not specified in the standard. The problems with the ICC standard become evident during conversions and as a result, you will not be able to predict results with 100% accuracy.

WORKING WITH LIGHT AND COLOR 4.8

LIGHT AND COLOR 4.8.1

Light is an important factor in determining how the eye perceives colors. Even if the brain often forgives color variations in different light sources, the practical consequences of using different types of light can be relatively significant, both when photographing images and when viewing and editing images during production. The thing that makes the type of light so important in these instances is the fact that its color composition can vary drastically. The colors of the objects we see are, as mentioned earlier, the result of the light reflected off those objects. The color of the reflected light is affected by the color composition of the incoming light. There is a big difference in the appearance of an object seen in reddish light, as opposed to that same object seen in bluish light. A surface that looks red under white light will be perceived as orange if illuminated by yellow light, for example.

Because of this, it's important to view photographs and printed products in the correct light. The color of light is usually expressed as a "color temperature" measured in Kelvin (K). A normal, neutral lighting has a color temperature of about 5,000 K. This is approximately the equivalent of daylight and is used as a reference light when viewing images, proofs and prints. A higher color temperature gives off a colder, bluish light, while a lower temperature provides a warmer, more yellow light.

There are several solutions to managing light in a work place. You can have light boxes and viewing boxes with the correct color temperature for viewing transparencies, reflectives, proofs and prints. The ideal solution is to light the entire workspace with lighting that has the right temperature and composition.

COLOR AND LIGHT PHENOMENA 4.8.2

The eye can also fool us. A particular color can be perceived in different ways depending on the color it is placed next to. A single color may be perceived as two totally different colors when placed next to different shades. This phenomenon is called contrast effect. There is also the situation in which two colors that look identical in a particular light become completely different in another light. This phenomenon is referred to as metamerism and is a result of the composition of the light and how the printing ink filters it.

▶ CORRECT VIEWING LIGHT PART 1
Because the color of a surface depends, in part, on the color temperature of the light falling on it, the same surface can appear as different colors under different lights.

▶ CORRECT VIEWING LIGHT PART 2
Two colors that look exactly the same under one type of light can look like completely different colors under another kind of light. This phenomenon is called metamerism.

▶ VIEWING BOX
It is important to view original artwork, proofs and prints in the correct light.

▶ LIGHT INDOORS
The light indoors can vary drastically. There are big differences in color temperature between a flash (right face), tungsten lighting (left face) and florescent lighting (background).

▶ DIFFERENT FILMS GIVE DIFFERENT RESULTS
Film by different manufacturers gives different results. There are variations in color and contrast.

LIGHT AND FILM 4.8.3

Photographic film is very sensitive to differences in the color temperature of light. For example, if you are photographing in tungsten light (typical bulblight) with a film adjusted for daylight and flash, the resulting images will have a strong yellow tint. Photographic films also differ in how they reproduce color. Some will produce colors that are

▶ THE KELVIN SCALE

Kelvin is a measurement of temperature used to describe light sources. When using Kelvin to describe a light source you aren't referring to the actual temperature of the light source. What color temperature means is that the illumination of a particular light source is perceived in the same way as a completely black object heated to the corresponding temperature in Kelvin.

The temperature unit Kelvin begins at absolute zero, −273 degrees Celsius or −459.4 degrees Fahrenheit. Thus the Kelvin scale cannot go below zero.

This also means that a temperature stated in degrees Celsius is equal to the temperature stated in Kelvin, (K) −273 degrees. For example, 5,000 K = 4,727 degrees Celsius. To calculate the temperature in Fahrenheit the following formula is used: F=9/5 (K−273)+32. Thus 5,000 K would equal 8,541.6 degrees Fahrenheit.

▶ CONTRAST EFFECT PART 1
Here we see an example of the color contrast effect. The color of the blue star when surrounded by green appears completely different from how it looks when surrounded by orange.

▶ CONTRAST EFFECT PART 2
A hue is perceived in a particular way because of its surroundings. The three stars in the upper row have the same hue, but appear to have different hues because of their different surroundings. The same goes for the stars in the row below.

▶ CORRECT FILM FOR CORRECT LIGHT
Photographs taken in tungsten light (typical bulblight) with daylight film will have a yellow cast, while a film adjusted to tungsten light will produce more accurate colors.

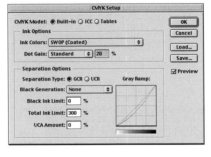

SIMULATING A PRINT ON THE SCREEN
Settings for on-screen print simulation work the same way in Adobe Illustrator 9.0 and Photoshop 6.0. First, select screen profile. It's done under Apple –> Control panels –> Colorsync –> Display.

Then go to View –> Proof Setup –> Custom. First select your desired ICC-profile for the simulation. If selecting Preserve Color Numbers, the image's colors will maintain their color values when converting from one color space to another. For example, a CMYK-image on the screen will be displayed the way it will look in print unless you re-separate the image with the ICC-profile selected for the image separation. This is useful if you want to check if an image can be used without re-separating it (i.e. no CMYK to CMYK conversion) [see 4.7.15]. After that, select conversion method (usually Perceptual).

The options under Simulate only exist in Photoshop and not in Illustrator. They provide a simulation of paper-white (white point) and the blackest in the print (black point). If you don't cross off Ink Black, black will always be displayed as darkly as the screen is capable of regardless of print simulation.

SIMULATING A PRINT IN ADOBE PHOTOSHOP 5.5
In Photoshop versions pre-dating 6.0, settings are established differently.

Under File –> Color Settings are RGB and CMYK Settings. You select the color space you want to work with under RGB Settings. Adobe RGB is a common choice.

Under CMYK Settings you set the CMYK Model you would like to work with, Built-in, ICC or Tables. Which model to select is specified by the printer. You will find more about how to establish the settings on page 93.

more saturated, while others may emphasize a certain color over the rest. It's always good to experiment with how different films behave in the circumstances you work under.

COLOR MANAGEMENT IN SOFTWARE 4.9

When using image-related software it is important to manage colors in such a way that they look real on the monitor and come out as expected in the print. Some software are better at doing that than others, and certain applications have no support whatsoever for color management. We'll take a closer look at Adobe Illustrator and Adobe Photoshop.

ADOBE ILLUSTRATOR AND ADOBE PHOTOSHOP 4.9.1

Today you can simulate the tonal changes that ocurr during the printing process in both Adobe Illustrator and Adobe Photoshop [see Images 5.8.4 and Printing 13.4.1]. Starting with Adobe Photoshop 6.0 and Adobe Illustrator 9.0, these settings are exclusively done using ICC profiles. In earlier versions, there are also other ways of setting the simulation. In the adjacent illustration we explain these settings.

In earlier versions, the settings used for simulating the print on the monitor are also used to adjust for printing – i.e., during the conversion from RGB into CMYK [see Images 5.8]. Starting with Illustrator 9.0 and Photoshop 6.0 these settings are established separately [see page 93]. ■

IMAGES

5.

CHAPTER 5 IMAGES IMAGES ARE A CENTRAL PART OF GRAPHIC PRODUCTION. IT REQUIRES SKILL TO CREATE IMAGES THAT COME OUT WELL IN PRINT. IMAGES ARE DIGITIZED WITH A SCANNER OR DIGITAL CAMERA, THEN EDITED AND PREPARED FOR PRINTING. MANY DECISIONS HAVE TO BE MADE DURING THE COURSE OF THE PRODUCTION WITH REGARD TO IMAGES.

▶ PIXEL GRAPHICS
Digitized photographic images consist of tiny squares of color, called pixels. The eye cannot perceive the pixels unless the image is greatly enlarged.

▶ OBJECT GRAPHICS
Object graphics consist of curves and lines. Images can be enlarged without affecting the quality.

Working with digital images requires knowledge of chromatics and printing. In this chapter we will cover the scanning of images, image editing, color converting, adjusting the images for print and different types of image compression. We will also look at different types of scanners and digital cameras.

We will start by looking at the basic types of digital images and file formats. There are two main types of digital images: object graphics and pixel graphics. Object graphics consist of mathematically calculated curves and lines that create surfaces and shapes, while pixel graphics are images consisting of pixels of different colors, squared to picture elements.

OBJECT GRAPHICS 5.1

Logotypes, news graphics and illustrations are examples of images that often consist of object graphics. Object graphics can include simple curves, straight lines, circles, squares, typefaces and other graphic objects. These can, in turn, have outlines of varying thickness and be filled with different colors, patterns and gradients. Object graphics are sometimes wrongly labeled "vector graphics." This term is derived from a time when vectors were used in graphic software. Simply speaking, a vector is a straight line between two points. In this technique, a series of short, straight lines is used to create the illusion of a curve. When you enlarge such images, however, the straight lines become visible and the curves appear jagged. Today object graphics are based on bezier curves. Bezier curves are softly bent curves that can assume any curved shape.

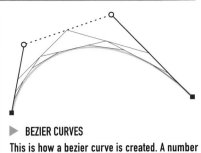

► **BEZIER CURVES**
This is how a bezier curve is created. A number of anchor points determine the shape of the curve. Object graphics are mainly based on bezier curves.

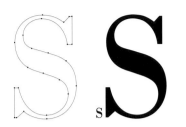

► **BEZIER GRAPHICS**
Bezier graphics are based on curves and, as a result, you get perfect outlines in rounded objects.

► **VECTOR GRAPHICS**
Vector graphics are based on straight lines and, as a result, you get jagged outlines in rounded objects.

Object graphics consist of filled-in areas with outlines. Mathematical values tell the computer to draw a certain type of line or curve from one point to another in the image. You get a very exact figure with a perfectly sharp outline that can be enlarged without affecting the quality. Only the limitations of the printer or the monitor you use affect the image quality. Object graphics use very little memory because only the location and design information must be defined – very simple values. This also applies to the colors used in object graphics, which are also expressed numerically.

OUTLINES AND LINES 5.1.1
Lines and outlines in object graphics can assume any color. You can also specify how thick the lines should be, the style of the lines (solid, dotted, etc.) and the shape of the corners (curved, squared, etc.).

FILL 5.1.2
Curved and closed objects can be filled with colors, color shifts and patterns. The colors are expressed numerically in terms of the ink coverage required for the respective printing inks. You can select fill patterns and color shifts from a predetermined menu.

PATTERNS 5.1.3
A pattern consists of a small group of objects repeated in a square pattern. It is easy to make your own patterns.

GRADIENTS 5.1.4
Color shifts are transitions among several colors at set distances. Gradients can either be linear or circular.

KNOCKOUTS 5.1.5
A curve that is placed within a closed object – a circle within a square, for example – can be selected as a knockout. In this example, the selection means that a circle knocks out a

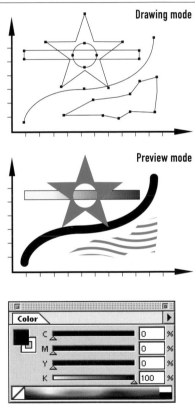

► **CREATING OBJECT GRAPHICS**
In Adobe Illustrator, objects with outlines are created in an invisible coordination system. Using the color palette you can provide the graphics with different attributes such as fill, width, outline, knockout, pattern and tone.

▶ BEZIER CURVES

In the image, you can see how bezier curves construct a letter and a logotype. From each anchor point you can grab a handle and modify the image.

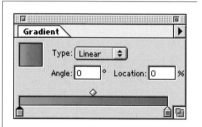

▶ GRADIENT

In Adobe Illustrator, you can create tonal transitions between two or more colors. A similar function exists in Macromedia Freehand.

▶ KNOCKOUTS

An object graphic can contain transparent parts called knockouts. In the image, the background photograph is visible through the circle knocked out in the center of the rectangle.

▶ CONVERTING PIXEL GRAPHICS INTO OBJECT GRAPHICS

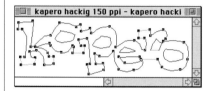

▶ Line art with a low resolution becomes jagged. It can be improved by converting it into bezier curves.

▶ Line art is converted into object graphics in a computer program (in this case Adobe Streamline).

▶ The result is an image with sharp outlines that can be enlarged as much as desired. The image can also be edited, for example in Adobe Illustrator.

▶ Photographs can also be converted into object graphics—but with a different result.

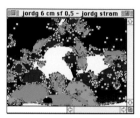

▶ Adobe Streamline divides the image into a number of colors consisting of monochromatic and curved surfaces.

▶ The image gets a poster-like appearance. In this case, we have divided the image into 10 different colors, creating 171 curved objects with a total of 836 anchor points.

transparent hole in the square. As a result, whatever you put behind the square will be visible through the circular hole.

APPLICATIONS FOR OBJECT GRAPHICS 5.1.6

Object graphics are created in illustration software such as Adobe Illustrator and Macromedia Freehand. There are also programs that take pixel graphics and converts them to object graphics. Adobe Streamline is one example. They are usually used to convert pixel-based logotypes into object graphics so they can be used in all possible sizes. Object graphics are usually saved in the image format EPS. You can also save them in whatever format the software uses, but then the object may not be able to be placed in a page layout application.

EPS FILES FOR OBJECT GRAPHICS 5.1.7

EPS files can contain both pixels and objects (more about that later). An EPS image that only contains object graphics consists of two parts: the objects and a pixel-based preview image in the file format PICT (on Macintosh) or BMP (on Windows). The preview image can be in black and white or in color and always has a resolution of 72 ppi (pixels per inch), because that is the monitor's standard resolution. It is used when placing EPS images into documents.

The objects in the EPS file are, as we mentioned earlier, independent of the image size. Therefore, the file size remains the same regardless of the measurements of the images. If, on the other hand, you make a large object-based image and save it in EPS format, the file size of the preview image will also be large – it is usually the preview image that takes up the most memory. If you don't have a lot of storage space for object-based EPS images, you can either choose to shrink the format before the image is saved in order to have a smaller preview image, or you can choose to save the preview image in black and white. A black and white preview image is less clear than a color preview image, but the quality of the printout is not affected.

PIXEL GRAPHICS 5.2

When photographs or illustrations are scanned into a computer, pixel-based images, or pixel graphics, are created. A pixel graphic is divided into tiny squares of color, almost like a mosaic. These tiny squares of color are referred to as pixels. Pixel graphics can also be created directly in the computer or by a digital camera.

RESOLUTION 5.2.1

If you assume that a pixel-based image is printed in a certain size, the image will consist of a certain number of pixels per centimeter or per inch (ppi). The resolution of an image is measured in ppi. This refers to the number and size of the pixels that make up a particular image. Sometimes the unit dpi is used (incorrectly) instead of ppi. Dpi, which means dots per inch, is the unit used to describe the output resolution in printers and imagesetters. If the resolution of an image is low, the pixels will be large, and you will clearly see that the graphic consists of a mosaic-like pattern. At a higher resolution, however, the eye cannot perceive that the image is made up of pixels. There is an appropriate high-level resolution for most images; if you make the resolution higher than that, you will not get a better quality image but it will take up more storage space.

COLOR MODES 5.2.2

Pixel-based images can be black and white or color and contain different number of colors colors. One usually says the images have different color modes. The simplest color mode is line art, which only contains two colors: black and white. Another example is the four-color image, which contains up to 16.7 million different colors. In between, you find grayscale images like black and white photographs; duotone images for tinted black and white images; indexed color images for the web; and images in RGB mode for image editing, the Web and multimedia. Every pixel in the image requires different amounts of memory depending on which color mode the image is saved in. The necessary memory

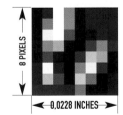

▶ IMAGE RESOLUTION
A pixel-based image always has a set resolution (pixels per inch, or ppi). In the example above, the image has 8 pixels/0.0228 inches= 350 pixels per inch, or 350 ppi.

LINE ART (BLACK) GRAYSCALE (BLACK) DUOTONE (BLACK+YELLOW) FOUR COLOR (C+M+Y+K)

▶ COLOR MODES
Here are examples of the same image in different color modes. You can also see which printing colors are used in the respective color mode.

▶ LINE ART
Line art consists of black or white pixels but no mid-range tones.

▶ RESOLUTION FOR LINE ART IMAGES

Line art images require higher resolution the better printing quality you would like:
Laser printout, newsprint 600 – 800 ppi
Fine uncoated paper 800 – 1,200 ppi
Fine coated paper 1,200 ppi – ∞

▶ GRAYSCALE IMAGES
Grayscale images consist of pixels of various tones of gray. Grayscale is appropriate for black and white photographs.

is expressed in bits per pixel; the more bits per pixel you have, the greater the number of different hues and colors a pixel can assume, thereby providing the image with more nuances.

LINE ART 5.2.3

Line art are images that only contain black and white pixels. Examples of such images are one-color logotypes or graphic illustrations like woodcuts. Screen fonts (the images of the typefaces displayed on the computer monitor) are line art images of letters [see Typeface 3.1.3]. Texts and images transmitted via fax are translated into line art.

Line art images are not screened when output [see Output 9.1], so the resolution rules for pixel-based images don't apply [see 5.4.9]. Line art requires a high resolution so that the image does not appear jagged due to all the pixels. The printing process determines the level of resolution needed. Around 600 ppi is appropriate for laser printouts and simpler prints. 1,000 to 1,200 ppi reproduces most details in a sheet-fed printing press on uncoated paper. Optimal print conditions and coated paper require more than 1,200 ppi for best results. When scanning a pre-printed and screened black and white image in the line art mode, you need to increase the resolution to 1,200–1,800 ppi to maintain the shape and size of the halftone dots, depending on the screen frequency [see 5.5.6]. Keep in mind that the upper range of the printer determines the maximum ppi you can print with. For example, a 1,200 ppi line art image printed on a printer with 600 dpi will not look better than a 600 ppi line art image.

GRAYSCALE IMAGES 5.2.4

A grayscale image contains pixels that can assume tones ranging from 0 to 100% of a particular color. The tonal range from white (0% black) to black (100% black) is divided into a scale with a number of different steps, usually 256, which is standard when working with PostScript. This makes the grayscale mode appropriate for black and white photographs that are going to be screened.

DUOTONES/TRITONES – TINTED GRAYSCALE IMAGES 5.2.5

As the name duotone indicates, two printing inks instead of one are used in these instances. If you want to reproduce fine details in a black and white image, make it softer or tint it a color other than black, you use duotones. Usually you print with black plus one spot

▶ DUOTONE
A duotone image has white and black parts and the scale in between is tinted in a color.

▶ "FAKE" DUOTONE
A grayscale image printed on a tinted area is called a "fake" duotone. The white parts of the grayscale image get the color of the tinted area.

▶ GRAYSCALE IMAGE IN COLOR
A grayscale image can also be printed using a spot color instead of black.

color of your choice. To ensure that the image does not become darker when the second ink is added, the black tones have to be lightened correspondingly. Image-editing software calculates the relationship between the first and second printing inks. Of course, you can also print with two spot colors instead of black and one spot color. If you print a grayscale image with three printing inks, it is called a tritone image, when it is done with four inks it is called quadtone.

When converting a grayscale image into a duotone image, the same pixel image is used for both printing inks. From a technical point of view, the same grayscale image forms the basis, but at output the image is separated into two colors – the black printing ink and the spot ink. Information about the spot colors is also added to the file, but duotones do not really take up that much more memory than black and white images.

It is important that the two halftone images output from a duotone image have the correct screen orientation. This means that the angles should be spaced to avoid moiré [see Output 9.1.6]. The program from which you are outputting the images can adjust the screen angles. With QuarkXPress, it is recommended that you set the screen angle for your spot color at the same angle you would use for cyan or magenta.

"Fake" duotones are black and white images printed over a colored tint area. You can also choose to print a grayscale image with a spot color. A duotone image should be saved in EPS format. The TIFF format does not work with duotones.

CREATING A DUOTONE IMAGE 5.2.6

Start with an image in grayscale mode. Select Duotone in Photoshop Image –> Mode –> Duotone. There are a number of useful pre-selected duotone combinations to choose from. If you want to create your own, you should select the printing inks you would like to use in the image. You do that by clicking on the color sample. You will then get a menu to select colors from. To change the ink percentage of different tones, click on the diagram of the ink you want to use and modify the curve. You will see the corresponding changes in the tonal range at the bottom of the window. Tritone and quadtone images can be built by defining additional colors and curves. Keep in mind that the printing color you have selected in Photoshop has to be defined with exactly the same name in your document in the page layout application.

▶ A black and white digital image consists of pixels in different shades of gray. The scale in between black and white is divided into a number of steps.

▶ Normally digital grayscale images consist of 256 different tones. As a result, the eye cannot perceive any distinct steps in the grayscale.

▶ Here is a "grayscale" for a duotone image with black and cyan. The darkest areas are black and the brightest are white. Because the scale between the black and white is tinted in a color, the image maintains its contrast compared to a grayscale image.

▶ DUOTONE SUMMARY

• Pixel-based grayscale image printed with two colors

• The relationship between the two colors is determined by curves

• Only works in EPS format

• Orientation of halftone screens is important

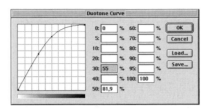

> **DUOTONE OPTIONS**

When creating an image in duotone mode, you have to start by selecting which colors you would like to print the image with. In this case, we are using two of the four process colors.

> **DUOTONE CURVE**

Two curves determine the allocation of the two spot colors. Under the curve you can see the result.

> **SAVING THE DUOTONE IMAGE**

The duotone image has to be saved as an EPS image. No special adjustments need to be made.

> **RGB MODE**

The RGB mode is based on the combination of light from three colors. The eye perceives this combination as color.

RGB 5.2.7

Red, green and blue, or RGB, are the colors used to scan a color image [see 5.9.1]. These are also the colors the monitor reproduces. Therefore, when images are previewed on the monitor – in multimedia presentations, for example – the RGB mode is usually used. Each pixel in the image has a value for how much red, green and blue it contains. The eye perceives this combination as a certain color [see Chromatics 4.4.1]. You could say that an RGB image consists of three separate pixel images. Technically, these are three images in the grayscale-mode that represent, respectively, red, green and blue. Because of this, an RGB image takes up three times as much memory as a grayscale image of the same size and resolution. In order for an RGB image to be printed, it has to be translated into the printing inks cyan, magenta, yellow and black, known as the four-color mode [see 5.7].

CMYK 5.2.8

When printing photographic images or other color images, the ink colors cyan, magenta, yellow and black are used; this is known as four-color printing. The transition from RGB mode to CMYK mode is called conversion. Each image in the four-color mode technically consists of four separate grayscale images. Each one of these defines the amount of each respective printing ink used during the printing process. A four-color image takes up 33% more memory than the same image in RGB mode because it consists of four separate files, rather than three [see 5.8].

INDEX COLOR MODE 5.2.9

Occasionally, you might want to use only selected colors in a digital image. You might do this because you want to keep the file size down or because the image is displayed on a monitor that can only manage a limited number of colors. Index color mode is used in these instances. GIF images for the Web are created in index color mode, for example.

An image in index color mode can display up to 256 different colors, which are defined as a palette in which each palette box contains a color and a number. This means that all the pixels in a particular image have a value between 1 and 256, based on the color palette. Therefore, in index color mode, an image only contains one pixel image of the same size

▶ INDEX COLOR MODE
This image only contains 256 colors, which is appropriate for displaying it on the monitor. To the right is Macintosh's system palette displaying 256 colors.

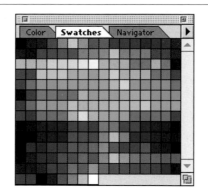

as a grayscale image, plus a palette. Usually you start with an RGB image, the colors of which are approximated as closely as possible by the 256 colors in the predefined index palette. You can also use palettes with fewer than 256 colors to further reduce the image file size. This is often done for web pages. Indexed images are usually not appropriate for color photographs, which contain far more than 256 colors.

▶ COLOR MODE AND MEMORY: HOW MUCH MEMORY IS NECESSARY?

Line art	1 bit per pixel	$= 2^1 = 2$ tones; black and white
Grayscale	8 bits per pixel	$= 2^8 = 256$ gray tones
Index color	(from 3 to) 8 bits per pixel	$= 2^8 = 256$ colors
Duotones	8 bits per pixel	$= 2^8 = 256$ gray*
RGB	$8+8+8 = 24$ bits per pixel	$= 2^8 \times 2^8 \times 2^8 = 256 \times 256 \times 256$ $= 16.7$ million colors
CMYK	$8+8+8+8 = 32$ bits per pixel	$= 2^8 \times 2^8 \times 2^8 \times 2^8 = 256 \times 256 \times 256 \times 256$ $= 4.3$ Billion colors **

*The image is still based on a pixel–based image in grayscale.

**The image comes from the RGB mode and has, as a result, 16.7 million colors. Because no additional colors are created when it's separated, you will still have 16.7 million colors.

AN ARITHMETICAL PROBLEM:
A 10×515 cm image with a resolution of 300 ppi contains 120 pixels per centimeter (1 inch=2,5 cm). This means that it contains a total of $(10 \times 120) \times (15 \times 120) = 2,160,000$ pixels. Because 8 bits is 1 byte, it is now easy to calculate the file size for this image in the different color modes. Line=270 KB, Grayscale/Index/Duotone=2.16 MB, RGB=6.48 MB, CMYK=8.64 MB

▶ CMYK MODE
The CMYK mode is based on combining the four printing inks by printing halftone dots on top of each other. The result is a color image.

FILE FORMATS FOR IMAGES 5.3

Pixel-based images can be saved in a number of file formats. Some of them have more or less become industry standards. They are primarily differentiated by which color modes they can handle as well as the level of features they are capable of. The most common image file formats are Photoshop, EPS, DCS, TIFF, Scitex CT, PICT, GIF and JPEG. Some are only used on Macintosh and others only on Windows. The two formats generally used in graphic production are TIFF and EPS.

PHOTOSHOP 5.3.1

This pixel-based image format is primarily used during the actual editing of the image. It cannot be used for output. One of the advantages of Photoshop is that it can save images in layers, which allows for more creativity in image retouching. Many other programs can read Photoshop-formatted files.

EPS 5.3.2

Encapsulated PostScript, or EPS, manages both object graphics and pixel graphics. This file format is used both with Adobe Illustrator and Adobe Photoshop. There are a number of useful functions in the EPS format for pixel graphics. Images can be selected with mask channels and the file format can store information about the halftone screen type and screen frequency as well as transfer functions for print adjustments.

The EPS file consists of two parts: a low-resolution preview image, and a PostScript-based image that can contain both objects and pixels. The preview image (PICT) is used when placing the image in the page layout software. EPS file formats are different for Windows and Macintosh. The high-resolution pixel part of the EPS file can be JPEG-compressed without losing any of its EPS functionality. As the name indicates, the Post-Script code is encapsulated in a file. Therefore, files in the EPS format are relatively protected, but it also means that you cannot edit an image once it is placed on a page. EPS handles line, grayscale, RGB and CMYK images as well as object graphics.

DCS AND DCS2 5.3.3

Desktop Color Separation, or DCS, is a version of the EPS-format for four-color images. DCS has all the functions that EPS has. The major difference is that a DCS file is divided into five parts: a low-resolution image for placing an image in PICT format, and four high-resolution images, one for each printing color (C, M, Y and K). DCS2 is a development of the DCS format enabling you to save an image in a certain number of files based on the number of colors the image contains. For example, if you have a four-color image with two spot colors the image is saved in seven separate image files: a low-resolution image for mounting, and six high-resolution images, one for each printing color (C, M, Y, K, Spot 1 and Spot 2). DCS2 is an appropriate format when creating artwork containing spot colors, commonly occurring in productions involving packaging.

One advantage with DCS is that the prepress company or printer can send low-resolution images to the designer or editor who is placing the images into the document. The high-resolution images simply replace the low-resolution ones when the document is output. A little warning when it comes to DCS: because the file consists of five parts, there is increased risk that part of the file will disappear or be damaged.

TIFF 5.3.4

Tagged Image File Format, or TIFF, is an open image format for pixel-based images. The file consists of a file head and information describing the image content, size and how the computer should read the file – a kind of instruction manual for how to open the image. TIFF images have the advantage of being able to be LZW-compressed directly from Photoshop [see 5.4.2]. The TIFF format also differs from Windows to Macintosh. TIFF handles line and grayscale images in RGB and CMYK modes.

SCITEX CT AND SCITEX LW 5.3.5

Scitex CT (Continuous Tone) for color and grayscale images and Scitex LW (Line Work) for line images are two less common formats used by scanners, image editing systems and RIPs from Scitex. Photoshop can also handle these formats.

PICT 5.3.6

Picture format, or PICT, is exclusively a Macintosh format. Mac computers use this format internally for icons and other system graphics. It is also used to create low-resolution mounting images in EPS and OPI systems. PICT images are not appropriate for print production and are primarily used for line, grayscale and RGB images.

GIF 5.3.7

Graphic Interchange Format, or GIF, is a file format primarily used on the Web. An American ISP, CompuServe, originally created the GIF format to make images small enough to be easily sent via telephone lines. A GIF image is always in index mode, can consist of line as well as grayscale images and can contain anywhere from 2 to 256 different colors. The number of possible colors is determined by how many bits are assigned to a pixel: 1 to 8 bits are possible. The colors are selected from a palette, which can be adjusted to the actual color content of the images or be drawn from set palettes for Macintosh or Windows. There is also a set palette for the web that represents a combination of Macintosh and Windows palettes.

JPEG 5.3.8

The Joint Photographic Experts Group, or JPEG, format is a compression method for images that also works as its own image format. The advantage to the JPEG format is that it is the same on all computer platforms. JPEG works for grayscale, RGB and CMYK modes [see 5.4.4].

PDF 5.3.9

Portable Document Format, or PDF, manages both object graphics and pixel graphics. Adobe Photoshop 6 and Adobe Illustrator 9 can save and edit images in high-resolution PDF. PDF will most likely become more commonly used because it combines the best characteristics of the EPS format and Photoshop, is better standardized and can be read across all platforms.

▶ TIFF +/−

+ Color, contrast and brightness can be modified in the page layout software

+ Can be LZW-compressed

+ Slightly smaller file size than EPS

− Cannot contain mask channels or halftone screen information

---

▶ POSSIBLE COLOR MODES FOR THE VARIOUS IMAGE FILE FORMATS

TIFF – line art, grayscale, RGB, CMYK

EPS – line art, grayscale, RGB, CMYK, object

PICT – line art, grayscale, RGB, object

GIF – index color maximum 256 colors

Scitex CT – grayscale, CMYK

Scitex LW – line art

JPEG – RGB, CMYK

▶ THE CONSTRUCTION OF IMAGES BASED ON FILE FORMAT

TIFF – File head and bitmap file

EPS – Encapsulated PostScript information and preview in PICT

GIF – Color palette and compressed bit map information

JPEG – Visually reduced and Huffman - coded file

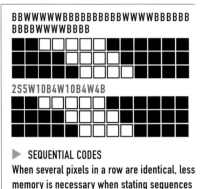

BBWWWWWBBBBBBBBBBBWWWWBBBBBB
BBBBWWWWBBBB

2S5W10B4W10B4W4B

▶ SEQUENTIAL CODES
When several pixels in a row are identical, less memory is necessary when stating sequences of pixels (2 5 10 4 10 4 4) than when stating the color of each pixel (1 1 0 0 0 0 0 1 1 1 1 1 1 1 1 1 1 0 0 0 0 1 1 1 1 1 1 1 1 1 1 0 0 0 0 1 1 1 1). This is the basis for sequential coding.

COMPRESSION ⁵·⁴

Images often take up a lot of storage space in the computer. Most of the time this is not a problem, but when transporting images, particularly via network and telephone lines, it is important to minimize the memory used to ensure fast transmission times. Therefore, images are usually compressed. There are two types of image compression: lossless and lossy. Aside from these, there is also the possibility of using certain common file compression programs, which can be used on all file types.

LOSSLESS IMAGE COMPRESSION ⁵·⁴·¹

This type of compression reduces the size of an image file without reducing image quality. When the image is uncompressed, it will look exactly like it did before compression. From a purely technical point of view, the description of the way in which the image is digitally stored is simplified.

A simple type of lossless compression is sequential coding. It is used for line art, which only consist of black and white pixels. Normally the code states the color of each individual pixel. A row might look like this: black, black, black, white, white, white, white, white, white, white, white, white, white, white, white, white, black, black, black, black, black, black. If the image is compressed with sequential coding, the row would be defined like this instead: 3 black, 14 white, 6 black. This takes up considerably less memory. Normally, images consist of many continuous parts of the same color, which means that compression can save a lot of space. Other examples of lossless compression methods include Huffman and LZW-compression (after the scientists Lempel, Ziv and Welch, who developed the method). Huffman coding is used in a modified version in fax machines.

▶ Uncompressed line image = 321 KB

▶ Uncompressed four-color image = 2 100 KB

▶ Same image LZW-compressed = 66 KB

▶ Same image heavily JPEG-compressed = 61 KB

▶ COMPRESSION AND FILE SIZE
Here are examples of how LZW compression affect the file size of an image. LZW-compression is lossless and has the greatest effect on line art while grayscale and color images are only compressed to half their original size.

LZW COMPRESSION 5.4.2

LZW compression can be used for images saved in the TIFF-format. It takes a couple of extra seconds to place an LZW-compressed TIFF image than it does to place a non-compressed TIFF image. LZW can handle line, grayscale, RGB and CMYK images. An LZW-compressed line image is reduced to about 1/10 its original size, while grayscale, RGB and CMYK images are reduced to about half of their original size.

LOSSY IMAGE COMPRESSION 5.4.3

There are types of compression that remove information from the image. Generally, they remove image information that cannot be perceived by the human eye. It can be a matter of tiny changes in a color or details in a surface that is mostly one color. You could say that you are simplifying the image. If you compress an image too much, however, you can remove too much information. The loss in quality is clearly visible; the image loses sharpness and begins to look like it is constructed of monochromatic fields of different sizes.

JPEG 5.4.4

The most common type of lossy image compression method is JPEG. The abbreviation JPEG stands for Joint Photographic Experts Group, after the group that designed the method. JPEG compression allows you to set the amount of information that can be removed from the image and thereby control the level of image compression. At the lowest levels of compression – when the image loses the least information – the file is reduced

▶ **LZW +/–**
+ Does not ruin the image
+ Can be used in TIFF and placed directly on the page
+ Works well for line art
– Does not reduce file size much
– Takes longer to open and save

▶ Uncompressed image, 2.100 KB

▶ JPEG Lightly compressed, 840 KB

▶ JPEG Medium compressed, 165 KB

▶ JPEG Heavily compressed, 61 KB

▶ **JPEG – IMAGE QUALITY AND FILE SIZE**
Lossy compression may sound dangerous but the fact is you can JPEG-compress without any visible difference in the end result. Of course, heavy compression is visible but if you're compressing lightly it is very difficult to notice a difference. In addition, you have a lot to gain in file size, which might be a great advantage when storing or transmitting images via the Internet. (The partial enlargements above are shown 3 times their original size.)

to about 1/10 of its original size and the loss cannot be perceived with the eye. When an image is compressed more, you would perceive the change if you compared the two images. With JPEG compression you are able to compress an image as much as you like, but the quality of the image can be reduced considerably as a result. If you edit an image in JPEG-format, it will be compressed every time it is saved. Therefore, images that will be edited repeatedly should not be saved in JPEG format.

JPEG is an independent format that works just as well on Macintosh as on Windows and other platforms. As a result, JPEG files can be moved with ease. The EPS format enables you to compress images using the JPEG format. The result of JPEG-compressing an EPS image is a normal EPS file with all its advantages and disadvantages. The high-resolution pixel image is JPEG-compressed but the file has a normal preview image.

FILE COMPRESSION 5.4.5

All types of data files can be compressed, with differing results in regards to the file size. Such file compression is completely lossless, meaning that no information is lost. You simply convert the file to a more efficient way of using ones and zeros. There are many programs that compress files this way, including Compact Pro, Stuffit, ZIP and Disk Doubler. Of course, image files can be compressed this way as well.

SCANNING IMAGES 5.5

In the following section, we will review what you need to know about scanning images into a computer, including the definitions of tonal range, tone compression and gamma. Resolution, screen frequency and sampling value are other terms of central importance. To begin with, we will look at what you should keep in mind when working with different types of original images.

ORIGINAL IMAGES 5.5.1

Original image refers to the original material that is scanned into the computer to create a digital image. An original image can be a paper print (reflective art), a slide or a negative (transparent art), or even a hand-drawn illustration, etc.

Different original images are appropriate for different situations. When you intend to print an image in large format or partially enlarge an image, it is important to select large originals. The maximum resolution of the scanner sets limitations on how much you can enlarge an image. If the scanner has a low resolution, you will not be able to enlarge an image very much. The size of the original is particularly important when using slides or negatives because the grain of the film can become clearly visible if the image has to be enlarged too much.

Different originals also have different life spans. A Polaroid picture will probably only keep its quality for a couple of years, while a correctly treated black and white paper print stored in a cool, dry and dark place can survive for more than 100 years.

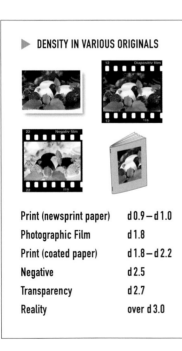

▶ DENSITY IN VARIOUS ORIGINALS

Print (newsprint paper)	d 0.9 – d 1.0
Photographic Film	d 1.8
Print (coated paper)	d 1.8 – d 2.2
Negative	d 2.5
Transparency	d 2.7
Reality	over d 3.0

TONE RANGE 5.5.2

The tone range refers to the number of tones that can be captured by a particular type of original. Slide films have the highest tone range of the materials discussed here, and are often used as originals when scanning because they contain the most information. Tone range is expressed in density units, and is a measurement of the maximum contrast between the lightest and the darkest areas of an image. An original slide usually has a tone range of 2.7–3.0 density units. By contrast, a print on a fine, coated paper has a tone range of around 2.2 density units, a print on newsprint paper has a tone range of approximately 0.9 density units and a print on paper based on a negative has a tone range of around 1.8 density units.

TONE COMPRESSION 5.5.3

Paper printouts generally cannot reproduce as much tonal information as an original image. Thus, when reproducing a film original, you need to compress the tone range of the original image to that of the paper you intend to print on. When you scan the image you need to take the tone range of the selected paper into consideration and make adjustments accordingly. In practice, a low tone range in print means that small tonal transitions that you can see in the original image are no longer visible when it is printed. Wider tonal variations will be perceived as distinct steps instead of smooth transitions. Tones that are too similar in value will blend together in the print.

TYPES OF MOTIFS 5.5.4

Tone compression results in a loss of image information. To use the image information in the best possible way, you can control the tone compression and prioritize certain areas of the image, giving them a higher tonal range than others. You should assess each image before scanning it in order to decide which parts of the image to prioritize. For example, if you have original artwork with a lot of detail in the dark areas, you can prioritize the tone range of those dark areas and compress the lighter areas more, thus preserving the important information in the image.

We have divided images into three categories or motifs: snow images, mid-range images and night images. A snow image is bright overall and has a lot of detail in the bright areas. The mid-range image has details mostly in the mid-range areas. A night image is a dark image with lots of detail in the dark areas.

▶ **Tone compression**
Because tone range is lower in the print than in reality, it must be compressed. When you compress, tones are lost and you need to prioritize which tones are most important.

▶ **SNOW IMAGE**
The snow image is bright and has a lot of detail in the bright areas.

▶ **MID-RANGE IMAGE**
The mid-range image has details mostly in the mid-range areas.

▶ **NIGHT IMAGE**
A night image is a dark image with a lot of detail in the dark areas.

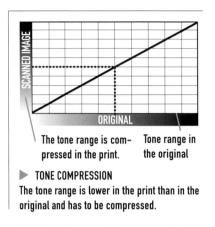

The tone range is com-
pressed in the print.　　Tone range in
　　　　　　　　　　　the original

▶ TONE COMPRESSION
The tone range is lower in the print than in the
original and has to be compressed.

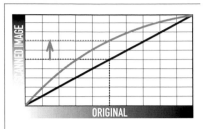

▶ GAMMA CURVE FOR SNOW IMAGES
This gamma curve has a gamma value
lower than 1.8 and is used for snow
images. The bright tones are prioritized
while the dark tones are compressed.

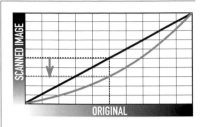

▶ GAMMA CURVE FOR NIGHT IMAGES
This gamma curve has a gamma value
higher than 1.8 and is used for night images.
Here the dark tones of the image are prioritized while the bright tones are compressed.

▶ RECOMMENDED SCREEN FREQUENCY
Below is a list of the recommended
screen frequency for the different paper
types and printing methods:

Paper

Newsprint paper	65 – 85 lpi
Uncoated	100 – 133 lpi
Coated, matte	133 – 170 lpi
Coated, glossy	150 – 300* lpi

Printing methods

Offset	65 – 300* lpi
Gravure	120 – 200 lpi
Screen	50 – 100 lpi
Flexographic	90 – 120 lpi

* Water-free offset

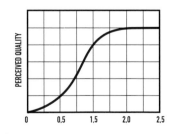

▶ THE SAMPLING FACTOR
Increasing the sampling factor above 2 will not
result in a better image. Instead, the image file
will just take up a lot of memory and can become
awkward to work with in the computer.

THE GAMMA CURVE 5.5.5

You can adjust the tone compression of an image with the help of a gamma curve. The gamma curve allows you to see how the tone values of the original artwork are translated into tone values for the print. A linear gamma curve does not affect the translation of tones, while gamma curves with various curvatures control the translation of tones in different ways.

The gamma value states the orientation and the position of the gamma curve. Normally, a gamma value of 1.8 is recommended for mid-range tones, because it approximates how the human eye perceives color. A night image, on the other hand, has to be scanned with a high gamma value so that the details in the dark areas of the original will appear in the print. The trade-off is reduced detail reproduction in the bright areas of the image. A snow image should be scanned with a gamma value less than 1.8 so that all the detail in the bright areas of the original image is reproduced in the print. The quality of the details in dark areas of the snow image will be compromised somewhat as a result.

RESOLUTION AND SCREEN FREQUENCY 5.5.6

When scanning, you must specify the resolution of the image. The resolution is stated in pixels per inch, or ppi. Two things determine the scanning resolution: the screen frequency you wish to print with, and whether or not you need to change the size of the image. The screen frequency is determined by the printing method and paper you use.

THE SAMPLING FACTOR 5.5.7

The relationship between the image resolution and the screen frequency of the print is called the sampling factor. It has been determined that the optimal sampling factor is 2 – i.e., the resolution of the image should be twice as high as the screen frequency. For example, an image that will be printed with a screen frequency of 150 lpi (lines per inch) should be scanned with a resolution of 300 ppi. If the sampling factor is less than 2, image quality will be compromised, although it is difficult for the eye to perceive this until the sampling factor starts to get below 1.7. If the sampling factor gets down to around 1, the pixels

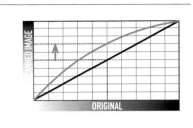 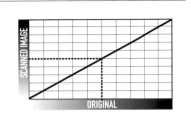 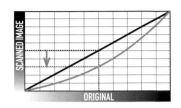

▶ **GAMMA LOWER THAN 1.8**
The images below are scanned with the recommended gamma curve for snow images.

▶ **GAMMA EQUALS 1.8**
The images below are scanned with the recommended gamma curve for mid-range images.

▶ **GAMMA HIGHER THAN 1.8**
The images below are scanned with the recommended gamma curve for night images.

▶ **SNOW IMAGE**
The snow image maintains detail in the bright areas of the image but compromises the level of detail in the dark areas.

▶ **SNOW IMAGE**
The snow image loses part of its detail in the bright areas of the image.

▶ **SNOW IMAGE**
The snow image loses all of its detail in the bright areas of the image.

▶ **MID-RANGE IMAGE**
The mid-range image loses part of its detail in the dark areas of the image.

▶ **MID-RANGE IMAGE**
The mid-range image maintains detail in the mid-range areas of the image but compromises the level of detail in the dark and bright areas.

▶ **MID-RANGE IMAGE**
The mid-range image loses part of its detail in the bright areas of the image.

▶ **NIGHT IMAGE**
The night image loses detail in the dark areas of the image.

▶ **NIGHT IMAGE**
The night image loses part of its detail in the dark areas of the image.

▶ **NIGHT IMAGE**
The night image maintains detail in the dark areas of the image but compromises the level of detail in the bright areas.

created by the scanning process will be clearly visible in the printed image. On the other hand, increasing the sampling factor above 2 will not result in a better image. Instead, the image file will just take up a lot of memory and can become awkward to work with [see below].

THE SCALING FACTOR [5.5.8]

If you want to enlarge the entire image or even partial areas of an image in relation to the original, you have to take this into consideration when selecting the scanning resolution. The relationship between the size of the original image and the print is called the scaling

▶ **THE SAMPLING FACTOR**

▶ The image is 1,382KB

▶ The image is 957KB

▶ The image is 627KB

▶ The image is 479KB

▶ The image is 380KB

▶ The image is 297KB

▶ The image is 182KB

▶ The image is 116KB

▶ The image is 66KB

▶ Above are examples of the same image with different sampling factors. Research shows that a sampling factor above 2 does not result in a better image, just a larger file size. It has been determined that a sampling factor slightly higher or lower than 2 provides the optimal relationship between file size and image quality. The effect of a low resolution in relation to the screen frequency (low sampling factor) is most evident in diagonal outlines, for example in the upper corner of the open lid. Generally low resolution results in blurriness and extremely low resolution in clearly visible pixels. These images are screened at 100 lpi to make the effect of a low resolution clearly visible.

factor. If, for example, you are printing an image at three times the size of the original, the scaling factor will be 3. This means you must have three times the scanning resolution as you would if the image was printed in the same size as the original.

THE OPTIMAL SCANNING RESOLUTION 5.5.9

The scanning resolution is determined by multiplying the screen frequency, the sampling factor and the scaling factor. For example, if you have an image you want to print with a screen frequency of 150 lpi at 170% of the original size, the optimal scanning resolution will be $150 \times 2 \times 1.7 = 510$ ppi. You should select the resolution on your scanner that is closest to the optimal value in order to get fast, good scanning. In this case, you would probably select 600 ppi, as the preset resolutions are usually expressed in even hundreds. Keep in mind that the resolution of the image equals double the screen frequency, while the scanning resolution equals the resolution of the image multiplied by the scaling factor. In the example above, the image resolution would equal 300 ppi, and the scanning resolution would equal $1.7 \times 300 = 510$ ppi. Most scanning applications have a function that automatically calculates the optimal scan resolution if you provide the screen frequency and the scaling factor.

HOW MUCH CAN YOU ENLARGE AN IMAGE? 5.5.10

Your ability to enlarge images is determined by the original artwork and the maximum scan resolution of the scanner. The maximum scan resolution is the smallest unit of length that the scanner head is constructed for. If a scanner has a maximum resolution of 1,200 ppi, it means that it can scan an original image at a maximum of 1,200 dots per inch.

Using the previous example, and assuming that the scanner has a maximum scan resolution of 1,200 ppi, an image that is printed at 150 lpi requires an image resolution of 300 ppi if we are using the optimal sampling factor of 2. This means that you can maximally enlarge the image: 1,200 ppi/300ppi = 4 times. In other words, an image that is going to

> **OPTIMAL SCANNING RESOLUTION**
> Optimal scanning resolution =
> screen frequency (lpi) × sampling
> factor* × scaling factor (%)
>
> * The sampling factor should be 2

> **SCREEN FREQUENCY AND IMAGE FORMAT**

	A6	A5	A4	A3	File size in RGB:	
500 ppi/250 lpi	4	5	6	7	1 – appr 2.25 MB	5 – appr 36 MB
350 ppi/175 lpi	3	4	5	6	2 – appr 4.5 MB	6 – appr 72 MB
240 ppi/120 lpi	2	3	4	5	3 – appr 9 MB	7 – appr 144 MB
170 ppi/85 lpi	1	2	3	4	4 – appr 18 MB	

As soon as you change the size of digital images the resolution, and thereby the screen frequency, is affected. The table shows the relationship between file size/image format and image resolution/screen frequency. In a digital image enlarged 200%, for example from A6 to A4, the resolution is cut in half and it can only be printed with a maximum of half the screen frequency of the original image. An image scanned in the A6 format for 250 lpi, i.e. 500 ppi, can be enlarged to A5 for 175 lpi, A4 for 120 lpi or A3 for 85 lpi (=number code 4 above).

> **TO ENLARGE IMAGES**
> If an image is enlarged three times its size, the resulting image requires 9 pixels for an area of the motif that only required 1 in the original size. Thus, it takes 9 times more memory to store and edit the enlarged image compared to the smaller one.

be printed at 150 lpi and read with a scanner resolution of 1,200 ppi can be enlarged 400% at most. If you are scanning an image that you want to print in a large format, it makes sense to use a large original image. If the original image you use is too small, you run the risk of not being able to enlarge it enough.

PLACING AN IMAGE 5.5.11

When placing an image in a page layout application, you can change its size. You should keep in mind that the resolution of the scanned image is dependent on its size, which means that any changes you make to the size in the page layout application will affect the resolution. For example, when you enlarge an image in a page layout application, its resolution is lowered.

For example, an image scanned with sampling factor 2 is enlarged to 150% in the page layout application. As a result, the sampling factor is lowered to 2/1.5 = 1.33—much too low. If we allow for a minimum sampling factor of 1.7, it would be possible to enlarge the

▶ SCALING FACTOR

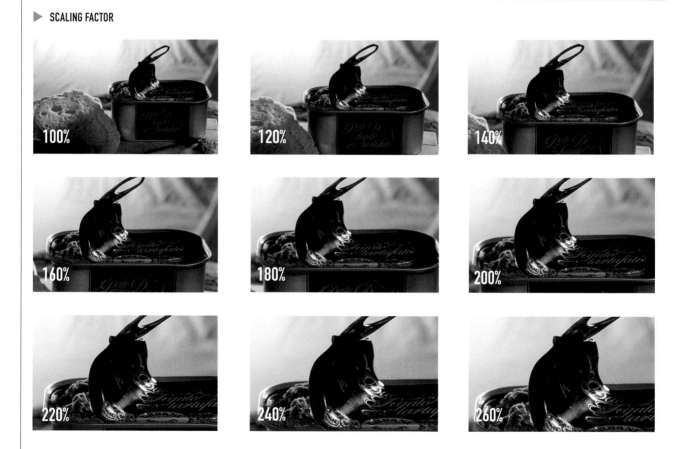

▶ Above are examples of an image with different scaling factors. Research shows that enlargements up to 120% provide a good result. With enlargements of more than 120% you'll get a clearly visible quality loss. The effect is most evident in diagonal outlines, for example in the upper corner of the open lid. Generally, great enlargements result in blurriness and extreme enlargements in clearly visible pixels.

image to 2/1.7 = 1.18 = 118%. This calculation expresses the outside range of how much you can enlarge an image without visible quality loss; the general guideline for enlarging images in a page layout application is 115–120%.

If you would like to enlarge the image more, you have four alternatives: scan it again with a higher resolution, lower the screen frequency in the print, accept decreased quality or interpolate a higher resolution in an image editing application. The interpolation will not provide the same quality as if the image had been scanned with the correct resolution, but you will get a better result than if printing the image with a resolution that is too low [see 5.6.3].

STORING AND RE-USING DIGITAL IMAGES 5.5.12

The scanning resolution limits image size and maximum screen frequency. CMYK conversion limits the field of application for an image. Images that are intended for many different purposes should therefore be stored non-converted at high resolution. These types of images could also be called digital artwork. You can choose to store an un-converted image in RGB or CIELAB. When it is prepared for print it has to be converted. Theoretically, you can never escape the size limitations of a scanned image, but with a high enough resolution you can create a digital artwork that can be used for most purposes. If an image is continually used in the same type of production, it can be stored converted.

IMAGE EDITING 5.6

There are a number of image editing procedures that are regularly executed during graphic production to ensure good image quality. However, most image editing procedures cause a loss of information in the image, compromising fine details, colors, etc. This means you can destroy an image if you are careless or perform too many tasks. It is therefore important to edit an image as little as possible and to perform the steps in the correct order. You would also want to keep a smooth workflow. Despite the fact that all steps technically "destroy" the image, the final result will generally give the impression of a better image. That is the whole purpose of image editing.

To avoid unnecessary loss of image information, adjustments to brightness, contrast and color should as much as possible be performed when the image is scanned. We will now review the steps of image editing, using a scanned image as our example.

THE ORDER OF THE STEPS 5.6.1

We recommend the following order when it comes to editing an image: first, shrink and crop the image to its final content and size – this will make the rest of the work faster and simpler. Next, make any aesthetic adjustments to the image that affect the print as a whole, followed by those affecting only specific areas of the print. Finally, make any changes needed to accommodate the printing process you plan to use, such as setting the sharpness and the color conversion.

▶ **IMAGE REPRODUCTION STEP-BY-STEP**

The recommended procedure when adjusting a recently scanned image in Adobe Photoshop:

All images:

1. Crop the image precisely.

2. Set the correct resolution.

3. Set the black and white points.
   Levels... (Ctrl+L).

4. Set brightness and contrast with
   Curves... (Ctrl+M).

Color images:

5. Set the color balance.
   Color balance (Ctrl+B).

6. Set hue and saturation with Hue-
   /Saturation or Selective
   Color.

All images:

7. Do all applicable selections, masks
   etc.

8. Save the image if it is going to be
   archived and used for other products.

9. Sharpen the image with
   Unsharp Mask.

Color images:

10. Separate the image based on the
    print prerequisites.

All images:

11. Save the image in an appropriate file
    format.

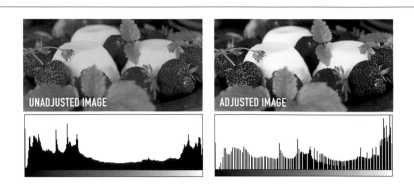

UNADJUSTED IMAGE

ADJUSTED IMAGE

▶ TO DESTROY AND IMPROVE AT THE SAME TIME

On the left is a recently scanned, unedited image without any loss of information. The histogram under the image describes its distribution of tones along the entire tone range, dark tones to the left and bright tones to the right. The height of the columns describes the number of pixels for each tone. To the right is the same image after it has been edited. In the histogram under the image, you can see that quite a number of tones have disappeared from the image—gaps occur in the histogram. The image becomes "lossy" because it loses image information. However, it still looks better to the eye. As soon as images are edited, some image information disappears. It is not a problem unless you edit the image too much. If it's edited repeatedly or in the wrong order, even more tones disappear and the image will end up with a loss of quality.

1. CROP THE IMAGE 5.6.2

Start by making sure the composition of the image is correct. Remove any unnecessary parts of the image by cropping it so you're not working with a larger image surface than you need. A smaller image makes for faster editing. Keep in mind that if the image requires bleeds, it needs to extend 1/4" beyond the edge of the page.

2. CORRECT RESOLUTION 5.6.3

After scanning, and particularly if the image is retrieved from a digital archive, etc., the resolution of the image has to be adjusted to that needed for the final print. We covered the process for calculating the optimal resolution earlier in this chapter. The adjustment is simple. Just make sure that Photoshop is set to use "Bicubic Interpolation" when you edit the images. It is the best method in Photoshop for scaling and rotating images, i.e., those operations in which the pixels are recalculated.

3. SET THE BLACK POINT AND WHITE POINT 5.6.4

Because the print has a more limited tonal range than reality and the original image, you want to enhance the tonal range of the print as much as possible. This is primarily done by setting the correct black and white points. The black point and white point settings determine the contrast of the image, ensuring that what appears as white in the digital image also appears white in print, and that the black areas in the image will print a true black.

Under the menu Image –> Adjust –> Levels, there are several ways to set the black and white points. Sometimes the automatic adjustment is enough to do the trick. The

▶ CROP THE IMAGE
In most image editing applications the symbol for cropping looks like two triangles.

program determines the lightest and darkest area in the image and sets them as the white and black points, respectively. To see which areas of the image will be completely white, you can press the alt key and click on the white or black triangle that you adjust the white levels with. This will show you those areas that don't have any color versus those that have a full amount of printing ink. Keep in mind that Preview cannot be checked off in order for this function to work. The percentages that white and black point should be printed with can be set. The values vary depending on the print process but for an offset print, the white point should not be less than 3%.

4. ADJUST BRIGHTNESS AND CONTRAST 5.6.5

In most cases, you will probably want to adjust the brightness and contrast of the image, if only in certain areas. For example, you might want to lighten up just the dark areas and

▶ **BLACK- AND WHITE POINTS**
You can adjust black and white points in the image by using Levels.
Click on Auto or adjust manually according to the procedure below.

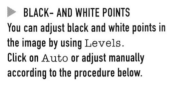

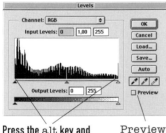

Press the alt key and click on the white or black arrow to adjust the white- or black points.

Preview cannot be checked off in order for this function to work.

▶ **CHECKING WHITE POINT**

When checking the white point only the entirely white parts of the image are displayed as white — everything else is black. The reverse applies when the black point is checked.

```
C = 12 %
M = 12 %
Y = 12 %
K =  3 %
```

```
C = 7 %
M = 5 %
Y = 5 %
K = 3 %
```

▶ **WHAT IS WHITE?**
The brain decides what is perceived as white in an image. The motif determines the interpretation. If the brain knows that a certain area of an image should be white it is perceived as white even if it's not, as in the image above.

maintain the brightness and contrast of the rest of the image. The best way to adjust brightness and contrast in Adobe Photoshop is to go to Image -> Adjust -> Curves.

5. ADJUST COLOR CASTS [5.6.6]

An image with an erroneous gray balance will wind up with what is called a "color cast," which means that the entire image will appear to be tinted a certain color. There are several tools for adjusting the gray balance in order to eliminate possible color casts. One can be found under Curves, Color Balance and Variations under the menu Image -> Adjust.

Color Balance allows you to regulate each respective color, while Variations allows you to view several versions of the image with different compensations for the color cast. All colors in the image are affected (unless you have marked only a specific area for changes). Variations allows you to modify just the highlights, midtones, or dark areas of an image. You can also modify the hightones of the images under Variations.

In order to achieve the correct gray balance and remove color casts quickly you can try the following procedure. First, display the palette Info under Window -> Show Info. Set the palette so you can see CMYK values. Find an area in the image that should be neutral gray tone. Measure the area with the eyedropper tool and compare that to the correct gray balance values, then adjust the entire image until the part of the image that should be neutral has achieved those values [see 5.8.2 and Print 13.4.3]. Correct gray balance values for a variety of print method/paper combinations should be available from your commercial printer. You can find some general recommendations further into this chapter [see

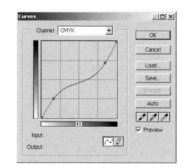

▶ **BRIGHTNESS AND CONTRAST**
By using Curves you can adjust the brightness and contrast of the image. To some extent you can also adjust the white and black points.

When the curve's shape changes the image's appearance changes accordingly. In this case, a flatter curve provides a "softer" image and a steeper curve a "harder." Keep in mind that the beginning and end stay in the same place, thus the white and black points are not affected.

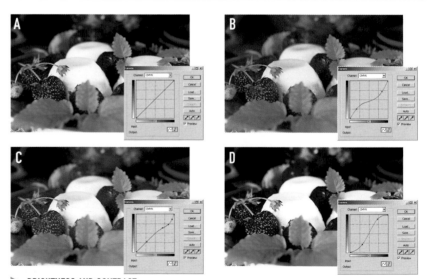

▶ **BRIGHTNESS AND CONTRAST**
A: The image is not adjusted thus the curve is straight. B: The image has been "softened" by flattening the mid-section of the curve. Black and white points are not affected. C: The dark areas of the image have been brightened. The rest of the image is not affected. D: The image has been made "harder" by sharpening the mid-section of the curve.

▶ GENERAL COLOR ADJUSTMENTS

The example above shows an image before and after general color adjustments have been made. In the image to the left, there is a cast of cyan. In the image to the right, the image has been adjusted so the neutral parts of the image have determined a change of all the colors in the image.

5.8.2]. When you have achieved the right gray balance in the most important areas of the image, the rest of the image should be correct as well. If the light varies throughout the image, you may need to make partial adjustments depending on the light in a particular area.

6. ADJUST CERTAIN COLORS 5.6.7

Sometimes you might want to adjust particular colors in an image. Often it is natural reference colors, like skin tone, the color of the grass or the sky, etc., that need to be corrected. The tool Image -> Adjust -> Hue/Saturation enables you to perform independent adjustments to a color's hue, saturation and brightness. This tool also enables you to make general changes to the image, like increasing the overall color saturation. You can also use this same tool for more manipulative operations like changing the color of an individual strawberry, flag, or other specific objects in an image.

7. RETOUCHES, SELECTIONS 5.6.8

Before the image is saved, you should remove any imperfections, such as dust flecks, etc., and conduct any additional retouches or montages [see 5.6.10]. If you want to make selections in the image, now is also the time to do so.

8. STORE THE IMAGE 5.6.9

If the image needs to be stored for future products you should do it now, while it is still in RGB mode. As soon an image has been adjusted for a specific print it is difficult to reuse efficiently for other purposes.

9. SHARPEN THE IMAGE 5.6.10

If the image appears "soft" it is generally due to a lack of sharp transitions between the dark and light hues in an outline. In order to increase the impression of sharpness in the overall image, you have to find these soft tonal transitions and sharpen them. This type of artificial sharpening is conducted on most images to varying degrees. An image is softened when it's converted into halftone screens and in the printing process. Because of that you need to sharpen the image even more.

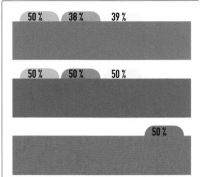

▶ GRAY BALANCE

Equal amounts of the three primary colors do not provide gray balance. What we can see above is a comparison to a neutral tint area consisting of 50% black.

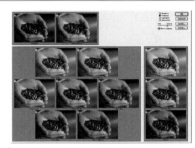

▶ ADJUST COLOR CASTS PART 1

Variations is one of three tools for general color adjustments in the image. It helps you to see how the image changes (see above).

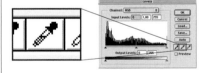

▶ ADJUST COLOR CASTS PART 2

By selecting the gray eyedropper tool in Levels and clicking on the part of the image that has to be neutral, you can adjust color casts.

▶ ADJUST COLOR CASTS PART 3

In Color Balance you make general color changes in the image by adjusting the color cast.

BEFORE

AFTER

▶ **SELECTIVE COLOR PART 1**
In Selective Color or Hue/Satura-
tion you can change selected colors in the
image. You can even make strawberries unripe!

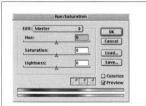

▶ **Selective Color Part 2**
Hue/Saturation is the easiest tool
for adjusting individual colors. For example, check off green if you want to change
green colors.

▶ **TIP – AVOID PIGS' FACES**

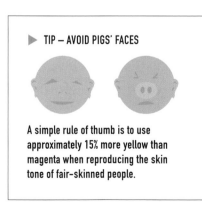

A simple rule of thumb is to use
approximately 15% more yellow than
magenta when reproducing the skin
tone of fair-skinned people.

"Unsharp Mask" is the best sharpening filter in Adobe Photoshop. This same filter is also available in many other image editing programs. This tool has three settings:
• Radius
• Threshold
• Amount

Radius

When setting the radius, start by finding out how long or short the tonal transition is that blurs the image. Long tonal transitions are always present because they are included as natural scales in the motif. The absolutely shortest tonal transitions should always be sharp. However short tonal transitions probably won't be visible in the screened image so sharpening is pointless. In Unsharp Mask you make adjustments for short tonal transitions in the Radius setting. There, quite simply, it is stated how short the tonal transitions should be, in number of pixels, to be sharpened. The radius should normally be between 0.8 and 1.6. Keep in mind that the resolution is important. If the resolution in the image is too high, the sharpening will not be particularly noticeable in print.

Threshold Value

Only transitions between two actual details should be sharpened. Those transitions are defined as the difference in brightness between two surfaces. The question is: How big of a difference is necessary for the transition to count as an outline that should be sharpened? You set a threshold value for how big the difference has to be for the sharpening to take place. The reason is if you sharpen too fine tonal differences, things like the original grains in the film or natural structures in the surfaces of the motif will be sharpened and give an unnecessarily rough impression.

Threshold levels in Unsharp Mask should normally be around 7–9. If the image is very grainy, you can raise the threshold to around 20–30. The measurement Threshold levels is stated as the difference in gray tone required for a transition between areas to be considered an outline. Because the image consists of 256 tonal steps from white to black, the Threshold levels is stated in the minimum difference between these tonal steps necessary for the tonal transition to be sharpened.

Amount

How much sharper the tonal transitions can be made when sharpening is determined by the setting Amount. If you set too low a value in Amount, the image is provided with too little extra sharpness. With too high a value in Amount, an extra dark edge will occur on the dark side of the outline and a light edge on the light one, creating a "halo effect." The amount should generally be between 100 and 200%.

Above we have provided you with recommended values to be used in Unsharp Mask. You should however try to find which settings are best in each situation. When it comes to very blurry images, it can be difficult to provide extra sharpness with the above recommended values. It is because the small differences in Radius and Threshold don't exist in such a blurry image. You could try with a higher Radius and a lower value in Amount. It is important when evaluating the image on the screen that the image preview is set to 1:1 or 100%. This means that every pixel in the image is displayed as a screen pixel. This provides the best opportunity to form an opinion about the image.

▷ Unsharp mask in Adobe Photoshop has three settings: amount, radius and threshold.

▷ Here are examples of soft and sharp transitions in an image. The difference between adjacent areas determines if it should be an outline that needs sharpening (sharp transition) or a tonal transition (soft transition) that should remain as it is.

▷ The three factors amount, radius and threshold can be illustrated as in the figure to the right.

Radius is a measurement of how large un-sharp areas of the image have to be for the sharpening to take place. The measurement is stated in amount of pixels that the blurry transition is wide, in this case four pixels. Only the areas around the selected radius are sharpened.

Threshold determines how different the brightness values between two pixels must be before they are considered edges and are sharpened.

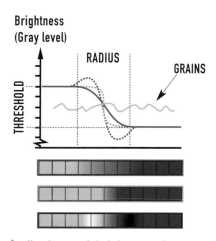

The measurement is stated in the minimum difference between tonal steps necessary for the tonal transition to be sharpened.

With the threshold function you can fine-tune the settings to avoid sharpening intentionally grainy surfaces.

Amount is simply the value of how much an image should be sharpened. If the sharpening amount is too high, it can cause a distracting outline effect.

▷ Here is a row of pixels from an unsharp area of an image (blue). An unsharp area means that the transition between light and dark is soft (the blue, flat curve).

In order to sharpen the image, try to make the soft transitions steeper (green curve).

If you sharpen the image too much, a halo-effect occurs along the outline (red curve).

▷ The second image above has been sharpened too much. It causes a distracting effect around outlines because a light line becomes visible on the light side of an outline and a dark line on the dark. Below is an example clearly depicting the contrast effect.

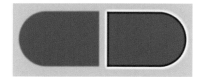

10. SEPARATION [5.6.11]

When CMYK converting, you have to define print adjustment values in advance because the conversion has to be adjusted according to the particular printing process [see 5.8]. The actual CMYK conversion is quite simple. In Adobe Photoshop, you only need to select Image -> Mode -> CMYK. The CMYK conversion is then done automatically.

11. SAVE THE IMAGE IN THE RIGHT FORMAT [5.6.12]

There are really only two image formats that are used in graphic production, TIFF and EPS. There is no noticeable difference in quality between the two formats, and they both take up about the same amount of memory. They are primarily differentiated based on the features they handle. For example, an EPS file can also be saved as a DCS file [see 5.3.2, 5.3.3 and 5.3.4].

TOOLS IN ADOBE PHOTOSHOP [5.7]

In this section we will briefly review some of the most common tools used to edit images in Adobe Photoshop.

THE PAINT TOOLS [5.7.1]

All paint tools in Adobe Photoshop can be set according to size (boldness). With tools like the paintbrush that allow for soft edges you can also set the shape and softness of the edges. All tools have unique controls that control aspects of the colors, like opacity, etc.

THE RUBBER STAMP [5.7.2]

When you want to remove a section of the image and replace it with a similar surface from another part of the image, the rubber stamp is the tool to use. It is mostly used to remove grains of dust and similar things but it also allows you to paint with another part of the image. Select the rubber stamp, press the Alt key and click on the area you want to paint with. Then you can fill in the areas you want with the selected surface. The place you retrieved the surface from is marked with a small cross.

THE SMUDGE TOOL [5.7.3]

The smudge tool is used to blur, or soften, one area into the next in one direction.

THE BLUR AND THE SHARPEN TOOL [5.7.4]

If you want to make an area of the image blurry you use the blur tool. The more you go over the image surface with this tool the blurrier it gets. The tool is very useful for removing outlines or softening details you want to make less prominent. The sharpen tool performs the opposite function, making areas of the image sharper. The tip does not, however, improve the overall image quality.

DODGE AND BURN [5.7.5]

Dodging and burning are two tools borrowed from the photography darkroom. Dodging an area of the image makes it lighter, while burning an area of the image makes it

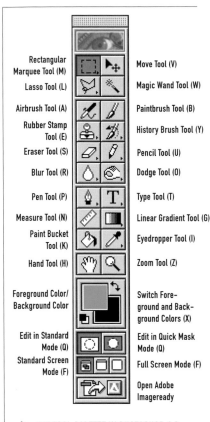

Rectangular Marquee Tool (M)	Move Tool (V)
Lasso Tool (L)	Magic Wand Tool (W)
Airbrush Tool (A)	Paintbrush Tool (B)
Rubber Stamp Tool (E)	History Brush Tool (Y)
Eraser Tool (S)	Pencil Tool (U)
Blur Tool (R)	Dodge Tool (O)
Pen Tool (P)	Type Tool (T)
Measure Tool (N)	Linear Gradient Tool (G)
Paint Bucket Tool (K)	Eyedropper Tool (I)
Hand Tool (H)	Zoom Tool (Z)
Foreground Color/ Background Color	Switch Foreground and Background Colors (X)
Edit in Standard Mode (Q)	Edit in Quick Mask Mode (Q)
Standard Screen Mode (F)	Full Screen Mode (F)
	Open Adobe Imageready

▶ **THE TOOL PALETTE IN PHOTOSHOP 6.0**
Many of the tools have optional tools— a small arrow on the tool buttons shows if such menu exists. Hold down the alt key and click or hold down the mouse button to get the optional tools.

You can quickly select each tool by pressing the key in parenthesis.

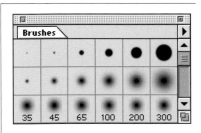

▶ **PAINTBRUSH AND PENCIL**
In the options menu for Paintbrush and Pencil you can select different brush shapes and sizes as well as create your own shapes.

darker, similar to the effects you can achieve when using these techniques on photographic paper in the darkroom.

AIRBRUSH, BRUSHES, PENS, ERASERS 5.7.6

These are the tools used for drawing and painting. The pen draws in full color; the brush can paint with different opacities, shapes and degrees of softness. The airbrush works the same way as a real airbrush, softly adding more and more color to an area as you keep brushing over it. The airbrush is appropriate for creating shadows and similar things. The eraser simply erases the image in a certain place, and can be used in a variety of different shapes. A convenient function of the eraser is Erase to History. Instead of completely erasing the surface you are crossing out, it returns the image to the surface it had the last time it was saved.

PEN TOOL 5.7.7

This tool is used to create bezier curves for selections with paths. The bezier curves can also be used to create selections.

GRADIENT 5.7.8

The gradient creates a soft tone between the foreground and background colors you select. It is particularly useful for creating a tonal selection in Quickmask.

QUICKMASK 5.7.9

Quickmask allows you to quickly and simply place a selection within an image. Click on the Quickmask icon to paint over the parts of the images that you select (or those that shouldn't, depending on how Photoshop is set). You can use any paint tools you like when creating the mask. This means that you can create selections that provide different effects. Click on the other Quickmask icon to return to normal settings. The mask will be visible as a contour line. You can also click on the Quickmask icon if you have a selection you would like to edit as a mask.

LAYER 5.7.10

The layering tool is useful for creating manipulations and collages. It is also useful for those times when you want to create graphics consisting of several parts – an image with text, an object and shadows, for example – that you want to keep separate until you are finished.

PAINT BUCKET AND MAGIC WAND 5.7.11

The paint bucket and the magic wand have similar functions. Though the magic wand creates a selection, while the paint bucket fills a surface with the foreground color, both of these functions are executed in the colors you select. The range of the immediate colors is determined by the Tolerance function in the Options menu.

▶ **HOW TO CREATE A QUICKMASK**

Find the tool "Quickmask" (the second from the bottom on the tool palette).

Enter Quickmask mode by clicking on the symbol on the right.

Use the paint tools to create a mask (in this case covered with red).

Go back and create an outline of the mask by clicking on the left.

▶ HOW TO CREATE A SELECTION WITH PATH IN ADOBE PHOTOSHOP

1. Start with an image in which the object you want to select has sharp contours.

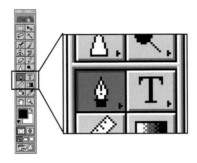

2. Select the Pen Tool from the tool palette.

3. Create a path with the pen tool. The path can consist of one or many objects. For best results, place the path somewhat inside of the contour of the object you want to select.

4. Save the path by double clicking on Work Path in the floating palette Paths. Give the path a clear name. You can save several paths in an image but only use one for a selection.

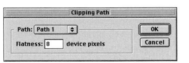

5. Choose to use the saved path as Clipping Path. A low value on the number of discrepant exposure points results in a slower rasterizing process. A value around 8–10 is usually recommended.

6. Save the image. You must use the EPS format.

7. Voila! The image is displayed as a selection when you place it in the page layout application or output as a selection according to the path you created. The entire digital file is however intact and visible if the image is edited in Photoshop (step 3).

SELECTIONS [5.7.12]

There are two ways to make a selection: make the background of the image white or use "paths." If you are using the first method, you can take advantage of the absence of sharp outlines in the subject, necessary when selecting an image with a short depth of field. Aside from making the selection you can add/maintain the shadow behind the subject and use the method in all image formats. EPS is the only format that handles selections with paths. The disadvantage of making the background white is that the background is removed forever. In addition, if you place the selected image on top of another image it will be surrounded by a white square. It is thus more common to select images using paths. By using the pen tools, you draw a bezier curve around the motif. You can also create a curve within the curve in order to "punch" holes in the selected motif. For example, in an image of a ring, you would draw a curve around the ring and punch a hole in the middle where it needs to be transparent. The edges of an image selected with paths will be completely sharp.

ADJUSTING FOR PRINTING [5.8]

When you look at an advertising campaign in which the same image appears in a newspaper, a weekly magazine, on a billboard downtown, or on a bus, etc., you should be aware that all these pictures are adjusted specifically for each purpose. Technically, they are actually five completely different digital images, treated and adjusted for their respective purposes. Generally a digitized image that has been adjusted for printing can only be used for the type of product it was created for.

The most common way to present color images on paper is to print with four colors: cyan, magenta, yellow and black. By mixing these colors you can put forth many realistic colors, but far from all [see Chromatics 4.4.2]. In theory, it's enough to use three colors to represent images: red, green and blue. If you printed all three, in full tone, on top of each other you would, theoretically, generate black. In practice, the result is more of a dark brown tone because the printing inks don't adhere to each other completely and because the printing inks don't contain perfect pigments. This phenomenon is called trapping [see Printing 13.4.4]. Therefore black is added to compensate for the shortcomings of the three inks and to be able to print with one color instead of three and, by doing so, reducing misregistration.

Scanners and computers work with three colors to represent images: red, green and blue [see Chromatics 4.4.1]. In order to be able to print a digital image you must convert the image from the three colors it was scanned with to the four you use to print with. This is known as CMYK conversion. You can conduct CMYK conversions in the RIP, the scanner application, or in a separate image editing application like Adobe Photoshop.

When converting images from RGB to CMYK, they are also adjusted for the specific print process and material that will be used. The three main factors to consider when converting/making adjustments for printing are paper type, printing process and halftone screen type. All three set special requirements on how the conversion should be done. They also determine how the black should be generated in relation to the other three process colors, i.e., which level of GCR/UCR should be used [see 5.8.3]. Printing process, and sometimes the paper type, determines the gray balance of the image. All three fac-

▶ **ADJUST YOUR TOOLS**
In the Options menu you can adjust the tools you are working with. All tools have different settings.

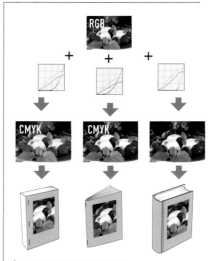

▶ **SIMILAR BUT DIFFERENT**
An image needs to be separated using a unique curve for each printing occasion. As a result, the same image has to be adjusted and edited differently depending on its intended use. A color-separated image is therefore difficult to use in a situation different from what it was originally intended for.

▶ **WHAT AFFECTS THE CMYK CONVERSION?**
The three main factors to consider when converting/adjusting for printing are:
- Paper stock
- Printing process and printing ink
- Halftone screens

> **TOTAL INK COVERAGE**
The image above has high ink coverage in the dark areas, is based on the four process colors, and has a total ink coverage of 343%.

> **RIGHT AND WRONG GRAY BALANCE**
The bottom image has the right gray balance whereas the top image has the wrong gray balance and, as a result, a distracting color cast.

tors (paper type, printing process and halftone screen) affect the dot gain that occurs in the printing process and in the production of the plates. When converting an image you have to set the values for ink coverage, GCR/UCR, gray balance, dot gain and color standard, among other things. Following is a review of these steps.

INK COVERAGE 5.8.1

In regular four-color printing you have four colors (CMYK) and each component color at a full tone achieves a tonal value of 100%. With each color at 100% you could, theoretically, get a total ink coverage of 400% (for example in a black tint area, consisting of 100% cyan, 100% magenta, 100% yellow and 100% black), although this is impossible to achieve in practice [see Print 13.4.4]. Coverage of 400% is undesirable anyway, as too much ink can result in smudging, long drying times and other phenomena.

When converting an image, you can set the value you want for maximum ink coverage. During conversion, the image is recalculated based on the values you choose. If, for example, you choose maximum ink coverage of 300%, no area in the image will have ink coverage of more than 300%. Depending on the paper type and the printing process, 240% to 340% is an appropriate setting for ink coverage. If the product is varnished when printed, you need to count the varnish as an additional color and thereby reduce the maximum ink coverage in order for the varnish to properly adhere.

GRAY BALANCE 5.8.2

If you print with equal amounts of the three colors C, M and Y, this will result in a surface that is not neutrally gray, although theoretically it should be. This has to do with the color of the paper, the fact that the printing inks don't stick to each other completely (and therefore, the order in which the printing inks are applied to the printed surface also matters), the differences in dot gain among the printing inks and because of uneven pigments and transparancy in the printing inks.

If the gray balance is not correct, natural reference colors in images such as grass, sky, or skin tone will look off. An image with an erroneous gray balance will have a color cast. To achieve the correct gray balance you have to adjust the image to adjust for the abovementioned discrepancies. A common value for gray balance is 40% cyan, 29% magenta and 30% yellow. This combination usually provides a neutral gray tone on regular coated sheet-fed press paper [see Printing 13.4.3].

UCR, GCR AND UCA 5.8.3

If you print the colors C, M and Y with the correct gray balance you will get a neutral gray hue. This ink combination can be substituted with black ink and you will still get the same gray color. It allows you to reduce the total ink coverage. This is called Under Color Removal, or UCR. UCR only affects neutral areas of the image.

Even colors that are not neutrally gray consist of a gray component. If we take an example consisting of C=90%, M=25%, Y=55%, the gray component of this color composition is C=25%, M=25%, Y=25%. If you substitute this gray component with black (K=25%) and mix it with the remaining amount of cyan (C=65%) and yellow (Y=30%) you will, in theory, get the same color. This type of substitution is called Gray Component Replacement, or GCR. You can vary the level of GCR so that you only substitute

Examples of gray balance values for a coated, white paper:

C	0	5	10	20	30	40	50	60	70	80	90	95	100
M	0		3	4	11	20	29	38	48	58	68	78	83	88
Y	0		4	5	12	21	30	39	49	59	69	79	84	89

Examples of gray balance values for an uncoated paper for newsprint:

C	0	5	10	20	30	40	50	60	70	80	90	95	100
M	0		2	4	10	19	28	37	47	57	67	77	82	87
Y	0		1	3	8	17	26	35	45	55	65	75	80	85

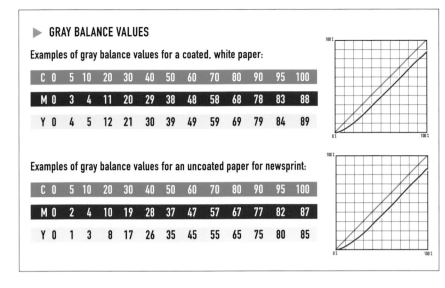

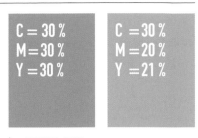

► NEUTRAL GRAY

In practice, a CMY combination of 30/30/30 will not come out as a neutral gray. A CMY combination of 30/20/21 however usually comes out neutral gray.

some of the gray component with black. In the above-mentioned example, this might mean substituting a smaller portion of the gray component, for example C=10%, M=10%, Y=10%, with K=10%, then mixing the black ink (K=10%) with the remaining portions of cyan, magenta and yellow (C=80%, M=15%, Y=45%).

The purpose of GCR is to reduce the total amount of ink used without changing the color. This makes it easier to reach gray balance in print and thereby get a more even print quality. GCR conversions also result in fewer problems with smudging in the printing press because the total amount of ink in the press is reduced. Images that are particularly sensitive to color changes should therefore be converted with GCR. Black four-color images, i.e., black and white images based on the four process colors, are one example of sensitive images.

When you substitute black for other colors, the darkest tones of the image can look washed out. To avoid this, you can add a little bit of color to the darkest tones. This is called Under Color Addition, or UCA. UCR, GCR and UCA can be set using a CMYK conversion application for images like Adobe Photoshop or Linocolor.

DOT GAIN 5.8.4

Dot gain is a technical print phenomenon wherein the size of the halftone dots increases during the printing process. In practice, this means that an image that has not been adjusted to account for dot gain will appear too dark when it is printed. To achieve optimal image quality in print, you must therefore compensate for dot gain when the image is CMYK converted. In order to do this you should find out the dot gain for the paper and printing process you are using from the printing house.

The size of the halftone dots increases when they are copied to the printing plate. This is only applicable to negative film and plate. If you are using positive film and plates, the opposite effect takes place – the dot size decreases. Dot gain also occurs in the printing when the ink is transferred from the printing plate to the paper. Different papers have different characteristics that affect dot gain and therefore the conversion has to be adjusted

► GCR – HOW IT WORKS

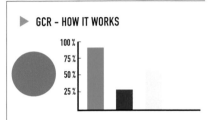

Above color combination consists of C = 90%, M = 25% and Y = 55%. The total ink coverage is thus 170% (90+25+55).

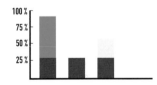

The color combination has a common gray component consisting of C=25%, M=25% and Y=25%. The gray component is replaced with the corresponding amount of black, i.e. K=25%.

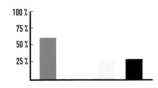

The result is a color combination providing the same result but with considerably lower total ink coverage, in this case 120%.

► IMAGE WITHOUT GCR

CMYK

=

CMY

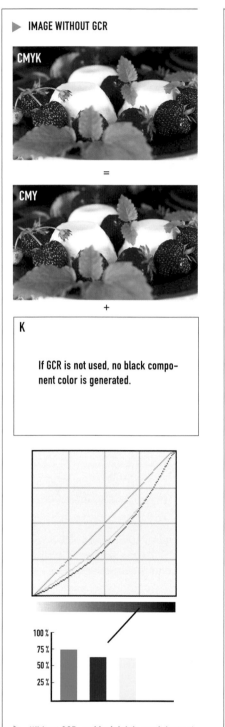

+

K

If GCR is not used, no black component color is generated.

► Without GCR, no black ink is used. Instead, black tones are created by C, M and Y.

► IMAGE WITH LIGHT GCR

CMYK

=

CMY

+

K

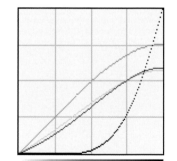

► With light GCR some parts of the primary colors' common gray component is substituted with black printing ink.

► IMAGE WITH MEDIUM GCR

CMYK

=

CMY

+

K

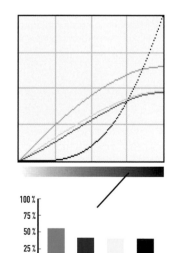

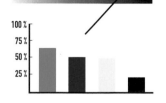

► Medium GCR means that a large part of the primary colors' common gray component is substituted with black printing ink.

▶ IMAGE WITH MAXIMUM GCR

CMYK

=

CMY

+

K

▶ With maximum GCR all parts of the primary colors' common gray component is substituted with black printing ink.

▶ IMAGE WITH UCR

CMYK

=

CMY

+

K

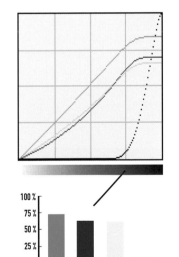

▶ UCR substitutes the common components of the primary colors with black in the neutral, dark areas of the image.

▶ WITH OR WITHOUT GCR

Normally, images with or without GCR should provide identical results. But if the amount of printing ink varies or is uneven in the printing press, an image converted with GCR will be less affected.

▶ An image without or with light GCR mainly consists of the primary colors. It's therefore considerably more sensitive to color fluctuations in the print and even minor changes can give the image a noticeable color cast.

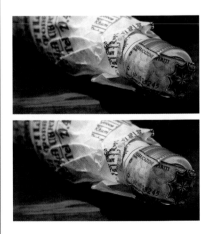

▶ Because an image with GCR consists of fewer tones comprised of the primary colors, the gray balance is not as affected by color fluctuations in the print. This means that the same image printed on different sheets remains identical.

► **BLACK AND WHITE IN FOUR-COLOR**
A black and white image can be converted and printed with CMYK to get softer tones and a better depth in the image. In this case, it is particularly important to use the correct gray balance value because it's easy to get color casts.

to account for these factors. If an image is erroneously adjusted – i.e., for a fine, coated paper (which has a low dot gain) when it will be printed on newsprint paper (which has a high dot gain) – the image will print too dark. There is also an optical dot gain, caused by the way light is reflected by the paper.

The printing process used also affects the level of dot gain. For example, web-fed presses are characterized by a higher dot gain than sheet-fed when printing on the same paper quality. A high screen frequency always results in a higher dot gain, assuming the same printing process on the same paper. Certain types of paper are more appropriate for certain screen frequencies. Paper manufacturers usually recommend an appropriate screen frequency for their different papers.

Dot gain is usually measured in 40% and 80% tones. A common value for dot gain is around 23% in the 40% tone for a 150 lpi screen and coated paper (negative film). Dot gain is always measured in absolute percentage units. Using the above example, this means that a 40% tone in the film will result in a 63% tone in the actual print (40% + 23% = 63%).

COLOR STANDARDS 5.8.5

When you convert an image into CMYK, you need to consider the color standard used. Different countries and parts of the world use their own definitions of the printing colors cyan, magenta, yellow and black. In the United States for example, SWOP is standard whereas in Europe the European scale is used. Within these color standards there are different options based on paper type and printing method, such as Eurostandard-Coated for a coated paper printed with colors according to the European scale. When you convert into CMYK you set the color standard used when printing and the image will be converted according to the color characteristics of these particular printing inks.

PRINT SPECIFICATIONS 5.8.6

In order to make high-quality reproductions, you need to know a number of values for the CMYK conversion. The printing house should be able to provide values for dot gain, color standard, GCR/UCR, ink coverage and gray balance for the paper you choose. The illustration on page 92 shows some printing house conversion recommendations for newsprint paper, uncoated paper and coated paper. Another way to obtain conversion values is to generate ICC profiles. An accurately generated ICC profile contains settings for all necessary values.

► IMAGE NOT ADJUSTED
This image is not adjusted for dot gain and is therefore too dark.

► IMAGE ADJUSTED
This image is adjusted for dot gain and the desired result is achieved.

PRINT PRODUCTION IMAGES

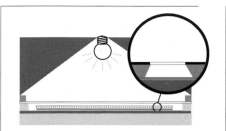

▶ DOT GAIN WHEN PRODUCING THE PRINTING PLATE
Because the light spreads between the film and the printing plate, halftone dots are enlarged/shrunk when copied to the printing plate.

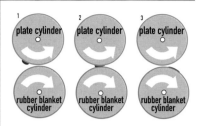

▶ DOT GAIN IN THE PRINTING PRESS
Halftone dots are compressed, and thereby enlarged, in the printing nip. As a result, tint areas and images become darker.

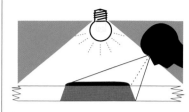

▶ OPTICAL DOT GAIN
Optical dot gain is an optical effect depending on how the light is reflected and spread on the paper.

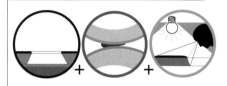

= TOTAL DOT GAIN

▶ TOTAL DOT GAIN
The total value of dot gain/dot reduction when producing the printing plate and printing as well as the optical dot gain.

HI-FI COLOR 5.8.7

New color conversion techniques have been developed recently based on more colors than the four traditional process colors, resulting in the need for six-, seven- or eight-color conversions. These processes make possible a greater tonal range and are capable of reproducing a considerably larger part of the color spectrum. The printed images resemble the original ones more closely as a result. Often the four primary colors, CMYK, are used with an additional two, three or four colors. Hexachrome is the most common of these new techniques and is based on six colors, CMYK plus the additional colors green and orange.

SCANNERS 5.9

In order to transfer original images to the computer for viewing and editing, you use a scanner, which reads the original image and converts it into a digital image. There are two main types of scanners: drum scanners and flatbed scanners. In a drum scanner, the originals are mounted on a glass drum, while in a flatbed scanner they are placed on a flat glass surface, much like they would be in a copier. Scanners range in price from a couple hundred dollars up to a fifty thousand dollars. What differentiates them is primarily the quality of the scan, productivity and how advanced their control programs are.

HOW DOES A SCANNER WORK? 5.9.1

When scanning an image, the scanner divides the surface of the original image into a checkered pattern, in which every little square corresponds to a scanning point. The denser the bitmap you select (the higher the resolution), the more image information the scanner will record – resulting in a larger file. Each scanning point is converted to a picture element (pixel) in the computer. The scanning resolution is measured in the number of pixels per inch (ppi) [see 5.5.9]. The scanner illuminates each point with white light. The light that is reflected (if you are using reflective art) or transmitted (back lit, if you are using transparent art) from the scanning point will pick up the color from the respective point on the original image.

The reflected or transmitted light is then divided into three components – red, green and blue – by color filters, providing the RGB value for any given color. Different intensities of red, green or blue light beams create different colors [see Chromatics 4.4.1]. When

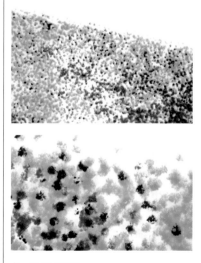

▶ HI-FI COLOR
The four primary colors, CMYK, are supplemented with an additional two, three or four colors. That way the color range will be considerably higher. Hexachrome, used as an example above, is the most common of these techniques and is based on six colors: CMYK, green and orange. In the image, the halftone dots of all six colors are visible.

DOT GAIN

You can measure dot gain with a densitometer and a color bar. Dot gain is usually measured with 40% and 80% tones as reference values.

Dot gain is always stated in absolute percentage units. Thus a dot gain of 23% means that a tint area of 40% will result in a 63% tone in the actual print.

To define a tint area as 40% in the print, you draw a horizontal line from 40% in print until the line intersects with the curve stating the dot gain. From the point of intersection you then draw a vertical line down to the film axis, which states the value.

Using the example above, this means that a 40% tone has to be adjusted to 25% (coated), 20% (uncoated) or 15% (newsprint) in order to come out correct in the actual print.

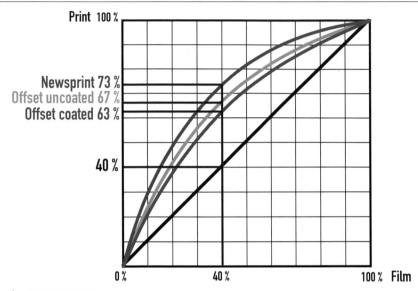

DOT GAIN CURVES

The curves show the dot gain across the entire tone for three different types of papers using negative film. The horizontal axis states the tone value on film while the vertical states the tone value in print. To read how a certain tone value is affected by dot gain, draw a vertical line from the tone value on film until it intersects with the respective dot gain curve. When you then draw a horizontal line from the point of intersection, you will get the tone value in print. The image shows how a 40% tone is affected by dot gain. It will come out as 63% on coated paper, 67% on uncoated paper and 73% on newsprint paper.

RECOMMENDED VALUES FOR SEPARATION

NEWSPAPER	around 85 lpi
dot gain	33%-neg/26%-pos
GCR	high
ink coverage	240–260%

UNCOATED PAPER	around 120 lpi
dot gain	27%-neg/20%-pos
GCR	low—medium
ink coverage	280–300%

COATED PAPER	around 150 lpi
dot gain	23%-neg/16%-pos
GCR	light/UCR
ink coverage	320–340%

COLOR CONVERSION WITH ICC PROFILE IN ADOBE PHOTOSHOP

You can set color management in Adobe Photoshop under Edit –> Color Settings. To separate images using ICC profiles is the most common method today. The separation is determined by three factors, profile (CMYK), Engine, and Intent.

Select the appropriate ICC profile developed for your particular print prerequisites or select a standard profile corresponding to the conditions at hand under Working Spaces –> CMYK. In the profile there is information about dot gain, gray balance, maximum ink coverage, color standard and the level of GCR [see Chromatics 4.7.6].

You set how existing colors and profiles should be handled under Color Management. Normally, Preserve Embeded Profiles is preset, which means that colors in an image already containing an embedded profile are not converted but handed off as they are.

You set the Color Management Module under Conversion –> Engine [see Chromatics 4.7.7]. Adobe Photoshop has its own Color Management Module but you can also choose modules available from other manufacturers.

Under Conversion –> Intent there are four conversion methods to choose from: perceptual, saturated, relative or absolute. The four methods are appropriate for different types of images. Perceptual conversion for example, is most commonly used for scanned photographs [see Chromatics 4.7.8-4.7.11].

If you have selected Use Black Point Compensation when converting, the darkest color value in the image will be represented by the darkest color value in the new color space. This is particularly interesting if you convert from a small color space into a wider, for example a CMYK to CMYK conversion.

To perform the actual separation, go to Image –> Mode –> CMYK. The example shows how to convert from Adobe RGB into the printing profile Eurostandard Coated.

ADOBE PHOTOSHOP'S BUILT-IN SEPARATION SYSTEM

Adobe Photoshop's built-in separation method is the traditional method for separating images and is used if you don't have access to an ICC profile. It is based on selecting an ink standard and setting values for dot gain, amount of GCR and UCA, maximum amount of black ink coverage as well as maximum ink coverage.

As usual, go to Edit –> Color Settings. Select Curves... –> CMYK –> Custom CMYK and you will be able to set the above factors.

You select printing inks based on predefined printing ink standards. SWOP is used in the United States and the European scale in Europe. Alternatively you can choose to define your own printing inks under Ink Options –> Custom... by using CIELAB or CIExyz values.

You set ink coverage and GCR under Separation Options. In this case, we have selected light GCR and high ink coverage of 340 %.

There are two ways of compensating for dot gain in Adobe Photoshop, Standard and Curves....

Standard is the most common method. It is a simple way of stating dot gain but has some restrictions. Photoshop always selects a dot gain value when you select Ink Colors but it rarely corresponds to reality and has to be corrected. You only need to state dot gain in the 40 %-tone; the software calculates additional values. Dot gain is only stated as a value for all colors and, as a result, does not take variations in dot gain between different printing inks into consideration.

Curves... is a more precise method of stating dot gain because it allows you to set dot gain in 13 different percentages in addition to setting separate values for cyan, magenta, yellow and black.

► DRUM SCANNER
The original artwork is mounted on a glass drum.

► FLATBED SCANNER
The original artwork is placed on a flat glass plate.

► THE PRINCIPLE OF SCANNING
The scanner illuminates a surface with white light and the reflected light is divided into three components — red, green and blue — by color filters. The combination of the reflected light translates into RGB values stating the particular colors.

the reflected or transmitted light is divided into the three basic components, the scanner translates the intensity of each respective component to a numerical value between 0 and 255. The light intensity of each primary color determines the numerical value between 0 (no light at all) and 255 (full intensity). Each primary color can thus be reproduced in 256 tonal steps/intensity levels. Each scanning point on the original image will be a pixel in the computer. The color of the pixel is described by the mixture of the three color values in RGB that combine to approximate the color of the scanned point on the original. For example, the mixture red=0, green=0 and blue=0 will appear black (no light) and red=255, green 255 and blue=255 will appear white (maximum intensity). When all the scanning points in the original image have been read by the scanner, the result can be thought of as a mosaic made up of tiny picture elements. This mosaic is called a "bitmap."

DRUM SCANNERS 5.9.2

The drum scanner gets its name from the large glass drum on which the original artwork is mounted for scanning. The maximum size of the original varies depending on the manufacturer, but is usually A3 (11" × 17"). For obvious reasons, a drum scanner can only scan flexible original images. If, for example, you want to scan a book cover, you have to photograph it first. Otherwise you have to scan it in a flatbed scanner. Slides have to be taken out of their frames before they are mounted on the glass drum. Drum scanners are usually very large and expensive but provide high quality and productivity. They are generally used by prepress service providers and commercial printers who need to produce high-quality results in large volume.

FLATBED SCANNERS 5.9.3

During the last couple of years, flatbed scanners have become much more common. Original images are placed flat on a glass plate, which is an advantage if you have inflexible originals. As with drum scanners, the maximum size of the original is usually A3 (11" × 17"), though it can vary depending on the manufacturer. Flatbed scanners are usually cheaper and easier to work with than drum scanners. They are available in a number of price and quality ranges, from a couple of hundred dollars up to tens of thousands of dollars. The best and most expensive flatbed scanners are comparable to the best drum scanners in terms of image quality.

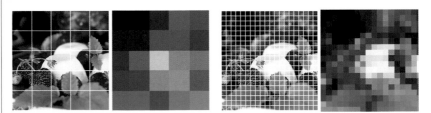

► SCANNING IMAGES
When scanning an image, the scanner divides the surface of the original image into a checkered pattern in which every little square corresponds to a scanning point. The denser the bitmap you select (the higher the resolution), the more image information it will record — resulting in a larger file. Each scanning point is converted to a picture element in the computer, also called a pixel. The scanning resolution is measured in number of pixels per inch (ppi).

SCANNING ^{5.9.4}

Drum scanners scan images by illuminating them and reading them with a read head containing photo multipliers or CCD cells [see fact box], which sense the intensity in the reflected/transmitted light. The drum rotates at high speed while the read head moves slowly along the surface of the image. Images in a flatbed scanner are read by a number of CCD cells that move forward in measured steps along the surface of the original image, scanning an entire row of the image at one time.

SINGLE-PASS AND THREE-PASS SCANNERS ^{5.9.5}

Most scanners can capture the red, green and blue color components simultaneously. This is called single-pass scanning. Some scanners, known as three-pass scanners, scan colors one by one. A single-pass scanner is therefore almost always three times as fast as a three-pass scanner. Another advantage to single-pass scanning is that you will have better registration between the colors.

MECHANICS AND ELECTRONICS ^{5.9.6}

The mechanics and electronics of the scanner are crucial in determining the precision you can scan images with. The optical precision affects color reproduction and sharpness, while the mechanical precision is important to ensure that the image capture is consistent over time. Poor optical precision results in dirty color reproduction and blurriness, while poor mechanical precision can cause striping and misregistration between colors.

PHOTO MULTIPLIERS AND CCD CELLS ^{5.9.7}

The quality of the photo multipliers or CCD cells in a scanner is important for ensuring the correct translation of light signals. CCD cells can have difficulty distinguishing tonal differences, especially in the darker parts of an image. CCD cells also have a tendency to age, which reduces their ability to reproduce colors and tonal transitions precisely. High-quality CCD cells with a long life span are extremely expensive to produce.

▶ **THREE WAYS OF LOOKING AT SCANNERS**
You can classify scanners in three different ways depending on their construction.
- Single-pass or three-pass
- Photo multipliers or CCD cells
- Flatbed or drum

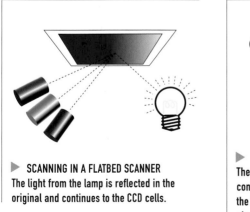

▶ **SCANNING IN A FLATBED SCANNER**
The light from the lamp is reflected in the original and continues to the CCD cells.

▶ **SCANNING IN A DRUM SCANNER**
The light passes through the original film and continues through the rotating drum. After that, the light is led via a mirror to the CCD cells or photo multipliers at the center of the drum.

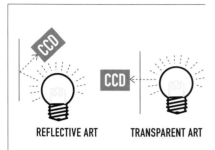

REFLECTIVE ART   TRANSPARENT ART

▶ **SCANNING**
When an image is scanned, light is either reflected or transmitted through the original image. Reflective images reflect the light while slides or negatives let the light through.

▶ **CCD AND PHOTO MULTIPLIERS**
The translation of light intensity into digital signals is either done by CCD cells (CCD stands for Charge Coupled Device), light-sensitive cells that "feel" the intensity of the light and convert it into a digital, electronic signal, or by photo multipliers. Photo multipliers operate similarly to CCD cells but generate an analog, electronic signal.

▶ **256 TONES**
The computer usually works with 1 byte (=8 bits) per primary color. 8 bits in the binary system correspond to the values 0 to 255 in the decimal system (2^8=256, making 256 values possible).

RANGE 5.9.8

The "range" of a scanner refers to its ability to reproduce the tonal range of an original image, including tiny color changes. The range of the scanner is limited by the sensitivity of its photo multipliers or CCD cells. To understand the limitations of a scanner's tonal range you can compare it to the tonal range of an original artwork. For example, a slide has a maximum tonal range of 2.7 density units [see 5.5.2]. A scanner with a lesser tonal range than the original can never reproduce it in an optimal way. Drum scanners often have a somewhat wider tonal range than flatbed scanners, and theoretically, should provide a somewhat better quality. A scanner with less tonal range may not be able to perceive tonal nuances, particularly in dark areas of an original image, resulting in a digital image with uneven tonal transitions and a lack of contrast.

BITS PER COLOR 5.9.9

The number of bits assigned to each color is usually referred to as the "bit-depth" of a scanner. There are scanners with bit-depths of 10, 12 or 14 bits per color. This means that instead of just 256 tonal steps, a bit-depth of 10 bits allows for 1,024 tonal steps, 12 bits 4,096 steps and 14 bits 16,384 steps. The eye is not able to perceive all these steps, but the extra bits can store important information about an image that is particularly sensitive, like shadow details in a dark image, for example.

RESOLUTION 5.9.10

Another indicator of a quality scanner is its resolution. A high-quality scanner can capture images at more than 3,000 ppi. High resolution is important when you want to enlarge an image considerably. For example, a regular small-format slide (24–36 mm) that you want to enlarge ten times has to be scanned with a resolution of 3,000 ppi in order to maintain an acceptable image quality and to be printed with a screen frequency of 150 lpi.

IMAGE SCANNING SOFTWARE 5.9.11

Most scanners come with advanced programs which allow you to set different specifications for the scanning process. A good image-scanning program should include a range of settings for sharpness, separation and print adjustment, selective color correction, scan resolution, dot gain and cropping. It should also be able to handle and create file formats such as TIFF, EPS, DCS and JPEG, as well as the color spaces RGB, CMYK and CIELab. Many of these factors can be addressed in a later stage of production, but you often benefit in terms of both quality and production time by executing these settings in correlation with the scanning. A poorly captured image can be difficult, even impossible, to adjust after it's been scanned [see 5.5.9].

DIGITAL CAMERAS 5.10

Digital cameras are closely related to scanners. The difference is that, with cameras, you don't work with an original image – you "scan" a subject directly into the camera/computer. The advantage to digital cameras is that the image is digitized directly in the camera and is immediately available for further digital editing. Because film is not used you don't have to spend time on developing and scanning. Since the image is immediately digital, it can be sent over a telecommunications network with ease. Digital photography is already to a large extent used by press photographers, because they can quickly and conveniently deliver their images to the editorial office. The disadvantage to digital cameras is that the image quality will not be as high as that of a traditional original image scanned with a high-quality scanner.

The technology of a digital camera is actually based on the same principle as a scanner: white light is reflected off an object and divided into three components (red, green and blue). The difference is that there is an actual object reflecting the light instead of an original image. There are digital cameras in all price ranges, from a couple of hundred dollars up to tens of thousands. The cheapest cameras provide considerably lower resolution and a lesser image quality than the more expensive ones. Digital cameras are generally divided into three categories: consumer cameras, digital SLR (Single Lens Reflex) cameras and studio cameras.

CONSUMER CAMERAS 5.10.1

The simplest and cheapest kind of digital cameras are intended for the consumer market. They are cheap, but do not provide the highest quality. These cameras are often as small as regular pocket cameras. The images they produce are best suited for screen display because of their low resolution. These cameras have a firm matrix with CCD cells. The optics are firm, the camera is fully automatic and in most the storage memory cannot be exchanged. The camera has to be "emptied" of images when the memory is full so that new ones can be stored. Some of these cameras do allow you to use an exchangeable floppy disk, a small hard disk or a "flash memory card" on which the images can be stored. 1600×1200 pixels is a common resolution for this type of camera, which is usually enough to print a postcard-sized image with a screen frequency of 150 lpi. These cameras usually cost a couple of hundred dollars.

SLR CAMERAS 5.10.2

A digital system camera is a modified SLR camera. The digital portion of this camera is really only a digital camera back, which replaces the camera back that is normally placed on these cameras. The digital back holds a matrix of millions of CCD cells. You can think of this CCD matrix as digital film. Just like film, it is light sensitive and registers and transforms red, blue and green light components into digital signals.

The exposure works, in principle, like it does with a regular camera—it relies on a shutter with a certain shutter speed. As in the traditional case, you set the shutter speed and the aperture. When the shutter is opened the light sensitive CCD matrix is exposed/illuminated, registering the image. Some digital SLR cameras require three exposures per image, or a three-pass, one for each primary color (RGB), and are therefore not appropriate for moving subjects. Such cameras are also called three-shot cameras. Cameras that capture the necessary information in one exposure are called one-shot cameras. Image resolution in digital system cameras is predetermined by the CCD matrix and is dependent upon the number of CCD cells. This means that you cannot increase the resolution, should it be necessary. These cameras are more expensive than consumer cameras and can usually achieve an image resolution high enough to print an A5-sized print ($5" \times 8"$) at a screen frequency of 150 lpi. The amount of image data they store is usually around 15 to 20 MB per file.

Consumer camera

Studio camera

▶ DIFFERENT TYPES OF DIGITAL CAMERAS
There are three types of digital cameras: consumer, SLR and studio cameras. Consumer cameras are usually the cheapest and studio cameras the most expensive.

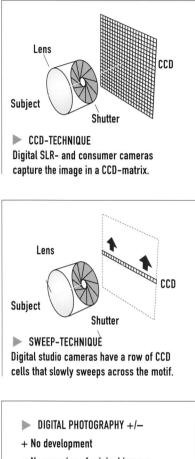

▶ CCD-TECHNIQUE
Digital SLR- and consumer cameras
capture the image in a CCD-matrix.

▶ SWEEP-TECHNIQUE
Digital studio cameras have a row of CCD
cells that slowly sweeps across the motif.

▶ DIGITAL PHOTOGRAPHY +/−

+ No development
+ No scanning of original images
+ Easy to distribute images
+ Fast
− Somewhat lesser image quality
− Difficult with moving subjects

STUDIO CAMERAS 5.10.3

The largest and most expensive version of the digital camera is the studio camera. This type of digital camera generally achieves the highest resolution and the best image quality of all the different types of digital cameras. Instead of a matrix of CCD cells, it uses a line of CCD cells. Exposure is based on the image scanning technique, so that the line of CCD cells move along the camera body as it records the image. The CCD cells are photosensitive and register the image similarly to a flatbed scanner.

This technique is considerably slower than consumer and SLR cameras and the exposure time (scanning time) can amount to several minutes. In exchange, you get a considerably higher resolution and often a better image quality than what consumer and SLR cameras can produce. As with a scanner, you can set the desired resolution. The amount of image data stored when the camera is set at its highest resolution is usually around 100 to 150 MB, which is enough to generate an A2-sized (17" × 22") print with a 133 lpi screen. Because the exposure takes a long time, this camera is not appropriate for moving objects, and is primarily intended for product photography in a professional studio where the quality of the images must be extremely high. It is generally more expensive than the other types of cameras, often costing over $10,000.

LIGHTING 5.10.4

As with all photography, appropriate lighting is very important in creating a good image in digital photography. The digital format requires that you are more careful with contrasts than you would with traditional film lighting, but other than that, the procedure does not differ much from traditional photography.

QUALITY 5.10.5

The image quality you can achieve with digital cameras is starting to improve. For simpler catalogue productions and other printed products that don't require absolute perfection, digital photography can be a cost-effective tool. In addition, you can generate a large number of images quickly and make your selections without having to bear film and developing costs. ■

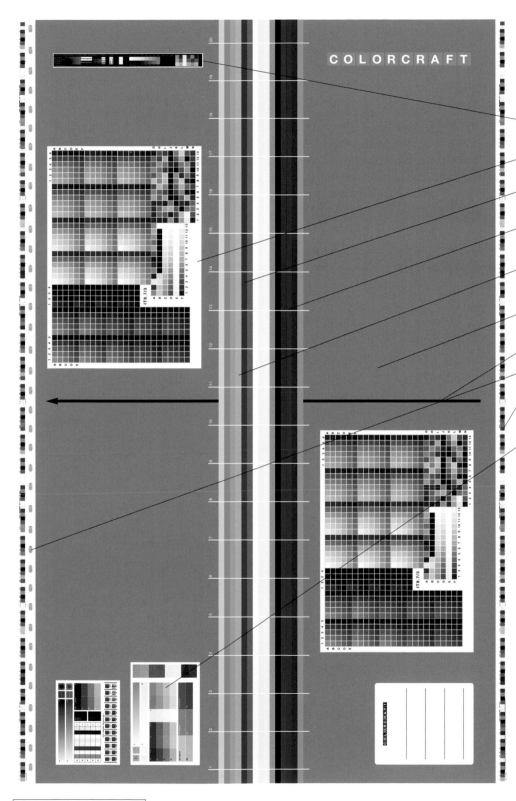

▶ TEST FORM

You print a test sheet to secure optimal print quality and to generate ICC profiles. On the left is an example of a test sheet.

Digital UGRA strips are used to check plate exposure.

IT8 test forms are used to generate ICC profiles.

Print contrast is checked to calculate the optimal ink coverage.

Trapping is checked to make sure the inks stick to each other.

Dot gain fields are used to measure the dot gain.

The stabilization area is used to stabilize and increase the ink consumption across the sheet.

Print direction.

Visual check of gray balance.

Quality control of the printing press.

Miscellaneous fields are used for detecting mechanical errors in the printing press (doubling and slurring) [see Printing 13.5].

DOCUMENTS

6

CHAPTER 6 DOCUMENTS CREATING DOCUMENTS AND PRODUCING ORIGINAL ARTWORK FOR PRINT PRODUCTION IS CONSIDERABLY MORE DIFFICULT THAN ONE MIGHT IMAGINE. KNOWLEDGE OF THE PRINT'S PREREQUISITES AND LIMITATIONS IS REQUIRED. YOU SHOULD ALSO HAVE SKILLS IN USING THE SOFTWARE AND IN HOW TO OUTPUT CORRECTLY.

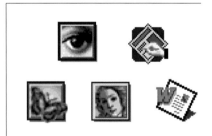

▶ SOFTWARE FOR GRAPHIC PRODUCTION
Different programs are used to create pixel- and object-based images, texts and pages. Even if the programs to some extent overlap, it's better to use a program designed for your particular assignment to obtain the best result. For example, it is better to stay away from doing page layout in word processing programs.

If you are creating a document for print production you should be aware that designing a layout is only one important element of the process. It is also as important to be able to output and print the completed document. Documents that are improperly crafted can cause increased costs and delays in production, or result in an unsatisfactory final product.

This chapter will provide you with information necessary to successfully prepare a document for print. Topics include: typeface management, definition and choice of colors, management of images and logotypes, knockouts, overprints, and spreads and bleeds. Developing a "final check-list" to review before sending a document to output will also be discussed. First, however, we will look at the different software you might use to produce originals.

SOFTWARE FOR PRODUCING ORIGINALS 6.1

When producing your original document, you need to use several types of software: word processing applications for writing text, image editing applications for editing images, illustration applications for creating illustrations, and page layout applications for merging the various segments into complete pages. It is important to choose applications that are common in the industry so that others may easily access and continue working with the files. It is also important to choose applications that work well for graphic production.

WORD PROCESSING APPLICATIONS 6.1.1

Microsoft Word is the most commonly used word processing application. WordPerfect is also used to some extent. Using these applications, text may be created that can later be moved into page layout applications. Older versions of Microsoft Word and Word-Perfect are generally preferred for document production because page layout applications cannot always import files from the newer program versions. The same thing applies if you want someone to be able to open the file in another word processing application. It is important to note that images in text documents cannot be imported to a page layout application, nor can typography.

PAGE LAYOUT APPLICATIONS 6.1.2

QuarkXPress, Adobe InDesign and Adobe PageMaker, the most common page layout applications, are generally equivalent in capabilities. They all merge text, illustrations and images into complete pages to create the original artwork, which is then output as the final films or files that are the basis for printing. All three applications are appropriate for graphic production because they are based on the page description language Post-Script [see Output 9.3.3]. These applications are generally used on the Macintosh platform, but are also available for Windows.

IMAGE EDITING APPLICATIONS 6.1.3

For pixel-based images, the application Adobe Photoshop is the industry standard. Other applications are available but they usually only manage Photoshop's image format. You should save images in EPS, DCS (five-file EPS) or TIFF format [see Images 5.3].

ILLUSTRATION APPLICATIONS 6.1.4

For creating illustrations and object-based images, Adobe Illustrator and Macromedia Freehand are the most frequently used applications. The images should be saved in EPS format [see Images 5.1.7].

LESS APPROPRIATE SOFTWARE 6.1.5

Software such as Microsoft Word, Corel WordPerfect, Microsoft PowerPoint and Microsoft Excel are not based on PostScript [see Output 9.3.3]. They are, therefore, inappropriate to use in the production of original artwork for printing. This does not mean that the applications are problematic in and of themselves, however.

FONTS 6.2

There are two types of fonts that are generally used in graphic production: PostScript and TrueType. PostScript Level 1 is the most common and best standardized of the two. TrueType typefaces are not PostScript-based and therefore not as suitable for output as PostScript Level 1 typefaces. When printing a document with a TrueType typeface on a PostScript-based printer, the typefaces will be converted to bezier curves. This conversion may cause changes in the typography. In practice, it results in erroneous line arrangement in the printout, even though it looks correct on the screen. If you choose to work with PostScript Level 1 typefaces (the standard for graphic output), you minimize

---

▶ **APPROPRIATE FILE FORMATS**

Text: Word, RTF, ASCII

Pixel-based images: DCS, EPS, TIFF

Object-based images: EPS

Page documents: QuarkXPress files, Adobe PageMaker files

Print-ready documents: PDF, PostScript, EPS

▶ **DIVIDING UP LARGE DOCUMENTS**

Both Adobe PageMaker and Quark-XPress have limitations on the number of pages you can have in a document. You might have to divide a document into several smaller ones. The division also makes the work smoother and the documents easier to handle.

▶ **SUGGESTIONS FOR TYPOGRAPHY**

Make sure not to use the functions italic, bold, outline, etc. in the page layout applications. Take the corresponding versions directly from the typeface instead. Otherwise it may result in errors when outputting.

▶ **CORRECT FONT FILE PART 1**
Even if two font files from different manufacturers have the same name there can be considerable differences between them. It is therefore important that everyone working on the same document use the same font files.

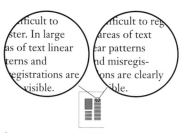

▶ **CORRECT FONT FILE PART 2**
Unpleasant surprises like changes in the text and line arrangement can be a consequence of switching between fonts with the same name but by different manufacturers.

the risk of typeface problems. Because PostScript fonts are bezier-based, they can generally be enlarged without compromising the quality [see Typeface 3.4.1].

Typefaces from different manufacturers can differ from each other despite identical names; therefore it is important to stay with the same manufacturer. If you substitute a typeface from one manufacturer for one with the same name from a different manufacturer, you might encounter unpleasant surprises such as changes in the text and line arrangement. The number of different typefaces is impossible to state. No supplier provides all of them or all versions of them. When delivering a document, the producer of the document will often include a copy of the fonts used. This is legal as long as it is understood that providing the fonts is for the one-time use in outputting the job. It is seen as a way to assure that the typeface remains constant and the printing will be free of problems [see Typeface 3.2.2].

WORKING WITH COLORS 6.3

When producing an original artwork, you often work with a number of colors in your document. We will briefly review the most important things to keep in mind when working with colors. We will discuss the terms spot colors and process colors and when to use them.

CHOOSING COLORS 6.3.1

When choosing colors for your document, you must decide if you are going to work with process colors, spot colors, or both. Process colors are the four printing inks (cyan, magenta, yellow, black), and spot colors are special premixed printing inks. The latter are available in a wide range of different colors and are usually identified by the color model Pantone [see Chromatics 4.5.5].

Use spot colors when:
• you only want to use one or two colors for your printed product
• you want to use colored text that is not black
• it is important that a particular color will turn out exactly right; for example, on logotypes and tint areas

Use process colors when:
• you are printing color images
• you are using more than two colors

Process colors and spot colors are both used when:
• you want to use one or more spot colors in addition to the four process colors in order to achieve a particular design effect
• you are printing gold, silver, flourescent colors or other colors that you cannot print with process color combinations
• it is important that a particular color will turn out exactly right; for example, on logotypes and tint areas

Important note: the computer monitor's representation of color prints is poor; therefore you should avoid choosing the colors directly from the screen. Whether working with process or spot colors, it is better to use printed color guides.

WORKING WITH PROCESS COLORS 6.3.2

Working with process colors involves using the subtractive color model: the colors cyan, magenta, yellow and black (C, M, Y, K). These can be combined to create a variety of different colors [see Chromatics 4.5.2]. Color guides for process colors indicate the various combinations of CMYK that can be printed on a particular paper. There are color guides for coated and uncoated papers, as well as for newsprint paper. You should use the color guide that best corresponds to the paper on which you are printing. When combining process colors, do not create combinations containing too much ink. Depending on the printing process and the paper, you cannot really print with more than 240 to 340% ink (theoretically, the maximum ink coverage is 400%). A fine sheet-fed print can usually take approximately 340% ink coverage, while newsprint is usually limited to approximately 240% coverage. You can get the exact values from your printer [see Printing 13.4.5].

When printing many colors on top of each other, you will never get a perfect match; you get a so-called "misregistration." With large objects like images, illustrations, tint areas or large text, it can hardly be noticed. However, with objects like small text, fine linear patterns or illustrations with fine details, misregistration is much more evident, and objects appear blurry as a result. Because of this, it is not recommended that process color be used on text or linear patterns. If it is important that a text or linear pattern has a particular color, it is better to print it with a special spot color, instead. The same phenomenon can occur if you are using negative texts or linear patterns against a colored background or an image. In these cases, you should select a single process color, for example black, or a spot color for the background. If you want to put negative text against a colored background (image or tint area), it is better to choose a sans serif typeface. Roman typefaces have fine serifs that may disappear completely if printed against a colored background. The degree of misregistration differs considerably in different printing methods. Newsprint has more misregistration than regular sheet-fed print [see Printing 13.5.1].

▶ COLOR GUIDE FOR CMYK
You should not select colors based on what they look like on the screen. Instead, you should use a color guide printed on a paper similar to the one you will be using. In the color guide you will also find the colors' CMYK combinations.

Text consists of thin lines. If the text is colored using many component colors like in this one, it is easy to get misregistration.
It is safer to set the text in one of the component colors or in a spot color because it is impossible to get misregistration.

▶ MISREGISTRATION IN TEXT
Avoid coloring small text with four-color combinations because it is easy to get misregistration.

You shouldn't use Romanesque typefaces for small-sized, negative text against a colored background because the fine lines in the letters are distracted

A larger grotesque typeface with thicker lines looks better.

▶ NEGATIVE TEXT IN FOUR-COLOR TINT AREAS
Avoid small-sized, roman typeface in negative text on tint areas consisting of many component colors.

If you place text on a monochromatic background, you will not get misregistration. It is always safe to set negative text on areas that only consist of one color.

▶ AREAS PRINTED WITH ONE COLOR ARE SAFE
To avoid misregistration in negative text, you should set it against a monochromatic background.

| K 100 %, C 50 %, M 50 % | = | K 100 % | + | C 50 % | + | M 50 % |

| K 100 %, C 50 % | = | K 100 % | + | C 50 % | + |

| K 100 %, M 50 % | = | K 100 % | + | + | M 50 % |

▶ **DEEP BLACK PART 1**
By mixing 100% black with 50% cyan and 50% magenta you get a deeper black tint than if only using black. With only cyan and black, the shade will also be deep black but with a cooler effect. With black and magenta you will get the corresponding deep black but with a warmer tint.

▶ **THE PROCESS COLORS ARE TRANSPARENT**
This is the premise for the subtractive color combination and it means that a printed object will be visible through the component color printed over it.

▶ **ALSO BLACK IS TRANSPARENT**
A tint area consisting of 100% black ink will not be able to cover objects consisting of any of the other component colors. It requires a deep black tint to get full coverage.

▶ **DEEP BLACK PART 2**
If a four-color image is placed against a black frame or area printed with black, the area will appear paler than the image. It is particularly evident when using paper of a lesser quality.

▶ **BLACK AND WHITE AGAINST FOUR-COLOR**
Another common problem is that a grayscale image usually looks pale against a saturated background or a four-color photograph.

A black tint area that is supposed to be deep black requires an ink coverage of 100% black and around 40% cyan or magenta (magenta will give you a slightly warmer black tint, cyan produces a cooler effect). A tint area with ink coverage of only 100% black will look gray in comparison. It is important, however, that cyan and magenta areas are contracted – in other words, made smaller than the black tint area – so there will not be visible misregistration [see 6.7]. If you place a color photo against a dark black area you should use the above-mentioned method so that the background does not look washed out next to the dark tones in the photo. Another situation in which to use a deep black tint (composed of black and cyan or magenta) is when you want to cover other elements. Process colors are "transparent." This means that an object that is printed with process colors, then covered by another tint area, will generally show through. The mixture of black and magenta or cyan covers these objects sufficiently.

WORKING WITH SPOT COLORS 6.3.3

If you are working with spot colors and process colors, or with more than two spot colors, you should find out how many inks the printer's printing presses can print with. If, for example, their printing presses only can print four colors, a product printed with one spot color in addition to the process colors needs to be printed twice. This can have a radical effect on the printing price. Many printers have printing presses that can print with five, six or eight colors. If you print a printed product with four colors and two spot colors in a six-color press, you can print all six colors at once.

When printing standard four-color plus one or two spot colors you can, for example, combine four-color images with texts, logotypes or tint areas in spot colors. Another common way to simultaneously print spot and process colors is to combine black with a spot color. For example, it is usually done when printing letterhead and business cards. Based on special Pantone color guides, you can select spot colors and see how they will look in print. These color guides are available for coated as well as uncoated paper [see Chromatics 4.7.1].

Each print color will fall on its own film when outputting. The number of films corresponds to the number of plates and, therefore, the number of inks in the printing press. If working with four-color images and two spot colors, the document will be printed with six colors: the process colors (CMYK) of the images as well as two spot colors. One way to determine if you have the right number of printing inks in your document is to make color-separated printouts on a laser printer. Each color you have used will appear on a separate printout, just as it does when outputting to film. For example, if the original contains a four-color image and two spot colors, you will get six printouts, four for the color image and two for the two spot colors you have selected. If there are other colors that are defined in the color box they will also be printed, even if you have not used them in your final document. These colors must be removed before giving the material for output to film. Otherwise you run the risk of having to pay for the output of empty pages resulting from the unused colors. In your correspondence with the printing house, you need to let them know which spot colors you have used.

WHEN YOU ARE CONVERTING A SPOT COLOR TO PROCESS COLORS:
• Check the Pantone guide against a process color guide and find the CMYK color combination that resembles the spot color the most. There are Pantone guides that show Pantone colors and their corresponding CMYK combinations
• Check off Spot Color in the color definition for the spot color
• Set the CMYK color combination that you have selected based on the color guides

Adobe PageMaker, Adobe InDesign and QuarkXPress can automatically CMYK convert spot colors in a document. When this happens, the applications' own conversion values are used, but they rarely provide good results. Therefore, it is recommended that you go through and convert the spot colors yourself where necessary.

WORKING WITH VARNISH 6.3.4
Occasionally, you might want to use varnish on some objects (a logotype, for example) to create a special effect [see Off Press Processing 14.12.2]. In your original document, you work with varnish in the same way you do spot color. Define a special color for the varnish and state which objects should have that color. To check that your instructions are correct, do a laser printer output with the "varnish color" only. The black areas on the laser output will be varnished in the final print.

▶ **PANTONE GUIDE**
There are special pre-printed Pantone guides to help you choose the correct Pantone color. In this type, you can tear out color samples. There are also color guides that show suggestions of CMYK converted versions of the colors in the Pantone guide.

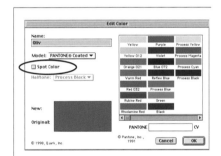

▶ **CMYK CONVERTING PANTONE COLORS**
When printing with four colors, you can use the Pantone colors in QuarkXPress, Adobe InDesign or Adobe PageMaker.

It is important to make sure the color is CMYK converted when output. Adobe PageMaker, Adobe InDesign and QuarkXPress can automatically convert spot colors in the document. In the example above from QuarkXPress, you should not mark the box for spot color. The program's own conversion values are used and it rarely provides a good result. You should check the colors in a color guide and manually convert the colors by entering the value for each process color.

WORKING WITH IMAGES 6.4

Along with colors and typography, images are an important component of originals. Prior to beginning production of an original, you should make a manuscript of images, decide the size of the images to be used, and determine if the images should be edited in a particular way. It is also important to select the right image format and to know how to deal with linked images in the document.

IMAGE FILE FORMATS FOR PRINTING 6.4.1

Scanned images are defined in the RGB color model. In order for images to be printed, they must be converted from RGB (the color model that is used on monitors and in scanners) to CMYK (the color model that is used for printing), known as CMYK conversion. In order to do this, you must adjust the images for the paper and the printing process that will be used [see Images 5.8].

There are three image file formats that are appropriate for printing: EPS, DSC, and TIFF. Images that are not saved in these formats must be resaved before they can be printed. In order to print them, they must be converted into CMYK and saved in one of the above-mentioned formats, using a program like Adobe Photoshop [see Images 5.3].

PLACING AND EDITING IMAGES 6.4.2

When placing images in a page layout application, first decide the size that you want the printed images to be. This is important because the quality of the image is dependent upon the degree to which a scanned image is enlarged. You can usually enlarge an image in the page layout application to around 120% without a noticeable loss of quality. This is assuming that the resolution was optimal at 100%. If the image has to be enlarged more than 120%, it is best to scan it again to get the larger size, rather than enlarge it in your page layout application [see Images 5.5.11].

Another reason that it's important to predetermine the final image size is that the resolution of the scanned image affects the possible size of the overall document, the size of the printed image, and the screen frequency used to print. If the final size of the printed image is unknown, images are usually scanned with a high resolution to avoid image quality problems if it turns out the image needs to be enlarged a lot. However, this can get expensive – the cost of scanning images often depends on their size and resolution, and the higher the resolution, the more expensive the scan. An image scanned with an unnecessarily high resolution will not result in a better final product, but it will cost more time and money.

It is easy to change images in page layout applications by rotating or skewing them, but you should be aware that such changes will cause the outputs to take much longer because the RIP will have to recalculate high-resolution images every time. Instead, adjust your images in an image editing application before placing them in the page layout application.

LINKED IMAGES 6.4.3

When an image is placed in a page layout program, a low-resolution version of the image is created in the document. This low-resolution image has a reference, called a link, to its

high-resolution image. When you output the document, the program uses the link to find the high-resolution image and replaces the low-resolution one. The link is based on the name and location of the high-resolution image in the computer's file structure. If you rename image files after you have placed them in your page layout application, the link will be broken. If you do make changes, you can update the links by telling the program where the image files are now located. You can check that all the image links are correct by going to Usage –> Pictures in QuarkXPress and File –> Links in Adobe PageMaker and Adobe InDesign. You can update image links by clicking Update and telling the program where the image files are located.

Adobe PageMaker allows you to save placed images directly in the document file instead of linking them. However, this practice can result in large and unwieldy documents. Moreover, you cannot make corrections to images that are saved directly in the document.

WORKING WITH LOGOTYPES 6.5

Spot colors are commonly used when designing logotypes. When printing with four-color, you need to CMYK convert the spot colors. To do it correctly, use a color guide. Find the process color composition that best corresponds to the spot color in the logotype. Most companies today usually put out a four-color logotype to avoid the possibility that a logotype is converted differently from one time to another.

Logotypes are usually object-based and are not saved as pixel images. This means that they are defined by mathematical curves and can be rescaled without losing quality. Logotypes that are saved as pixel images should be converted to curves. This can be done using Adobe Streamline [see Images 5.1.6].

KNOCKOUTS AND OVERPRINTS 6.6

When one object needs to be superimposed over another (for example, a text over a tint area), you can choose to print the object directly on top of the tint area, or "knock out" a hole in the tint area the same shape as the object, which is then printed on the resulting blank surface. In the first example, called an "overprint," the ink used to print the overlying text is mixed with that of the underlying tint area, creating a new color. In the second example, called a "knockout" [see figure], the text will be in the color defined by the

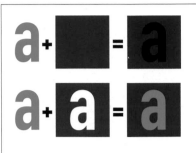

► OVERPRINT vs KNOCKOUT PART 1
As you can see, when overprinting the colors are mixed into undesirable color combinations.

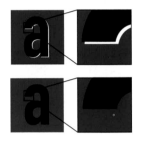

► OVERPRINT vs KNOCKOUT PART 2
When the color of the object is not sensitive to color changes, for example black, you should use overprinting to avoid gaps.

► TRANSPARENT INK WHEN OVERPRINTING
Because printing ink is transparent, the underlying object may show through. It can cause problems such as in the image above.

page layout program. If you don't specify otherwise, the page layout program usually automatically uses the knockout procedure. Using the knockout procedure sometimes causes distracting gaps or misregistration to occur. To avoid this, you may need to use traps or overprints (see below).

When the contrast between a dark object and a light background is substantial, it is best to overprint rather than knockout. With black text, overprint is always recommended. Then it is impossible to get misregistration between the objects. It is also faster to output the page. Overprinting is also recommended when there are thin lines or small text, if the colors can be combined appropriately.

When trapping, the dimensions of the objects change slightly. This effect becomes more evident the smaller the object is because the trap is the same regardless of the object's size. That's why you should, as much as possible, use overprint rather than traps for small objects. Be aware that black text overprinted on both a tinted area and a white background will be two different shades of black – darker over the tinted area than over the white area. This can be avoided by knocking-out the black text. The entire text will be printed against a white background and will be the same color as a result.

TRAPS AND CHOKES 6.7

As mentioned earlier, some degree of misregistration will always occur when several colors are printed on top of each other. This is because the dimensions of the paper change during the print process [see Printing 13.3.6]. When knockouts are used, the misregistration will appear as a white or colored gap between object and background. Even small misregistrations can be distracting. The problem is most noticeable in web-fed printing presses and flexography printing.

To solve this problem you can use trap and choke processes. In the trap process, an object is enlarged slightly so it overlaps another object. For example, in a situation where a tint area is directly aligned to another tint area, it is possible to avoid a white gap between them if one tint area is spread so it slightly overlaps the other. Most common applications for production of originals, such as Adobe PageMaker, QuarkXPress, Adobe InDesign and Adobe Illustrator have built-in trap tools. There are also powerful specialized applications such as Imation Trapwise and Island Trapper. However, these applications are expensive and take up a lot of memory, which makes them suitable only for larger production environments.

While trapping involves enlarging the foreground object in a color overlay, choking requires that the knockout, or the hole, be shrunk. Both functions provide an overlap between object and background, which prevents a gap from appearing if there is a small misregistration. The level of trapping is determined by the size of the misregistration in the printing process. The greater the misregistration, the larger the trap. The overlap that occurs when using chokes and spreads creates a new, darker color. As a result, you get a visible outline, which sometimes can be distracting. However, such an outline is usually preferable to a white gap. This outline is more evident when the contrast between the foreground and background is great.

The darkest parts of an object or background determine the shape the eye sees. Therefore, spreads and chokes are used on the lighter parts to prevent the eye from perceiving that an object has changed shape. For example, if a choke is used on a yellow background under a dark blue text, the text will keep its optical shape. If a trap were used on the blue text, it would be noticeably distorted. In the examples to the right, we have used two different process colors to simplify things.

If the color of the object and the background are similar, traps are not needed. In this case, misregistration creates a gap in a color that is very close to that of both the overlay and the background's color. Traps are not needed for two primary colored objects when one of the object's colors has higher ink coverage than the other.

Page layout applications can only trap simple objects like text overlaid on tint areas. Effective use of traps on more complicated objects (for example, those with color shifts and patterns where the trap has to be changed step by step in accordance with the color shift) requires access to more powerful trapping applications.

HOW MUCH SHOULD YOU TRAP 6.7.1

It is difficult to give a general recommendation as to which values should be used for trapping because values are specific to each printing process and paper stock. Check with the company printing the product as to recommended trap values if you are doing the trapping yourself. Trap values are usually between 0.1 and 0.5 points, depending on the printing process. When delivering digital material for printing, it is important to inform the printer that you have done the trapping yourself or that you need them to do it.

BLEEDS 6.8

Images or tint areas that reach all the way to the paper edges are called bleeds. It is important that these objects stretch slightly outside of the page format so that they will remain as bleeds after the printed product has been cropped and postpress processed. If objects do not extend outside the format, there is a risk that they will not reach all the way to the edge of the page after it has been postpress processed. As a consequence, there will be a white, unprinted area between the image or the tint area and the paper edge. Because printing and postpress processing are never exact, a safety margin (bleed) is required. A bleed of at least 1/8" is recommended.

CROSSOVER 6.9

Sometimes you want to place an image or other object on a full (two-page) spread. Often during printing, the two pages of the spread will be on different sheets or on different

▶ **OVERPRINT SMALL TEXT**
You should overprint small text to avoid changes in shape when knocking out and trapping.

▶ **MISREGISTRATION WHEN KNOCKING OUT**
With knockouts and misregistration you will get white or miscolored gaps.

▶ **TRAPPING AND CHOKING**
When trapping, the object is enlarged. Choke requires that the knockout be shrunk.

▶ **DISCOLORED OUTLINE**
When trapping and choking you will get a discolored outline. If two objects have similar shades the area of overlapping will have a darker shade, which sometimes can be distracting.

Print Production = Print Production+

Print Production = Print Production+

▶ **STYLISTIC CHANGES IN DARK OBJECTS**
The eye easily registers changes in the shape of dark objects. To avoid distracting shapes you should, as in the case above, shrink the background. In the upper example, the dark text has been trapped causing a distracting shape.

▶ **ONLY TRAP HALF OF THE OBJECT**
To avoid getting discolored objects, you should only trap where necessary.

▶ **TRAPPING IS NOT NECESSARY**
If an object and a background have a similar combination of process colors, the gap that appears at misregistration will get a similar color. That's why you don't need to trap or choke the object or the background.

parts of the same sheet, not printed immediately next to each other [see Off Press Processing 14.3.1]. Spreads that are printed this way are called crossover bleeds. When the final print is postpress processed and folded, it can be difficult to get perfect registration between the two pages. Avoid placing particularly delicate objects, such as small texts or thin rules, on two-page spreads. Images placed diagonally across the spread are also very susceptible to misalignment. Images and objects that cross over a spread should not be sensitive to small color changes. The color combination in the print often wanders a bit through the run and also between different makereadies. Thus, the two different parts of the image, placed on adjacent pages, can differ in color.

PROOFING AND HANDING OFF DOCUMENTS 6.10

Before handing off your original documents for the next step, it is important to proof them one last time. Then, collect all the files belonging to the document (images, illustrations, logotypes and fonts) and place them in a folder. Both QuarkXPress, Adobe InDesign and Adobe PageMaker have functions for saving documents that collect all pertinent objects and place them in a folder. In QuarkXPress, this is done by going to "File" and selecting "Collect for output." Then all the documents with images are collected in the folder you refer them to. In addition, a report is created that contains information about all fonts, images and colors that have been used, as well as additional information about the document. In Adobe InDesign, the function can be found under File –> Package. When using this function, the document is first proofed, a process called Preflight [see Review and Proofing 10.4] and then placed in a folder with images, typefaces and a report.

When you send materials out it is important that you label all items clearly. All Zip and Jaz disks should have labels with information about their contents and ownership. You should also purge the storage media of old versions of the files and anything that does not pertain to the production. Files should be named and structured so the service bureau can easily find the material. When delivering files via any kind of data communication process (for example, a modem, ISDN or the Internet), compress your files. Generally it is a good idea to compress all files belonging to one document into one single file. This speeds up the process and you're more likely to have a successful transfer if you only send

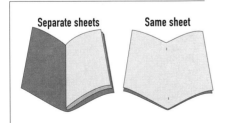

▶ **FULL (TWO-PAGE) SPREADS**
The left spread consists of two separately printed sheets. The right spread consists of pages from the same sheet (a center spread).

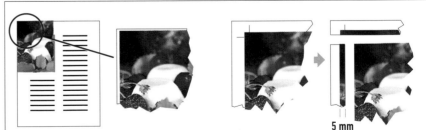

5 mm

▶ **BLEEDING IMAGE**
When placing an image at the very edge of your document, there will most probably be a white border around the image. The solution is to place the image at least 1/8" outside of the page and then cut the sheet clean after it's printed. That way, the image will extend all the way to the edge: it will "bleed."

▶ PART 1
You will always get a certain variation in color composition on the printed sheets and even between the left and the right side of a sheet. That's why you should avoid placing objects or images with sensitive colors across a two-page spread.

▶ PART 2
You will never get a 100% registration between two separate pages. That's why you should avoid placing objects or images diagonally across a double-spread.

▶ PART 3
You should also avoid thin lines that bleed across a double-spread. Thicker lines are less sensitive to misregistration.

one large file. The file should be "self-extracting"; the recipient should not need a decompression program to access and work with the files. Keep in mind that compressed files can sometimes be difficult to receive on computer platforms different from the originating machine. This situation must be dealt with on a case-by-case basis, since different systems have different characteristics [see Images 5.4.5]. Always include printouts of the printed product, even if you send the material via the web or Internet. Regular black and white printouts are usually sufficient, but make certain that the printout is of the most recent version of the document. Printouts allow you to double-check that the document you are delivering is correct, and they provide an opportunity for the people handling the next step in the process to discover possible errors at an early stage. For four-color productions, it is useful to do a four-color laser output. You can then check that any knockouts and overprints are correct. In addition, images saved in RGB will only be printed in the black output print. ■

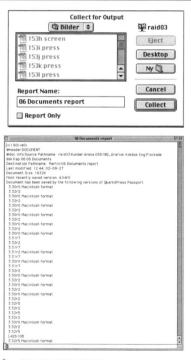

▶ COLLECT FOR OUTPUT
QuarkXPress has a function for saving the document and collecting all the accompanying objects and images. All files are placed in a folder with a content report.

▶ OUTPUT A COLOR-SEPARATED DOCUMENT
A good way of checking that the document is
correct is to print it color-separated on a
black and white laser printer. You set it under
File –> Print...

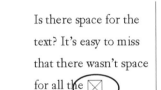

▶ IS ALL TEXT INCLUDED? PART 1
Is there space for the text? It's easy to miss
that there wasn't space for all the text in a
text area. QuarkXPress shows this symbol
when all the text is not displayed.

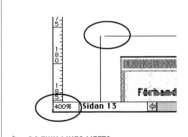

▶ DO THIN LINES MEET?
Enlarge your document to check that all thin
lines and frames really meet as they are
supposed to do.

▶ SEND THE MOST RECENT VERSION
When including printouts of your document, make sure to send the most
recent version. Don't make any changes
after it's been printed. If you do, you're
running the risk of confusing the service bureau and having them correct the
document based on an old version.

▶ IS ALL TEXT INCLUDED? PART 2
Adobe PageMaker alerts you when there isn't
space for all the text in a text area by showing
a red arrow at the bottom of the text area.

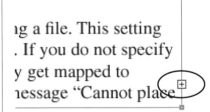

▶ IS ALL TEXT INCLUDED? PART 3
Adobe Indesign alerts you when there isn't
space for all the text in a text area by showing
a red plus sign at the bottom of the text area.

▶ CORRECT TOLERANCE FOR THE CLIPPING PATH
When creating a mask you have to set its tolerance. 8 pixels is usually appropriate.

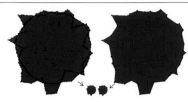

▶ TOO MANY ANCHOR POINTS
Avoid too many anchor points. In the illustration of an uneven halftone dot in the chapter
Review and Proofing, there were too many
anchor points. You will get the same result
with fewer points (small dots) and it is faster
to rip.

▶ PREFLIGHT
This is the name of Adobe InDesign´s function
that checks document links, typefaces, etc. It
can also collect the document for output;
gather all accompanying fonts, objects and
images, place them in a folder and create a
report.

Below are additional suggestions of things to keep in mind when handing off your document for further treatment.

THE DOCUMENT

- ☐ Check that there aren't any undesired empty pages in the document.

- ☐ Thin lines should be defined with an exact measurement and not as "fine" or "hairline."

- ☐ Enlarge to check that thin lines and frames meet as they are supposed to do.

- ☐ Try to collect all pages in as few documents as possible to reduce the startup effort when the document is handed off for further processing.

- ☐ Check that the pagination is done with uneven numbers on the right pages — it can easily change when the document is recomposed.

- ☐ Clean out objects that remain outside of the page area.

- ☐ Define the format of the document in the size as the final format of the printed product. You can't, for example, work with A3 sheets in a document for an A4 signature. Instead, select the A4 view.

THE FILES

- ☐ Different program versions and plug-ins can create problems between creator and recipient.
  Check that the recipient is able to receive your files.

COLOR

- ☐ In the page layout application, empty the color menu of all colors not used when printing. Otherwise, additional films may be output in vain.

IMAGES

- ☐ Check that images are linked to the images used and not to sketches (unless you have agreed to have someone replace your images).

- ☐ Is the image correctly cropped?

- ☐ Make sure that the background color isn't defined in image blocks with selected images.

- ☐ TIFF images should be set with a white background in the image area. If not, jagged outlines may appear in the shades against white.

- ☐ Mask channels, paths and illustrations can't have too many anchor points or be set with too low "tolerance."

- ☐ Spot colors (for example PMS colors) used in linked images must have exactly the same name as in the original document for a smooth output process.

- ☐ TIFF images in gray scale and line position can be colored in QuarkXPress. It doesn't work with EPS images.

TYPOGRAPHY

- ☐ Check the printout for text rearrangements.

- ☐ Is there space for the text? It's easy to miss that there wasn't space for all the text in a text area.

STORAGE MEDIA

- ☐ Choose a storage media that is an industry standard.

STORING AND ARCHIVING

7

CHAPTER 7 STORING AND ARCHIVING   THERE ARE MANY TYPES OF DIGITAL STORAGE MEDIA, APPROPRIATE FOR DIFFERENT FILE TYPES. FOR EFFICIENCY'S SAKE, IT'S WORTH TAKING THE TIME TO DEVELOP A METHOD FOR STORING YOUR FILES THAT ALLOWS FOR EASY ACCESS AND USE.

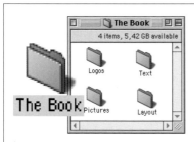

▶ STRUCTURE FOR NAMING FILES
When storing files, it is important to work out a system for naming folders and files so they can be easily identified as on-going projects. Organizing files and folders by order numbers or customer/project names is common practice.

When you save a file that you are working with on the computer, that file must be stored somewhere. Files are usually stored on the computer's hard drive or on a server, depending on the system set-up. Files can also be saved on other storage media, such as CDs or tapes. These media are generally less expensive than hard drives, and are convenient for storing files that must be shared or transported among users not connected to a network server, or for archiving files that you do not need on your hard drive. Archiving old files in this way also frees up space on your hard drive or server for more frequently accessed material.

In this chapter, we will cover different types of storage media, including hard drives, magnetic and optical disks, and tapes. We will discuss which media are best suited for different storage situations. Finally, we will look at the process of archiving and the use of archiving programs and databases.

STORAGE SYSTEMS 7.1

The graphic production process often involves working with a large number of files of different types: text, layouts, logotypes, images, fonts, illustrations, print-ready files, etc. Because of this, it is important to have an organized file structure in place. A good structure makes it easy to access the files you need and clearly indicates the most recent version of each document.

When several people are working on a network and saving files on the same server, it is particularly important to have a structured system for storing and naming files – otherwise, chaos will ensue and no one will be able to find anything. Ideally, there should be a system for saving files used by everyone on a daily basis, as well as for regularly archiving seldom-used files in order to free up memory on the server. Individual computer hard drives are relatively expensive and are not really appropriate for long-term storage. Files you do not use on a daily basis should be archived on less expensive storage media like Zip disks or CDs. When you want to work with an archived file, you simply need to load it back up on your hard drive or server. It is important to create naming, storage and archiving conventions that clearly indicate the most current version of each file, in order to minimize the risk of files being deleted or archived while they are still in use.

STORAGE MEDIA ⁷·²

Most people store the files they use frequently on their computer's hard drive. When you want to archive files, exchange files with other users or move data, you need other types of storage media. There are a number of different storage media, appropriate for different situations. Because these media differ in both cost and operation, it is important to understand their specific functionalities, advantages and disadvantages in order to choose the right one for the task at hand.

CHOOSING A STORAGE MEDIUM ⁷·²·¹

Your choice of storage media should be based on how you intend to use the stored information. Storing information during production, short-term archiving, long-term archiving, creating back-up files, and storing information for transportation and/or distribution all demand different things from a storage medium. When choosing a medium, certain factors should be taken into consideration: cost, storage capacity, read/write speed, access time, security, life span, standardization and availability. A medium's access time refers to how long it takes for your computer to find a file stored on that medium. Read/write speed is a measurement of the amount of data that can be read or written per second by a particular storage device. Security concerns how sensitive the medium is to damage from things like electromagnetic fields or physical shocks and jolts. The life span of a storage device is determined by how long information can be stored on it and still be read, and also by how physically durable the medium is. If a storage device is so commonly used that the industry has developed a standard version, made and sold by a variety of manufacturers and stores, the device is considered to be standardized and widely available.

TYPES OF STORAGE DEVICES ⁷·²·²

Storage devices fall into two main categories: magnetic and optical. There are also magnetic/optical hybrids combining the magnetic and optical techniques. One difference between magnetic and optical media is that magnetic media are erasable and can be reused, while optical media are not rewriteable. Because of this, optical media are generally more appropriate for archiving purposes. Magnetic storage media work best for use during production and transportation. Magneto-optical drives reside on the desktop computer just like the local hard drive, which makes them easy to use. Following is a closer look at some of the different types of storage devices.

▶ FOLDER STRUCTURE FOR STORAGE
When storing different types of files in a common space, it's helpful to have a folder structure that makes it easy to find the different files.

▶ STORING FILES

Different uses for file storage:
- Production
- Distribution
- Transportation
- Short-term archiving
- Long-term archiving
- Safety copying/Backup

▶ COMPARISON OF STORAGE MEDIA

Important factors to consider when selecting a storage medium include:
- Cost per MB
- Storage capacity
- Read and write speed
- Access time
- Durability
- Life span
- Distribution
- Compatibility/Standardization

Significance of Factors	Production	Distribution	Transportation	Archiving/short	Archiving/long	Safety Copying
Speed	very high	medium	high	medium	low	low
Safety	low	very high	medium	high	very high	high
Life span	low	very high	low	high	very high	medium
Distribution	low	very high	high	low	low	low
Cost/MB	low	very high	low	high	very high	high

Efficient production requires optimal read/write speeds and access times. Files archived for a short time should be stored on inexpensive yet relatively fast media. Long-term archiving requires a medium that is durable and is usually relatively expensive. Safety copying/backup is best done on an inexpensive medium with large storage capacity. When transporting files between workstations or offices, it is important that the storage medium be one that is in wide distribution, to ensure that the recipient will be able to use the format they receive. Read/write speeds are also important considerations for media that will be used to transport files. Widespread distribution of files requires a medium with a high degree of standardization and security.

HARD DRIVES 7.3

Hard drives are the fastest storage medium when it comes to access time and read/write speed. They are generally used for storage during the course of a project, when speed is a priority. All computers have a built-in hard drive, called a local hard drive. If you need more hard drive space, you can add peripheral hard drives to your Macintosh computer via the SCSI, FireWire or USB port. Peripheral hard drives can also be used for the transportation of larger amounts of data.

A hard drive is made up of a number of disks stacked on top of each other. Each disk is coated with a magnetically sensitive layer. When you save information to the hard drive, these surfaces store information in magnetic "tracks" that the computer then reads and interprets as a series of ones and zeros. The hard drive's read/write head travels very close to the rotating disks when recording or reading information, making it sensitive to jolts while in operation. If the hard drive is jolted while in use, the read/write head may collide with the disks and damage the information on them. This is known as a "head crash" [see The Computer 2.2.12].

MAGNETIC DISKS 7.4

The floppy disk is the most common type of removable magnetic disk, despite its relatively small storage capacity (up to 1.4 MB). Most of today's personal computers have built-in floppy drives. Floppy disks are increasingly being replaced by CDs and Internet transmissions.

Other types of removable magnetic disks include Jaz and Zip disks. These disks are fast and have the capacity for large amounts of data. Syquest disks were, for a long time, the most wide-spread solution but are no longer produced. They have been replaced by Jaz and Zip disks, useful for transporting large files like page layout or image files. These disks are built like the disks in your computer's hard drive, and work in the same way. They

► HARD DRIVES

It is appropriate to use a hard drive for storage when:

• Storing and working with files while in production

• Transporting large amounts of data

► HARD DRIVES +/–

Advantages and disadvantages of hard drives:

+ They are very fast

– They are relatively expensive

– They are sensitive to damage from magnetic fields

– They are sensitive to damage from jolts

PRINT PRODUCTION STORING AND ARCHIVING

▶ **HARD DRIVE**
A hard drive consists of a number of magnetic disks on which data is recorded and read by a number of read/write heads.

▶ **HARD DRIVES ARE MADE UP OF DISKS**
Sensitive disks are stacked closely together, with information stored on both sides.

▶ **MAGNETIC DISKS**

Appropriate uses for magnetic disks (does not apply to floppy disks):

• File storage during production

• Transportation of large amounts of data

require compatible read/write drives which are relatively inexpensive, but the disks themselves can be quite pricey (on a cost per MB basis).

TAPE 7.5

Tape is also a magnetic medium. There are many different kinds, but the most common include DLT (Digital Linear Tape), DAT (Digital Audio Tape) and Exabyte. Tape is a relatively slow medium, but its cost per megabyte is low and it can store large amounts of data. It is generally used as a backup medium but it can also be effective for long-term archiving, especially when you have to store large amounts of data. All tapes require compatible read/write devices connected to the work station. Tape is not a particularly standardized medium; for example, there are often several different programs for a single type of tape. In order for a computer to read a tape, it often needs to have the exact program originally used to save the content of the tape. This makes tape an inefficient means of distributing files.

Tapes store information sequentially, which means that in order to access the information you need, you have to locate the place on the tape where it was recorded. This means that you do not have immediate access to files like you do with magnetic disks and optical storage media. Tape access times can be several seconds, compared to access times of a few milliseconds for magnetic or optical disks. On the other hand, tapes have relatively fast read/write speeds.

▶ **MAGNETIC DISKS +/–**

Advantages and disadvantages of magnetic disks (does not apply to floppy disks):

+ They are widely distributed

+ The reading devices are fast and inexpensive

+ They are highly standardized

+ They have a protective cover

– The disks themselves are expensive (on a cost per MB basis)

– They are sensitive to damage from magnetic fields and dust

– They are sensitive to damage from jolts

▶ **STORAGE CAPACITY OF VARIOUS DISKS**

• Floppy disks – 1.4 MB

• Zip disks – 100, 200, 250 MB

• Jaz disks – 1 or 2 GB

▶ **FLOPPY DISK**
A floppy disk holds 1.4 MB.

▶ **JAZ DISK/DRIVE**
A Jaz disk holds 1 or 2 GB.

▶ **ZIP DISK/DRIVE**
A Zip disk holds 100, 200 or 250 MB.

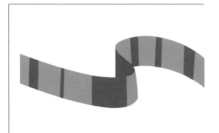

As with magnetic disks, the tape's surface is magnetized, making it sensitive to damage from electromagnetic fields. Tape is also exposed to physical wear and tear when it is written to or read. Manufacturers estimate the life span of most tapes at around 5-10 years.

OPTICAL DISKS 7.6

Optical disks do not have magnetized surfaces like those media we have just discussed. This means that they are insensitive to damage from electromagnetic fields and, there-fore, safer for long-term storage. Optical disks are generally not rewriteable or erasable, which also makes them a very safe option for archiving. Though not as fast as magnetic disks, they have a life span of anywhere from 10-30 years, and are relatively inexpensive. There are three types of optical disks: CDs (Compact Discs), DVDs (Digital Versatile Discs) and MO cartridges (Magnetic Optical cartridges).

THE CD 7.6.1

The CD is the most common type of optical storage medium and the most standardized of the optical media. Most computers have built-in CD drives, and are able to read CDs with-out any special programs. Because the CD is standardized, widely distributed, and cannot be erased, it makes an excellent medium for electronic publishing. Distribution and archiv-ing are two other appropriate uses for the CD. CDs do require careful handling, because the disks can be scratched or damaged fairly easily. CDs generally have a storage capacity of 650 or 700 MB.

CD-ROM (Compact Disc-Read Only Memory) is the medium of choice for digital pub-lishing, for example encyclopedias or games, and distribution, for example of computer software. When a CD-ROM is produced, a master disc is created. Then a printing form of the master disc is made from which you print all the CDs needed for distribution.

▶ A CD
A CD can hold up to 650 MB of data, and is not rewritable.

▶ SEQUENTIAL STORAGE
Optical disks store data in sections, similar to hard drives and magnetic disks.

With the advent of the CD-R (Compact Disc-Recordable), it is now possible to produce CDs with your own computer. All you need is a special CD read/write drive and the accompanying software. To burn a CD with 700 MB of data takes 2 to 20 minutes depending on how fast the read/write drive is, and though a CD can be added to in more than one session, these files cannot be erased or replaced. If you only need a couple of copies, the CD-R technique is a relatively efficient and inexpensive way to archive files. Another development of this technology is the CD-RW (Compact Disc-Rewriteable). These rewriteable CDs allow you to delete or record over existing files.

Photo CD is a CD-R technique launched by Kodak. Photo CD allows you to store up to 100 images of five or six different resolutions on a CD. The images are stored in a special compressed format called YCC. Photo CD has a number of different applications within the graphic production process.

A CD physically consists of three layers: a foundation layer of polycarbonate, an information layer coated with reflective aluminum, and a protective layer of varnish. Like an analog record album, information stored on the CD is laid out in a continuous spiral track. Along the spiral track are pits and elevations that have been burned into the CD's surface by a powerful laser. A low-powered laser illuminates and "reads" these variations, and the computer translates them into a series of ones and zeros. Transitions from pits to elevations are interpreted as ones, whereas no change in transition is interpreted as zeros.

DVD (DIGITAL VERSATILE DISC) 7.6.2

The DVD (Digital Versatile Disc or Digital Video Disc) is a new storage standard for optical discs. The DVD is based on CD technology, but DVDs store information more densely, giving them the capacity to hold much more data than a CD. DVDs can also be single-sided, like CDs, or double-sided (storing information on both surfaces of the disc). Single-sided DVDs can store anywhere between 2.6 to 3.93 GB of data, and double-sided discs can store up to 5.2 GB. Future DVDs will have even greater storage capacity. Although the data stored on a DVD is read with a laser beam (just like the CD), a special DVD reader is needed to read the densely packed information. A DVD reader, however, is also capable of reading CD-ROMs. DVDs can store music, text, images – even moving pictures. In fact, DVDs and DVD players are expected to replace conventional videotapes and VCRs as the medium of choice for home entertainment. In the graphic production industry, DVDs are generally used for distribution and long-term archiving.

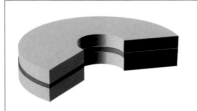

▶ CONSTRUCTION OF A CD
A CD consists of three layers: a foundation layer of polycarbonate, an information layer, with a reflective aluminum coating, and a protective layer of varnish.

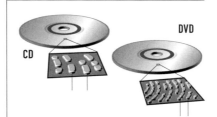

▶ HOW CDS AND DVDS STORE INFORMATION
CDs and DVDs record data in a continuous spiral pattern of pits and elevations. The tracks on a DVD are denser than those on a CD, and can therefore store more data.

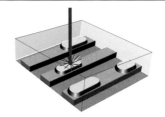

▶ READING DATA ON A CD
A low-powered laser reads the tracks on a CD or DVD, and the computer interprets the changes in elevation as a series of ones and zeros.

▶ DVD ABCs

Different types of DVDs and their uses:
- DVD-Video – video
- DVD-Audio – music
- DVD-ROM – data
- DVD-R – archiving
- DVD-RW, DVD-RAM, DVD+RW – archiving

▶ DIFFERENT USES FOR DVD-R
- Distribution of large amounts of data
- Short-term archiving
- Long-term archiving

▶ DVD +/-

Advantages and disadvantages of DVDs:
+ Inexpensive
+ The reading devices are also inexpensive
+ They are insensitive to damage from magnetic fields
+ They have a long life span
+ High storage capacity
- They don't have a protective cover

There are several different types of DVDs. Video is stored on DVD-video, music on DVD-audio, and all other types of data on DVD-ROM. Writable DVDs are known as DVD-Rs. There are three different kinds of rewriteable DVDs: DVD-RW, DVD-RAM and DVD-RW.

MAGNETO-OPTICAL CARTRIDGES 7.6.3

Magneto-optical cartridges (MO cartdriges) are a hybrid of optical and magnetic media. These rewriteable cartridges are covered with a protective layer of plastic, which makes them less vulnerable to scratches and damage than CDs or DVDs. MO cartridges can store up to 1.3 GB of data. The disks store information on two sides, and each side must be read separately (you have to turn them over), so you only have access to half the total storage capacity at one time. Magneto-optical technology is relatively well standardized, although not to the same level as CD technology.

MO cartridges require compatible read/write devices connected to the work station. While MO cartridges are relatively inexpensive, the read/write devices can be pricey, which makes this system practical only if you have a large number of MO cartridges in use. MO cartridges are primarily used for transporting larger amounts of data and for archiving (short or long term) purposes.

To record data on an MO cartridge, a high-powered laser must first heat up the cartridge to 200 degrees Celsius in order to alter the direction of the cartridge's magnetic field. It's important to note that the direction of the magnetic field can only be changed when the disc is heated. As a result, MO cartridges are insensitive to the influence of external magnetic fields at room temperature. When you want to write over information already stored on an MO cartridge, the old information must be erased before the new information can be recorded. This means that rewriting information on a disk takes twice as long as reading it. MO cartridges are read by a low-powered laser reflecting off the surface layer of the disk. The reflection is affected by the changing directions of the recorded magnetic field, and the computer is able to interpret these variations as a series of ones and zeros.

A high-powered laser heats up the cartridge, altering the direction of the magnetic fields on its surface.

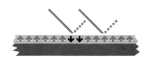

A low-powered laser reflects against the surface layer. The computer interprets the different directions of the magnetic fields as ones and zeros.

▶ MO CARTRIDGE
MO cartridges exist in 5.25 or 3.5 inch formats and hold up to 1.3 GB of data.

COMPARISON 7.7

Because each type of storage medium has its advantages and drawbacks, the decision of which to choose is determined largely by what you want to use it for, be it production, transportation, distribution or archiving.

PRODUCTION 7.7.1

During the actual production of a project, it is recommended that you store all project-related files on a computer's internal hard drive, external hard drives or on a network server. These methods allow efficient access to files you'll be using every day.

TRANSPORTATION 7.7.2

For transporting files between different locations, magnetic disks are appropriate because they are well standardized and widely distributed, as well as rewriteable. CDs are good for transporting data as well, because they are also highly standardized and widely distributed. Since CDs are generally not rewriteable, you can be confident that the data you record on them will not be erased or changed by mistake. Magneto-optical disks are also suitable for transportation, but are not as widely used as magnetic disks or CDs. Internet transmission is becoming the most popular method for transporting files.

DISTRIBUTION 7.7.3

If you want to distribute a digital product to many different users, CDs are highly recommended since they cannot be erased, are well standardized and have a long life span.

SHORT-TERM ARCHIVING 7.7.4

Magnetic disks are convenient for storing files you only intend to archive for a short time; they are inappropriate for long-term storage, however, because of their sensitivity to damage from magnetic fields. CD-Rs and magneto-optical disks are also good for short-term archiving because of their durability.

LONG-TERM ARCHIVING AND SAFETY COPYING/BACKUP 7.7.5

When archiving large amounts of data on a long-term basis or backing up files for safety, we recommended that you use either tapes or optical discs. Tapes are inexpensive and

---

▶ USES OF MO CARTRIDGES

MO cartridges are an appropriate choice for:

• Transportation of large amounts of data

• Short-term archiving

• Long-term archiving

▶ MO CARTRIDGES +/−

Advantages and disadvantages of MO cartridges:

+ They are insensitive to damage from magnetic fields

+ They have a long life span

+ They have a protective cover

− The reading devices are expensive

− Write speeds are slow

▶ A COMPARISON OF DISK STORAGE CAPACITY

CD – up to 700 MB

DVD – up to 17 GB

MO Cartridges – 3.5 inches: 128/256 MB; 5.25 inches: 650/1,300 MB

---

have large storage capacity, but they also have a shorter life span than optical discs. Because of this, we'd recommend choosing optical discs, like the relatively inexpensive CD-R, when security and longevity are your chief concerns. Hard disks and magnetic cartridges are less appropriate for long-term archiving because of their high cost per megabyte of storage space.

ARCHIVING 7.8

Now we'll take a closer look at archiving programs designed to help you keep track of an extensive archive of files.

DIGITAL ARCHIVING 7.8.1

A digital archive stores files, and information about those files. Digital images and text are two of the most commonly archived types of files, but archives can contain any kind of file: page layouts, sound files, applications, etc. When we talk about a "digital archive" we are referring to a system consisting of an archive program, a database containing information about the stored files, and the actual medium on which the files are physically stored.

Digital archiving has many advantages over traditional, manual archiving, or filing. One of the biggest advantages is that a digital archive takes up considerably less space than a physical one. A few CDs or tapes can store perhaps hundreds of files. And unlike a traditional filing system, digital archiving does not confine you to a hierarchical structure. A digital archive can take advantage of the computer's ability to create cross-references among all sorts of different entries. For example, an image of a cat and dog sitting together is only physically stored in one place in a digital archive. Yet, this single picture might be accessed via a number of different searches – under their subject matter "cat" and the subject matter "dog" and perhaps even "cats and dogs", depending on how the system is set up.

▶ **DIGITAL vs MANUAL ARCHIVES**
Digital archives allow you to access data from multiple paths by using cross-references, whereas manual filing systems restrict you to a hierarchical structure.

▶ **ATTRIBUTES OF COMMON STORAGE MEDIA**

	Hard drive	Floppy disk	Zip/Jaz	DAT/DLT tape	CD-R/CD-RW/DVD	MO cartriges
Read and write speed	high	low	high	medium	High/medium	medium
Sensitivity	high	high	high	medium	low	low
Life span	medium	short	short	medium	long	long
Storage capacity	80 GB	1.3 MB	250/2 000 MB	4–80 GB	650/650/5200 MB	1.3 GB
Storage technique	magnetic	magnetic	magnetic	magnetic	optical	magneto-optical
Distribution	high	high	medium	low	high	low
Standardization	ok	good	ok	poor	good	ok
Application field 1	production	transportation	transportation	backup	archiving	archiving
Application field 2	transportation	distribution	production	archiving	distribution	transportation

An archive program is really just a system for simplifying the management of a database. This database stores all the information about the files in the archive. This information usually includes things like the file names, the date each file was archived, the size of each file, the images contained in each file, where each file can be located, etc.

The database is typically stored on a hard drive, while the archived files are stored separately on media such as CDs, or magnetic tapes. This allows you to do a quick search of the archived files without having to pull out and go through all the CDs or tapes you stored the actual files on.

When you actually archive a file, the file itself is transferred to the storage medium you've chosen. The file is recorded and described by the archive program, which then stores this information in the local database. If you are archiving an image file, the program creates a small, low-resolution copy of the high-resolution image. These low-res images are called 'thumbnails'. The thumbnails stored in the database allow you to easily identify and/or locate the actual high-resolution image files in the archive. Each archived file also has a "registration box" where you can enter descriptive information and categorize the file. You can then use the search function which allows you to locate files based on the information you entered.

CLASSIFICATION, DESCRIPTION AND STRUCTURE 7.8.2

If you are creating digital archives for long-term storage, or your archive contains an especially large number of files, you might find it helpful to organize them according to a given structure so you can easily find them again. One way to do this is by classifying each file according to specific searchable traits. You can classify a file by describing it in as much detail as possible in the registration box. For example, the registration box for an image file might contain a number of different fields, including filename, ID number, photographer, customer, owner, date, resolution, measurements, etc., all entered by the person who archives the file. Usually there are fields for keywords and text descriptions as well. When you want to describe an image with keywords, the program provides a dictionary of terms you can use for classification. You can also add new words to the dictionary, if necessary. You can type anything you want in the text description fields, such as a short sentence describing the file. Classification is a critical step in the archiving process, and can determine how functional your archive really is. A well-organized archive is particularly important if outside users will be searching for files, since they won't have the advantage of being familiar with what they are searching for.

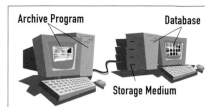

▶ **3 PARTS OF A DIGITAL ARCHIVE**
A digital archive generally consists of three parts: an archive program, a database and a storage medium.

▶ **THUMBNAIL-SIZED IMAGES**
When you conduct a search in an archive program, the results are listed on-screen with accompanying thumbnail images.

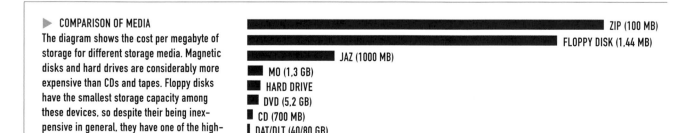

▶ **COMPARISON OF MEDIA**
The diagram shows the cost per megabyte of storage for different storage media. Magnetic disks and hard drives are considerably more expensive than CDs and tapes. Floppy disks have the smallest storage capacity among these devices, so despite their being inexpensive in general, they have one of the highest costs per megabyte.

ZIP (100 MB)
FLOPPY DISK (1.44 MB)
JAZ (1000 MB)
MO (1.3 GB)
HARD DRIVE
DVD (5.2 GB)
CD (700 MB)
DAT/DLT (40/80 GB)

Each object entered into an archival database gets a registration card. This 'card' stores all the pertinent information about the file, which will enable you to search for this file at a later date.

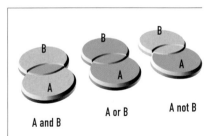

▶ SEARCH BOX
When you conduct a search for a file in your archive database, you will get a search box that allows you to enter the criteria of the item you are searching for. You can combine several search criteria with boolean variables like "and," "or" and "not."

▶ BOOLEAN VARIABLES
Boolean variables involve creating partial matches with variables like "and," "or" and "not." The illustration on the left shows the results of a search using the "and" variable; the one in the center, the "or" variable; and the illustration on the right shows results of the same search using the "not" variable.

SEARCHING 7.8.3

There are many ways to search for a file in a digital archive. Programs often have a search function containing a number of predefined fields in which you can type what you're looking for. Sometimes this function is combined with a search menu containing keywords, which allows you to choose the word that best describes what you are looking for. This makes it easier to select criteria that will increase the probability for a successful search.

Digital archives use boolean variables (see illustration) to manage the outcome of searches. Two or more search words can be combined with the boolean variables "and", "or" and "not" and achieve different search outcomes. For example, when you do a search for "dogs and cats", the search result will include images containing both search criteria – in other words, only images containing both dogs and cats, not those with only cats or only dogs. If you do a search for "dogs or cats", you will get all the images that were classified as dog images, as well as all those classified as cat images, in addition to all those with both dogs and cats. If you do a search for "dogs not cats", you will get images containing dogs only. Search results are often displayed as a list with accompanying thumbnail sized images, so you can easily identify the file you were searching for. ■

▶ DIGITAL IMAGE ARCHIVE +/−

The advantages and disadvantages of digital image archiving (compared to manual archiving):

+ The archive is relatively easy to search
+ Searches are quick
+ Not limited to a hierarchical search structure
+ There is a high probability of successful search results
+ The archive program allows for precise classification of files
+ There is no physical wear and tear on original images
+ A digital archive takes up relatively little space
+ You can search the archive in many different ways
+ It is easy to make backup copies

− You do not have access to the physical artwork, and the image quality is reduced
− Computer knowledge is required to set up a digital archive
− Technical problems can prevent access to information stored in the archive
− Image files require a large amount of storage space
− There are limitations on how you can use digitally stored images, in terms of size and resolution etc.
− Because technology is constantly changing and there are so few standards in the computer industry, the content of the archive needs to be updated regularly in order for it to remain accessible.

NETWORKS AND COMMUNICATION

8

CHAPTER 8 NETWORKS AND COMMUNICATION **TO ENABLE FILE TRANSFERS BETWEEN COMPUTERS AND TO ALLOW SEVERAL USERS TO SHARE THE SAME PERIPHERAL EQUIPMENT (PRINTERS, SERVERS, IMAGESETTERS, TO NAME A FEW), COMPUTERS ARE USUALLY CONNECTED TO A NETWORK. IN A NETWORK, DATA (SUCH AS FILES OR PRINT JOBS) ARE EXCHANGED BETWEEN COMPUTERS AND PERIPHERALS THROUGH A SERIES OF DIGITAL SIGNALS.**

In this chapter, we will discuss concepts like LAN and WAN, network components, and the basics of transmission technique and capability. We will also look at different types of networks, dial-up connections and the Internet. First, we will define what a network is.

WHAT IS A NETWORK? 8.1

There is more to a network than just the physical cables. A network can be defined by meeting one or more of the following criteria:

1. *The presence of network cable(s) and special network interface cards in the computers.*
2. *The presence of a network protocol that manages network communication.*
3. *With a network you are able to:*
• Share units such as printers, servers and modems with other computers in your network
• Make the information on your hard disk available to other computers in your network
• Share a common database with other computers in your network
• Send messages between computers in your network via electronic mail services such as an intranet

LAN AND WAN 8.2

Networks are sometimes defined by their geographical reach. A network limited to a room or a building is usually called a local area network, or LAN. LANs commonly used in the graphic production industry include Localtalk, Ethernet and fiber-optic networks (FDDI).

▶ **NETWORKS**
By connecting peripheral devices to a network, you can share units such as printers, servers and modems with other computers in your network. For example, all computers in a network can share one printer.

Networks that range over long distances are called wide area networks, or WANs. A company with offices in many different cities might use a WAN to connect all of its locations. Telephone lines can be used to connect several LANs to one WAN. Data can then be sent from one location to another over the WAN, using, for example, telephone wires.

▶ **LAN**
LAN, or local area network, is limited to a room or a building.

WHAT MAKES UP A NETWORK? ^{8.3}

A network consists of a number of components, including cables, network interface cards, network protocols and different network devices. Cables physically connect the machines. The network interface facilitates communication between the computer and the cables. Network protocol contains the rules for how this communication should be conducted. Network servers and other network units such as repeaters, hubs, bridges, switches and routers are the physical components needed to build a network. We will now look more closely at the different elements of a network.

NETWORK CABLES ^{8.3.1}

The type of network cable used in creating your network is important because it determines the speed of the network, i.e., how long it takes to transfer data. The type of cable also determines how large a network can be (different types can carry data over different distances), as well as how secure those transmissions are. There are three main types of network cables: twisted-pair, coaxial and fiber-optic cable.

The twisted-pair cable is the most common and least expensive of the three main types. It consists of insulated copper wires twisted around each other, identical to a regular telephone line. Twisted-pair cables can carry a signal for about 100 meters. After that, electrical noise weakens the signal and the information may have to be retransmitted. This noise is caused by the electrical fields surrounding electrical cables and devices, among other things. To provide protection against noise in twisted-pair wiring, shielded twisted-pair wiring has been developed. The shield consists of a protective foil sheath wrapped around the wires.

The second type of cable, coaxial cable, consists of a copper wire shielded with plastic insulation. The insulation is wrapped in a protective copper insulation, which makes the cable insensitive to noise. A coaxial cable can carry a signal for up to 185 meters. Coaxial cable is very common, and although it is more expensive than twisted-pair cable, it is considerably less expensive than fiber-optic cable.

Fiber-optic is the third type of network cable. Electronic signals are converted to light pulses in the network interface, which then travel through the glass fibers of the cable. This means that fiber-optic cable is completely insensitive to electronic noise. A fiber-optic cable can carry a signal for up to 20 kilometers, and allows higher transmission speeds than the two other cable types. Transmissions via fiber-optic cables are secure because they can't be bugged. Fiber-optic cables are very costly and require expensive fiber-optic compatible hardware.

Cable choice is generally a question of price versus capability. It is common to combine different types of cables in the same network. In some parts of the network, simple twisted-pair cable is sufficient, whereas areas carrying heavy data traffic over long distances might require capabilities only fiber-optic cable can offer.

▶ **WAN**
WAN, or wide area networks, can connect local networks over long distances to create a common network for a company based in many different geographical locations.

▶ **NETWORK COMPONENTS**

A network generally consists of:

- Cables
- Network interface cards
- Network protocols
- Network devices such as servers, repeaters, hubs, bridges and routers

---

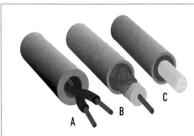

NETWORK INTERFACE CARD 8.3.2

The network interface card is a circuit board, usually installed in a card slot on the computer. The card handles the communication between the computer and the network cables. Different network types require different network interface cards [see The Computer 2.2.8].

NETWORK PROTOCOL 8.3.3

In order for all the units in a network to communicate with each other, they have to speak the same language. This is where a network protocol comes in. A network protocol is a set of "rules" governing how computers and other units in a network communicate with each other – similar to the rules of grammar for a particular language. In other words, a network protocol defines how information is packaged when transmitted through a network.

Some network protocols are more standardized than others and can be used on several network types. Appletalk and TCP/IP are the most common network protocols in the graphic production industry. Appletalk and Ethertalk are Apple's network protocols and are often used in networks involving many Apple Macintosh computers. Appletalk is used with Apple's own network solution Localtalk. Ethertalk is used in Ethernet networks [see 8.6].

When networks have a combination of Apple Macintosh, Windows and Unix computers, it is common to use TCP/IP, or Transmission Control Protocol/Internet Protocol. TCP/IP is also the protocol used when communicating via the Internet. TCP/IP is the most standardized network protocol and is compatible with most networks. There are additional network protocols, but we will not cover them in this book.

NETWORK DEVICES 8.4

In addition to the elements already discussed, a network also involves one or more servers and a variety of other connected units. The server is a computer in the network that handles the users' common tasks. Repeaters, hubs, bridges, switches and routers are examples of different network devices that are used to expand and/or divide a network into different zones or segments, or to connect different networks. What follows is a short discussion of the most common network devices.

SERVERS 8.4.1

A server is a central computer that all the other computers in a network are connected to. It is usually a powerful computer that administers all the network devices. It can handle a number of different tasks.

The most common use for a server is storing files shared by many users. Certain applications can allow a server to administer printer or imagesetter outputs, also known as spooling. Software can also enable the server to provide information on network traffic and capacity, as well as identify which users are connected, and even track their network activity.

The server can also be connected to the Internet with a modem, IDSN line, DSL, etc. The users in the network can then dial up external computers (and vice versa) via the server. Using these telecommunications devices you can expand your LAN or WAN. Email is often managed by a server.

A network server can manage network security using password programs that allow for different levels of access to the information stored on the server. For example, all users but one might be given access to open files, but not to save or delete them. Only the user designated to save and delete files is enabled to do so. The risk that files will be modified or deleted by mistake is greatly diminished.

It is simple to administer and automate data backup via the server. One example of server-based backup systems is a "mirror" hard drive. There are two hard drives on the server, but you always work with the same one. When saving or changing the content of one drive, a program on the server copies or "mirrors" the changes to the other drive. Both hard drives always have the same content. If your primary drive crashes, all your data is still stored on the mirror hard drive. You can also use other media for backup, such as magnetic tapes and optical discs [see Storing and Archiving 7.7.5].

Since servers handle frequently and commonly used functions, if you have a large network, you might consider dividing the workload among several servers to maintain optimal functionality and security of your system.

REPEATERS 8.4.2

Repeaters are used to extend the geographical reach of a network. As mentioned above in our discussion of cables, there are physical limitations to a network because a signal carried over cable weakens as it travels further from its source. A repeater strengthens the signal and allows the network to extend beyond the limitations of cable alone. The repeater strengthens all signals in the cable regardless of origin or destination.

HUBS 8.4.3

Hubs are units used to connect different parts of the network. Network units such as bridges and routers are connected via hubs. There are two types of hubs: active hubs and passive hubs. Active hubs function as repeaters and strengthen the signals that pass through them, while passive hubs only serve as connecting units between network devices. Some hubs are built so that each connected device can be assigned a constant level of network bandwidth. Devices connected via such hubs are not as affected by fluctuations in network traffic.

BRIDGES AND ROUTERS 8.4.4

Bridges and routers are used to connect designated parts of a network called network zones or network segments. They only transfer information from one segment or zone to another. This helps minimize unnecessary traffic over the entire network and reduces the competition for network bandwidth.

TRANSMISSION TECHNIQUE AND CAPACITY 8.5

When working with a network, transmission speed is an important consideration. Transmission speed is measured in bits per second, which refers to how much data can be transmitted over the network in a given amount of time. Theoretically, the transmission

▷ **NETWORK UNITS**

Examples of different network units are:
- Servers
- Repeaters
- Hubs
- Bridges
- Routers

▷ **TASKS FOR SERVERS**

The most common tasks for servers usually are:
- File management
- Output management
- Network supervision
- Communication and email
- Security services (access)
- Safety copying/back up

▷ **TELECOMMUNICATION IN A NETWORK**

It is common to connect modems, ISDN or Internet to a server. It enables users of the network to dial up external computers and vice versa. That way you can connect your LAN to a WAN. Email management is usually also done by a server.

▶ **NETWORK UNITS**
Network units are usually assembled in a "rack" like in the image above. Units like routers, hubs and switches look similar.

speed of the network is primarily dependent upon what kind of network and cable you are using.

In reality, transmission speed also depends on which network protocol you are using, how the network is constructed and what the traffic volume is. Traffic volume is determined by how many users are connected to the network at any one time and the size of the files being utilized and transmitted. Because computers share the network capacity the transmission speed, the bandwidth, slows down when the traffic volume is high. The bandwidth is the maximum, theoretical transmission speed of a particular means of communication.

HOW DOES A TRANSMISSION WORK? 8.5.1

Ethernet is one common type of network, and we'll use it here as an example to discuss how a network transmission occurs. To send a file from one machine to another via an Ethernet network using the Ethertalk protocol, the originating unit begins by inquiring if the machine it wants to send information to is currently available on the network. When it gets a positive answer, the originating unit divides the file into several "packets" of data. In Ethernet networks the size of the packet is usually between 64 and 1,514 bytes.

Each packet is constructed so that the first segment of each packet contains the address information of the sending and receiving units and the last segment contains a description of the contents of the package. This enables the receiving computer to determine that the transmission is complete and all information has been received. The actual information that the packet is transmitting is carried between these two segments. When a packet is received, the sender is notified that the next packet can be sent. The last packet of the file contains information that concludes the transfer.

WHAT AFFECTS THE TRANSMISSION CAPABILITY OF THE NETWORK? 8.5.2

A typical network involves a number of users who might want to send information over the network at the same time. Ethernet only allows for transmission of one packet over the network at a time. As soon as a packet has been sent, the network is blocked until the package has arrived at the correct address. Then it is available again and a new packet can be sent from another computer.

If two users send a packet at the same time, their transmissions will collide and neither packet will reach its destination. To prevent such collisions, a "random number" generator manages the transmission of the packets; this device nearly eliminates the risk for collisions. The more computers in the network, the more possibilities there are for collisions. The more packets transmitted, the more network bandwidth used.

Aside from traffic consisting of file transmissions and print jobs, there is also something called network control traffic. All connected machines have to constantly inform each other that they are available on the network. They do this by frequently sending small questions and answers to each other. The more machines you have in the network, the more network control traffic is generated.

▶ **FILE TRANSFER IN A NETWORK**
To send a file from one machine to another, the originating unit begins by inquiring if the machine it wants to send information to is currently available on the network. When it gets a positive answer, the originating unit divides the file into several "packets" of data. The last packet of the file contains information that concludes the transfer.

MAKING THE BEST USE OF NETWORK CAPACITY 8.5.3

A common way of reducing network traffic is to divide your large network into a number of smaller independent networks called zones. The equivalent procedure in the Windows

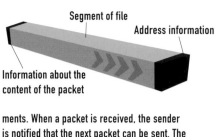

Segment of file

Address information

Information about the content of the packet

ments. When a packet is received, the sender is notified that the next packet can be sent. The last packet of the file contains information that concludes the transfer.

world is called segmentation. Each zone functions as its own self-contained network, which means, among other things, that no control traffic needs to be sent between machines in two different zones. In addition, the traffic load of one zone is not affected by the traffic load of another. If, for example, you put high traffic image editing computers in one zone, and less demanding page layout computers in a second zone, the users in the second zone would not notice any reduction in their network capacity. Zones make a big difference in network performance: an Ethernet network that has not been divided into zones might only achieve half the efficiency of a network with well-designed zones.

Another advantage of zone-divided networks is that they are not as sensitive to technical or mechanical failures. If a cable malfunctions in one zone, only that zone is affected; the rest of the network can continue to function without it. There is a lot to gain by giving careful thought to how your network is constructed.

NETWORK TYPES 8.6

In this section we will briefly cover the most common types of LANs and Internet connections used in the graphic production industry. Local networks included here are Localtalk, Ethernet and Fiber Distributed Data Interface (FDDI); the Internet connections we will cover are modems, ISDN lines and cable connections.

LOCALTALK 8.6.1

Localtalk is the simplest of Apple's networks. Localtalk is so slow that it is hardly used anymore. The only data it can transmit at a reasonable speed are text documents. The theoretical transmission speed is 230 kilobits per second, or 28.75 kilobytes per second, which is about 40 times slower than a regular Ethernet category 3 network [see 8.6.2]. A Localtalk network generally uses the network protocol Appletalk and twisted-pair cabling.

ETHERNET 8.6.2

Ethernet category 3 is the most established network standard in the graphic production industry today. It has a theoretical transmission speed of 10 megabits per second, or 1.25 megabytes per second. An Ethernet network usually uses either Ethertalk or TCP/IP as a network protocol. All types of cabling can be used with an Ethernet network.

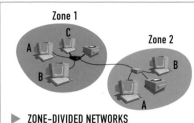

Ethernet category 5, or Fast Ethernet, is an updated version of Ethernet category 3. It has a theoretical transmission speed of 100 megabits per second, ten times faster than Ethernet category 3. Ethernet category 3 is easily upgradeable to Ethernet category 5.

FDDI 8.6.3

FDDI, or Fiber Distributed Data Interchange, is a standard for fiber-optic networks. An FDDI network can theoretically transmit up to 100 megabits, or 12.5 megabytes, per second. FDDI networks are expensive and require fiber-optic cable. The network protocol TCP/IP is usually used. FDDI networks are generally used by companies that transmit vast amounts of data, and/or require very high security for their transmissions.

SCSI 8.6.4

SCSI stands for Small Computer Standard Interface and is pronounced "scuzzy." It is not an actual network, but a computer's own interface for communication with peripherals like external hard drives, scanners, etc. Communication via SCSI cable is very fast at 24 megabits, or 3 megabytes, per second. There is a new version of the SCSI standard called SCSI-2, or Fast-SCSI, which provides transmission at 80 megabits, or 10 megabytes, per second. SCSI cables are limited to 6 meters in length, and are therefore not appropriate for networks [see The Computer 2.2.13].

DIAL-UP CONNECTIONS 8.7

Dial-up connections use existing telephone lines. With a dial-up connection, you can communicate between computers or entire networks over long distances. Communicating over telephone lines requires a piece of hardware called a modem, which converts computer data into signals that can be transmitted via telephone cables. There are two types of modems, analog modems (for older telephone lines) and ISDN lines (for a digital network). All types of dial-up connections require special software.

ANALOG MODEMS 8.7.1

Modems allow computers to communicate over regular telephone lines. With an analog modem, a computer can simply dial up another computer over a phone line. An analog modem converts digital information to analog tone signals that the telephone system can transmit. The receiving modem interprets the signals and converts them back to digital information.

The modem is connected to the modem port of the computer [see The Computer 2.2.9]. Most computers today come with built-in modems. In order to be able to use a modem you need communication software, which is usually included when you purchase the hardware. Analog modems provide relatively slow transmission speeds. The fastest modems on the market today transmit information at a speed of 56,600 bits, or 7.2 kilobytes, per second.

ISDN 8.7.2

ISDN, or Integrated Services Digital Network, is a mode of telecommunication that has become increasingly popular within the graphic production industry. ISDN is based on the same premise as a regular modem, the dial-up connection. However, ISDN takes advantage of digital advancements in the regular analog telephone system.

With ISDN you can reach higher transmission speeds than with modems, which works well for text documents and low-resolution images, but it is still relatively slow when sending large amounts of information. ISDN transmission is done via two "channels" and the maximum speed is 128 kilobits, or 15 kilobytes, per second.

Unfortunately, ISDN is not particularly standardized. There are three different ISDN interfaces for Macintosh computers on the market (Planet, Leonardo and OST), as well as various communication software applications. To ensure error-free communication, it is generally required that both sender and recipient have the same ISDN interface and communication program. Commonly used communication programs include Easy Transfer, Leonardo Pro and ISDN-Manager.

THE INTERNET 8.8

The "Internet" is the name for the global network that connects millions of LANs and WANs worldwide. TCP/IP is the network protocol for the Internet. The Internet can be reached from almost any computer, either via a dial-up connection or directly through a cable connection.

CABLE CONNECTION 8.8.1

Cables offer a direct connection to the Internet via a network cable built into the local network.

DIAL-UP INTERNET CONNECTION 8.8.2

When using a dial-up Internet connection with an analog modem or ISDN, the computer's modem dials up the modem of your Internet service provider on the other end, and it "connects" you to the Internet.

A dial-up Internet connection is only connected to the Internet during the time you are calling. When dialing with an analog modem, you have to wait for the modem to connect every time you want to access the Internet. This takes approximately 15-30 seconds. ISDN takes a second to connect.

The Internet is based on a platform that transmits information to its destination over one of many different paths, which increases the probability of a successful transfer. The Internet first attempts to send information the fastest way possible, but if the transmission does not get through that way, it may take a different, slower path. As a result, it sometimes takes a little longer to receive email or view a web page.

APPLICATIONS ON THE INTERNET 8.8.3

There are several types of applications that utilize the Internet – the World Wide Web, email and FTP are the most common. All of these programs work regardless of the type of computer you have or your geographical location. In other words, it's just as easy to

▶ MODEM
An analog modem converts the computer's digital information to analog tone signals that the telephone system can transmit. The receiving modem interprets the signals and converts them back to digital information.

▶ ISDN

An ISDN modem doesn't need to convert the computer's digital signals to analog tone signals, like a regular modem would. ISDN uses its own digital telecom network, an advancement of the regular analog telephone system.

send an email or read a web page on a Macintosh as on a Windows or Unix computer, etc. Small glitches, such as erroneous character substitution, do occur, but these are being eliminated as applications improve.

WWW 8.8.4

The World Wide Web (also called www, w3 or just, "the web") allows you to "browse" through linked web pages containing various combinations of text, images, sound, moving images and interactive programs. The most common web browsers are Netscape Navigator and Microsoft Internet Explorer.

EMAIL 8.8.5

Email is electronic messages sent between two computers. A message can also be sent to more than one email address at a time. The most common email programs for Macintosh are Microsoft Outlook, Eudora, Claris E-mailer and First Class. Netscape Navigator and Microsoft Internet Explorer also handle email.

Email can carry "attachments" between computers. Any digitized file can be attached to an email–text document and low-resolution images are frequently translated into email attachments.

In order to speed up the process of sending large file attachments, files can be compressed before they are sent. Compression programs can merge many files into one, making transmission faster and more secure [see Images 5.4.5 and Documents 6.10].

FTP 8.8.6

FTP, or File Transfer Protocol, is a standard for transmitting files between two computers on the Internet. You can log on to another computer with FTP and put/get files from your own. Both the sender and recipient must have FTP programs. Common FTP programs are Anarchie and Fetch. Newer web browsers can also handle FTP. FTP is the fastest protocol for transmitting files via the Internet.

INTERNET SPEED 8.8.7

The speed at which you can send email, transfer files or view web pages on the Internet can vary tremendously. Generally, it is always slower to work on the Internet than on a local network. A dial-up connection combined with a standard modem at 56.6 kilobits per second only allows you to transfer compressed files at a rate of 6 kilobytes per second, compared to a local network with theoretical speeds of 10 to 100 megabits per second. A cable connection can reach speeds up to ten times faster than an analog modem.

TRANSFERRING FILES 8.8.8

FTP and email attachments are the two primary methods for transferring files via the Internet. There is a major difference between the two methods. With FTP you fetch a file from an FTP server; with an email attachment, the file is transmitted to the recipient's email account. Email attachments must pass through the email servers in several places. FTP requires a user name and password for accessing the server. With FTP you can deliver the file to its destination yourself, or have the recipient pick it up.

▶ **FTP – File Transfer Protocol**
FTP, or File Transfer Protocol, is a standard for transmitting files between two computers on the Internet. You can log on to your computer with FTP and send/receive files from another. Both the sender and recipient must have FTP programs.

▶ **WWW – World Wide Web**
"The web" allows you to "browse" through linked web pages containing various combinations of text, images, sound, moving images and interactive programs.

Below is a chart of theoretical transmission speeds for different types of networks and telecommunications. It also contains examples of file sizes and their transmission speeds. Note that you can never reach these transmission speeds in reality — 60 to 70% of the stated value is more realistic. Errors, superfluous information and high network traffic, etc., contribute to reducing the transmission speeds.

	SPEED (kilobit/s)	SPEED (kilobyte/s)	10 megabytes
Modem	56.6	7.1	24 min
ISDN 1×	64	8	21 min
ISDN 2×	128	16	11 min
Localtalk	230	28.8	5.8 min
Cable connection	512	64	2.6 min

	SPEED (megabit/s)	SPEED (megabyte/s)	10 megabytes
Cable connection	2	0.25	40 sec
USB	12	1.5	6.6 sec
SCSI	24	3	3.3 sec
SCSI 2	80	10	1 sec
Ethernet	100	12.5	0.8 sec
FDDI	100	12.5	0.8 sec
FireWire	400	50	0.2 sec

When you use Internet services within a company or organization, it is called an Intranet. In these cases, the web is used to handle internal information. If you allow external users to access parts of your Internet-based network, that portion of the system is known as the Extranet.

PROTECTION FROM NETWORK INTRUSION [8.8.9]

Networks with an external connection, i.e., a modem or the Internet, should be protected from intrusion. This is often done by providing the computer that handles communication with something called a "firewall." A firewall is a specialized program that only allows authorized traffic to pass through the communication systems. There are many types of firewall applications on the market. ∎

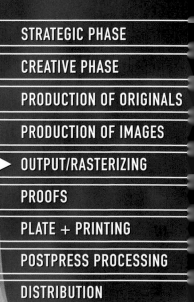

OUTPUT

9

CHAPTER 9 OUTPUT

WHEN THE DOCUMENT IS FINISHED IN ITS DIGITAL FORMAT, IT IS READY FOR OUTPUT ON PAPER, FILM OR PLATES. YOU WILL COME ACROSS TERMS LIKE POSTSCRIPT, RIP, OPI AND PDF. IT'S TYPICAL TO ENCOUNTER CERTAIN PROBLEMS AT THIS STAGE OF GRAPHIC PRODUCTION, SO IT'S IMPORTANT TO FAMILIARIZE YOURSELF WITH THE BASICS OF OUTPUTTING.

'Output' is the general term for various types of print outputs. In this chapter, we will cover the basics of outputting. You may output your document to a printer or an imagesetter, and you can also print to a file. However you decide to output, there is one common step: the digital document must be translated to a file format that can be output or displayed on the screen. This format is called a page description language (PDL). Adobe PostScript is the current industry standard PDL. PDF is another file format from Adobe that is becoming a standard for both physical outputs and screen display. We will look more closely at both formats, as well as OPI, which is a common type of production and output program used in the graphic production industry.

Before outputting a project onto the films used for printing, you can do either a digital or manual imposition. If you choose to work digitally, you arrange the individual pages on the computer and output film that will already be imposed. If you want to do a manual imposition, you output each page on a separate film and then manually arrange them into a film assembly. We'll cover the basics of imposition later in this chapter. Finally, we will look more closely at different types of output devices, including printers and imagesetters.

First, however, we will review the process called rasterizing, the process of converting text and image into halftone dots using halftone screening, which is the foundation for all output and printing techniques.

HALFTONE SCREENING ^{9.1}

A photograph consists of continuous tones – tonal transitions of color hues. A printing press cannot produce continuous tones. Instead, it combines printed and non-printed surfaces to achieve a similar effect, almost like a stamp. Halftone screens are used to simulate gray tones with black and white inks. Halftone screens deceive the eye into believing it sees continuous tonal transitions by dividing the printed image into very small parts, which the eye blends to look like continuous tones when the image is viewed from a normal distance. Smaller divisions result in better image quality.

A halftone screen consists of small dots in closely spaced rows. The size of the dots varies depending on the tones you want to simulate. In light areas, the dots are small; in dark areas, the dots are larger. The denser the dotted rows are, the higher the "screen frequency" is. A high screen frequency means the image is divided into smaller parts (smaller dots in the halftone screen) and, as a result, you will get finer tonal transitions and finer detail in printed images. A black surface is completely covered with dots, giving 100% ink coverage. A surface that is white does not contain any dots – 0% ink coverage. A gray surface has an ink coverage of anything between 1 % and 99%, depending on the shade of gray.

Halftone screens are calculated by a processor, a Raster Image Processor (RIP), then exposed on graphic film in an imagesetter. Most imagesetter manufacturers have developed their own particular halftone screening techniques, which means slightly different results may occur depending on the brand of equipment used to rasterize. Different halftone screening techniques include Agfa Balanced Screening (ABS), High Quality Screening (HQS) from Linotype Hell, and Adobe Accurate Screening (AAS).

HALFTONE DOTS ^{9.1.1}

A halftone dot consists of a number of exposure dots in the imagesetter. The resolution of an imagesetter is measured in dpi (dots per inch). The exposure dots are placed in square patterns called halftone cells. The halftone dot is composed from the center of the halftone cell and works its way out. The number of exposure dots used to build the halftone dot determines its size. The smallest consists of one exposure dot and the largest of all exposure dots within the halftone cell. The size of the halftone cell is determined by the screen frequency.

SCREEN FREQUENCY ^{9.1.2}

The screen frequency is a measurement of the number of halftone cells per line. It is measured in lines per inch, or lpi (sometimes this is denoted as l/in, lines per inch, or l/cm, lines per centimeter). The lower the screen frequency, the larger the halftone cell and, consequently, the larger the halftone dot. This means that a halftone dot with a 50% coverage in a 60 lpi screen is four times as big as the same halftone dot in a 120 lpi screen.

The higher the screen frequency, the finer the details in the resulting image. The paper and printing method used help determine what screen frequency you can print with. Paper suppliers usually provide screen frequency recommendations for different types of paper. The printing house can also provide this information. If the screen frequency you use is too high for a certain kind of paper, you run the risk of blurring the halftone dots, which will result in a loss of detail and contrast in the print. 150 lpi is a

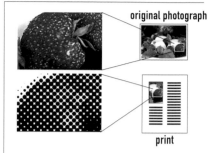

▶ **HALFTONE SCREEN—SIMULATION OF GRAY TONES**
A printing press cannot produce continuous tones, like in a photograph with smooth tonal transitions. It can only print with color or without color. To reproduce gray tones in print, you use halftone screens instead. Halftone screens consist of small dots in closely spaced rows. Their size varies depending on which tone you want to simulate. Halftone screens deceive the eye into believing it sees continuous tones although only black and white have been used.

▶ **CONTINUOUS TONAL TRANSITIONS**
In the upper gray scale, we have simulated a continuous tonal transition. The tonal transition is, in reality, not continuous but because the halftone screens are so fine the transitions are not visible.

In the lower gray scale, we show the same tonal transition but with a lower screen frequency. The brain also perceives this example as a continuous tonal transition. You can see that the gray scale is composed of differently sized dots in black and white, the two colors you can print with black printing ink.

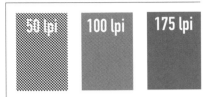

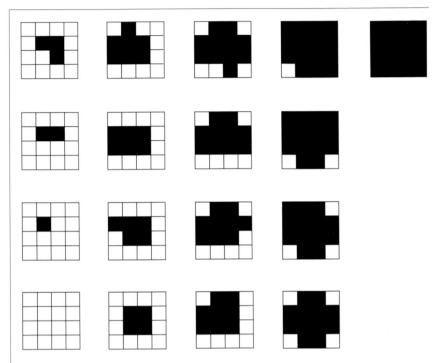

THE STRUCTURE OF THE HALFTONE DOT
Inside a halftone cell, the halftone dot is constructed by exposure dots that fill the cell from the center and outwards always following the same pattern. The number of exposure dots that fit in the cell determines the number of sizes a halftone dot can assume, i.e., the number of gray tones the halftone screen can simulate. The halftone dot shown can simulate $4 \times 4 + 1 = 17$ tones (+1 is derived from the unfilled halftone cell).

SCREEN FREQUENCY
Screen frequency is stated in lpi, lines per inch, and is a measurement of the number of halftone cells per inch. The lower the frequency, the larger the halftone cell and the halftone dot. Above are examples of different screen frequencies. At 50 lpi the eye is still able to perceive the halftone dots but at 175 lpi the surface is perceived as a continuous tone.

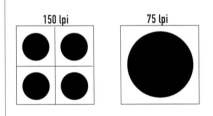

SCREEN FREQUENCY DIVIDED IN HALF
If you divide the screen frequency in half, the halftone cell will be four times as big. As a result, a halftone dot in the same gray tone, will be one fourth the size in a 150 lpi screen compared to the 75 lpi screen.

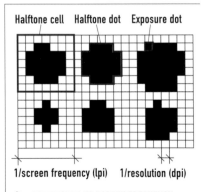

RESOLUTION VS SCREEN FREQUENCY
The difference between output resolution (dpi) and screen frequency (lpi) is illustrated above.

common screen frequency for high-quality products like brochures and annual reports and 85 lpi is common for low-quality products like newsprint.

OUTPUT RESOLUTION 9.1.3
When film is output on an imagesetter, you must set an output resolution. Imagesetters have a number of default settings, which state the resolution in dpi, the number of exposure points per unit of length. Common resolutions are 1,200, 2,400 and 3,600 dpi. The desired screen frequency and tonal range should determine the resolution you choose for outputting on an imagesetter. The higher the screen frequency you want to use for the final print, the higher output resolution you have to choose. Higher resolution results in a broader tonal range, but prints out more slowly than a low-resolution output.

TONAL RANGE 9.1.4
Tonal range refers to the maximum number of gray hues you can get with a particular screen frequency and output resolution in the imagesetter. The relationship between the screen frequency and the output resolution determines the tonal range that can be reproduced. The formula for calculating the tonal range is: number of gray hues = (output res-

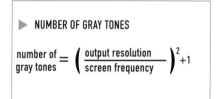

► THE BRAIN IS TOO SLOW!

When the resolution is too low, soft tonal transitions (upper illustration) may come out as separate stripes of the different tones. This phenomenon is known as banding effects, or striping effects.

olution/screen frequency)^2+1. Using this formula, a 133 lpi screen frequency with a 2,400 dpi setting in the imagesetter would have $(2,400/133)^2+1 = 327$ gray hues.

A grayscale image in the computer generally consists of 256 gray hues, and a four-color image has 256 hues in every component color [see Images 5.2.4 and 5.2.8]. In order to reproduce all these hues, you should select a resolution that provides at least 256 gray hues. In this case, the above-mentioned example, which provides 327 gray hues, is more than enough. In reality, the human eye cannot distinguish between 256 gray hues. 64 gray hues is usually the limit to what the eye can see. The gray hues of the computer and the imagesetter are created according to a linear function: each gray hue represents an equal-sized step in the total tonal range. By contrast, the eye's perception of gray hues is logarithmic, which essentially means that the eye is differently sensitive in different parts of the grayscale – it can more easily distinguish tonal differences in the lighter part of the spectrum than the darker part. Thus, in order to compensate for the more sensitive parts of the eye, you have to be able to reproduce more than 64 linear hues. It is difficult to determine the exact number of hues needed, so it is recommended that you have at least 100 hues per component color, and therefore that you select an output resolution capable of producing that number of shades given the desired screen frequency. To use the previous example again: with a 133 lpi screen, a resolution of 2,400 dpi would be more than enough. On the other hand, if you chose a setting of 1,200 dpi, the imagesetter would only reproduce 82 gray hues – too few for optimal results. 1,200 dpi would be an appropriate setting for an 85 lpi screen however; according to our formula, the imagesetter would reproduce 200 gray hues with that combination [see illustration].

Given these parameters, you might think that 100 shades of gray would be enough. Why then, do digital images contain as many as 256 hues – sometimes more? When an original image is opened in a program like Adobe Photoshop it contains color information consisting of the full 256 hues. As the image is edited, some of that tonal information is destroyed. Therefore, you need that extra image information when editing, more so than at output. Normally, 256 hues are enough to maintain image quality during the editing process, but if there are repeated edits or extensive retouching to certain parts of the image, there may not be enough information left in the edited image to allow for a good reproduction [see Images 5.6].

So, why not always choose the output setting with the highest possible resolution? That way you never have to worry about having a sufficient tonal range, right? The rea-

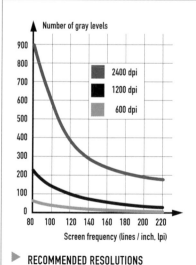

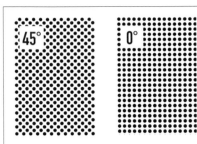

► PATTERNS AS PERCEIVED BY THE BRAIN
The brain is easily distracted by patterns, particularly those involving 0 and 90-degree angles. To make patterns less obvious, halftone screens are therefore tilted at 45-degree angles.

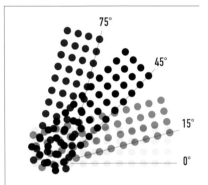

► SCREEN ANGLES OF THE PROCESS COLORS
Black is the most distracting color for the brain and its screen is tilted to 45 degrees, the angle that distracts the brain the least. Yellow is the least distracting color for the brain and its screen is tilted to 0 degrees, the angle that distracts the brain the most.

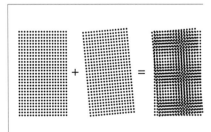

► MOIRÉ
Moiré is a regular pattern that occurs when two individual patterns are placed on top of each other. It is easily perceived by the eye and can be very distracting in the print.

son we don't do this is because printing at a high resolution requires more time and does not necessarily provide better results. For example, it takes twice as long to output a document at 2,400 dpi than at 1,200 dpi, and three times as long to output at 3,600 dpi. Setting the resolution too low however, results in an insufficient tonal range and inferior reproduction of tint areas and images. If you want a tonal range of at least 100 shades of gray, you can use screens up to 100 lpi with an output resolution of 1,200 dpi. 2,400 dpi is enough for 200 lpi screens, and so on.

SCREEN ANGLES 9.1.5

The brain can easily perceive patterns involving 0 and 90-degree angles. Halftone screens are therefore tilted at 45-degree angles to make patterns less obvious. When printing with four colors, the screen for each component color is placed at a different angle in order to avoid a moiré effect [see below]. Because black ink generally has the highest contrast with the printing surface, it also makes the strongest impression on the brain. Therefore, the screen for the black ink is tilted to 45 degrees, the angle that distracts the brain the least. Yellow has the lowest contrast, so its screen gets the "worst" screen angle, or 0 degrees. The angles of the cyan and magenta screens are oriented as close to 45 degrees as possible, in opposite directions. For offset printing, the recommended screen orientations are 45 degrees for black, 15 degrees for cyan, 75 degrees for magenta and 0 degrees for yellow. This gives you an even displacement of 30 degrees among the three most visible colors. These suggested angles only apply to offset printing. Other printing methods like screen printing or gravure printing require different orientations.

MOIRÉ 9.1.6

Proper orientation of the screens is very important for ensuring a quality print. Improperly set screen angles can result in an effect known as moiré. Moiré is an obvious, regularly occurring pattern in the print, which can be easily perceived by the eye. It is very distracting. Today's halftone screening techniques avoid moiré by assigning each component film a slightly different screen frequency. Often the screen angles are also adjusted to compensate for this effect. This makes it considerably more difficult for the different halftone screens on the films to interfere with each other.

Sometimes you will also find moiré in isolated parts of an image, an effect called "object moiré." This is not the result of an error in setting the screen angles, but because

► WRONG SCREEN ANGLES CAUSE MOIRÉ
If an image is output with improperly set screen angles, moiré can be visible in the print.

► OBJECT MOIRÉ
Sometimes patterns in an image coincide with those of the halftone screens and cause object moiré.

PRINT PRODUCTION OUTPUT

patterns in the image coincide with those of the screens. Object moiré is relatively unusual but does occur occasionally in sensitive images like checkered or patterned fabrics, for example. A similar phenomenon can be observed when someone appearing on a TV screen is wearing a checkered or patterned suit.

HALFTONE SCREEN ROSETTES 9.1.7

When the screen angles used in printing are well-registered, the resulting print has a rosette-like pattern. If you look closely at a printed image, this rosette pattern is more or less visible to the naked eye, depending on the ink coverage and the color combination of the print. Although rosettes might be distractingly obvious in some parts of a printed image, this is considered a "normal" screen phenomenon, unlike moiré. In general, the lower the screen frequency, the more visible the rosettes.

All analog proofs, and some digital, allow for a sharp reproduction of halftone dots, and rosette patterns can be very evident as a result—even though they may not appear that way in the final print. For example, if you were to do an analog proof of a newspaper advertisement at 85 lpi (a low screen frequency), the rosette pattern might be distracting, reproduced in sharp detail on the fine paper of the proof. When the advertisement is actually printed on low-quality newsprint paper, however, the dots will not appear as sharp and the rosettes will not be as evident.

HALFTONE DOT TYPES 9.1.8

Not all "dots" are round. Dots can be round, elliptical or square, though round dots are most common. Depending on the printing method, and sometimes on the printed product, square or elliptical dots might be a better choice. The corners of square dots meet at a tonal value of 50%. The eye can sometimes perceive this transition in softer shades. Round dots work the same way, but meet at a darker tone, approximately 70%. Because of their shape, elliptical dots meet at two different tonal values, 40% where the pointed ends meet and 60% where the long sides meet. You will thus get two critical points of interaction in the tonal transitions and elliptical dots can sometimes create lines in the image where the dots meet. There are halftone screens that combine different dot shapes in different screen percent values. Agfa Balanced Screening, for example, combines round and square dots in order to get the benefits of both shapes.

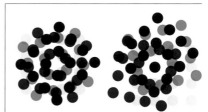

Open center   Dot in center

▶ HALFTONE SCREEN ROSETTES
When the screen angles used in printing are well-registered, the resulting print has a rosette-like pattern. There are two main types of rosettes: those with an open center and those with a dot in the center. Which one is better is disputed.

▶ SCANNING SCREENED IMAGES
When scanning printed (already screened) images, you run the risk of generating moiré because the screens of the image and of the print coincide.

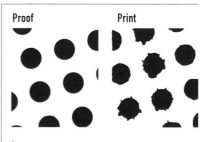

Proof   Print

▶ SHARP HALFTONE DOTS
Analog proofs and water-free offset prints provide sharper halftone dots than wet offset. The halftone screen rosettes may be perceived as distracting because they are so sharply reproduced.

▶ HALFTONE DOT SHAPES

• Elliptical dots:
They are recommended for several types of objects. For example, they can be used for both flesh tones and products in the same image. Elliptical dots are prone to create patterns.

• Square dots:
They can be used for images high in detail and contrast, for example images of

jewelry. Square dots are less appropriate for flesh tones.

• Round dots:
They are recommended for bright images, with, for example, flesh tones. Round dots are less appropriate for areas with a lot of detail in shadows.

The choice of dot shape also depends on the printing method used.

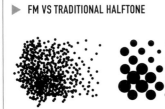

▶ PART 1

In FM screening, the halftone dots are the same size but the distance between them differs. In traditional screening, the halftone dots have the same distance to each other but differ in size.

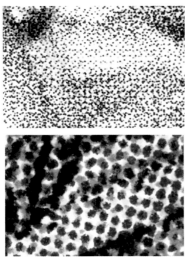

▶ PART 2

In the enlarged screens above, you can see the difference between FM and traditional screening.

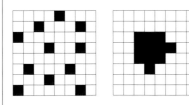

▶ PART 3

In the FM technique to the left, the exposure dots are spread out in the cell. In the traditional to the right, the dots are collected in the center. Both halftone screens have the same gray tone, approximately 17% (11/64).

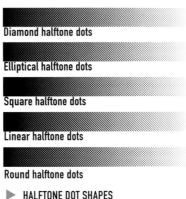

Diamond halftone dots

Elliptical halftone dots

Square halftone dots

Linear halftone dots

Round halftone dots

▶ HALFTONE DOT SHAPES

The different halftone dot shapes have different characteristics, visible in fine tonal transitions.

▶ ELLIPTICAL DOT CRISIS

Because of their shape, elliptical dots meet at two different tonal values, 40% where the pointed ends meet and 60% where the long sides meet. You will thus get two critical points of interaction in the tonal transitions causing linear patterns.

FREQUENCY MODULATED SCREENING [STOCHASTIC SCREENING] 9.1.9

The big difference between stochastic screening and traditional halftone screening is that the number of dots per surface unit varies, rather than the size of the dot. The name used by the graphic production industry, "stochastic screening", is somewhat incorrect, however. Stochastic means random, and the screens are not random. A better name for this technique is Frequency Modulated screening, or FM screening.

In FM screening, all halftone dots are the same size. The halftone dots are approximately the same size as the smallest dots in traditional halftone screening. A dark area in a traditional halftone-screened image contains large dots, while the same area in an FM screened image contains a large number of dots instead. It may seem like these dots are randomly placed within the screen, but in reality, a program places the dots according to mathematical calculations. Different dot sizes are available for different types of paper. Smaller dot sizes are used for paper with a smoother surface, which requires a higher output resolution. Larger-sized dots are more appropriate for low-quality paper and low-resolution printing. The sizes available depend on the supplier. For example, Agfa has dot sizes of 14, 21 and 36 micrometers.

FM screening generally allows for better reproduction of details than traditional halftone screening. This is particularly evident when using FM screens on low-quality paper where you would otherwise have relatively low screen frequency. On the other hand, tinted areas and soft tonal transitions can appear blotchy with stochastic screening. With this type of screening, there are no screen angles, and therefore no problems with moiré or distracting rosettes. As with traditional halftone screening, different manufacturers have developed their own versions of this technology, including Cristalscreening from Agfa, Diamond Screening from Linotype Hell, and Full Tone Screening From Scitex.

In general, FM screening requires a more controlled process at all stages. A dust-free environment is very important when developing the plates based on films. The first time you do an FM screening you should preview the results with a proof run to secure the result. Dot gain curves and full-tone densities will look different from a production based on traditional halftone screening. It is important to have a good dialogue between prepress staff and the printer both before and during production.

There are few analog proof systems that can produce proofs based on FM screening techniques. An alternative is to use digital proofs and check the films very carefully.

OTHER SCREENING TECHNIQUES 9.1.10

In addition to the above-mentioned techniques, there are other specialized screening techniques, like line screening and divided halftone dots. The latter technique divides each normal-sized dot into four smaller dots, giving the impression of double the screen frequency with the same tonal range in the large halftone cell.

PAGE DESCRIPTION LANGUAGE 9.2

A page description language (PDL) is a graphic programming language that describes the layout and appearance of a page. When printing a document, the file format used to create it (i.e., QuarkXPress, Adobe InDesign, Microsoft Word) has to be translated to a file format that the Raster Image Processor (RIP) or imagesetter can understand. A PDL is used to describe the elements a page contains (text, images, illustrations, etc.) and the location of these elements on the page to the processor or printer. It also enables the RIP to translate the page description into halftone screens.

A number of different page description languages have been developed by different manufacturers. Today's graphic production industry uses software and hardware from many different manufacturers, so the ideal page description language is one that works with all machines, regardless of the brand, and allows them to communicate freely with each other. Some examples of such page description languages are AFP from IBM, PCL from HP or CT/LV from Scitex. However, PostScript from Adobe currently dominates the market, and has therefore become known as the de facto industry standard. PostScript is an open standard, which means that other companies besides Adobe can use PostScript.

POSTSCRIPT 9.3

PostScript started out as a programming language, but for our purposes it's easier to think of it as a system consisting of several different parts. The system has three main components: translation of files into PostScript code, transfer of PostScript code, and processing (rasterizing) of the PostScript code. PostScript code used to be based on 7-bit text files (ASCII) but can now be saved as 8-bit binary code [see The Computer 2.4].

When you print a document, the file is first translated into a PostScript code. This means that a PostScript file is created, which is then sent to a PostScript-compatible output device with the help of a PostScript printer driver, which processes the file with a RIP [see 9.1 and 9.3.4]. All three steps are equally important in achieving a good final result. Adobe created a book called "The PostScript Language Reference Manual", which contains complete PostScript specifications for those who want to make PostScript-based machines or programs. Unfortunately, problems with so-called PostScript "clones" often occur with both RIPs and printer drivers. The problem usually shows up as changes to the original line arrangement when a file is saved and rasterized. Therefore it is recommended to use vendors that sell the original Adobe systems.

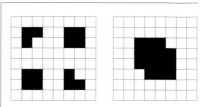

▶ DIVIDED HALFTONE DOTS
If you have a screen with divided halftone dots, the screen derives from four separate units within the halftone cell (left). The cell maintains its number of grey tones but the resolution appears to have doubled. Compare it to the traditional screen with one single unit (right). Both examples shows a 20% grey tone.

▶ LINE SCREEN
Often used for effect, the line screen method generally provides low image quality. The screen consists of lines rather than dots.

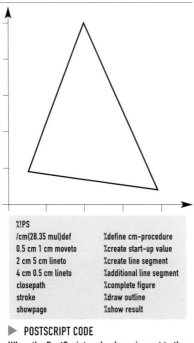

```
%!PS
/cm{28.35 mul}def      %define cm-procedure
0.5 cm 1 cm moveto     %create start-up value
2 cm 5 cm lineto       %create line segment
4 cm 0.5 cm lineto     %additional line segment
closepath              %complete figure
stroke                 %draw outline
showpage               %show result
```

▶ POSTSCRIPT CODE
When the PostScript code above is sent to the printer, it will create a triangle (see illustration above). The text after "%" is a comment and doesn't print.

▶ ASCII TAKES UP MEMORY

A file in ASCII format takes up more memory than a binary file but can be read as a regular text file.

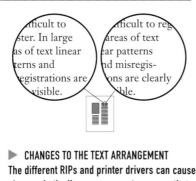

▶ CHANGES TO THE TEXT ARRANGEMENT
The different RIPs and printer drivers can cause changes in the line arrangement, an error that is rarely noticed until it's too late.

You can also save a document in PostScript format. Doing this "locks" the appearance of your document. You cannot open the document from the PostScript file, nor can you edit the PostScript file. If you want to make changes, you have to make them to the original file and save it as a completely new PostScript file [see How to Create a PostScript file on page 148]. Some programs, like imposition and trapping programs, are based on the PostScript format. A document must first be saved as a PostScript file before it can be edited with these types of programs. It should be noted that these programs only allow you to add or remove information from a document, not change the actual content of the document.

PostScript is similar to a programming language. Because of this, there is no single way to describe layout with PostScript. In some PostScript files, a large amount of information is located in the beginning of the file, or "file head". This information often serves the purpose of making the code that follows it more efficient; it allows long commands to be shortened in the subsequent code. Adobe Illustrator uses this technique, and you can see the difference it makes when you compare files saved in the Adobe Illustrator format with those saved in an EPS format. The EPS file is then smaller than the Adobe Illustrator file.

POSTSCRIPT IS OBJECT-BASED 9.3.1

PostScript is an object-based page description language, which means a page is described based on the objects it contains. The objects in a particular PostScript file—be they typeface or graphic objects like lines, curves, shades, patterns, etc.—are all described with mathematical curves. An image that consists of pixels – a scanned photograph, for example – is stored in a PostScript file as a bitmap with a PostScript file header.

Because the objects in PostScript are based on bezier curves you might assume that you can shrink or enlarge the pages without losing image quality. This is partly true – if there are no pixel-based images in the file, you can enlarge or reduce without a problem. However, if a pixel-based image is included in the file, you cannot enlarge the page without reducing the quality, as enlarging a bit-mapped image lowers its resolution [see Images 5.5.9, 5.5.10 and 5.5.11].

POSTSCRIPT AND TYPEFACE MANAGEMENT 9.3.2

When creating a PostScript file for output or to be saved for further editing, you can include the fonts with the file or choose to use fonts that are already stored in the output device. In PostScript 2 output devices, there are 35 standard fonts, while PostScript 3 output devices have 136. If it is a recurring print using the same fonts, it might be easier to have the fonts downloaded in the output device. This allows the PostScript file to be smaller and therefore faster to create, move and output.

CREATING POSTSCRIPT FILES 9.3.3

Every time you output a document from the computer to a PostScript-compatible printer, a PostScript file is created. It contains all the information of what the page will look like when it is printed. Instead of outputting a file to an output device, you could choose to save it as a PostScript file on the hard disk using a similar procedure.

There are essentially two ways to convert a file to PostScript, depending on the type of program you are translating it from. The most common way is to create the original files in PostScript-based programs like Adobe InDesign, Adobe PageMaker, Adobe Framemaker, QuarkXPress, Adobe Illustrator, and Macromedia Freehand, among others. These programs translate the actual file to PostScript when you output it. Before outputting, however, you must select a printer driver and a PostScript Printer Description, or PPD. This gives the program access to information about the specific output device you are using, including its resolution, page setup, etc., and the PostScript file is adjusted accordingly (this applies to for example LaserWriter printer driver 8 or higher and PC printer driver 4x or higher). The program gets help from a printer driver to send the file to the output device you have selected. Printer drivers are selected using the Chooser function on a Mac.

QuarkXPress uses a Printer Description File instead of a PPD. It works the same way as a PPD but you select this option from within QuarkXPress. In order to avoid confusing it with Adobe's PDF file format, we will refer to this option only as Printer Description File.

Programs that are non-PostScript based, like MS Word, WordPerfect, MS PowerPoint, etc., use printer drivers to create PostScript files. Printer drivers are assisted by a PPD, which adds information about the printer, just like the examples above. When using non-PostScript based programs, there can be unexpected changes in the appearance of a document when the PostScript file is created. These are often the result of differences between various PPDs and printer drivers or because the printer driver is a poor translator of the PostScript language.

Generally, you should use Adobe's own printer drivers (LaserWriter 8X for Mac or Adobe's printer driver for PC) or ask your graphic service provider what they recommend as a printer driver. You might also find that it's best to work with the same printer driver and PPD during the creation of the document and the PostScript file. You can usually see any errors in the page arrangement directly on the screen when changing printer drivers.

Because of the previously mentioned problems when using non-PostScript-based programs, it might be better to deliver completed PostScript files to the RIP. The PostScript file locks in all the appropriate settings, which allows you to avoid potential changes in the appearance of your document. In contrast, when you use a PostScript-based program, the settings of the layout are saved directly in the file format of the program and are not reliant on a particular printer driver. Thus, the layout is not affected by the printer driver, and transfers between different computers and printer drivers are not a problem. Files created in a PostScript-based program can also be handed off for rasterizing without affecting the layout.

POSTSCRIPT RIPS 9.3.4

RIP stands for Raster Image Processor. A RIP consists of two main parts, a PostScript interpreter and a processor translating the pages into raster images (bitmaps). The interpreter receives and translates the PostScript information, whereupon the processor creates a bitmap of every color separation of the page. There are two kinds of RIPs: hardware and software RIPs. Hardware RIPs are actually computers specially designed for rasterizing. Software RIPs consist of a special rasterizing program that can be installed

▷ **CHANGE THE SIZE OF A PAGE**
If a page only consists of object-oriented graphics its size can be changed without considerable loss in quality when it's converted to PostScript. In QuarkXPress and Adobe InDesign it's done under File –> Page Setup.

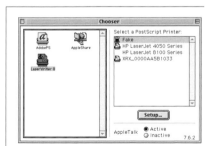

▷ **SELECT PRINTER DRIVER**
Under the "Chooser" behind the Apple symbol you select the printer driver. LaserWriter 8.x is one of the most common.

on a standard computer. Hardware RIPs are usually faster because they are specifically designed for rasterizing, while software RIPs are more flexible because they can be used with any standard computer. A PostScript-compatible RIP can execute additional operations such as decompression and separation of images in conjunction with rasterizing.

Documents created in programs like QuarkXPress and Adobe InDesign are described using the format specific to that particular program. In order to look at a document on the screen, the program's code has to be translated into a language the screen can understand. When outputting your document, the program code is translated into PostScript code with the adherent settings. The RIP receives the PostScript information, interprets what needs to be done on the page and performs all the calculations. When an entire page has been calculated, including images, typeface, logotypes, etc., a bitmap for each print color (four for a CMYK print, for example) is created. The bitmaps (based on ones and zeros) then let the imagesetter know which exposure dots should be exposed. When printing separated films, each page is calculated four times, one for each color.

The more complex a page is, the longer the calculations and rasterizing takes. A complex page might contain numerous fonts, complicated illustrations with several layers of information, vector-based images with many anchor points, rotated or scaled images, or images that were not cropped in the image editing application but in the desktop publishing application. Such pages can take a long time to rasterize even if the file size is small. On the other hand, exposure in the imagesetter always takes the same amount of time, regardless of the file size or the complexity of the document.

POSTSCRIPT LEVEL 1 [9.3.5]

Level 1 is the basis for the three current versions of PostScript and was launched in the mid-eighties. The two latter levels are based on the same page description language as Level 1, but each subsequent version contains additions and improvements. The different levels are compatible with each other, a PostScript 3 RIP can convert a Level 1 file and vice versa. On the other hand information is lost when you go from a higher to a lower level. PostScript Level 1 is a relatively simple page description language, compared to the other two. For example, Level 1 does not support color management.

POSTSCRIPT LEVEL 2 9.3.6

Not until Level 2 could PostScript products support color management. Earlier, some specially designed products from different manufacturers supported color management, but with the advent of PostScript Level 2, all products were able to support CMYK color mode and images in RGB and CMYK. New functions were also added, including support by device-independent color models (CIE), improved screening techniques, compression and decompression filters, and increased support for the unique functions of specific printers.

POSTSCRIPT 3 9.3.7

With PostScript 3, the most recent version of PostScript, Adobe removed the word "Level" from the name. Improvements to PostScript 3 focused on optimizing the rasterizing of PostScript files, and on making adjustments for the Internet. The number of fonts that can be installed in output devices was increased from 35 to 136, which allows for faster processing, since it is now unnecessary to attach fonts to the file.

When rasterizing in Postscript 3, each object in the PostScript file is treated separately in order to increase processing speed. PDF is also used during rasterizing. When the RIP begins processing a file, the file is converted to a list on which each page is a separate item (organized page by page). This list is a PDF file. The difference this makes is that pages can be processed one by one – you are page independent, compared to earlier versions, where the entire file had to be processed at once.

At the same time, the transition to PDF removes unnecessary information, like parts of images that have been cropped, for example. This also helps to shorten processing time. PostScript 3 RIPs can also process PDF files directly, without using PostScript.

Adobe has developed a new rasterizing technique, PostScript Extreme, which takes advantage of files being page independent. You can divide the rasterizing of the different pages among different processors. Then the less complex pages don't need to wait to be finished because of a page that takes a long time to convert.

Among the additions made to PostScript 3 for the Internet is the capability to provide PostScript output devices with Internet addresses. This means that you can output to an output device via the Internet, regardless of where you are. PostScript 3 also supports an improved way of outputting straight from HTML files.

PDF 9.4

In 1993, Adobe launched the file format PDF, or Portable Document Format. The idea was to create a file format that was platform- and program-independent. This means that documents look the same on the monitor and in a printout no matter what platform – MacOS, Windows, Linux or Unix, etc. – is used to create or read them. PDF files are used for anything from images and proof management to digital publishing, e-publications, digital forms, etc.

A PDF file is essentially "locked", which means you cannot edit the file. We say "essentially" because you can actually make some changes in Adobe Acrobat, using the Touch-Up Tool. There are also utility programs that facilitate editing PDF files.

▶ POSTSCRIPT AND ERROR MESSAGES

If something is wrong with the PostScript file you will usually get an error message when you're trying to output.

These messages can be difficult to interpret. Here are some helpful suggestions for finding the most common errors:

- Check that you have used the correct PPD or Printer Description Files.

- Check that you have used the correct printer driver, generally Laserwriter 8.x.

- Try to print on another PostScript output device. That way you can check if something is wrong with the actual output device.

- Remove the images from the document and print. That way you'll know if any of the images are causing the problem.

- Make sure the fonts are activated when outputting the PostScript file.

- Translate the PostScript file into PDF by using Acrobat Distiller. If it's a PostScript error, the translation into PDF will fail and you can check the log file to see what caused the problem.

▶ HOW TO CREATE A POSTSCRIPT FILE

When creating a PostScript file you start with the same procedure as when you output your document on a printer. Below are instructions for creating a PostScript file in Quark-XPress. The screen shots may differ depending on the program version and printer driver you're working with but the settings are the same. You use a similar procedure when creating a PostScript file in PageMaker or InDesign.

1. Select LaserWriter 8.x under the Chooser. Select a PostScript printer and click on Setup.

2. Set PPD (Postscript Printer Description) by clicking on Select PPD.

The selected PPD will be tied to the selected printer until you change the PPD.

In PageMaker, InDesign and QuarkXpress you can also change PPD under Print. This selection will be tied to the document and not to the printer.

3. Now you will see a window with all PPD files installed in the system folder on your computer. Select the file you want to use and click OK. Select Acrobat Distiller PPD if you are going to use the PostScript file to create a PDF file.

4. Go to File –> Print Setup in QuarkXPress. Fill out the window according to above. Separations and registration should be off if you are using the PostScript file to create a PDF file.

5. If you click on Setup in the preceding window this view will pop up. Nothing should be checked. Printer description should be Acrobat Distiller if you are using the Post-Script file to create a PDF file.

6. Click on Page Setup and choose PostScript Options under Page Attributes. Fill out the window according to above, nothing should be checked.

Click OK.

7. Click on Printer and choose File as Destination and Save as File under General. Fill out the window according to above. Make sure that all the typefaces are included.

8. In the next window displayed, you decide where to save the PostScript file.

When clicking on Save the computer will start creating the PostScript file. The file will have the suffix .ps.

The corresponding file in a Windows environment has the suffix .prn.

► HOW TO OUTPUT A COLOR-SEPARATED PRINTOUT

Sometimes it makes sense to check multi-colored documents by printing a color-separated output on a black and white printer. The basis is the same as for a regular output or for creating a PostScript file.

Below are instructions for creating a color-separated file in QuarkXPress. The screen shots may differ depending on the program version and printer driver you're working with but the settings are the same. You use a similar procedure when creating a Color-separated printout file in PageMaker or InDesign.

1. Select LaserWriter 8.x under the Chooser. Select your usual black and white printer and click on Setup.

2. Set PPD (Postscript Printer Description) by clicking on Select PPD.

The selected PPD will be tied to the selected printer until you change the PPD.

In PageMaker, InDesign and QuarkXpress you can also change PPD under Print. This selection will be tied to the document and not to the printer.

3. Now you will see a window with all PPD files installed in the system folder on your computer. Select a PPD file that fits your printer and click OK.

4. Go to File -> Print. Fill out the window according to above. When you check "Separations" each component color in the document will be printed on a separate sheet. If you haven't emptied your color box of non-separated colors in four-color documents or of colors you're not using in a spot color document, these colors will be printed as well [see Document 6.3.3].

If you don't select Separations the document will print composite; all the colors are printed on the same output. If you print composite on a black and white printer, all the colors will be printed as grayscale on the same sheet. If you print composite on a four-color printer, the four-color printer will automatically separate the colors and print all colors on one sheet. When selecting to output with registration marks each page contains information about which component color has been printed. That could make the proofing easier.

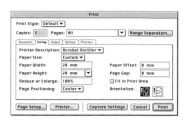

5. If you click on Setup in the preceding window this window view will pop up. Select a printer description and make sure to select a paper size that your printer can manage.

6. Click on Page Setup and choose PostScript Options under Page Attributes. Fill out the window according to above, nothing should be checked.

Click OK.

7. Click on Print and your color separated printout will start.

► WHAT CAN BE PROOFED?

- That colors in the document are separated.
- If there are colors in the color box that are not used.
- Overprint and knockouts.
- That images are separated, RGB images will only come out in the black printout.
- Bleeds.

The PDF format is closely related to PostScript but differs from it in a number of ways. The PDF format is better standardized than PostScript. As a result, a page in PostScript that might be described in many different ways will only be described one way in PDF. This makes it easier for the RIP to interpret the appearance of the page, greatly reducing the risk of errors when printing. Another important difference between PDF and PostScript is that with PostScript, all the pages of a given document are dependent on each other; you can't just print one page in a PostScript file, all pages have to be output each time. In PDF files the pages are separated, enabling you to output each page of a document individually.

To create a PDF file, you first create a PostScript file, which is then converted into PDF. When converting, the code and superfluous PostScript information are removed. Both images and text can be compressed, and, as a result, the PDF file takes up less memory than the original PostScript file. Compressibility and platform-independence make the PDF file format suitable for digital distribution and publishing. PDF is on its way to taking over PostScript's role within graphic production and is today one of the most common formats for digital delivery of advertisements and other products for printing.

THE ADOBE ACROBAT FAMILY 9.4.1

Adobe has developed an entire program family around the PDF file format. The most common programs are Acrobat Reader, for reading PDF files; Adobe Acrobat, for editing and proofing PDF files; Acrobat Distiller, for creating PDF files; Acrobat InProduction, used in graphic production; Acrobat Catalog, for archiving and searching PDF files; and Acrobat Capture, for converting scanned paper documents into PDF files. Adobe also has a printer driver, PDF Writer, with which you can create PDF files directly from a page layout application. In addition to the above-mentioned programs, there are utilities based on the PDF format available from program developers other than Adobe.

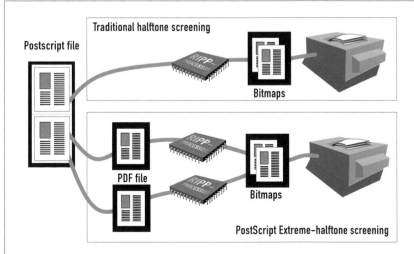

▶ POSTSCRIPT EXTREME
When the file is rasterized, it is first translated to a PDF file. With PostScript Extreme, each page of the document is processed separately (lower image). The file is "page-independent." If you're using traditional PostScript technique however, the entire file is processed sequentially (upper image).

Acrobat Reader

Acrobat Reader is the most frequently used of these programs and is a requirement for reading PDF files. The program is free and can also be used to output PDF files on paper (available for downloading at http://www.adobe.com). When outputting, Acrobat Reader translates the PDF file into PostScript and sends it to the output device. Post-Script 3 RIPs can rasterize PDF files directly – you don't even need to open the file, you simply send it directly to the printer.

Adobe Acrobat

Adobe Acrobat enables the user to add to or edit a PDF file. It's essentially an Acrobat Reader with a number of additional functions. For example, Acrobat allows you to create links between different pages, different documents, and even links to pages on the Internet. In this way you can create interactive documents based on a file initially intended for printed matter. You can also create forms and fields for digital forms.

In the graphics industry, PDF is also used for proofing. Adobe Acrobat has a number of useful support functions for working with digital proof management. One of these functions enables you to add yellow "post-its" to a document with comments regarding the content or composition of a page. Other useful functions include the ability to high-light or underline selected parts of a document, as well as a function that compares selected documents to ensure that changes have been made. In addition, you can sign and approve PDF files. Adobe Acrobat also allows you to make certain types of changes to existing text and images [also see 9.4.4].

Acrobat Distiller

Acrobat Distiller is the program necessary for creating PDF files. The program is essentially a software-based RIP, which translates PostScript files into PDF files. It also allows you to select, among other things, the level of compression, the typeface management and the resolution of illustrations and images for all your PDF files [also see 9.4.2].

Acrobat InProduction

Acrobat InProduction is a program designed specifically for working with PDF files in a graphic production environment. It allows you to proof, create four-color separations, and color-convert PDF files, as well as define crop marks, bleeds and trapping factors. Several similar software programs are available from leading graphic software manufac-turers such as Agfa, Heidelberg, etc.

Acrobat Catalog

Acrobat Catalog enables you to create index files with which to organize a large number of PDF documents. If you have indexed your documents in Acrobat Catalog you can conduct keyword searches among thousands of documents in Adobe Acrobat. Acrobat Catalog is a very useful program for archiving.

ACROBAT CAPTURE

Acrobat Capture is a program that can interpret scanned text. Using a technique called

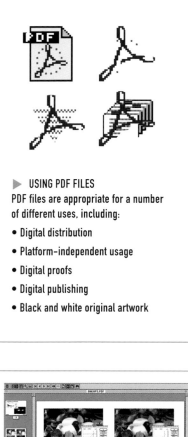

▶ **USING PDF FILES**
PDF files are appropriate for a number of different uses, including:

- Digital distribution
- Platform-independent usage
- Digital proofs
- Digital publishing
- Black and white original artwork

▶ **TO LOOK IS FREE!**
Adobe Acrobat Reader is a free program for viewing PDF files. You can navigate the file by clicking on the thumbnail images to the left.

Optical Character Recognition, or OCR, the program identifies text and converts it into actual typography, which results in compact, well-designed and searchable PDF files.

UTILITIES

There are a number of utility programs for Adobe Acrobat developed by independent software manufacturers, known generally as "plug-ins." Plug-ins can expand the functions of the programs in the Acrobat family. Examples of plug-ins used in graphic production are Crackerjack and PitStop from Enfocus. Crackerjack enables you to conduct four-color separations directly from Adobe Acrobat. PitStop enables you to edit PDF files. PitStop allows you to change most things, including text, colors, the placement of objects and images, and object shapes. There is also a preflight function, which creates printable error reports. PitStop is also available as an independent program in a server version.

ADOBE PHOTOSHOP AND ADOBE ILLUSTRATOR

Both Adobe Photoshop and Adobe Illustrator have increasingly been upgraded in terms of creating and editing PDF files. As a result, many of the aforementioned utility programs will probably be replaced by functions in Adobe Photoshop and Adobe Illustrator.

CREATING PDF FILES 9.4.2

The work of creating a PDF file starts with creating pages in a page layout, illustration, word processing or presentation application. Once you have these pages, you create a PostScript file using the appropriate program [see page 154]. Note that a special PPD file, Acrobat Distiller PPD, is necessary to interpret the PostScript file with Acrobat Distiller. The complete PostScript file is then opened in Acrobat Distiller, which converts the file into PDF. It is important to determine the correct settings in Acrobat Distiller in order to optimize the PDF file with regard to its intended use. For example, if the PDF file is only intended for screen display, you can leave out typeface, lower the resolution and compress images to keep the file size down. If, on the other hand, the content of the file is intended for printing, you should only compress images a little bit (if at all) in order to maintain optimal image quality. The most important settings for creating a PDF file are located under Settings –> Job Options. Here you can select general and advanced settings as well as settings for typeface, compression and color management [see " How to create a PDF file" on page 159].

Using Acrobat Distiller is absolutely the best way to create PDF files but you can also use a special printer driver, called PDF Writer, to create PDF files. Just as you would select a printer from the "Chooser" in the Apple menu, you select "PDF Writer" from among the printer drivers. Now, if you choose to output, the document will be saved as a PDF file. PDF Writer is recommended for simpler text documents. As soon as you have pages with a more complex content, like images, illustrations or typographic text, you should create a PostScript file instead and use Adobe Acrobat Distiller to create the PDF file. PDF Writer does not use PostScript and sometimes has difficulty interpreting complex pages. Adobe InDesign, Adobe Photoshop and Adobe Illustrator can also save documents and images directly as PDF files.

▶ HOW TO CREATE A PDF FILE

When creating a PDF file you should always start by making a PostScript file of the original document.

Below are instructions for creating PDF files in Acrobat Distiller. When making a PDF file you should take into consideration whether the file should be used for printing or screen display. A PDF file for screen display is considerably smaller than a PDF file for printing.

You can also create a PDF file via PDF Writer available under the Chooser. It is not a good way of creating PDF files and is only appropriate for text documents.

1. Start Acrobat Distiller and make your settings for printing or screen display. Then select File -> Open and find the Post-Script file you will be using. Tell the program where it should be saved. When you click on Save, the Distiller starts working and the PDF file is created. The file will get the suffix .pdf.

▶ DISTILLER SETTINGS FOR SCREEN DISPLAY

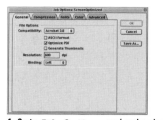

1. Go to Job Options and make above adjustments under General.

2. Click on the tab Compression and make the following adjustments. The images are sampled down to 72 ppi (dpi) (screen resolution) and will be compressed medium-high.

3. Under the tab Fonts you select above settings.

4. Under the tab Color you select to convert images. It involves removing print-specific information from the images.

5. Under the tab Advanced you select above settings.

▶ DISTILLER SETTINGS FOR PRINTING

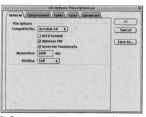

1. Go to Job Options and make above adjustments under General.

2. Click on the tab Compression and make the following adjustments. The images are down-sampled to 300 ppi (dpi) and will be slightly compressed.

3. Under the tab Fonts you select above settings. Note that Embed All Fonts should not be crossed off.

4. Under the tab Color you select above settings. That way print-specific information will remain in the document.

5. Under the tab Advanced you select above settings.

PROOFING PDF FILES 9.4.3

When you receive a PDF file intended for graphic production, you should start by proofing it. The first step is to open the PDF file and proof it on the screen. However, PDF files may look correct on the screen and still contain hidden errors. Because of this, you also need to conduct some general technical tests, tests concerning the typeface in the PDF file, and print technical tests.

General Information

You can check general information about the PDF file by opening it in Acrobat and then selecting File –> Documents Info –> General.... This allows you to see the filename, as well as other information added to the file, like title, subject, keywords, etc. The most important information is contained under the headings "Creator," "Producer" and "PDF version." These items tell you what program was used to create the original PostScript file (for example, QuarkXPress 4.0), what program created the PDF file (for example, Acrobat Distiller 4.0) and which version of the PDF format your file is in (for example, 1.3, 1.2 or 1.1).

The PDF version of the file is particularly important because PDF version 1.2 and 1.1 lack pertinent information for use in graphic print production. PDF version 1.3 is the only one of the PDF formats that can be used for professional graphic production (NOTE! To create a correct and smoothly operational PDF file version 1.3, it has to be written with Adobe Acrobat Distiller 4.05 or a more recent version).

The information about what program created the original PostScript file is interesting because it allows you to see if certain information from the PostScript original was excluded from the PDF file. A PDF file created from Microsoft Word, for example, will not contain CMYK color information because Word does not manage that. As a result, the resulting PDF file has to be four-color separated before it can be output.

Typeface

Typeface is always a central topic in graphic print production. Acrobat Distiller allows you to choose if you want to include typefaces in the PDF file or not. If you choose to do so, you can do it fully or partially – i.e. only include the characters used in the document. When you create PDF files intended for printing, you should choose to include all typefaces in the PDF file. If you don't include all the typefaces, Acrobat's typeface replacement system, based on the Multiple Master technique, kicks in [see Typeface 3.4.3].

Adobe Acrobat Distiller 4.0 allows typeface creators to block their typefaces from being included in PDF files. Many typeface manufactures use this function because of the copyright uncertainties surrounding typefaces, and, as a result, you cannot include their typefaces when creating a PDF file. All of Adobe's typefaces can be included, however. Acrobat allows you to easily check how the typefaces are being handled in a particular PDF file. File –> Documents Info –> Fonts... will give you a list of the typefaces used and to what extent they are partially, fully or not at all included in the PDF file.

When checking typeface in a PDF file, it is important to have all other typefaces on your computer turned off. A PDF file contains information about which typefaces are used in that particular file. If they are opened on the computer's system as well, they will also be activated in the PDF file. As a result, the file will look correct even though typefaces are missing. InProduction and PitStop enable you to view the typeface information included in a file independent of the rest of your computer.

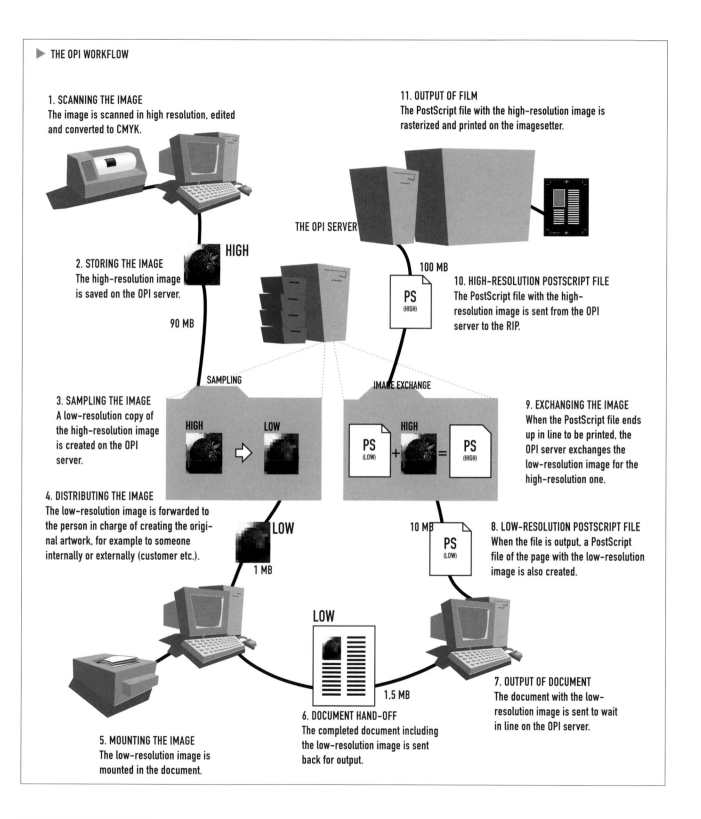

▶ THE OPI WORKFLOW

1. SCANNING THE IMAGE
The image is scanned in high resolution, edited and converted to CMYK.

11. OUTPUT OF FILM
The PostScript file with the high-resolution image is rasterized and printed on the imagesetter.

HIGH

2. STORING THE IMAGE
The high-resolution image is saved on the OPI server.

THE OPI SERVER

100 MB

10. HIGH-RESOLUTION POSTSCRIPT FILE
The PostScript file with the high-resolution image is sent from the OPI server to the RIP.

PS (HIGH)

90 MB

SAMPLING

IMAGE EXCHANGE

3. SAMPLING THE IMAGE
A low-resolution copy of the high-resolution image is created on the OPI server.

HIGH → LOW

PS (LOW) + HIGH = PS (HIGH)

9. EXCHANGING THE IMAGE
When the PostScript file ends up in line to be printed, the OPI server exchanges the low-resolution image for the high-resolution one.

4. DISTRIBUTING THE IMAGE
The low-resolution image is forwarded to the person in charge of creating the original artwork, for example to someone internally or externally (customer etc.).

LOW

1 MB

10 MB

PS (LOW)

8. LOW-RESOLUTION POSTSCRIPT FILE
When the file is output, a PostScript file of the page with the low-resolution image is also created.

LOW

7. OUTPUT OF DOCUMENT
The document with the low-resolution image is sent to wait in line on the OPI server.

1,5 MB

6. DOCUMENT HAND-OFF
The completed document including the low-resolution image is sent back for output.

5. MOUNTING THE IMAGE
The low-resolution image is mounted in the document.

Preflight Check

Preflight refers to a review of different technical factors affecting the printing process, including format, color positions, separations, crop marks, bleeds and trapping [see preflight]. There are a number of different programs available for preflight checking PDF files. Some programs are specialized for checking PDF files but there are also general preflight programs, for example from Adobe InDesign, QuarkXPress and Adobe PageMaker. The most common program is probably Adobe's Acrobat InProduction which helps you proof, four-color separate and color-convert PDF files as well as define crop marks, bleeds and trapping. Keep in mind that most preflight programs can only discover errors in the document, not correct them. For example, a PDF file that is not correctly created for printing essentially has to be recreated. Errors in the file have to be corrected in the program that the original pages were created in, for example QuarkXPress or Adobe PageMaker. You can make some simple corrections directly in the PDF file; in principle you have the same possibilities correcting directly in the PDF file as when manually correcting print-ready original films. Enfocus PitStop and Adobe InProduction are two examples of preflight programs for PDF files.

EDITING PDF FILES 9.4.4

Although PDF files are essentially locked in terms of editing, you can make certain small revisions. The degree to which you are able to edit a document is determined in part by the security settings assigned to the PDF file when it was created.

Security Settings

When saving a PDF file you can designate a security setting, which protects the file in various ways. The security settings for a particular PDF file can be set under File –> Documents Info –> Security…. PDF files can also be password-protected in order to control the type of access different users have to the document. You can control output, document changes, the copying of text and images, as well as the ability to add or change notes or fields of entry. You should keep in mind that if you allow for output a user can

---

▶ DIGITAL IMPOSITION +/–

+ Less labor intensive

+ Faster workflow

+ Precise registration

+ You can save imposition templates that can be reused.

– If you want to do a completely digital imposition, all material that is the basis for the printed product has to be digital. For example, print advertisements (usually delivered on film) have to be delivered digitally. If not, you have to leave empty pages in the digital imposition and mount the advertisement manually.

– If an error occurs on the film or plate, the entire imposition has to be output again, a time-consuming process. You can also output a new film for the page with the error, cut the old one out and manually mount the new one.

DIFFERENT TYPES OF IMPOSITIONS

The printing press is the costliest unit per hour in the graphic production process. You should try to minimize the time spent in the printing press by utilizing large paper sheets and as much space of the paper sheet as possible. Most printing presses have a maximum paper format of 4, 8, 16 or 32 pages depending on the sheet size used [see Paper 12.1.1].

When printing a book or a booklet, for example, several pages are arranged next to each other on the same printer's sheet. The arrangement of the pages on the sheet is called imposition and varies according to the paper formats the printing press can accommodate.

As an example to illustrate the different imposition variations, we are using an 8-page 8 1/2" x 11" booklet, which consists of two 11" x 17"-sheets, folded in the middle and stapled together with two staples in the fold.

Each 11" x 17"-sheet accommodates four 8 1/2" x 11"-pages, two on each side. After taking the off press processing into consideration, an 8-page booklet can be imposed in two different ways: by folding and stapling two separate 11" x 17"-sheets or by cross folding, stapling and cutting clean one 19" x 25"-sheet.

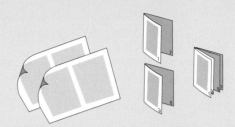

8-page booklet made from two 11" x 17"-sheets.

8-page booklet made from one 19" x 25"-sheet

IMPOSITION FOR AN 8-PAGE, 8 1/2" x 11"-BOOKLET FOR A 11" x 17" PRINTING PRESS

If a printing press' largest format is 11" x 17" you need to impose for four 11" x 17"-pages. You will have to execute four makereadies in the printing press because each 11" x 17"-sheet runs through the printing press twice, one for each side of the sheet. When the print run is completed, you will end up with two 4-page 11" x 17"-sheets with two 8 1/2" x 11"-sheets on each side of the sheet. The sheets are then folded, one by one, and stapled into an 8-page 8 1/2" x 11"-booklet [see illustration to the right].

Four film assemblies   **Two printed sheets**

IMPOSITION FOR AN 8-PAGE, 8 1/2" x 11"-BOOKLET FOR AN 19" x 25" PRINTING PRESS

If a printing press' largest format is 19" x 25", you need to impose for two 19" x 25"-pages. You will have to execute two makereadies in the printing press because each 19" x 25"-sheet runs through the printing press twice, one for each side of the sheet. When the print run is completed, you will end up with an 8-page 19" x 25"-sheet with four pages on each side of the sheet. The sheet is then right-angle folded and stapled into an 8-page 8 1/2" x 11"-booklet [see illustration to the right].

Two film assemblies   **One printed sheet**

IMPOSITION FOR AN 8-PAGE, 8 1/2 x 11"-BOOKLET FOR A 23" x 35" PRINTING PRESS

If a printing press' largest format is 23" x 35", you need to impose for one 23" x 35"-page. You will only have to execute one makeready in the printing press because each 23" x 35"-sheet runs through the printing press twice, one for each side of the sheet, but without changing the printing plate. All eight pages fit on a single printing plate. Pages 1, 8, 4, and 5 are imposed on one half of the 23" x 35"-sheet and 2,7,3 and 6 on the other. After the 23" x 35"-sheet has been printed on one side, it turns and the other side is printed with the same plate, a procedure called halfsheet work or work and turn. When the print run is completed, you will end up with a 16-page 23" x 35"-sheet with eight pages on each side of the sheet. The sheet can then be divided into two identical 8-page sheets, right-angle folded and stapled into an 8-page 8 1/2" x 11"-booklet [see illustration to the right].

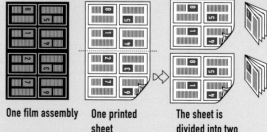

One film assembly   **One printed sheet**   **The sheet is divided into two parts**

The number of colors the product is printed with does not affect the procedures described above as long as the various printing presses have the same amount of printing units.

The entire work procedure takes for granted that you know where each page should be placed on the printer's sheet so the pages in the complete printed product end up in the correct order. In other words, you need to know how the printed product should be imposed.

THE INK SETTINGS AFFECT THE IMPOSITION

If all the pages in a printed product are not printed with the same amount of component colors, it is generally cheaper to print on different printing presses. For example, because a one-color printing press has a lower cost per hour than a four-color printing press you are better off printing one-colored pages in a one-color printing press, etc.

When you produce the originals you can, if you know in advance the format the product is printed with, study the imposition and take advantage of the ink settings. Let's use the example of the 8-page booklet. It should be printed with black ink except for page 3, which is in four colors. The side of the print sheet that contains page 3 has to be printed in a four-color printing press. In the examples below, you can use four-color on all pages placed on the same side of the sheet as page 3 without generating additional costs (we have not taken the costs for color separation into consideration).

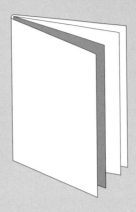

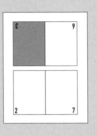

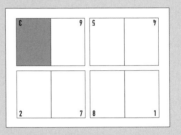

In an 11" x 17"-printing press, the entire page that contains page 3 has to be printed in a four-color printing press. Even if page 6 only contains one color, it will also be printed in the four-color printing press.

In a 19" x 25"-printing press, the entire page that contains page 3 has to be printed in a four-color printing press. Pages 2, 6 and 7 are thus also printed in the four-color printing press.

In a 23" x 35"-printing press, all the pages of the booklet are on both sides of the 23" x 35"-sheet. All the pages on the entire sheet has to be printed in a four-color printing press regardless if they contain color or not.

▶ THE MAKEREADY

A "makeready" involves all the activities performed until you get the first, approved printed sheet. Because the printing press has a high cost per hour, you should minimize the number of makereadies and execute them quickly. The following factors should be executed in the makeready [see Printing 13.3].

- Printing plate makeready
- Setting the feeder
- Registering the sheets
- Pre-setting the ink screws
- Ink-humidity balance
- Registration
- Ink coverage
- Correspondence to the proof

always create a new PS file in Adobe Acrobat and then use Acrobat Distiller to create a new PDF file. The resulting file will not contain any of the safety settings you designated and can therefore be fully controlled by the user.

When sending a PDF file to a graphic production company for production you should set the security specifications to allow for any and all changes because you might need them to make last-minute corrections. By contrast, when sending a PDF file for review and proofing it is often appropriate not to permit changes to the file. However, you should allow the user (the proofreader) to add notes and copy text (in order to paste it into a note, for example).

Text Editing

Text editing can be easily done in Adobe Acrobat. It is limited, however, in that you can only make changes to individual lines – i.e., you cannot change the line arrangement. You can add a new line within the text, but line breaks and hyphenation have to be done manually. To edit text in Acrobat, you have to have the correct typeface installed. If you don't, the typeface of the edited text will be replaced with another typeface from the computer you are using. Text editing in Acrobat is normally not recommended and should only be done minimally and when absolutely necessary. Any significant changes to the text should be done in the original file.

Editing Images and Object Graphics

Images and object-oriented graphics can be altered in Adobe Acrobat using the "Touch-Up" tool. The tool allows you to mark the images you wish to change. Images can then be moved, cropped, removed or copied and pasted into other parts of the document. You can also open individual images or illustrations in Adobe Photoshop or Adobe Illustrator, edit them, and save them directly into the PDF file, which will automatically update itself with the changes.

Mounting PDF Files

Most page layout applications in use today can mount PDF files as images. With older versions of these programs, you might mount a PDF file by exporting it as a PostScript or EPS file. When you export a PostScript file you should include all typefaces used in the document. You can choose to export in PostScript Level 1, PostScript Level 2 or PostScript 3 code. When you choose PostScript Level 1, the file will be decompressed (the PDF file contains compressed data) and the PostScript file will be considerably larger (with regard to data) than the PDF file. If you export in PostScript Level 2 or PostScript 3 code, the resulting file will only be slightly larger than the original PDF file because PostScript Level 2 and PostScript 3 code support compressed data. You can also export a page from a PDF file as an EPS file. This means that the page is exported as an image in EPS format. You will have one EPS file for each page you export. It is important to choose PostScript Level 1 when exporting EPS files because most programs cannot decompress an EPS file.

▶ SHEETS AND FIBER DIRECTION

Off press processing affects the format of the paper used and the necessary fiber direction in the paper.

You also need to take gripper edges and trim areas into consideration.

▶ TAKE THE PRINTED IMAGE INTO CON- SIDERATION!

If you have large, heavy tint areas in the print, you may want to try to avoid imposing too many pages on one sheet in order to prevent the print on the different pages from affecting each other negatively.

OUTPUTTING PDF FILES ^{9.4.5}

It is important to understand how Adobe Acrobat works when it comes to outputting PDF files, so we will review some of the most common issues below.

OPI

Adobe Acrobat has support for OPI comments, which means that you can work with PDF files in an OPI production flow [see 9.5]. In practice, you can create PDF files with low-resolution OPI images. When the low-resolution PDF file is output, the low-resolution image is replaced with the high-resolution image. Unfortunately, not all OPI programs follow the standard for OPI comments, which means you have to double check to see if this procedure works with your particular OPI program.

Color Separation

In order to output four-color separations directly from Adobe Acrobat you will need to use a plug-in like CrackerJack from Lantana, Adobe InProduction or PDF OutputPRO from Callas. These programs enable you to conduct color separations similar to those in QuarkXPress, InDesign and PageMaker. Another alternative is to color separate your PDF files in the rasterizing program, in correlation with the output (all PS3 RIPs support this "in-rip-separation"). There are also software applications designed solely to color separate PostScript and PDF files.

PDF files may contain elements defined in RGB or elements not yet color-separated into CMYK colors (images, text, graphics). If you want to execute a color-separated output, these elements have to be four-color separated first. This is a common occurrence with PDF files created in Microsoft Office programs because they do not support four-color separation. It can be difficult to visually check whether images in a PDF file are CMYK converted or not. Plug-ins, like "Quite a Box of Tricks" from Quite for Acrobat, allow you to check that images are separated, among other things.

Spot Colors

Starting with Acrobat 4.0 and PDF 1.3, spot colors are always included in the PDF file. In order to confirm that a PDF file contains spot colors, you need to run a preflight application such as Acrobat InProduction, Enfocus PitStop, "Quite A Box of Tricks," PDF OutputPRO from Callas or CrackerJack from Lantana.

Registration Marks

Adobe Acrobat cannot include registration or crop marks in the output. These marks need to be added with another program like Adobe's Acrobat InProduction.

BLEEDS

PDF 1.2 and previous versions did not allow you to define information about bleeds in the PDF file. To solve this problem, a larger page format was defined in order to "fool" Acrobat into including the bleed. Today this is no longer necessary. The bleed can be defined, as usual, when writing the PostScript file. This information is then included in the PDF file, which creates a page format identical to the PostScript document, including the specified bleeds. For example, a QuarkXPress page with a document format of 9 × 9" with 1/8" bleed will create a PDF file sized 9 1/4" × 9 1/4".

The PDF 1.3 specification contains a number of different page format definitions. These include output format, bleed format (the page including bleeds), final format and graphic format (freely selected surface on the page).

In order to access this information in the PDF file, the program that creates the Post-Script file must support these surface-definitions – something many programs don't do yet. This doesn't mean that you can't include bleeds in a PDF file, but other programs working with the PDF file may not be able to interpret how much bleed a PDF file contains.

TRAPPING

If you create PostScript files that are not color seperated in QuarkXPress, trapping values will not be included. This means that PDF files created from QuarkXPress documents won't contain any trapping information. However, there are separate programs that can provide trapping information for PDF files.

OPI ⁹·⁵

When several people are working on a graphic production project, it is common to store images and documents on a network server. When you move large, high-resolution image files from the server to your personal computer, the network is heavily taxed, and it takes a long time to place the image in your page layout. This heavy usage drastically reduces network performance and slows down everyone working on the network. When the document with the high-resolution images is output from the computer, the document and images are sent to the printer via the network and the network is once again heavily taxed. In addition, the computer from which the output is sent is "locked" during the output process. For extremely large documents with many images, this might be a matter of hours.

To reduce stress on the network and improve and speed up the output process, you can equip the server with an Open Prepress Interface program, or OPI. Most companies that handle large numbers of images use such programs. For each high-resolution image saved on the server, an OPI program will automatically create a small low-resolution copy with the same file name. These files generally have a resolution of 72ppi, the same as the monitor. When importing the image to your document, you use the low-resolution copy instead of the high-resolution image. Because of its low resolution, the image needs less memory and can be installed quickly. When the document is output, the output with the low-resolution images is sent to the server. These are exchanged for the corresponding high-resolution images and forwarded to the RIP.

In practice, this means that a network without an OPI system would take several hours to output a document, whereas with an OPI program, output from an individual computer to the network only takes a couple of minutes. The actual output to the printer is not faster, however. The OPI program is simply a way of letting the server, rather than the individual computers, handle the outputs. In addition, OPI reduces the stress on the network because it reduces the amount of information sent over the network.

The low-resolution images created by an OPI program are only intended for mounting in page layout applications. If you want to edit the images in any way, you have to open the high-resolution image in an image-editing program. OPI "comments" are saved in the document in which a low-resolution image is installed. These comments note the file name and where it is stored. If you move or change the names of these image files, the OPI server will not be able to find the corresponding high-resolution images at output.

The most commonly used OPI programs today are Color Central and Helios. Color Central is available for Mac and Windows, while Helios only exists for the Unix environment. Helios follows the OPI standard. PDF files also follow the OPI standard and you can use low-resolution OPI images in PDF files sent for rasterizing.

IMPOSITION 9.6

Printing on a printing press is the costliest procedure in the graphic production process. Therefore you should try to minimize the time your project spends in the printing press by using the largest sheets of paper you can. When printing documents with several pages, a number of pages are placed on a single sheet in order to make the most efficient use of the paper. After printing, the sheet is folded and cut down into several smaller pages. The pages must be placed on the paper in a way that preserves their correct relationship to one another when they are folded and cut. The process of placing pages correctly and adjusting them for off print processing is called imposition.

You can do manual or digital impositions. With a manual imposition, you use individual films for each page – every page of the printed product has been output onto a separate film. The pages are placed according to an imposition scheme and mounted with tape on a larger transparent film. The completed film assembly is then used to expose the printing plate. Digital imposition means that you impose and arrange the pages in an imposition program, such as Imation Presswise or Preps from Scenicsoft. The digital assembly is output to an imagesetter that can print large formats. The imagesetter will then print out an "imposed film." There are many advantages to digital imposition. The most important one is that you save time and manpower because the pages don't have to be mounted manually. If your printed product has many pages, the cost of manually arranging them can make up a considerable part of the total printing cost.

WHAT AFFECTS IMPOSITION? 9.6.1

There are many factors that affect how an imposition is done. The most important is the layout, which, among other things, dictates the format of the printed product and the placement of color images. This, in turn, determines the number of plates needed and the makeready of the printing press. You will most likely want to minimize the number of makereadies because each one takes time and costs money. The post processing is another important factor in determining how an imposition is done, partly because you want to minimize the makereadies for this process, and partly because the machines used have limits on the sheet size they can handle and the number of folds they can make. Budget and printing technique are other factors that affect the imposition process.

During the imposition, different marks and color bars are usually added to make the printing and off press processes easier.

- Color bars: to check the correct ink coverage in the print.

- Registration marks: to check that the different component colors are registered (placed exactly on top of each other).

- Crop marks: to show how the sheet should be cut to the correct format.

- Fold marks: to show where and in what direction to fold.

- Collation marks: to show the order of the sheets [see Off Press Processing].

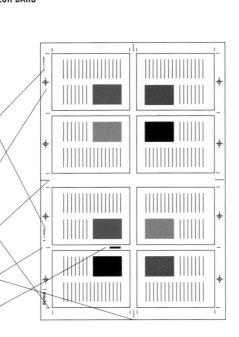

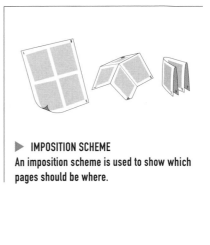

▶ IMPOSITION SCHEME
An imposition scheme is used to show which pages should be where.

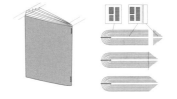

▶ CREEP
The pages of the folded product are pushed outwards causing the image area of the pages in the center to move further away from the gutter than those in the beginning and end [see illustration]. You have to compensate for this in the imposition process by adjusting the inner margin and then cropping the outer margin of the pages.

BUDGET AND IMPOSITION 9.6.2

You should always try to impose the pages as inexpensively as possible, which means minimizing the time spent on the printing press. If we use an eight-page folder as an example, a 23" × 35" press would probably be the least costly printing press format [see how the impositions of an eight-page folder for various printing press formats differ in number of makereadies, page 163]. The cost is dependent on the volume of the run and the hourly charge for the printing presses. A 23" × 35" press will be more cost effective than a 19" × 25" or 11" × 17" press for a larger run (one that takes longer). For a smaller project a 19" × 25" press might be better – it might take longer in a 19" × 25" press than an 23" × 35", but the hourly rate is much lower and the total cost will come out less. The makereadies don't really differ in the actual time needed, but the 19" × 25" press requires twice as many makereadies as the 23" × 35" press. The illustrations on page 170 show a comparison of the production times for the different printing presses.

OFF PRESS PROCESSING AND IMPOSITION 9.6.3

The imposition is directly affected by the format of the paper used, the machine direction of the paper and the kind of off press processing it will go through. The off press processing sometimes sets limits on the size of the paper that can be used. Again, you

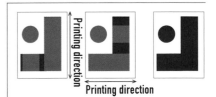

▶ GHOSTING
Tint areas are sensitive to other printed objects on the sheet. This phenomena is called ghosting and manifests as tracks of unwanted print in the tint areas. The right image shows the correct printed image and the two left images how ghosting manifests itself in the different printing directions.

▶ **MANUAL IMPOSITION**
When manually imposing the pages, the individual page films are taped to a large montage film. To make sure the pages are placed correctly, the mounting is done on a light table.

▶ **DIGITAL IMPOSITION**
When digitally imposing the pages, they are mounted on a digital printer's sheet. Above is an example of two such impositions.

want as few makereadies as possible during this process. For example, cross-folding a 16-page sheet takes the same amount of time as cross-folding an eight-page sheet, and you only have half the number of makereadies in the folding machine. This makes it possible to cut the folding cost in half. Gripper edges and trim areas for the off press processing also affect the imposition. The gripper edge is the extra space between the printed area and the edge of the paper that allows the printing press and the off press-processing machines to grip to move the sheet. The placement of the gripper edge is taken into consideration in the imposition and whoever is responsible for the off press processing usually delivers an imposition scheme in which the position and size of the gripper edges and trim areas are marked [see Off Press Processing 14.3.3.].

During folding, a phenomenon called creep (or shingling) may occur. This means the inner pages of the folded product are pushed outwards causing the image area of the pages in the center to move further away from the gutter than those in the beginning and end [see illustration]. You have to compensate for this in the imposition process by adjusting the pages [see Off Press Processing 14.3.3].

PRINTING TECHNIQUE AND IMPOSITION 9.6.4

If you have large, heavy tint areas in the print, you may want to try and avoid having too many pages on each side of a single sheet. Heavy tint areas require a lot of ink and can "steal" ink from other areas of the print. In addition, heavy tint areas are very sensitive to the effect of other printed areas on the same sheet. This phenomenon is called Ghosting and manifests as tracks of unwanted print in the heavy tint areas. Ghosting is most common in smaller printing press formats and can be avoided by rotating the imposition 90 degrees.

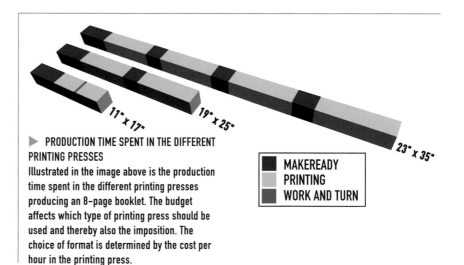

▶ **PRODUCTION TIME SPENT IN THE DIFFERENT PRINTING PRESSES**
Illustrated in the image above is the production time spent in the different printing presses producing an 8-page booklet. The budget affects which type of printing press should be used and thereby also the imposition. The choice of format is determined by the cost per hour in the printing press.

■	MAKEREADY
■	PRINTING
■	WORK AND TURN

COMMON IMPOSITION TECHNIQUES 9.7

You can impose a printed product in many different ways, and following is an overview of the most common imposition techniques.

GANG-UP 9.7.1

Depending on how many copies of the product you place on a sheet, this imposition is referred to as a 2-up, 3-up, etc. These impositions are usually used if the product only has one or two printed pages. You want to impose as many copies of the pages as possible on a single sheet of paper, in order to minimize the time your project spends on the printing press. For example, if your printed product consists of an 8 1/2" × 11" sheet and is to be printed in a 19" × 25"-press, you can impose the print 4-up. Printing a product gang-up can be done in combination with some of the imposition methods mentioned below.

SHEET WISE (WORK AND BACK) 9.7.2

The most common method of imposition is called sheet wise, or work and back. With this type of imposition, each side of the sheet gets its own makeready, i.e., two makereadies per sheet. The side of the sheet containing the first and last page on the sheet (if the printed product contains four pages or more) is called the first form. The sheet containing page 2 and the next to the last page is called the inner form. In the example of the eight-page folder, illustrations 1 and 2 on page 163 are sheet work impositions for the 11" × 17" and 19" × 25" presses.

WORK AND TURN (HALFSHEET WORK) AND 2-SET (2-UP) 9.7.3

(Work and turn) work and 2-set are two imposition techniques based on a situation where the sheet has space for at least twice as many pages as the printed product contains. These methods place a first form imposition on one half of the sheet and an inner on the other. This gives you a version of the 2-up, also called a 2-set or 2-on, because you get two printed products from one sheet. When the entire run is printed, the sheets are turned over and run through the printing press a second time. That way, both pages of the sheet can be printed with only one makeready – i.e., without changing the printing plate. Even if the printed product has four colors on one side and only one color on the other, it can still be cost effective to use this type of imposition instead of doing two makereadies in two different printing presses.

Work and turn, or halfsheet work as it is also called, is the most common of these two types of imposition. The printing press grips the same edge of the paper when printing both the front side and back side of the sheet. This makes it easier to get proper registration between the front and back of the sheet. With the 2-set technique, the same gripper edge is not used for both sides [see Print 13.2.3]. Instead, the sheet is turned over for the second run in the printing press and the gripper edge is moved to the other side of the sheet, making it more difficult to align the front and back sides of the print. In this case, even something as minor as having slightly different-sized sheets of paper in the press run can cause misregistration.

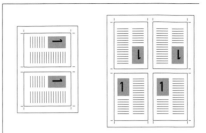

▶ GANG-UP
Here you can see a 2-up and 4-up imposition.

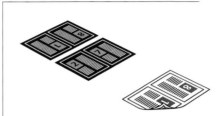

▶ FIRST FORM-INNER FORM
Each side of the printed sheet will need one makeready. Thus, you will need two imposed film sets per printed sheet.

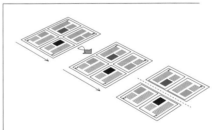

▶ HALFSHEET WORK (WORK AND TURN)
You place a first form imposition on one half of the sheet and an inner on the other. When the entire run is printed, the sheets are turned over and run through the printing press a second time. That way, both pages of the sheet can be printed with only one makeready – i.e. without changing the printing plate.

PRINTERS ^{9.8}

Today there are a large variety of printers on the market, ranging from inexpensive desktop printers for around $100 to professional printers costing hundreds of thousands of dollars. A PostScript-based printer is preferred for graphic production work, and is often more expensive than one which is not PostScript-based. Many non-PostScript based printers can be upgraded to PostScript printers, however. We will review the three most common types of printers: laser printers, ink-jet printers and sublimation printers.

LASER PRINTERS ^{9.8.1}

Laser Printers are the most common type of printer in use today. They work much like a copy machine because both are based on the xerographic process. There are many types of laser printers, from smaller black and white desktop printers and four-color laser printers to high-volume printers with a capacity of several hundred letter-sized pages per minute. The laser printer technique is also used in some digital printing methods.

THE XEROGRAPHIC PROCESS ^{9.8.2}

Laser printer technology is based on the xerographic process. This process is initiated by a rotating drum, or photographic conductor, which carries either a positive or negative

▶ LASER PRINTER

▶ PHOTOGRAPHIC CONDUCTOR

A material whose electrical charge can be affected by light.

▶ **THE XEROGRAPHIC PROCESS**
Regular copy machines and laser printers are based on the same technique, the xerographic process. In the xerographic technique, light changes the charge in a photographic conductor and toner, heat and physical pressure are applied.

What follows is the principle for how a (white-printing) laser printer operates.

▶ **THE COMPONENTS OF THE LASER PRINTER**
The numbers in the image refer to the following steps for conducting a print-out.

▶ 1. The photographic conductor is electrically charged before exposed by the laser beam.

▶ 2. The laser beam hits a rotating, octagonal mirror and passes across the width of the photographic conductor, row by row as the conductor is fed forward. When the laser beam hits it, the conductor loses its charge in that particular spot.

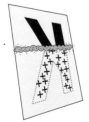

▶ 3. After it has been exposed to light, the photographic conductor absorbs toner in the charged areas. The toner may have a reversed charge to increase the attraction between the conductor and the toner.

▶ 4. The photographic conductor passes the paper, which has the same charge as the conductor but stronger. As a result, the toner is attracted and transferred to the paper.

▶ 5. When the toner has been transferred to the paper, it is only fixed to it with a weak electric charge. The toner is further fixed with heat and a light physical pressure.

▶ 6. The photographic conductor is cleaned.

► HIGH-VOLUME PRINTER
A high-volume printer prints black and white at a speed of 100–400 pages per minute with the possibility of alternating the paper stock (for example, using colored paper) while operating. High-volume printers often have simpler post processing procedures, such as stapling, built in.

electrical charge (the kind of charge differs depending on the brand). The drum has the same surface size as the paper you are printing on. With the help of a laser beam that passes across the drum the charge is removed from the areas that are to receive toner (or the areas that aren't – this also varies from brand to brand). The laser beam's exposure of the drum creates a charged reverse image. The drum is then exposed to toner, small color particles which stick to the charged image (the toner particles are either statically charged or neutral, depending on the brand of printer). The paper is then charged with a higher static value than the charged image on the drum. When the paper passes the drum, the toner is transferred to the paper because it has the higher charge. At this point, the toner is loose on the paper, bound only with a weak electric charge. The toner is heated and exposed to light physical pressure in order to permanently fix it – or "burn it" – onto the paper. The heat needed to fix the toner is about 200 degrees Celsius. In four-color printers, the above process takes place four times, once for each component color (CMYK).

THE EXPOSURE OF THE LASER PRINTER [9.8.3]

The drum is exposed with the help of a laser in the laser printer. In order to expose the entire drum as quickly as possible, a rotating, multi-edged mirror is used, often octagonal in shape. Because the mirror rotates, an edge of it can together with the laser beam expose the entire width of the drum at once. The laser beam is only broken when it reaches an area on the drum that should not be exposed.

When an edge of the mirror has exposed a line on the drum, a motor rotates the drum a small step forward so that next edge of the mirror can expose the next line. The mirror rotates quickly, often several thousand rotations per minute, which makes laser printers sensitive to jolts. There are several versions of laser printers that use a number of laser diodes to expose each dot on each line one by one, instead of a laser beam and a rotating mirror. These printers are called LED printers (for Light-Emitting Diodes).

▶ **XEROGRAPHIC PRINT**
To fix the toner, it is heated and "burned" onto the paper. When you print with toner halftone dots and text become somewhat blurry because the toner particles do not always land in the right place.

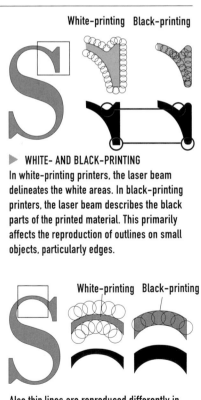

▶ **WHITE- AND BLACK-PRINTING**
In white-printing printers, the laser beam delineates the white areas. In black-printing printers, the laser beam describes the black parts of the printed material. This primarily affects the reproduction of outlines on small objects, particularly edges.

Also thin lines are reproduced differently in white- and black-printing printers. Thin lines become bolder in black-printing printers.

THE RESOLUTION OF THE LASER PRINTER [9.8.4]

The resolution in a laser printer mainly depends on three factors: the exposure dot of the laser beam, the size of the steps the engine takes, and how small the toner particles are. The exposure dot of the laser beam is determined by the actual laser and by the optics of the laser printer. There are printers that have different resolutions in different directions. This is because the engine can move in steps smaller than the size of the exposure point of the laser, or vice versa. Many current laser printers have a resolution of around 600 dpi. Toner is the factor that currently limits resolution the most. Smaller toner particles mean higher resolution. Toner particles are currently only a couple of micrometers in diameter. In LED printers the resolution is determined by how closely the laser diodes are spaced.

WHITE-PRINTING AND BLACK-PRINTING LASER PRINTERS [9.8.5]

Machines made by different manufacturers may utilize different technologies. For example, there is the difference between black-printing and white-printing. In black-printing printers, the laser beam describes the black parts of the printed material on the drum. In white-printing printers, the laser delineates the white areas—those that are not to be printed. White-printing printers create thinner lines than black-printing printers, which means that the same document printed in both types of printers will produce different results.

PAPER FOR LASER PRINTERS [9.8.6]

The paper used for laser printers must have certain characteristics. It cannot be too smooth, like a coated paper, because the toner will have difficulty adhering to the paper's surface. Neither can the paper lose its static charge too fast. If it does, the toner will not be attracted to the paper. Finally, it has to be resistant to high temperatures because of how the toner is heat-fixed to the paper surface. The gloss on coated paper can cause smoldering when heated.

The most common laser printers work with paper formats ranging from 8 1/2" × 11" to 11" × 17", weighing 20–32 lbs. Papers that are too thick can easily damage the printer. The stiffness of the paper is also important for feeding it through the printer successfully. Because you cannot use coated papers in laser printers, a number of special papers with a coated feeling have been developed. These kinds of papers are often relatively expensive. Most laser printers can be used for printing transparencies as well. You should use the transparency films recommended by the manufacturer, as they will be able to withstand the heat of the fixation process without melting.

BLANKS IN LASER PRINTERS [9.8.7]

Another type of paper frequently used in laser printers is offset pre-printed paper, or "blanks," like letterhead.

There are certain things you need to keep in mind when creating and using blanks in order to avoid problems with staining in the printer. When creating a blank, you need to make sure your paper is suitable for both offset and laser printers. You should avoid layouts with vertical lines and large, heavy tint areas because these can stain the fixation drum. Above all, allow the offset printing to dry completely before using the blanks in your laser printer. This can take up to two weeks.

When using blanks, you should also be aware that it is difficult to get exact registration between the proof and what is printed in the printer. It is difficult to make adjustments to the positioning of where the laser printer prints on the paper, and in general, the output will vary approximately +/- 1/24" (1mm) on the paper.

INK-JET PRINTERS 9.8.8

Ink-jet technology involves small drops of ink sprayed onto a paper surface. Ink-jet printing is often used when printing addresses on printed products, and there are also ink-jet desktop printers, four-color printers and digital proofs.

INK-JET TECHNOLOGY 9.8.9

Ink-jet printing is usually done using one of two techniques. One method squirts a continuous series of ink drops across the paper. The areas of the paper that should remain white, the beam is removed with the help of an electric field. The second method only sprays the ink on the areas of the paper that should be printed. In both methods, the ink drops are electrically charged and directed by an electric field to the right place on the paper. The ink drops are around 10 micrometers in diameter, depending on the manufacturer. The drops are smaller if the continuous method is used, giving you a higher resolution and a better tonal range.

INK-JET INK COMPOSITION 9.8.10

The ink used in the ink-jet printer is made up of a combination of approximately 60–90% solvent and various dyes. The solvents usually contain water and polythene glycol or a mix of both. The composition of the dye affects both the function of the printer and the end quality of the printout. One of the most common problems with ink-jet printers is that the ink dries in the nozzle that produces the drops. To avoid that, polythene glycol is added to the water-based inks. The dyes are either pure pigments or dissolved dyes. Pigment-based dyes tend to block the nozzles more but are also less sensitive to light and water once they are on the paper. Pigments allow for heavier color saturation than the dissolved dyes. The dissolved dyes are more sensitive to water and light but do not clog the nozzles. You should also be careful to avoid ink formulations that are poisonous, flammable or bad for the environment.

PAPER AND THE INK-JET PRINTER 9.8.11

The type of paper you use with the ink-jet printer is very important, because of the nature of the technology. In some ink-jet printers, only the paper supplied by the manufacturer can be used. The biggest problem that occurs is bleeding, when two colors bleed into each other. To avoid bleeding the ink must dry quickly. The paper has to be able to absorb the liquid components of the ink as soon as possible without the dye following them into the paper. If too much dye is absorbed into the paper, the color density can be adversely affected.

When the ink is absorbed into the paper it not only seeps down into the paper, but it spreads out as well. This effect can be compared to writing with a magic marker on a newspaper. When an ink drop is absorbed into the paper, it increases in size, usually to

▶ INK-JET PRINTERS
There are ink-jet printers that can print large formats, in this case an entire imposition. Some can also print on special materials, for example on textile (fabric) wrappers.

▶ ESSENTIAL PRINTER QUALITIES

Resolution:
Measured in dots per inch, dpi.

Speed:
How many pages can a printer print per minute, ppm (page per minute).

Mechanical precision:
How precisely the print-out is placed on the paper.

Color correspondence:
How well the colors of the four-color printer correspond to standardized scales.

Stability:
How often you need to calibrate the printer.

Color cost:
How much toner and ink is necessary and what is the cost.

Paper grade:
What kind of paper can be used and what is the cost.

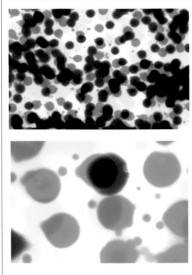

The ink-jet technique is based on a method which squirts small drops of ink onto the paper. The size of the drops are around 10 micrometers in diameter, depending on the manufacturer.

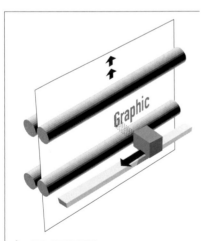

▶ INK-JET PRINTER
In ink-jet printers, an ink cartridge slides across the paper. In the places where the paper is supposed to be colored, a small drop is squirted out onto the paper. When one row is colored, the paper is fed forward and the next row is colored.

three times that of the original drop. Printing with an ink-jet requires paper that is stable dimensionally, so it does not wrinkle or pucker because of the liquid in the ink. Because most printer manufacturers recommend their own special papers, the selection is relatively limited and the paper itself can be expensive.

DYE SUBLIMATION PRINTERS 9.8.12
Dye sublimation printers, also called thermo-transfer printers, are based on a technique reminiscent of old-fashioned typewriters. With dye sublimation printers, however, color is not transferred to the paper by physical pressure (like the typewriter key hitting the ribbon), but by heating the ribbon. The dye sublimation printing technique is relatively expensive and primarily used for certain digital proofs and outputs on photographic paper or transparencies.

DYE SUBLIMATION TECHNOLOGY 9.8.13
The ink in the dye sublimation printer is neither liquid nor powder, but consists of paraffin or wax esters on a ribbon of either polyester film or condenser paper. The color ribbon is heated by a print head and the ink attaches to the paper because it has a rougher surface than the color ribbon. The print head consists of several small radiators surrounded by porcelain. Each radiator can be heated to different temperatures. This allows you to regulate the amount of ink transferred to every dot in the output.

PRINTER RIBBON 9.8.14
The ribbon in a dye sublimation printer is on a continuous roll, just like that of a typewriter. However, the cost of the ribbon for this type of printer is quite high. Color ribbons made with condenser paper are usually cheaper than polyester-based color ribbons but are of a somewhat lesser quality. The ribbons are usually about 10 micrometers thick, of which 4 micrometers is color.

PAPER FOR DYE SUBLIMATION PRINTERS 9.8.15
The choice of paper for the sublimation printer is relatively open, as long as you pay attention to the roughness of the paper. These printers require a paper with a relatively fine surface but it does not matter if the paper is coated or uncoated. A very rough surface contributes to lower printing quality.

HIGH-VOLUME PRINTERS 9.9
Many printers of this type have built-in post processing functions such as stapling. Productions printed with such equipment typically include reports, manuals, handbooks and educational material: i.e. printed products that are updated often, printed in smaller editions and higher numbers. Printed products produced in this way are often created in non-PostScript based programs like Microsoft Word. If using such programs, you should hand off the material as PostScript files [see 9.3.3].

COST OF HIGH VOLUME PRINTERS VS. OFFSET PRINTERS 9.9.1

High-volume printers are most cost-effective for printed products with many pages, printed in small editions. The closest competitor is offset printing on perfecting print presses, which prints on both sides of the sheet in the same press run. The financial breaking point is around 1,000 copies. The starting costs of high volume printing are relatively low but the price per unit is high.

The post processing cost is usually higher for offset printing because the sheets have to be folded, etc., while high volume printers use pre-arranged inserts. Manufacturers of off press processing equipment have also developed simpler processing systems that take advantage of using pre-arranged inserts, for example systems that can be connected to printers or used online.

QUALITY OF HIGH VOLUME PRINTERS 9.9.2

The most common high-volume printers have a resolution around 600 dpi, which is enough to maintain a reasonable quality for line art, screen shots and simpler photographs. High-volume printers are appropriate for documents containing mainly text.

IMAGESETTERS 9.10

An imagesetter generally works like a laser printer, but instead of printing on paper with colored powder, photosensitive film or paper is exposed and developed. An imagesetter usually has a higher resolution than a laser printer – around 3,600 dpi, compared to 600 dpi for an average laser printer. It's because the emulsion side of the film has a high resolution. In laser printers, the ink powder and paper type limit the resolution. An imagesetter exposes film, but you also need a separate machine to develop the film after it has been exposed. These machines are called online developers.

The imagesetter's RIP calculates the halftone screens, creating a large bitmap in which every exposure dot in the imagesetter is represented by a one or a zero (i.e., exposed or non-exposed surface). If you are printing in multiple colors a separate bitmap is created for each component color in the print.

A very fine laser beam exposes the areas of the film that should be exposed according to the information in the bitmap. Unexposed film is stored on a roll in a film cassette. The cassette feeds the film forward when an exposure needs to be made. When exposed, the film is rolled up on a new film cassette. This cassette is then inserted into the developer. The film is fed through a developing bath. Before it comes out of the developer, the film is cleaned and dried. If you have an online developer, the film goes straight from exposure to developing without being rolled up in between. There are also imagesetters that output to printing plates instead of film. They work in a similar way using a technique called CTP. The major advantage to this type of imagesetter is that you do not have to handle the film and printing plates manually [see Film and Plates 11.4].

▶ **IMAGESETTER**
By looks the imagesetter is anonymous. On the right the exposed film is fed forward into a developer – so called on-line development.

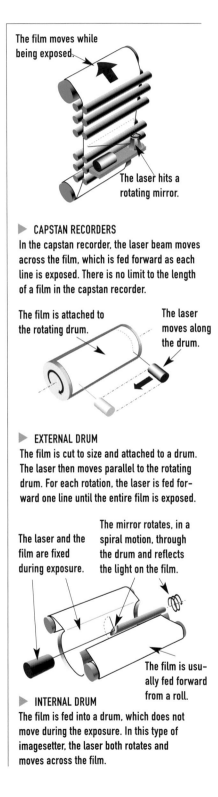

The film moves while being exposed.

The laser hits a rotating mirror.

▶ **CAPSTAN RECORDERS**
In the capstan recorder, the laser beam moves across the film, which is fed forward as each line is exposed. There is no limit to the length of a film in the capstan recorder.

The film is attached to the rotating drum.

The laser moves along the drum.

▶ **EXTERNAL DRUM**
The film is cut to size and attached to a drum. The laser then moves parallel to the rotating drum. For each rotation, the laser is fed forward one line until the entire film is exposed.

The laser and the film are fixed during exposure.

The mirror rotates, in a spiral motion, through the drum and reflects the light on the film.

The film is usually fed forward from a roll.

▶ **INTERNAL DRUM**
The film is fed into a drum, which does not move during the exposure. In this type of imagesetter, the laser both rotates and moves across the film.

THREE TYPES OF IMAGESETTERS 9.10.1

There are three basic types of techniques for imagesetters: Capstan recorders, and recorders with internal or external drums.

Capstan recorders store film in a cassette and feed it forward to be exposed. The film is exposed by a laser beam that shines through a quartz crystal. The quartz crystal is controlled by the information on the RIP bitmap, which tells it when to let the laser through or not. When the crystal lets the beam through, it hits an octagonal mirror, just like in a laser printer. The mirror causes the beam to sweep across the film in a line. When a line has been exposed, the film is fed forward and the next line is exposed. When the entire film has been exposed, it is rolled up into a new cassette. It is very important with this type of machine that the film is fed through precisely and that the rotation of the mirror is exact.

In the external drum technique, the film is cropped and stretched around a drum. The drum then rotates while the laser beam exposes the film. The laser beam is first directed through a quartz crystal and then reflected via a mirror that steps forward along the rotating drum. In these imagesetters, it is important that the film is attached to the drum in exactly the right way and that the mirror steps forward with precision.

In the internal drum technique, the film is fed into a drum, cropped, then "sucked" into place. The laser beam is directed through a crystal, then reflected off a mirror, which rotates on a screw inside the drum. The mirror moves step by step along the entire width of the film. When the film is completely exposed, a new sheet of film is fed into the drum and the exposed film is rolled up into a new cassette. The precision of the mirror's movement along the film is crucial to the success of this technique. It is the only technique in which the film remains still while being exposed, and it is therefore usually considered to be the most precise. It is the most common technique in use today.

In all types of imagesetters, precision and repeatability are very important factors. Repeatability is the imagesetter's ability to expose exactly the same way many times in a row. An imprecise imagesetter might result in misregistration between four-color films. Proper exposure and development of the film is crucial to the quality of the final print. Therefore, it is important that an imagesetter be calibrated and that the developing liquid in the developer is frequently changed. An imagesetter should be calibrated in a linear fashion, i.e., a 50% tone on the computer should be 50% on the film. An uncalibrated imagesetter can produce completely erroneous tonal values. Old developing liquid loses its ability to develop the film properly, resulting in insufficient or uneven inking. ■

REVIEW AND PROOFING

CHAPTER 10   REVIEW AND PROOFING   CREATING AND REVIEWING PROOFS IS IMPORTANT DURING THE ENTIRE PROCESS OF GRAPHIC PRODUCTION, STARTING AT A VERY EARLY STAGE. PROOFING ALLOWS YOU TO CATCH AND CORRECT MISTAKES IN ONE STAGE BEFORE MOVING ON TO THE NEXT, SAVING YOU TIME AND RESOURCES. MANY PEOPLE ARE "TOO BUSY" TO MAKE TIME FOR PROOFING. HOWEVER, WHEN THINGS REALLY GO WRONG, THEY OFTEN FIND THE TIME TO START THE WHOLE PROCESS OVER FROM SCRATCH.

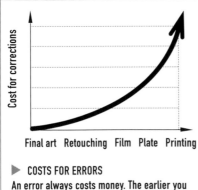

▶ COSTS FOR ERRORS
An error always costs money. The earlier you catch it, the less expensive it is to correct.

When creating a printed product, you want each stage to produce the desired result before moving on to the next. Several types of review and proofing systems can be employed to assure these results. For example, you can preview a printed product on the computer screen, via printouts, use preflight applications, create analog or digital proofs or even run a proof print on a printing press.

Throughout the project you can review text, layout and images right on your computer screen. Laser printer outputs are mainly used to review the text and layout before producing the films or plates used for printing. Preflight software can check that the document is ready to go to press. Analog and digital proofs are primarily used as final proofs before the actual edition is printed on a press. With particularly important productions, you can even make a proof in a printing press before the edition is printed. This is expensive, but justified in certain cases. You might also make proofs in a printing press if you need a high number of proof prints for each page.

All of these review and proofing procedures serve the same purpose: to ensure that every step goes as planned. The later in the production process you discover errors, the more expensive and time-consuming it is to correct them. It is therefore important to schedule time for review and proofing throughout the entire process, including the very early stages.

In this chapter, we will look at different review and proofing systems. We will also go through a review checklist and discuss the production of proofs. To begin with, we will cover some of the errors that can occur during the graphic production process.

COMMON ERRORS IN THE GRAPHIC PRODUCTION PROCESS 10.1

Any number of errors can occur during the preparation of digital documents used in graphic production. For simplicity's sake, we'll divide the most common mistakes into five main areas:
• Aesthetic errors, i.e., typographic mistakes like orphans and poor kerning
• Computer errors caused by programs, drives or operating systems
• Careless errors or those caused by inexperience.
• Errors caused by the prepress staff
• Mechanical errors like poorly calibrated imagesetters or errors in the OPI

The creation of analog proofs is really the only way to check all of these errors, but analog proofs are done at such late stage in the production process that it pays to eliminate as many of these errors in earlier stages as possible.

SOFT PROOFS [SCREEN PROOFS] 10.2

Carefully reviewing text and images on a well-calibrated computer screen is an effective and inexpensive first step towards ensuring a good result. Most image editing and page layout applications have tools designed to help you check different measurements. You can review typography, placement of images, illustrations, logotypes and text.

You can also screen-check hyphenation and line arrangement, format, type area, trapping, knockouts, overprints and bleeds [See Document 6.6, 6.7 and 6.8]. An experienced graphic production assistant can use an image editing program to review color matching, image edits, ink coverage, UCR/GCR and dot gain adjustments [see Images 5.6].

One way to create a soft proof to show the client is to save your document as an Acrobat PDF file [see Output 9.4]. A PDF file can be easily distributed via email to people whose feedback you need. With the program Adobe Acrobat, digital notes can be added to the document. Also, if you can create a PDF file, it's most likely possible that you can rip and output a document on film or plate. [See 10.4.2].

LASER PRINTER OUTPUT 10.3

Laser printer outputs are primarily used to review typography, check the placement of images, illustrations and logotypes, and to fact-check text and correct spelling. Laser printer outputs also allow you to check hyphenation, line arrangement, format, type area

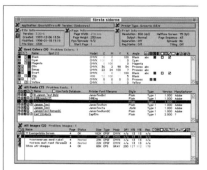

and bleeds [see Document 6.8]. These printouts are generally done on a PostScript-based laser printer in color or black and white.

A good way to determine if a document is ready to be rasterized is to make a four-color separated laser printout [see Output page 155]. This type of output enables you to check knockouts and overprints and the number of colors in the document. Images and exact colors are impossible to effectively review in a laser output because the resemblance is not close enough to a final print.

DOCUMENT REVIEWS AND PREFLIGHT SOFTWARE 10.4

The word "preflight" is borrowed from the aviation world, and refers to the preflight check a pilot performs on an airplane before takeoff. In the graphic production industry, "preflight" refers to the review of digital documents before they go into production. Special preflight software is used to check documents against a standard checklist. Preflight review might seem like an unnecessary step, but most digital documents sent to production arrive with errors that must be corrected. It can be devastating if an error is discovered as late as when rasterizing or outputting to film or plate, and it only gets worse if errors are discovered in later stages. Preflight programs help catch these errors as early as possible, reducing the risk of delays and cost overruns.

Preflight software can be divided into two main categories. The first group, which includes programs such as Markzware's Flightcheck and Extensis Flight Pro, checks QuarkXPress, Adobe InDesign and Adobe PageMaker documents and the accompanying illustrations, images and typefaces. The second group reviews and, if necessary, corrects the PostScript or PDF files before a document goes from the page layout program to the RIP. Digiscript from Onevision, Tailor from Firstclass NV, ProScript from Cutting Edge Technology and Pitstop from Enfocus are a few examples of this type of application. Each type of preflight program catches different kinds of errors. Those that check page layout files can find errors resulting from carelessness or inexperience. Applications that check PostScript and PDF files find technical errors caused by programs, drives or operating systems and can also catch certain errors made by the prepress staff.

PREFLIGHT SOFTWARE FOR CHECKING PAGE LAYOUT APPLICATIONS 10.4.1

These programs review QuarkXPress, Adobe InDesign or Adobe PageMaker files for the following:
• Links to images and illustrations in documents
• File formats of images and illustrations
• Colors used in documents and illustrations
• If some colors are defined as Pantone colors
• If the images are saved in RGB or CMYK mode
• Image resolution
• That all typefaces are active
• Number of anchor points in a curve
• Trapping and overprinting
• Font styles (bold, italic, etc.)

These programs also allow you to create "filters." Filters let you determine what the program should check for and what it should do when it finds errors. If an error is found, it is corrected in the program in which the document, illustration or image was originally created, for example in QuarkXPress, Adobe Illustrator or Adobe Photoshop.

PREFLIGHT SOFTWARE FOR CHECKING POSTSCRIPT & PDF FILES 10.4.2

These programs review the following:
- If it is possible to rasterize the file
- That all typefaces are included in the PostScript file
- That all images and illustrations are included
- Which colors are defined
- Image resolution

The Preflight software also modifies and optimizes PostScript code or PDF, making the files smaller and faster to rip. As in the programs mentioned above, you use filters to decide which factors the programs should look out for. Some programs can also make changes the PostScript file directly. For example, Acrobat Distiller from Adobe checks PostScript files. However, it is not a full-fledged preflight support. It is really only checking if it is possible to interpret the PostScript file.

PROOFS 10.5

Proofs are used to assure that prepress work is accurately executed, and they provide an opportunity to make necessary corrections before the printing plate is produced. Proofs act as a guideline for the printing house in terms of what the client expects the printed result to look like. Proofs are made using specialized techniques and can often simulate a press-printed product very closely. There are two categories of proofs: analog and digital. Analog proofs are made from the film used in the production of the printing plates. Digital proofs are printouts of the finished design on very high-quality color printers. Both kinds provide a good preview of the final print result in terms of image quality and color. To check the quality and content of the films, you need to make an analog proof.

There are a number of different names for proofs, some of which reflect the brand of equipment and/or materials used in their creation. Chromalin or Chroma, Colorart, Matchprint and Agfa-Proof are some common names for analog proofs. An analog proof is usually called a "chroma" regardless of what equipment is used. Iris, Rainbow, Approval or digital Chromalin are common names of digital proofs. Bluelines and whiteprints are special kinds of analog proofs, which are based on the films used for printing. Blueprints are blue and white and whiteprints are black and white, which means you cannot proof the colors. On the other hand, they allow you to do a final check of the imposition and content of the films [see Output 9.5].

The calibration of proofs is very important whether they are analog or digital. A poorly calibrated proof is next to impossible for the printing house to reproduce. It is therefore extremely important that the proof is calibrated to the requirements of the final print. You should be aware, however, that the final printed product will never correspond 100% to a proof. This is because proofs are created in a different way, using different materials (ink, paper stock, etc.) than the final print.

▶ **PROOFS**
Proofs are used to assure that prepress work is accurately executed, and they provide an opportunity to make necessary corrections before the printing plate is produced.

▶ **BLUELINE**
Bluelines are special kinds of analog proofs, which are based on the films used for printing. Blueprints are blue and white, which means you cannot check the colors. On the other hand, they allow you to do a final check of the imposition and content of the films.

PRESS PROOFS 10.6

To press proof means to print some sample copies of the print in the printing press before the actual edition is printed. Press proofs are generally made on a different printing press than the one used for the edition, but because they are created on similar equipment, press proofs provide the most accurate projection of the final result. Advertisement productions commonly produce proofs in this way, known as advertisement proofs. These ad proofs are usually done in sheet-fed offset presses, but the magazine in which the advertisement is included might be printed via web-fed offset, for example. Although the results will be very similar, this process will not produce an exact match between press proof and actual print. Doing a real press proof is often very expensive, and may not be cost-effective for most projects.

WHAT SHOULD BE CHECKED? 10.7

Now we'll look at a rundown of all the different things that need to be checked during the proofing process. We will also discuss the most appropriate times during the graphic production process to conduct these reviews.

PROOFING TEXT 10.7.1

Begin by reviewing the text of your document for content and correctness, first on screen, and again in laser-printed format. After this point, there should be no further changes made to the text. Changes to the text in later stages of production will be both time-consuming and expensive, so make sure that you get final approval of the text before moving on.

PROOFING IMAGES 10.7.2

In order to proof images on your computer, it is important to make sure that the computer screen is calibrated correctly. A computer screen uses something called an additive color model (RGB) to represent color, whereas printers use a subtractive color model (CMYK) [see Chromatics 4.4.1 and 4.4.2]. Therefore you will never have an exact color match between the screen and printed versions. However, with a well-calibrated screen you can get a surprisingly close approximation of the printed product.

The size and resolution of images can be checked with various image editing programs, which can also check retouching, image sharpness, and color correspondence. Adobe Photoshop includes tools that allow the user to check color value and saturation in any selected area of an image. To do this properly, a thorough knowledge of print reproduction is necessary. An experienced image scanner or image editor can use these programs to check image edits, color saturation, maximum ink coverage, UCR/GCR and adjust dot gain [see Image 5.6].

If your project requires high-level image quality, you should always have a proof of the images done. A proof is based on CMYK, which means you will get a closer color match to the final print. Digital proofs are excellent for checking images as long as they are carefully calibrated and produced according to the prerequisites of the print. Analog proofs are also excellent for checking images, but are generally more expensive than digital proofs because they must be produced from films. The advantage of analog proofs is that the images are rasterized and rendered in the same way as in the final print. In addition, analog proofs generally have a higher resolution than digital proofs, which can be important if you want to check fine tonal transitions. Color laser printouts are not recommended for checking images as they generally have poor color correspondence with the actual print.

PROOFING PAGES 10.7.3

When it comes to proofing an entire page of an original, a lot can be checked on the computer screen. It is important to check the typography and the placement of images, illustrations, logotypes and text. You can also check hyphenation and line arrangement, page format, type area, trapping, knockouts/overprints and bleeds [See Document 6.6, 6. 7 and 6.8]. You should also print out the pages (in either black and white or color) and check the items listed above one more time. It is preferable to generate a printer output that is the same size (100% including bleeds) as the finished printed product will be.

If you do a color printer output, you can also check that all the elements on the page have approximately the color you want (remember that this method is not the most accurate way of doing this). You can check that the color conversions are correct by making a four-color separated laser printer output [see Output page 155]. For a regular four-color page you should get four printouts per page, one for each printing color. If you are printing with one or more spot colors, you will get one page per spot color. If you get pages with spot colors you don't want, you've probably forgotten to separate one or more colors in your document, or have neglected to delete the colors you decided not to use. In four-color separated laser printer outputs, you can also check trapping and overprinting.

One of the last steps in traditional graphic production is the creation of graphic film. At this stage, you might want to create an analog proof to make sure that nothing went wrong with the film when it was rasterized, exposed or developed. A simple way to do this is to lay the approved laser printout over the analog proof on a light table. By doing this you can see right away if there are any discrepancies between the two. If you have done all the check-ups in the previous stages, you should not find any errors in the analog proof. The point of this type of review is to make sure that the film is correctly exposed and developed. In addition, the analog proofs lets the printing house know what you expect the printed product to look like.

REVIEWING PROOFS 10.8

There are variations in proof printing, including the printing method that is being simulated, the type of paper stock, the pigment of the colors, halftone screening, simulation of dot gain and trapping, to name a few.

DIFFERENT PRINTING METHODS 10.8.1

Certain printing methods, paper stocks colors and inks can be very difficult, if not impossible, to simulate in a proof. Offset printing on coated paper is the easiest to simulate with a proof print system. Other printing methods such as gravure printing, flexography or screen printing are considerably more difficult to simulate. This means that you can

▶ **PROOF OF IMAGES**

If your project requires a very high-end image quality, you should do a proof print of the images.

Otherwise, it might be enough to proof them on a well-calibrated monitor.

The more knowledge you have about image editing and print reproduction, the better able you are to proof images on a monitor.

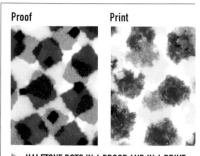

Proof   **Print**

▶ **HALFTONE DOTS IN A PROOF AND IN A PRINT**
Here we can see a magnified comparison of dots from an actual proof and an actual final print. The fine paper/base material that the analog proofs are made of makes the halftone dots look sharper and more exact than in the final print.

expect a closer correspondence between a proof and final print when it comes to offset printing than with any other printing method. Daily newspapers printed in web-fed offset presses can be difficult to simulate. As a result, it is common in such productions to make a proof print on a printing press.

PAPER/BASE MATERIAL 10.8.2

Analog as well as digital proofs are often made on the base material provided by the proof system manufacturer, which means that you have limited paper choices for these proofs. These papers are often white and glossy. If the paper you have chosen for the final printing is a coated, smooth, bright white paper, the proof print will yield very similar results. If, on the other hand, you are using a matte, uncoated or yellowish paper for the final printing, the colors of the proof will appear slightly different. In some proof printing systems you can use the same paper that will be used for the final edition, which is an obvious advantage in terms of matching the proof colors to those of the final print.

COLORS/INK COVERAGE/DENSITY 10.8.3

Proofs are created using a different type of ink than what is used in a printing press. Preferably, the colors should follow the American color model SWOP, but some proofs follow the European color scale. For similarity's sake, it is also important for the proof to simulate the density of the final print. The density is affected by how much ink the printing house can use on a given type of paper [see Print 13.4.2]. Proof systems usually have limited capabilities to simulate the print in this regard. Many proof systems have a set density, which is often higher than you will be able to print with in the final stage. This higher density results in a proof with a wider tonal range than the final print. Because of this, the proof will appear more brilliantly colored than the final printing. Digital proofs can usually approximate the density of a final print more closely than analog proofs.

LAMINATION 10.8.4

Most analog proofs can be laminated, a process that gives the proof a glossy surface and considerably brighter colors than those the printing press can achieve. For this reason, lamination is not recommended. A client who has seen a glossy, brightly colored laminated analog proof will undoubtedly be disappointed when they compare it to the final print.

HALFTONE DOTS, HALFTONE SCREENING PATTERNS, TONAL TRANSITIONS, MOIRÉ 10.8.5

Because analog proofs are done directly from the films that the print is based on, they are produced with exactly the same halftone screening technique. This means that you can check that halftone screening phenomena like moiré do not occur in your print. The fine paper/base material that the analog proofs are made of makes the halftone dots look sharper and more exact than in the final print. This can sometimes lead to disruptive rosette patterns in the proof. In the final print, these patterns are not as visible because the halftone dots are not as sharp.

Digital proof systems are very low resolution (often 300–600 dpi) compared to imagesetters (1,200–3,600 dpi). If you were to use a traditional halftone screening technique when making a digital proof you would get a poor tonal range [see Output 9.1.4]. Therefore a kind of FM screening technique is usually used [see Output 9.1.9], which means that you do not see any actual halftone dots in the proof. Because the digital proof is reproduced with a different halftone screening technique than the final print, you cannot detect possible halftone screening phenomena like moiré with this type of proof. The low resolution of digital proofs also means that subtle tonal transitions might appear different in the final print.

SPOT COLORS/PANTONE COLORS 10.8.6

Neither analog proof systems nor digital proof systems can simulate Pantone colors, which means that you are generally limited to the four primary colors: cyan, magenta, yellow and black. If you are using Pantone colors, you can do a proof with any of the primary colors instead. Of course, it does not provide you with the correct color impression, but you can check that everything looks approximately the way it should. This type of proof should be accompanied by a printed reference, such as a Pantone sample card from a color guide, to show how the actual colors will appear.

DOT GAIN 10.8.7

In order for the proof to resemble the final print as much as possible, it is important to be able to simulate the dot gain of the final print. Proof systems usually have a limited ability to do this, but some are better than others. In general, you can usually calibrate digital proofs more accurately than analog proofs when it comes to dot gain.

TRAPPING 10.8.8

When doing a proof, the phenomenon called "trapping" does not occur as it does in the final print [see Print 13.4.4]. In a proof the colors attach to each other completely, although digital proofs can generally be calibrated more accurately to reflect trapping than analog proofs.

CREATING A PROOF 10.9

The two main types of proofs, analog and digital, are produced in a variety of ways.

ANALOG PROOFS 10.9.1

There are three types of analog proofs: overlay, laminate and blueline proofs. All analog proofs are based on color separation (CMYK conversion), which means that the proofs are produced using several separate films. Overlay proofs are produced by exposing the print image on acetate film, with one sheet of film, or layer, for each color. After exposure, the acetate films are layered on top of each other. Brands of overlay proofs include Dupont Cromacheck and 3M Color Key. Laminate proofs are produced by laminating a base material with different pigment layers (CMYK) exposed one at the time using the films for the print. When you have laminated the base material with the first pigment layer, the corresponding film is placed and exposed in an exposure frame. Then the first color is developed in a special developing machine. The next color layer is laminated on top of the previous one, and its corresponding film is placed and exposed and so on. For

▶ **ANALOG PROOF**
After the proof has been exposed in an exposure frame, it is developed in a special developer. Shown here: Fuji's Colorart.

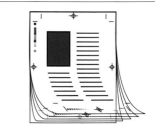

▶ **OVERLAY PROOF**
Overlay proofs are created by layering acetate films, one for each print color, on top of each other.

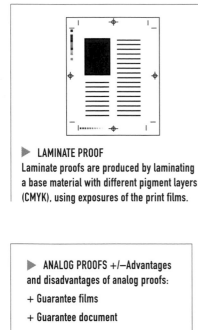

a regular four-color proof, the process is repeated four times before the final proof is done. Examples of laminate proofs include Fuji Color-Art, 3M MatchPrint, Dupont Chromalin and Agfa-Proof. Blueline copies are created by exposing the print films on UV sensitive paper. Bluelines are often produced on paper that is the same size as the final print, which allows you to check bleeds and imposition.

The calibration of an analog proof is monitored by checking exposure and development at regular intervals with color bars. Analog proof systems generally have a limited variety of printing options. Manufacturers may offer a number of different base materials/papers on which different types of prints can be simulated, but ink coverage and gray balance cannot usually be modified. The quality of the inks and base materials, as well as the developing and exposure equipment used in the process, are crucial to the success of the analog proof.

DIGITAL PROOFS 10.9.2

Traditionally, separation-based analog proof systems have been used to check the films used in the creation of the final printing plates, but digital proofs are gaining ground. Scitex Iris, 3M Rainbow and Kodak Approval from Kodak are a few examples of digital proof systems. With a digital proof you cannot check things like exposure and development to see if the film for the plates has been produced correctly or if the content of the films is accurate. Digital proofs essentially allow you to proof print the digital file from which the films will be created.

There are several methods of digital proof printing. Current techniques include ink jet, sublimation, and xerographic printing. A digital proof system is actually just a very high-end color printer [see Output 9.7]. The halftone screening technique used in producing digital proofs often differs from traditional halftone screening techniques. An ink jet printer uses a kind of FM screening [see Output 9.1.9]. The only current systems that use a traditional halftone screening technique is Kodak's Approval, Polaroid's Polaproof and Fuji Finalproof. Because every system manufacturer has its own halftone screening technique, the results might differ from the technique used when producing the film depending on the halftone screening technique used.

Digital proof systems are controlled by programs. These programs and their settings are determining factors for calibration and adjustment for the printing of the digital proof. These programs enable you to check dot gain, ink coverage and gray balance. You can pre-define a number of default settings that you select when printing. This allows you to adjust the digital proof to the requirements of the final print. The program, resolution, base material, halftone screening technique, colors, operational reliability and repeatability of the machine determine the quality of a digital proof [see Output page 175]. ■

FILM AND PLATES

11

CHAPTER 11 FILM AND PLATES **GRAPHIC FILM IS USED IN MANY PRINTING PROCESSES TO PRODUCE PLATES OR PRINTING FORMS. THESE FILMS FORM THE BASIS OF THE ACTUAL PRINTING PLATE OR PRINTING FORM USED TO MAKE THE FINAL PRINTS. THIS CHAPTER WILL FOCUS ON THE USE OF FILM AND PLATES IN OFFSET PRINTING, AS IT IS THE MOST COMMON PRINTING METHOD.**

Because the printing process is based on a principle of printing and non-printing surfaces, films and plates are as well. As a result, surfaces are printed with full ink or no ink at all [see Output 9.1]. In this chapter, we will discuss graphic films and printing plates, how they are produced and how they are used to produce printed products.

GRAPHIC FILM 11.1

Graphic film consists of a plastic backing coated with a light-sensitive emulsion layer. Graphic film is exposed in an imagesetter then developed using chemical developers. These chemicals are one of the big environmental burdens of graphic production. Because of this, many film manufacturers have put a lot of energy into developing "dry" films, which don't require the use of hazardous chemicals.

The developed film is then placed on a printing plate and exposed to light. The plate has a light sensitive polymer layer that reacts to the light exposure. The method is reminiscent of the way photographers create contact sheets. After the plate is exposed, it is developed with liquid chemicals. Manufacturers are also working on a "dry" version of these plates.

NEGATIVE AND POSITIVE FILM 11.1.1

There is both negative and positive film. When positive film is exposed and developed, all printing surfaces appear black, and all surfaces that are non-printing are transparent.

This type of film looks essentially like what the page would look like output from a laser printer. Exposed and developed negative film comes out exactly opposite – all printing surfaces appear transparent and those that are not to be printed are black.

The offset printing process can accommodate positive as well as negative film, and there are advantages and disadvantages to both. Some commercial printers prefer using positive film while others prefer to work with negative film. Geography seems to play a part in film preference – the United States mainly uses negative film whereas most of Europe uses positive film.

DIRECT AND INDIRECT PRINTING PROCEDURES 11.1.2

A distinction is usually made between direct and indirect printing procedures. Direct printing means that the printing ink is deposited onto the paper (or other material) directly from the printing form. In this case the image on the printing form has to be reversed so that it prints correctly on the paper, much like the way a stamp works. Examples of direct printing procedures include flexography and gravure printing.

Indirect printing involves transferring ink from the printing form to a rubber blanket, which in turn transfers the ink to the paper. The print image is correct on the printing form, and reversed on the rubber cylinder so that it is oriented correctly on the paper. Offset printing is an indirect printing procedure.

FILMS WITH POSITIVE AND REVERSED IMAGES 11.1.3

Indirect and direct printing procedures require different types of films. Direct printing uses films with positive images, right-reading emulsion up (RREU), whereas indirect printing uses films with reversed images, or right-reading emulsion down (RRED), as they are often called within the graphics industry. This is different than the distinction between positive and negative films; it refers instead to whether or not the text is reversed on the side of the film that contains the emulsion layer.

The terms right-reading emulsion up and right-reading emulsion down always assume that you are looking at the film from its emulsion side, the matte side. If the print image is reversed, you have a negative film; if the print image is correctly oriented, you have a positive film.

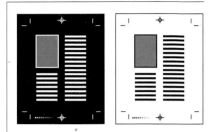

▶ NEGATIVE AND POSITIVE FILM
In negative film, all printing surfaces appear transparent and those that are non-printing are black. Positive film comes out exactly opposite.

▶ FIND THE EMULSION SIDE

If you are not sure which side has the emulsion layer, hold up the film against the light. The emulsion side is matte and the other side is shiny.

You can also try to carefully scratch the corner of the film with a sharp object. On the emulsion side you will be able to scratch off some of the emulsion, on the other side you won't.

The emulsion layer is sensitive to scratches and must not be damaged. Scratches in the emulsion layer will be directly transferred to the printing plate and the print.

▶ POSITIVE FILM VS NEGATIVE FILM

POSITIVE FILM	NEGATIVE FILM
+ It's easy to check the print image because it is positive	– Difficult to check the print image because it is negative
– Dust and dirt become printing surfaces and are transferred to the print	+ Dirt and dust don't become printing surfaces
Dot reduction when the plate is exposed	Dot gain when the plate is exposed

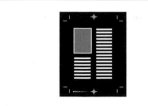

▶ PAGE FILM
Each page is output on separate films.

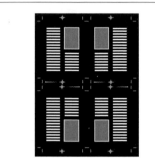

▶ IMPOSED FILM
The pages are imposed in the computer and output on the same film.

▶ FILM DENSITOMETER
Use a densitometer to check the density of graphic film.

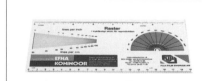

▶ SCREEN RULING METER
With a screen ruling meter, you can check screen frequency and screen angles on a film.

FILM SETS 11.1.4

When printing with many colors, you need one film for each printing ink. Such a collection of films is usually called a film set, or in the case of a four-color print, a four-color set.

MONTAGE AND IMPOSITION OF FILM 11.1.5

In a printing press, several pages of the printed product are usually printed together on the same large sheet. This means that the printing plate must contain all of the pages to be printed on any given sheet. When producing film originals, you can either output the individual pages on separate films or on "imposed film." When using many separate films, they are then mounted and imposed manually on a larger film. The final film assembly is used to expose the printing plate. With digitally imposed film, the pages are mounted and imposed on a computer using an imposition program before they are output. This allows you to output an imposed film set for an entire printer's sheet with which you can directly expose the printing plate [see Output 9.6].

OFFSET PLATES 11.2

There are a number of different types of plates. The most common offset plates are made of aluminum coated with a photosensitive polymer (plastic). There are also plates with base materials of polyester or even paper (known as quick printing).

▶ TO CHECK FILM

There are four technical factors you should check on a film:

1. DENSITY
The density of the film should be at least 3.5 to 4 density units. If the density is too low, the film will let through a little bit of light exposing the plate in places it shouldn't.

2. TONAL VALUES
The tone values of the film have to be checked so the screen percent values in the print come out correct. You can check it by measuring the 50% value on the color bar of the film with a densitometer. The tone should be around 50% when it's measured but a discrepancy of 2% is usually accepted.

3. SCREEN FREQUENCY
You can measure the screen frequency with a screen ruling meter.

4. SCREEN ANGLES
You can measure the screen angles with a screen ruling meter. (The angles should be oriented around C=15° M=75° Y=0° K=45° in a regular offset print.)

You should also check that the film doesn't have scratches and that it has the correct format.

POSITIVE AND NEGATIVE PLATES 11.2.1

There are both positive and negative plates. Positive plates are used for positive film, negative plates are used for negative film. Both positive and negative plates give you a positive print image after development.

PRODUCTION OF OFFSET PRINTING PLATES 11.2.2

To expose a printing plate, the emulsion side of the film is placed directly against the plate. The plate is then exposed for a certain number of seconds in an "exposure frame." It is important to have the timing exact in order for the exposure to come out correctly. Erroneous plate exposures can result in incorrect screen percent values (too high or too low depending on if the exposure time was too long or too short). Wrong exposures can also prevent halftone dots from transferring to the plate at all. You can determine the correct exposure time by using a control strip. The light source in the exposure equipment ages and its characteristics change over time. Therefore you should regularly check that the exposure times are still accurate. Newer exposure frames automatically revise the time according to the aging of the lamp.

Before the exposure takes place, the film is suctioned to the plate by a vacuum action. It is important that the film is closely and evenly placed against the plate with no air bubbles to ensure an even transfer across the entire plate. It is also important that the plate production takes place in a dust-free environment. Dust prevents the film and plate from lying flush against each other. In addition, larger dust particles can be visible on the plate, particularly with positive film and plates.

If you are using negative film and plates, the illuminated areas of the plate's polymer layer are hardened during exposure. A small dot gain or dot reduction occurs during plate exposure, depending the type of film (negative or positive) used. When you chemically develop the plate, the unexposed, non-hardened, non-printing areas are washed away. The non-printing areas are now represented by the uncoated surfaces of the plate base, and the printing areas by the polymer layer. If you are using positive film and plates, the exposed surfaces of the plate's polymer layer are washed away during development instead, giving you essentially the same results.

Because the polymer layer of the plate is photosensitive, plates must be protected from light or they will be destroyed. A normal wet offset plate lasts for between 70,000 and 1,000,000 prints depending on the manufacturer and the type of plate. Plates can also be hardened to last for a particularly large run.

▶ **PLATE EXPOSURE**
Before the exposure takes place, the film is suctioned to the plate by a vacuum action to ensure that the film and plate are lying flush against each other. The plate is then exposed with the lamp of the exposure frame.

▶ **PLATE EXPOSURE**
The plate is exposed with ultraviolet light in an exposure frame. When exposing, curtains are used to prevent the light from harming the eye.

▶ **PLATE DEVELOPER**
After the plate has been exposed in the exposure frame it's developed.

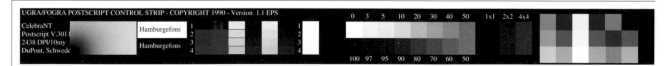

▶ **UGRA/FOGRA COLOR BAR**
With a color bar you can check that the plate has been exposed with the correct exposure time.

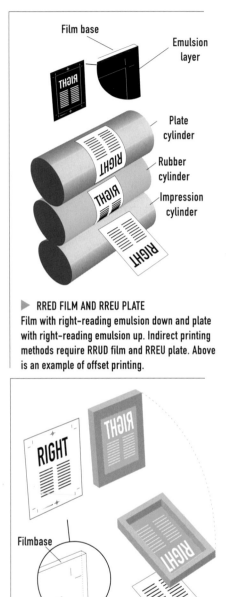

Film base

Emulsion layer

Plate cylinder

Rubber cylinder

Impression cylinder

▶ RRED FILM AND RREU PLATE
Film with right-reading emulsion down and plate with right-reading emulsion up. Indirect printing methods require RRUD film and RREU plate. Above is an example of offset printing.

Filmbase

Emulsion layer

▶ RREU FILM AND RRUD PRINTING FORM
Right-reading emulsion up and printing form with right-reading emulsion down. Direct printing methods require RREU film and RRUD printing form. Above is an example of screen printing.

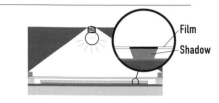

Film

Shadow

Film

Shadow

▶ DOT GAIN AT PLATE EXPOSURE
When using negative films and plates, the light does not penetrate the film vertically. As a result, it spreads to areas that are not supposed to be exposed and you will get dot gain on the plate.

▶ DOT REDUCTION AT PLATE EXPOSURE
When using positive films and plates, the light does not penetrate the film vertically. As a result, it spreads to areas that are not supposed to be exposed and you will get dot reductions on the plate.

PLATES WITH POSITIVE AND REVERSED IMAGES 11.2.3

When exposing the printing form, the emulsion layer of the film should always be placed directly against the printing form. A reversed print image on the film gives a correct print image on the printing form. When using an indirect printing method the plate leaves a reversed print image on a rubber blanket, which then transfers a correct image onto the paper. Direct printing uses right-reading film that exposes a reversed print image on the printing form, which in turn imprints a correct print image on the paper [see 11.1.2 and 11.1.3].

PLATE SETS 11.2.4

When printing with several colored inks, you need a separate plate for each color. This combination of plates is usually called a plate set, or in the case of a four-color print, a four-color plate set.

REGISTRATION 11.2.5

In order to line up all the component colors of a print precisely on top of each other, the film-plate-printing press chain has a registration system. For example, you will find a number of pins where the plates are tightened in the printing press. Holes are punched into the films and plates according to the location of these pins. When films are mounted into film assemblies, holes are punched into them. These holes correspond to the location of the pins in the printing press. There is also a steel ruler with pins spaced like those in the printing press on which you set the first film assembly and then mount the film for the next component color. On top of that, you set the film assembly for the next color, then the film for that color, and so on. This process ensures proper registration of all the colors.

Some imagesetters punch the film when it is exposed. That way you don't have to use mounting film when they have been imposed digitally. When you are exposing the plates, you use a similar steel ruler with pins. The plate is punched and both plate and film are mounted on the pins.

REPRINTING 11.3

Reprinting means printing additional copies of a project after the initial production run is completed. After a production is completed, the commercial printer is obligated to save the films used in the process for at least six months. If a customer anticipates that a project will need to be reprinted, they have to let the printer know that the films should be saved for a longer period of time. If the printer cannot store the films, the customer assumes that responsibility. When ordering reprints of old films it makes it easier for the printer if you can provide the date of the first printing and the name of the project, as well as any order number or invoice number associated with the job.

COMPUTER TO PLATE 11.4

In graphic production, you always want to eliminate unnecessary steps whenever possible. Outputting on film and copying it onto a printing plate is one such step, and it can be eliminated via a process called "Computer To Plate" or CTP. With CTP, the digital original is exposed directly onto the plate with a special platesetter. A platesetter essentially looks like a regular imagesetter for large film formats.

You can also transfer the digital material directly from the computer to the paper, eliminating the need for plates altogether. This technique is the basis of digital printing presses. Digital presses are most suitable for short print runs. Larger print runs still require a printing plate [see Printing 13.9].

PLATESETTERS 11.4.1

Platesetters essentially work as imagesetters for film. The machine is fed with printing plates instead of film. The emulsion layer differs slightly from that of traditional plates. There are two main types of plates, those that are exposed with light and those that are exposed with heat. Just like regular imagesetters, platesetters can be built with internal or external drums. There are also capstan or flatbed models [see Output 9.91]. Working with platesetters require that the basis for the printed product be digital. Digital imposition must be used [see Output 9.5]. In order to register a multi-color print, the plates are punched during exposure [see 11.2.5].

ADVANTAGES AND DISADVANTAGES OF CTP 11.4.2

In order to talk about the advantages of CTP, it is important to clarify what it is being compared to. Much of film-based production is still done via individual films (one film per page) that are manually mounted into finished impositions. Going from manual mounting to digital imposition obviously has certain advantages [see Output 9.5], but when you make the same comparison with imposed plates the advantages are less obvious. When comparing CTP technique to traditional production the latter process is defined as: output of digitally imposed film, film development, exposure of plates and plate development.

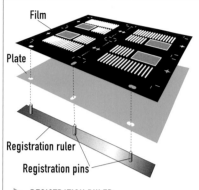

▶ REGISTRATION RULER
To be able to keep alignment between the plate and film, you punch holes in them. When mounting and exposing the plate as well as in the printing press, the material is attached to a ruler with pins.

▶ PLATE PUNCHER
A plate puncher punches holes in the plate before it's exposed.

▶ CTP EQUIPMENT
A modern platesetting system.

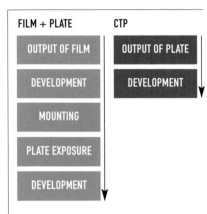

FILM + PLATE   CTP

OUTPUT OF FILM	OUTPUT OF PLATE
DEVELOPMENT	DEVELOPMENT
MOUNTING	
PLATE EXPOSURE	
DEVELOPMENT	

▶ **TRADITIONAL VS CTP FLOW**
Above you can see the film and plate production flows of traditional vs CTP. Because CTP productions have fewer steps, they have a faster flow.

▶ **PRECISION IN CTP**
With CTP you reach a lower dot gain and a better precision because the step between film and plate is eliminated.

Error margin Traditional		Error margin CTP	
film	+/− 2 %	plate	+/− 2 %
plate	+/− 2 %	print	+/− 4 %
print	+/− 4 %		
TOT	+/− 8 %	TOT	+/− 6 %

Advantages of CTP vs. Tradition Production

+ Reduced material consumption – no film or development chemicals needed.

+ Less manpower – no one is needed to process the film.

+ Faster workflow – entire steps of the production process are removed (exposing the plate and processing the film).

+ Environmentally friendly – CTP avoids the negative environmental aspects of chemical film development, as well as the costs related to recycling systems and peripheral devices. You should be aware, however, that CTP systems do require certain chemical developers, though not to the same extent as graphic film.

+ Better quality – CTP avoids potential losses in quality that may occur during film processing, including scratches in the film, and variations in the exposure. An imagesetter usually has an accuracy rate of +/− 2%.

+ Sharper dots.

Most of the above-mentioned advantages are of a technical and/or economic nature and primarily concern the printer itself. To the consumer, the saving is not yet particularly substantial, but in the long run printers using platesetters will likely be able to offer more competitive prices and shorter delivery times than traditional printers. CTP plates are currently more expensive than traditional plates, so part of the financial advantage disappears. However, as sales increase over time, the price of CTP plates will go down.

Disadvantages of CTP vs. Traditional Production:

– Restricted to digital format – CTP productions require that the basis for the printed matter as well as the imposition, be digital. Certain projects, like advertisements, would have to be delivered digitally.

– Re-making of plates – if for some reason a CTP plate is damaged, if an error occurs when it's ripped or if something has to be corrected after the plate is exposed, you have to create a completely new, imposed plate. It is more expensive to make a new plate than to discover and correct the error on the film. In traditional production, for example, if there is just a small error you can output the correction on a separate film and mount it manually.

– Reprinting costs – in traditional printing, the customer owns the rights to the imposed films for six months, whereas the customer does not own any rights to the digital files that are the basis for the CTP production. This means that the commercial printer does not have to save the CTP files. As a result, a reprint could, in theory, cost approximately as much as the first printing.

When using platesetters, you have to do digital proofs or output separate films and do analog proofs of all the images and pages to ensure that everything is correct before making the plate. If using analog proofs, you will benefit somewhat because it's less time-consuming and more managable. If outputting films, you will also benefit because it's easier to correct errors by outputting new films than to correct errors later in the production process.

Many of the disadvantages of CTP will be resolved in the near future. Efforts are already being made to digitize traditional production. Manufacturers have created printers compatible with CTP systems that can output rasterized files. These outputs act as a kind of blueprint to ensure that nothing goes wrong when rasterizing. The rasterized files can be saved so you don't have to start the process from scratch if there are errors, although they are large and take up a great deal of memory. Despite the drawback of their size, they can save you time because you don't have to re-rip the entire imposition. There are also systems that are able to exchange individual pages in ripped files, which provides increased flexibility.

In general, successful CTP-based production requires the following:
• Prepress-skilled personnel
• Imposition skills
• Entirely digital material
• Digital proofs
• Good quality-assurance systems
• Digital archives

DEVELOPMENT OF CTP 11.4.1

A platesetter is expensive and is primarily used by large commercial printers or prepress service providers, although inexpensive solutions designed for smaller companies are being developed. Thermal CTP plates will most likely become the standard. Most manufacturers are working on developing thermal plates that don't need to be chemically developed. These plates will be completely ready after exposure. This technology avoids developing liquids completely, which is a great advantage from an environmental point of view.

There are also CTP systems that expose the plates directly in the printing press. The platesetter is built into the printing press. The printing plate is automatically fastened to the printing cylinder and then exposed right there within the press. Heidelberg's Quickmaster DI is one example of this type of machine. It is likely that we will see more innovations like this in the future. ■

▶ CTP PROOF
Here you can see an ink-jet printer with a CTP system that can print rasterized files, a kind of blueprint for the CTP system. It's used to make sure that nothing unexpected happens when it is rasterized.

PAPER

12

CHAPTER 12 PAPER SELECTING A PAPER IS AN IMPORTANT PART OF THE PRINT PRODUCTION PROCESS. THE PAPER YOU CHOOSE NOT ONLY HAS A CERTAIN "FEEL" AND MAKES A CERTAIN AESTHETIC IMPRESSION, IT AFFECTS THE TEXT AND IMAGE QUALITY AS WELL AS FUNCTIONALITY OF THE PRINTING PRESS. OFF PRESS PROCESSING AND DISTRIBUTION COSTS CAN ALSO AFFECT THE PAPER SELECTION.

There are a number of different grades of paper, which are used for different purposes. We will limit our discussion to those used for graphic production, known as "fine papers." A paper's characteristics are of vital importance to the final printed result. Therefore you should select the paper as early as possible in the production process, preferably even before starting to work on the original artwork. This allows you to make all necessary adjustments to the production according to the paper selection, optimizing the quality of the outcome. Too often it happens that the paper is selected too late or that the decision is changed right before going to press. Many people also select paper without thinking about the consequences it has for the printed product that is produced. The choice of paper affects, among other things, readability, text and image quality, production of orig-

▶ SOME QUESTIONS YOU SHOULD ASK YOURSELF BEFORE CHOOSING PAPER:
- What "feel" do you want to communicate with the printed product?
- What is the expected life span?
- How much can it cost?
- What is more important, the readability of the text or image quality?
- Which screen frequency and tonal range should it have?
- Which printing method should be used?
- How should the printed product be off press processed?
- How should it be distributed?
- How important is the environmental impact for the buyer?

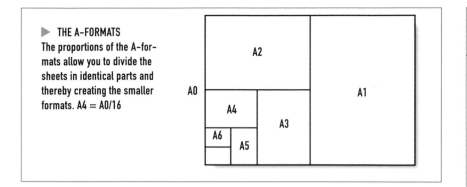

Book 25" × 38"	Bond 17" × 22"	Cover 20" × 26"	Grammage (g/m²)
30#	12#	16#	44
40#	16#	22#	59
45#	18#	25#	67
50#	20#	27#	74
60#	24#	33#	89
70#	28#	38#	104
80#	31#	44#	118
90#	35#	49#	133
100#	39#	55#	148
120#	47#	66#	178
33#	13#	18#	49
41#	16#	22#	61
51#	20#	28#	75
61#	24#	33#	90
71#	28#	39#	105
81#	32#	45#	120
91#	36#	50#	135
102#	40#	66#	158
91#	36#	50#	135
110#	43#	60#	163
119#	47#	65#	176
146#	58#	80#	216
164#	66#	90#	243
183#	72#	100#	271

▶ BASIS WEIGHTS
Basis weights for standard papers.

inal artwork, and reproduction, as well as the quality and durability of the printed product. We will cover these issues in more depth later in this chapter. We will begin, however, with a review of common paper terminology, and look at how paper is made and classified.

PAPER TERMINOLOGY 12.1

In order to understand how the type of paper influences the printed product, you should be familiar with the following terms: format, basis/substance weight, grain direction, dimensional stability, bulk and opacity.

FORMAT 12.1.1

When purchasing paper for a specific job it is best to stay with standard trim sizes to reduce the amount of waste [see cutting chart page 210]. There are a number of standard formats in the world of which the A-formats, i.e. A0, A1, A2, etc., are the most common. In the A-formats the relationship of the length of the page to the width is 1:√2 (the square root of 2 is approximately 1.414).

This means that a page that is 210 millimeters wide would be 210 × 1.414, or 297, millimeters high. The A formats are based on A0, which has a surface of 1 square meter and a width-to-length ratio of 1:√2. For example, when you divide an A0-sheet in half across the long side, you get two A1-sheets, each with a surface area of half a square meter and the same width-to-length ratio.

In the United States, stock paper sizes are much less standardized and are based on a combination of the size of the presses most commonly used and the most popular trim sizes for books.

BASIS/SUBSTANCE WEIGHT 12.1.2

In the U.S. a paper's weight is given in pounds per ream (500 sheets) calculated on the basis size for a specific grade of paper. For example, a 60 pound (60#) book paper is a paper for which 500 sheets at the basis size of 25" × 38" weighs 60 pounds [see table].

A paper's weight in grams per square meter [g/m²] is called grammage substance, or gsm, and is the most common measurement of a paper's weight outside of the United States. When talking about an 80-gram paper you are referring to a paper that weighs 80 grams per square meter. So, what does an 80-gram A4-sheet weigh? As explained above,

▶ Formula to convert basis weight to grammage:

$$\frac{\text{Basis Weight} \times 1406.5}{\text{Basis Size}} = \text{g/m}^2$$

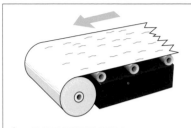

► GRAIN DIRECTION PART 1
Most of the paper's fibers orient themselves to the longitudinal direction of the paper web.

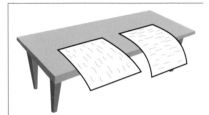

► GRAIN DIRECTION PART 2
The fiber direction of a paper sheet is visible when you let the paper hang over a table edge—the end that bends the most is opposite the fiber direction.

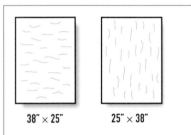

38" × 25"   25" × 38"

► GRAIN DIRECTION PART 3
The paper manufacturer's measurements tell you which machine direction the paper has. The first number in the measurement always indicates the side opposite the fiber direction.

you get 16 pieces of A4 from a single A0 sheet. The A0-sheet is 1 square meter. This means that the A4-sheet weighs 80 g divided by 16, or 5 grams.

GRAIN DIRECTION 12.1.3

When the paper is manufactured, most of its fibers orient themselves to the longitudinal direction of the paper web. This direction is usually referred to as the paper's grain direction. Because most fibers are oriented in one direction, it is more difficult for the paper to bend in that direction. You can take advantage of this trait when trying to figure out the grain direction of a particular piece of paper. Let the paper hang over a table edge—the end that bends the most is opposite the machine direction. You can also pinch along the paper edge between a finger and a nail. The edge that dents the most is opposite of the machine direction. Machine direction is important in certain printing methods. If it is difficult for the paper to bend and follow the intended path through the printing press, there is more of a chance that problems will occur when running the press. In this case, you would want to load the paper so that it bends easily, with the grain direction opposite the printing direction. It is also important to have the correct grain direction when folding paper. If you fold opposite the grain direction, the fibers are broken down and it looks as if the paper is cracking. Folding paper along the grain direction will give you a fine, smooth crease instead. [see Off Press Processing 14.2]

The paper manufacturer's measurements tell you which grain direction the paper has. The first number in the measurement always indicates the side opposite the grain direction. Consequently, a paper with the measurement 25" × 38" has a grain direction opposite its short side. Conversely, a paper with the measurement 38" × 25" has the grain direction opposite its long side.

DIMENSIONAL STABILITY 12.1.4

Because paper has a fiber direction and the fibers have particular dimensional characteristics, the paper takes on these characteristics. Wet paper fibers shrink and bond less lengthwise than widthwise as they dry. When paper fibers shrink simultaneously while drying, the paper web tightens in the machine direction and causes tension in the paper structure. The tension is higher in the fiber direction. Because the fibers' dimensional change is higher in the opposite direction and because there are no particular tensions across the paper web, the paper is much more inclined to change dimension opposite the fiber direction. Thus the paper changes asymmetrically when exposed to variations in humidity. This phenomenon means that you always get misregistrations in different directions in wet offset printing [see Printing 13.3.6 and 13.5.1]. However, a paper with good dimensional stability maintains its shape comparatively well throughout the entire print run and thereby reduces the risk of misregistration.

BULK 12.1.5

The relationship between the thickness of the paper and its weight is called bulk and is expressed in the U.S. as pages per inch (ppi). This may range from 200 to over 1,000 ppi depending on the type of paper, its basis weight and finish. Bulk is a measurement of how voluminous a paper is. Paper with a low ppi is lightweight, thick and porous, whereas paper with a high ppi is thin, heavy and compact. When using glue binding, paper with a higher bulk is preferred to that with a low bulk. In order to ensure a strong binding, the glue has to penetrate into the paper, which is easier with a porous, high-bulk stock. Papers with a high bulk generally feel stiffer and thicker than low-bulk papers with the same weight.

OPACITY 12.1.6

The opacity of a paper refers to how well light penetrates and is absorbed by the paper. A paper that is 100% opaque is completely non-transparent. The higher the opacity, the less transparent the paper. High opacity is often preferred for printed matter because you don't want text and images showing through both sides of a page. An example of a paper with very low opacity is wax paper.

It is particularly important that newsprint and uncoated papers have a high opacity. When printing ink is applied to this type of paper its oil component sinks into the paper, allowing the pigment to stick to the surface of the paper [see Printing 13.1.4]. Similar to a grease stain on paper, this oil can negatively affect the opacity and the pigment can show through to the other side. This primarily applies to newsprint where the oil component of the ink is relatively high.

WHAT PAPER IS MADE OF 12.2

When making paper you start out with pulp. Pulp consists of cellulose fibers extracted from wood. There are two types of paper pulp: chemical and mechanical. When making chemical pulp the cellulose fibers are extracted from the wood by boiling it with chemical ingredients. To make mechanical pulp, the wood is ground to extract the cellulose fibers. Chemical pulp usually consists of a mix of long-fibered pulp from coniferous trees (about 2-3.5 mm) and short-fibered pulp from deciduous trees (about 1-1.5 mm), whereas the main raw material for mechanical pulp is fiber from coniferous trees, primarily spruce.

During paper production, these short-fibered and long-fibered pulps are usually mixed together; the proportions depend on what characteristics the paper needs to have. The fibers of coniferous trees are relatively long, and they bond quite securely to each other because they tend to have several points of contact. This results in a stronger paper. Fibers of deciduous trees, which are a bit shorter and therefore form a somewhat weaker bond than coniferous fibers, are useful for better opacity.

> **WOOD-PULP/WOOD-FREE**

- Paper pulp consisting of more than 10% mechanical pulp and less than 90% chemical pulp is called "wood-pulp paper."

- Paper pulp consisting of less than 10% mechanical pulp and more than 90% chemical pulp is called "wood-free paper."

> **THE STOCK**

The stock is the mixture of ingredients required to make a particular paper. The stock consists of:

- Water
- Fibers
- Fillers
- Sizing agents
- Color

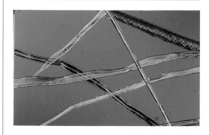

> **PULP FROM CONIFEROUS TREES**
Pulp from coniferous trees is long-fibered. The fibers are around 2-3.5 mm.

> **PULP FROM DECIDUOUS TREES**
Pulp from deciduous trees is short-fibered. The fibers are around 1-1.5 mm.

► BEATEN CELLULOSE FIBERS
Beating the fibers in the stock preparation makes for better bonding among the fibers, provides many points of contact, and results in a stronger paper.

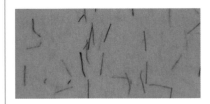

► PIECES OF A PLANT IN THE PAPER
Stock preparation is the time to add special effects like pieces of plants or paper.

► THE PAPER MACHINE
Paper machines are huge. Note the size of the people compared to the machine.

Paper pulp consisting of more than 10% mechanical pulp and less than 90% chemical pulp is used to make a paper called "wood-pulp paper," while paper produced from pulp consisting of less than 10% mechanical pulp and more than 90% chemical pulp is called, oddly enough, "wood-free paper." Wood-free print paper is strong and very white, and is used for most types of printed products. Wood-pulp paper often has a slight yellow-grayish tint and is used for publications like newspapers and catalogues. Wood-pulp paper yellows more quickly than wood-free. By adding less mechanical pulp to the chemical pulp, you increase the bulk and opacity of a paper while maintaining the whiteness and capability for good image reproduction. Doing this lessens the differences between wood-free and wood-pulp paper. Mechanical pulp is less expensive to produce than chemical pulp, so wood-pulp papers are generally less expensive for the consumer. The terms wood-free and wood-pulp are primarily derived from customs regulations that assign different tariffs to the different types of paper. Different countries have different standards for what is considered wood-free and wood-pulp respectively, with the result that this distinction is not as commonly used today.

Approximately 45% of America's total paper consumption is recycled. Cellulose fibers can be recycled five or six times and provide good raw material for new paper given the right process. In recent years, fine papers consisting of 100% recycled fibers have appeared on the market.

HOW PAPER IS MADE 12.3

After the paper pulp is made, three steps remain in the creation of the paper: stock preparation, the paper machine and post treatment.

STOCK PREPARATION 12.3.1

During stock preparation, the cellulose fibers are beaten, fillers and sizing agents are added and any desired color is added. Beating the pulp makes for better bonding among the fibers, and results in stronger paper. The most common fillers are ground marble or limestone ($CaCO_3$) and clay. These ingredients improve the opacity and the color of the print on the paper. The fillers also provide the paper with softness and elasticity. Sizing agents like alum and rosin make the paper more resistant to water absorption. They also help prevent ink from being absorbed into the paper and spread sideways, a phenomenon called "feathering." Stock preparation is also the time to add color or other special effects like flower petals, etc., to the paper.

► THE PAPER MACHINE
Here's a basic sketch of a paper machine. The stock is poured out onto the wire in the headbox. The paper is drained in the wire 35–50%. In the press and dryer section, the paper is dried 90–95%. After that, the paper can be glazed and rolled up on a roll.

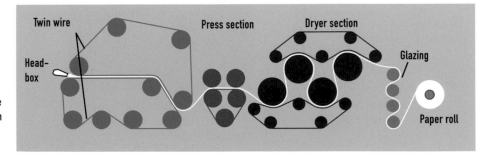

THE PAPER MACHINE 12.3.2

At the entrance of the paper machine, or "headbox," the pulp stock is about 99% water. The most extensive draining of the stock takes place in the twin-wire where the water is sucked up by two straining-cloths. The wire moves at high speed, which means that the paper has a very short time to be drained. In order for the paper pulp to reach the speed of the wire, the pulp has to accelerate from the headbox. This acceleration causes most fibers to orient in the direction of the machine. This causes the paper to manifest different characteristics lengthwise and crosswise, which in turn affects the dimensional stability.

It is the pulp flow from the headbox that determines the weight of the paper. By varying the flow and concentration of the stock that is poured out onto the wire, you can create paper with different weights. The "formation" of the paper is also created on the wire. If you hold up a piece of paper to a light source and it looks even – i.e. without "clouds" – the paper is considered to have a good formation. Good formation is important for good print quality, especially with offset printing, because of the paper's absorption of the oil component of the ink [see Print 13.1.4]. Offset printing on a paper with a poor formation manifests blotchiness in the color, especially in flat, even tint areas.

After the wire section, the paper is fed into the press section. This consists of a press cylinder that uses filters to remove more water. You can affect the bulk of the paper in the press section. In the next step, the paper is dried. The drying level depends on what the paper will be used for. Paper intended for sheet-fed offset printing, web-fed offset printing and photocopying all have different drying levels, for example.

If the paper is to be surface-sized, it is first dried in a dryer section. After that it is surface-sized in a size press and then dried again in the dryer section. The paper is surface-sized to give it a strong surface that can take the pressure it is exposed to when the ink is added in the printing press [see Print 13.5.2].

POST TREATMENT 12.3.3

The post treatment a paper receives is determined by what paper quality and surface characteristics it is intended to have. A post treatment that is executed in the paper machine is a "machine finish" or "calender finish." During this process, the paper is pressed to an even thickness and given a smooth surface to ensure quality prints.

To make the paper even more suitable for printing, it can be coated. The process of coating the paper can be compared to evening-out the surface with putty and a putty knife. The coating itself consists of a binder (starch or latex) and a pigment (fine kaolin clay or calcium carbonate). In addition, other ingredients are added to provide various characteristics. Coating improves both the optical and print qualities of the paper. You can also use a higher screen frequency when printing because the surface of the paper is smoother [see Output 9.1]. Coated paper absorbs ink more quickly and evenly, and the prints will have a glossier finish.

Paper can also be glazed to give it a very high gloss. Glazing provides for better image quality but reduces opacity and stiffness. During glazing, the paper is rubbed between different pairs of cylinders. This process is called calendering.

Finally, the paper is taken up on rolls or cut to sheets, depending on its intended use.

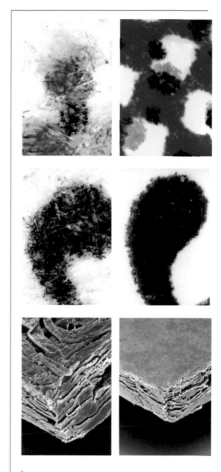

▶ UNCOATED VS COATED
In the images above, you see uncoated (to the left) and coated (to the right) paper. When the paper is coated, the optical characteristics and printability of the paper improve. You can use a higher screen frequency and get a higher gloss in the print because the paper absorbs the ink more quickly and evenly.

The coating consists of a binder (starch or latex) and a pigment (fine kaolin clay or calcium carbonate) and is applied to the paper in a thin layer. In addition, other ingredients are added to provide various characteristics. The process of coating paper can be compared to evening-out the surface with putty and a putty knife.

▶ ROLL
The paper is rolled up on enormous rolls in the end of the paper machine.

▶ PAPER PRICES DIFFER

• Paper sheets are more expensive than paper on a roll.

• Glossy papers are more expensive than matte or silk papers.

• Wood-free paper is more expensive than wood-pulp paper.

• Colored paper is more expensive than white.

• Paper with cotton fibers, rag paper, is more expensive than papers without.

▶ PAPER STOCK
It is usually worthwhile to use the papers the printing house normally uses and has handy in stock.

CLASSIFICATION OF PAPERS 12.4

Paper is categorized according to the following criteria: surface, type of pulp and weight.

COATED OR UNCOATED 12.4.1

Commercial printers commonly distinguish between coated and uncoated paper. Coated paper can be further divided into additional categories depending on the amount of coating it has: lightly coated, medium coated, highly coated or art paper. Paper can also be treated so it is matte or glossy. Examples of uncoated papers include stationery, photocopying paper and the paper used for paperback books. Most uncoated papers are surface-sized in order to ensure good surface bonding strength. Examples of coated papers include paper used for brochures, art books and magazines.

WOOD-FREE, WOOD-PULP, RECYCLED AND RAG PAPER 12.4.2

This classification is mostly based on how the paper is produced and is increasingly of lesser importance in modern graphic print production. Wood-pulp paper has a shorter life span, poorer surface strength and is not very white, but it does have higher opacity and bulk. Wood-pulp papers are generally less expensive than wood-free papers.

The increased demand for paper with recycled fibers has contributed to the existence of many different fine papers with recycled fibers as a base. The most common varieties are either 50, 75 or 100% recycled paper. Great improvements have been made in the printability and runability of recycled paper. It also turns out that recycled fibers give paper a high opacity.

If at least 25% of the paper pulp is made up of cotton fibers, the resulting paper is called rag paper. Rag paper is characterized by durability and a comfortable smoothness (it resembles fabric a bit), which it gets from the cotton fibers. Rag paper is appropriate for certain types of special prints. Lamination, for example, is one type of print often done on rag paper.

MATTE/SILK OR CALENDERED 12.4.3

Uncoated paper can be glossy or matte. Coated paper can also be slightly glossy or matte. Matte coated textures have been developed, called matte silk. The texture is smooth but non-reflective, which means that paper treated with this coating will produce prints with a combination of high image quality and readability.

PAPER OR CARDBOARD 12.4.4

Cardboard is a stiff paper product. Paper manufacturers usually define cardboard as a paper whith a weight greater than 80 lbs. If a paper exists both in a light paper weight and in heavier cardboard weight, the cardboard version is called fine cardboard. This type of cardboard is produced in the same way as paper.

Cardboard produced in special cardboard machines is called graphic cardboard. There are two types of graphic cardboard: multi-layered board and solid board. Multi-layered board is made up of several layers of different types of pulp. Solid board is also made up of many layers, but all the layers are the same type of pulp.

HOW TO CHOOSE A PAPER 12.5

When choosing paper there are many criteria to evaluate: the feel of the printed product, its intended life span and price, readability vs. image quality, the printing method and off press processes you intend to use, how the product will be distributed, the environmental impact, and the requirements of the printing house. All these aspects affect the choice of paper in their own way.

THE FEEL OF THE PRINTED PRODUCT 12.5.1

The choice of paper is very important in creating the feel you want your printed product to have. Your printed product has an intended purpose—for example, you want your material to sell something or to inform people, etc. Different papers can help you communicate completely different impressions, depending on the effect you desire. Often the choice of paper is also influenced by aesthetic trends.

THE LIFE SPAN OF THE PRINTED PRODUCT 12.5.2

As most people know, newsprint paper can't sit around for long before it starts turning yellow. Since newspapers are only meant to last a short time, this is not such a problem. On the other hand, if you want your printed material to last for a long time, there are two kinds of paper to choose from: age resistant and archive. The main difference between these two paper types is that archive paper has a higher strength, due to additional cotton fibers. In general, wood-pulp paper is more sensitive to aging than wood-free paper. However, you can add a calcium carbonate filler to make the paper more resistant to aging.

COST OF THE PRINTED PRODUCT 12.5.3

Paper prices vary widely depending on the quality of the stock. The price of paper also depends on what kind of agreement the printers might have with the different paper manufacturers and the quantity in which you buy the paper. Because of this, paper prices can vary significantly from printer to printer.

   You should keep in mind that with smaller runs, paper price has a relatively small effect on the total cost for the printed product, whereas paper costs play a crucial role in the total cost of large print runs.

READABILITY VS. IMAGE QUALITY 12.5.4

When printing images, you normally want to achieve as high a contrast as possible between printing ink and paper. However, when it comes to printed products in which text information is more important you have to abandon this ideal. Too much contrast between the paper and the printed text can cause eyestrain for the reader. Therefore, a slightly yellow-toned paper is generally recommended for printed products with a lot of text. The paper should also be matte or even uncoated in order to avoid distracting reflections. Textbooks are an example of a type of product usually printed on uncoated, yellow-toned papers.

   Images look best on coated, glossy, bright white paper because it provides maximum contrast. If you print images on colored paper or a paper with a low whiteness, be aware

▶ PRINTING ON COLORED PAPER
When you print on colored paper, the images have to be adjusted according to the color of the paper. In some cases it's impossible to avoid problems.

▶ PRINTABILITY

Printability is the sum of the paper's characteristics that creates the prerequisites for high print quality.

• The pores of the paper make it possible to absorb the printing ink properly and avoid smearing (the ink smears on the following sheet). At the same time, you don't want the print to go too deep and become visible from the backside of the paper.

• The surface of the paper shouldn't restrict the contact between the printing form, the printing surface in the printing press and the paper.

• The paper has to have an adequate surface strength to prevent paper fragments from tearing off, causing pickouts in the print. The pickouts are white spots in the print and are primarily visible in monochromatic tint areas.

• Porous paper absorbs the incoming light and provides high opacity.

• The brightness of the paper is important because it provides a high contrast between print and ink.

that it is difficult to compensate for the color of the paper in the printing process, and you will often get a lesser image quality as a result. Also keep in mind that colored text and illustrations can come out wrong when printed on colored paper. If the images and text are of equal importance, you usually compromise by using a matte, coated paper. To achieve an optimal image quality, the ink must be evenly applied to the paper so that it does not look blotchy. The smooth surface of a coated paper allows for an even application of ink.

SCREEN FREQUENCY AND TONAL RANGE 12.5.5

Every paper has limitations in terms of the screen frequency it can handle and its ability to reproduce the complete tonal range of an image [see Images 5.4.2 and 5.4.3]. Papers that can handle higher screen frequencies will give you better image quality. These two factors have to be taken into consideration when choosing a paper.

Paper manufacturers recommend maximum screen frequencies for their different papers. When images are scanned and color-separated, they must be adjusted to the screen frequency and tonal range of the particular paper you've chosen. Of course, this means that you have to make your paper selection before you scan your images.

PRINTING METHOD 12.5.6

Some printing methods require that the paper used have a certain machine direction in order to ensure smooth operation of the printing press. Different printing methods also have limitations as to the thickness and sheet size of the paper. Offset printing, for example, requires a paper with a high surface bonding strength. The viscous printing ink used in wet offset printing has a tendency to rip the paper fibers and, at the same time, the water used in the process weakens the paper. In dry offset, there is no water to weaken the paper but the ink has a higher viscosity [see Printing 13.1.5]. Gravure printing, on the other hand, requires that the paper have a very smooth surface to avoid problems with the application of the ink.

Printers who print with digital printing presses will recommend papers based on their own proof runs, and you should contact them for information before you begin produc-

▶ **WEIGHT STATED IN GRAMMAGE FOR A PRINTED PRODUCT IN A4 FORMAT**

		Number of pages (2 pages=1 sheet)							
	g/m²	2	4	6	8	12	16	24	32
Grammage substance	70	4,38	8,75	13,13	17,50	26,25	35,00	52,50	70,00
	80	5,00	10,00	15,00	20,00	30,00	40,00	60,00	80,00
	90	5,63	11,25	16,88	22,50	33,75	45,00	67,50	90,00
	100	6,25	12,50	18,75	25,00	37,50	50,00	75,00	100,00
	115	7,19	14,38	21,56	28,75	43,13	57,50	86,25	115,00
	130	8,13	16,25	24,38	32,50	48,75	65,00	97,50	130,00
	150	9,38	18,75	28,13	37,50	56,25	75,00	112,50	150,00

tion. Xerographic techniques (laser printer outputs or copying) work best with a slightly uneven paper surface, and uncoated paper is often recommended. This is because the toner powder used in these processes has difficulty adhering to coated paper. You cannot use regular coated offset paper in a laser printer, but paper manufacturers have developed special papers with a coated feel just for xerographic machines. In turn, these special papers are not particularly appropriate for offset printing. This type of paper does not absorb the oil component of the offset printing inks and the pigment has difficulty - adhering to the paper surface as a result [see Printing 13.1.4].

OFF PRESS PROCESSING OF THE PRINTED PRODUCT 12.5.7

Folding is affected by the paper type. You have to remember to fold the paper in the direction of the grain to ensure a smooth fold. If you fold against the grain, the fibers will break and it will look as if the surface of the paper is cracked [see Off Print Processing 14.2].

Thick or stiff papers always have to be scored before they can be folded. Scoring means that the fibers are delaminated along a line where the fold will be. After the paper is scored the fibers are easily displaced when folded and do not resist bending. Scoring can also save the day if you don't get the grain directions right [see Off Press Processing 14.7].

If you are using the glue binding technique when binding your printed product, the thicker and lighter the paper – i.e., the higher the bulk – the more durable the binding will be. Thicker paper simply has a larger surface area for the adhesive, and the paper's porous nature makes it easier for the adhesive to penetrate the paper, creating a deeper, sturdier bond. Coated and glossy papers are less appropriate for glue binding [see Off Press Processing 14.7].

DISTRIBUTION OF THE PRINTED PRODUCT 12.5.8

If you are creating a printed product that is to be distributed via postal mail, it's important to keep postage rates in mind when choosing paper. Selecting a paper with a lower weight might help you avoid a higher postage rate and save you a lot of money.

ENVIRONMENTAL IMPACT 12.5.9

It is said that 30% of a printed product's total negative impact on the environment stems directly from the paper used. Therefore it is a good idea to try and select a paper that has minimal negative impact on the environment. ■

Trimmed page size (inches)	Number of Printed Pages	Number From Sheet	Standard Paper Size (inches)
4 × 9	4	12	25 × 38
	8	12	38 × 50
	12	4	25 × 38
	16	6	38 × 50
	24	2	25 × 38
4 1/4 × 5 3/8	4	32	35 × 45
	8	16	35 × 45
	16	8	35 × 45
	32	4	35 × 45
4 1/2 × 6	4	16	25 × 38
	8	8	25 × 38
	16	4	25 × 38
	32	2	25 × 38
5 1/2 × 8 1/2	4	16	35 × 45
	8	8	35 × 45
	16	4	35 × 45
	32	2	35 × 45
6 × 9	4	8	25 × 38
	8	4	25 × 38
	16	2	25 × 38
	32	2	38 × 50
8 1/2 × 11	4	4	23 × 35
	8	2	23 × 35
	16	2	35 × 45
9 × 12	4	4	25 × 38
	8	2	25 × 38
	16	2	38 × 50

▶ CUTTING CHARTS
This chart shows how many pages one can expect
to get from some standard U.S. paper sizes.

PRINTING

13

CHAPTER 13 PRINTING

OUR EVERYDAY LIVES ARE FULL OF PRINTED PRODUCTS. MOST OF THEM ARE PRINTED ON PAPER, BUT THERE ARE ALSO PRINTED PRODUCTS ON MATERIALS SUCH AS PLASTIC, GLASS, ALUMINUM AND FABRIC. IN ORDER TO PRODUCE ALL THESE DIFFERENT PRODUCTS, COMMERCIAL PRINTERS HAVE DEVELOPED A NUMBER OF DIFFERENT PRINTING METHODS.

▶ CHOOSING A PRINTING METHOD

The choice of printing method is primarily determined by:

• Quality requirements

• Edition size

• Printing material

• Product type

• Print format

Most print products are printed on paper, but you can also print on other types of materials. The printing method you use for a particular project is usually determined by the quality requirements, the edition size, the printing material, and the format and type of printed product you are creating. In this chapter, we will cover the different printing methods and their characteristics. We will review a number of printing phenomena and how to evaluate the quality of a print. The emphasis will be on offset printing, which is by far the most common printing method in use today.

▶ DIFFERENT PRODUCTS REQUIRE DIFFERENT PRINTING METHODS

PRODUCTS AND MATERIALS	PRINTING METHOD	SCREEN FREQUENCY
Signs, clothing and bags. Various materials and surfaces, large surfaces, non-flexible surfaces	Screen Printing	50–100 lpi
Packaging	Flexographic Printing	90–120 lpi
Printed products in large editions, newspapers, catalogues, packaging	Gravure Printing	120–200 lpi
Most printed products printed on paper, for example newspapers, magazines, packaging, folders and brochures	Offset Printing	65–300 lpi

OFFSET PRINTING 13.1

All offset printing is based on the lithographic principle. There are two basic methods, wet offset, which is the most common, and dry or water-free offset, which uses silicone instead of water.

THE LITHOGRAPHIC PRINCIPLE 13.1.1

Lithographic printing works differently from stamp-type printing, in which the printing surfaces are separated from the non-printing surfaces of the image by differences in surface elevation. In lithography, printed and non-printed areas are separated by their different chemical characteristics. On a lithographic plate, the areas that print are usually made of a polymer, and the non-printing areas are usually expressed in aluminum. Because the ink used in lithographic printing is greasy, the surfaces that attract the ink are called olio-filial (from the Greek words for grease – "olio," and friendly – "filial"). Surfaces that repel the printing ink are called olio-phobic ("phobic" is Greek for "fearful").

In wet offset printing, water is used to help repel ink from the areas of the plate that shouldn't print. The non-printing areas attract the water, while the areas that print repel it. Because of this, the areas of the plate that print are called hydrophobic (hydro=water) and the areas of the plate that don't are called hydrophilic. In water-free offset printing, the non-printing areas are coated with olio-phobic silicone instead. As you can see in the image to the right, there is a slight difference in elevation between the printing and non-printing surfaces on a finished offset plate, but this is not responsible for creating the printed image.

DAMPENING SOLUTION 13.1.2

So that the ink does not stick to the non-printing areas of the printing plate, the plate is dampened before the ink is added with a thin, even film of water. Alcohol is added to the water in order to ensure that it covers the entire non-printing area without creating droplets. Usually, 8 to 12% isopropyl alcohol is added to the dampening solution in order to achieve the desired characteristics for dampening and cleaning printing plates.

To get a good print, the ink should to some extent be mixed with water before being applied to the printing plate. The water is emulsified in the ink, which results in a mixture of small, discrete drops of the two liquids – a mix of oil and water, so to speak. The dampening solution must also have the correct pH value and hardness in order to work properly. Hard water contains a number of different mineral salts, which, in large amounts, can cause pigments in the printing ink to dissolve. When the pigments dissolve, they can mix with the water coating the non-printing parts of the plate, thus transferring color to parts of the image that should remain non-printing. This phenomenon is known as "toning." The hardness of the water is regulated by adding a hardness regulator. You adjust the dampening solution to buffer, regulate, the pH value.

THE RUBBER BLANKET 13.1.3

Offset printing is an indirect printing method, which means that the ink is not transferred to the paper directly from the printing plate. The plate cylinder first transfers the print image onto a rubber blanket cylinder, which in turn transfers the image to the

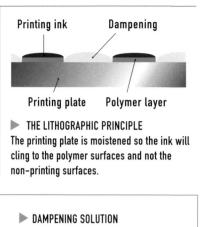

▶ THE LITHOGRAPHIC PRINCIPLE
The printing plate is moistened so the ink will cling to the polymer surfaces and not the non-printing surfaces.

▶ DAMPENING SOLUTION
Dampening solution is used in offset printing to:
- Make sure that the non-printing surfaces repel the printing ink
- Keep the plates clean of paper fragments
- Keep the plates cool during the printing process

▶ ALCOHOL IS ADDED TO THE DAMPENING SOLUTION
Alcohol is added to the dampening solution to help the water spread in an even film over the non-printing surfaces of the printing plate.

▶ TONING
Toning occurs when non-printing areas of the printing plate attract ink and become printing surfaces, causing unwanted blotches in the finished print (see background).

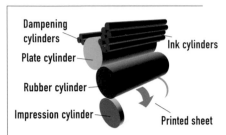

Dampening cylinders
Ink cylinders
Plate cylinder
Rubber cylinder
Impression cylinder
Printed sheet

▶ THE PRINTING UNIT

This sketch shows the basic workings of the printing unit in an offset press. This is how it prints:

1. Dampening solution is added and coats the non-printing surfaces of the printing plate.

2. Ink is added and adheres only to the printing surfaces of the plate.

3. The print image is transferred from the plate to the rubber blanket.

4. Paper is run between the rubber blanket cylinder and the impression cylinder and the rubber blanket transfers the inked image to the paper.

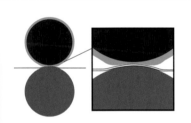

▶ THE PRINTING NIP

The rubber blanket is pressed in the "nip" between the rubber blanket cylinder and the impression cylinder.

▶ PRINTING INK

Printing ink has three important characteristics:

• Color

• Physical characteristics (viscosity, liquidity, etc.)

• Drying characteristics

---

paper. The paper passes between a rubber blanket cylinder and an impression cylinder. In indirect printing procedures, the image on the printing plate reads in the same direction as the final print, as opposed to direct printing methods like flexography and screen printing, in which the print is a mirror image on the printing form [see Film and Plates 11.1.2].

It is important that the rubber blanket can easily absorb the ink from the printing plate and transfer the ink to the paper. If the rubber blanket has difficulty transferring the ink to the paper, the paper surface can tear, causing what are called "pick-outs ," which appear as blotches in the printed areas of the image. The rubber blanket is subject to wear and damage and has to be changed frequently. Rubber blankets often need to be changed because of compression. For example, a blanket can be crushed by paper that has inadvertently folded over in the printing press. When this happens, the thickness of paper between the rubber blanket cylinder and the impression cylinder is too great and it compresses the flexible surface of the rubber blanket. A crushed rubber blanket loses elasticity in the compressed areas.

THE INK 13.1.4

The three most important characteristics of printing ink are:
• The chromatic characteristics of the ink, including its purity, its correspondence with the color standard used (The European Scale in Europe or SWOP in the USA), and the color saturation of the ink
• The physical characteristics of the ink, such as its liquidity and viscosity
• The drying characteristics on the paper used

The chromatic characteristics of the ink depend on its pigment. Pigment consists of small particles that can be both organic and inorganic in nature. For example, particles used in black pigment include chemical precipitates and soot. Pigments are suspended in a binding agent, which enables them to attach to paper. The binding agent gives the ink its liquid form and provides it with its lithographic characteristics. The physical characteristics of the ink, such as liquidity and viscosity, are also affected by the composition of the binder. The binding agent is also formulated to protect the pigments from dissolving in the dampening solution, which helps prevent toning.

Binding agents used in offset printing inks are made up of resin, alkyd and mineral oil. The combination of these materials helps determine the drying characteristics of the ink. When ink is first applied to paper, the paper absorbs the mineral oil in the ink, causing it to "set." This is considered to be the first phase of the drying process. It is important, however, that the paper does not absorb the pigment as well. If the pigment is absorbed, the colors will be less saturated. Hence, the pigment, the alkyd and resin in the ink form a kind of gel on the surface of the paper. This gel is just dry enough not to smear on the next print sheet when the sheets are placed on top of each other in the delivery bay.

The gel dries completely as the alkyd is oxidized. The alkyd undergoes a chemical reaction with the oxygen in the air. This is the second drying phase, called "curing," or oxidation. UV radiation is sometimes used to speed up the curing process. Printed sheets are also sometimes sprayed with drying powder in order to prevent smearing. The drying powder actually keeps the sheets physically separate so that the ink on one sheet cannot smear the sheet on top of it, and different grades of powder are used depending on the texture of the paper. Drying powders usually consist of starch or calcium carbonate ($KaCO_3$).

WATER-FREE OFFSET 13.1.5

Water-free offset printing essentially functions the same way as wet offset printing. As mentioned earlier, water-free offset printing uses a silicone layer instead of water to differentiate the non-printing surfaces of the printing plate from the printing surfaces. Water-free offset requires special printing plates, coated with a silicone layer. When these coated plates are exposed and developed, the silicone is washed off of the exposed areas revealing the printing surfaces of the plate. Water-free offset printing uses ink with a higher viscosity than that used for wet offset printing. Water-free offset presses are often rebuilt wet offset presses in which tempered cylinders have been added so that the temperature of the ink – and hence its printing characteristics – can be controlled.

One advantage of water-free offset printing is that you can print with a higher color saturation, or ink density, which results in a higher tonal range. Water-free offset also allows for sharper printed dots, which means you can print with a higher screen frequency. There is also a shorter makeready time with water-free offset printing because you don't have to set the ink and humidity balance. In addition, water-free offset printing is more environmentally sound than wet offset printing because it does not require alcohol additives in the dampening solution. A wet offset printing press is less expensive, however, because it does not require controlled temperatures. Another disadvantage of water-free offset printing is that pick-outs are more common, because of the greater viscosity of the ink and the fact that there is no water to clean off the rubber blanket [see 13.5.2]. Tradition also contributes to the continuing popularity of the wet offset printing method, but many feel that water-free offset printing will become more common in the future.

THE OFFSET PRINTING PRESS 13.2

There are two different types of offset printing: sheet-fed offset and web-fed offset. The most common printing method in North America is sheet-fed offset. Therefore we will from now on focus on sheet-fed offset and its function.

WEB-FED OFFSET PRINTING 13.2.1

Web-fed offset printing is usually used for creating prints of a somewhat lesser quality. It is most suitable for large-volume editions – say, for example, 50,000 units and up. You can rarely do any kind of advanced off press processing with web-fed offset printing; such processing is usually limited to the folding and stitching of printed products [see Off Press Processing 14.14.1]. Common web-fed offset products include newspapers, periodicals, folders and other prints of lesser quality.

SHEET-FED OFFSET PRINTING 13.2.2

With sheet-fed offset you can print almost any paper-based printed product. As the name indicates, printing is done on paper sheets. This method allows for an enormous selec-

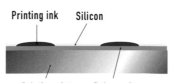

▶ **WATER-FREE OFFSET PRINTING PLATE**
The non-printing surfaces of a water-free offset printing plate are coated with silicone, which repels the greasy ink, making a dampening solution unnecessary.

▶ **WATER-FREE OFFSET PRINTING: +/−**

+ Sharper dots make it possible to print with a higher screen frequency

+ No need to balance the ink/humidity, which speeds up the makeready process

+ Allows for a higher maximum density, which gives you a wider range of colors

+ No dampening solution means less negative impact on the environment

− Pickouts are more common, in part because the ink is more viscous and in part because there is no dampening solution to keep things clean.

− The printing units need to be temperature-controlled, which makes for a more expensive printing press.

▶ **THE SHEET-FED OFFSET PRINTING PRESS**
In the foreground you can see the delivery bay where printed sheets are collected as they come out of the press. The four separate printing units (one for each color) are visible in the background.

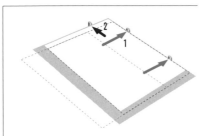

tion of paper in terms of both finish and quality. A wide range of high quality off-press processing is available for sheet-fed prints, including lamination and glue binding of the printed product. Common sheet-fed products include advertising brochures, annual reports, posters and books, as well as other high quality printed products.

We will now review the actual sheet-fed printing process, starting with how the sheets are transported through the printing press.

SHEET TRANSPORTATION 13.2.3

In a sheet-fed press, the mechanisms that grab the sheets and feed them through the printing press directly affect the final quality of the printed product. This machinery essentially has three main tasks:

- Pick up a single sheet of paper from the paper stack
- Make sure that only one sheet is fed into the press at a time
- Adjust—or register, as it is called—the paper in the machine so that all sheets enter into the printing press in exactly the same way. This is important in order to ensure that the image is printed in exactly the same place on each sheet of paper.

The part of the printing press that picks up sheets from the paper stack is called the feeder. There are several different types of feeders but the most common is a pneumatic feeder with suction heads that lift up the sheet. As the sheet is lifted, the heads separate the top sheet from the one below with a blast of air. This ensures that only one sheet is fed into the machine at a time. The feeder takes the sheet it has picked up and places it on the feed board. The paper on the feed board is checked again to make sure there is only one sheet. If more than one sheet is fed into the press at a time, there is a great risk of crushing the rubber blanket.

In order to ensure accurate off press processing of printed products, it is important that the placement of the printed image on the paper sheets is exactly the same throughout the run. If they are not, the accuracy of off press finishing like folds, staples, etc., will be compromised. In order to avoid this, the paper sheets are adjusted, or registered, on the feed board before they continue through the printing press. The sheets are registered against two edges, the front edge, called the gripper's edge, and one of the side edges, called the feed edge. The sheets are registered only along two edges because the size of the sheets usually varies slightly throughout a paper stack.

It is important to keep track of the corner formed by the two registration edges. When the sheets are to be printed on both sides, you should make sure that when the second side is printed, the same edges are used to register the paper. Otherwise, it is difficult to ensure that the front and back of the sheets will match up correctly throughout the run [see Off Press Processing 14.13.3]. As we mentioned earlier, it is also important for the off press processing that the print is registered throughout the run. Because of this, the corner formed by the gripper edge and the feed edge is usually marked on the stack of prints prior to off-press processing.

THE PRINTING UNIT 13.2.4

The part of the printing press in which the ink is transferred to the paper is called the printing unit. A printing unit in an offset press generally consists of three parts: a plate cylinder, a rubber blanket cylinder and an impression cylinder. The construction of the printing unit and its placement within the printing press varies, but for simplicity's sake we will look at four main versions: three-cylinder units, five-cylinder units, satellite units and perfector units.

Three-cylinder units are currently the most common units found in sheet-fed offset presses. A three-cylinder unit consists of an impression cylinder, a rubber blanket cylinder and a plate cylinder. This unit prints one color on one side of the paper at a time. For multi-color printing, several three-cylinder units – one for each printing color – are lined up after each other.

Some multi-color printing presses composed of three-cylinder systems can turn over the paper sheets with a converter unit, allowing some of the printing units to print on one side of the paper, while the rest of the units print on the reverse side. The technique of printing both sides of the paper in one run through the printing press is called perfecting printing. A perfecting press producing four-color prints on both sides of a sheet in a single run (4 + 4) would have eight three-cylinder units lined up with a converter unit in the middle.

Five-cylinder units are also used primarily in sheet-fed offset presses. The five-cylinder unit consists of two plate cylinders and two rubber blanket cylinders with one common impression cylinder. This setup allows the unit to print with two colors on one side of the paper.

Satellite units are mainly in web-fed offset presses, but are also suitable for use in sheet-fed offset presses. A sheet that runs through a satellite system is held with the same griper throughout the printing press, which facilitates registration between the printing inks. The satellite system generally consists of four plate cylinders, four rubber blanket cylinders and a common impression cylinder. This setup allows the unit to print four colors on one side of the paper. There are also satellite systems with both five and six units.

Perfector units are exclusively used in web-fed offset presses, and print on both sides of the paper in one run through the printing press. This unit has no impression cylinder; instead two rubber blanket cylinders, placed on either side of the paper web, act as impression cylinders for each other.

INK PYRAMIDS AND DAMPENING SYSTEMS 13.2.5

Ink pyramids (systems of ink rollers) and dampening systems (systems of dampening rollers) are common to all the systems described above. All ink pyramids and dampening systems are not designed like the ones on page 218, but the discrepancies among the different designs are relatively small and the general functions are the same.

CONTROL OF INK COVERAGE 13.2.6

Screws controlling the ink allow the printer to specify how much ink should be transferred to the printing plate in different zones across the plate. The ink screws regulate the ductor knife and thereby determine how much ink should be forwarded to the different zones. The screws on old printing presses were manually preset based on experience and a check of the printing plate or the proof print. Any adjustments to the different zones were then made according to measurements taken with a densitometer or spectrometer. Large and modern printing presses incorporate a control panel from which you can adjust the position of the screws and, thereby, the flow of the ink.

▶ **FIVE CYLINDER UNIT**
This type of unit is primarily used for sheet-fed offset printing. It consists of two plate cylinders and two rubber blanket cylinders that share a common impression cylinder.

▶ **SATELLITE UNIT**
A satellite unit is primarily used for web-fed offset printing. It usually consists of four plate cylinders, four rubber blanket cylinders and a common impression cylinder.

▶ **PERFECTOR UNIT**
The perfector unit is exclusively used for web-fed offset printing. This system does not have an impression cylinder. Instead, two rubber blanket cylinders act as impression cylinders for one another.

▶ **INK ZONES**
Each number in the ink duct corresponds to a specific ink zone.

INK PYRAMIDS AND DAMPENING SYSTEMS

The ink pyramid in a printing press is made up of several types of cylinders with different functions. The dampening system in a printing press has fewer cylinders than the ink pyramid but the cylinders are of the same type and perform the same functions:

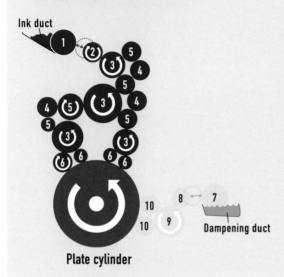

THE INK PYRAMID

1. The duct roller delivers ink from the ink duct to the ink pyramid. The duct roller rotates slowly and is made of steel.

2. The drop roller transfers ink from the duct roller to a distribution roller by "jumping" between the duct and the distribution roller. Thus, it is never in contact with both rollers at the same time. The drop roller is coated with rubber.

3. The distribution rollers make sure that the ink is evenly distributed on the printing surfaces in a thin film. As the distribution rollers rotate they also move side to side, spreading the ink. The first distribution roller picks up ink from the drop roller while the rest pick up ink from the driving rollers. The last distribution rollers transfer the ink to the form rollers. The distribution rollers are usually coated with plastic.

4. Transfer rollers transfer ink between the ink-absorbing and ink-delivering driving rollers. Transfer rollers have a rubber coating.

5. Driving rollers roll against the distribution rollers and either absorb or deliver ink, depending on their placement. Driving rollers are made of plastic-coated steel like the distribution rollers.

6. Ink form rollers transfer ink from the last distribution rollers onto the printing plate. They are rubber-coated.

THE DAMPENING SYSTEM

7. The dampening duct roller is made of chromed steel.

8. The dampening drop roller has a rubber coating covered with a sock of terry cloth or similar material, used for its ability to absorb liquid.

9. The distribution roller is made of steel.

10. The dampening form roller has the same coating as the dampening drop roller, i.e., rubber with a sock of terry cloth or similar material.

▶ THE CONTROL PANEL
The control panel enables the printer to control the ink screws in the different zones. Measuring the different zones against the color bar on the printed sheet will tell you which zones need to be adjusted.

Printers now have plate scanner systems that scan the printing plates before they are mounted in the printing press to provide information about each zone's ink coverage. This information is then digitally transferred to the printing press. This provides you with a fairly accurate presetting of the ink screws and results in a faster makeready. The most efficient way to preset the ink screws is to enter the ink coverage for each zone as specified by the digital file that the print job is based on. There are systems that can analyze this data, convert it for the printing press and use it to preset the ink screws. The standard for this procedure is called CIP 3.

▶ THE INK DUCT
Printing ink is evenly added to the ink duct and transferred to the duct roller.

▶ PLATE MAKEREADY
It is very important that the printing plate be inserted correctly in order to ensure proper registration of the prints.

▶ CONING
The phenomenon called "coning" happens when the print area of the first ink color laid down on a sheet is slightly wider than the print area of the last ink color printed on a sheet. This happens because the paper is compressed as it passes through each successive printing unit. Coning occurs both in sheet-fed and web-fed offset printing.

1. Correct print image on the printing plate.

2. The paper is compressed as it passes through the first printing unit and the printed image is transferred.

3. The paper gets its original shape back after printing is completed and the printed image shrinks.

4. In the second printing unit, the sheet is compressed and enlarged a little bit more and the print area of the second ink color lands inside the first one.

5. The appearance of the sheet after it has been printed in both units.

PRINT MAKEREADY 13.3

The term "makeready" refers to all the printing-related steps leading up to the first, approved print sheet. Because printing time is costly, you want this process to take as little time as possible, but there are a number of necessary steps:

• *Plate makeready*
• *Setting the feeder*
• *Registration of the sheets*
• *Presetting of ink screws*
• *Ink-dampening balance*
• *Registration*
• *Ink coverage*
• *Correspondence to the proof*

Always strive to minimize the number of makereadies – they can often take more time than the actual print run [see Output 9.6]. What follows is a more in-depth description of the makeready steps.

PLATE MAKEREADY 13.3.1

To help achieve accurate registration among the different inks, it is important that the printing plates are inserted into the press correctly. The registration pins and holes in the printing plate set the plates properly [see Film and Plates 11.2.5]. The insertion of the printing plate is often done manually, but printing presses with automatic plate changers are becoming more common.

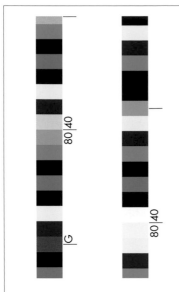

▶ COLOR BARS
Color bars allow you to measure and proof different quality requirements for the print.

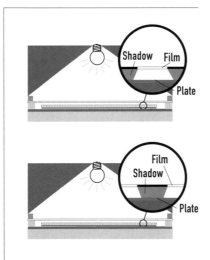

▶ DOT GAIN – PART 1
When you expose a negative plate, you will get dot gain (top). When you expose a positive plate, you will get dot reduction (bottom).

SETTING THE FEEDER 13.3.2

The feeder has to be set to the correct sheet format. The feeder must also be set so that it picks up no more than one sheet of paper at a time.

REGISTRATION OF THE SHEETS 13.3.3

It is important that the sheets of paper are accurately registered before going into the printing press. This helps ensure that the image is printed in the same place on every sheet throughout the run, and consequently, that the off press processing will be as accurate as possible.

PRESETTING OF INK SCREWS 13.3.4

Making changes to the appearance of the print by adjusting the ink screws is a relatively inefficient process. Therefore it is important that screws are preset as carefully as possible. The ink screws are either set manually or automatically, using information from a plate scanner or from the digital file the print is based on.

INK-DAMPENING BALANCE 13.3.5

It is important to set the ink-dampening balance correctly. Too much water creates an excess of emulsified water drops in the ink and can cause small, white dots in the print. On the other hand, too little water can cause tinting of the non-printing areas, also known as "dry-up."

REGISTRATION 13.3.6

When printing with several colors, accurate registration is of the utmost importance. Proper registration ensures that the individual printing inks are laid down on top of each other as precisely as possible. Unfortunately, because the format of the paper sheets changes slightly as they pass through the printing press [see illustration page 219], the press will never achieve 100% registration.

INK COVERAGE 13.3.7

The amount of ink transferred to the paper is referred to as the "ink coverage." Proper ink coverage is important; too much ink results in smearing, drying problems and lack of contrast in darker areas of the image. If the ink coverage is too low, the image will appear washed out. Ink coverage is measured with a densitometer [see 13.4.2]. If the ink coverage is too low in a specific area of the print, you have to change the basic setting for that area by adjusting the ink screws.

If the ink coverage of only one of the colors is too low, you can get color casting in the images. When this happens, you say that you have the wrong "color balance." The color balance is checked against gray test marks that become discolored when the color balance is off [see 13.4.3].

CONSISTENCY TO THE PROOF 13.3.8

The proof gives the buyer an idea of how the final result will look. It is also important to check that the printed result corresponds, as much as possible, to the proof. Therefore the print is usually fine-tuned against the proof. If the proof and the pre-press work are accurately done, major adjustments should not be required to reach a high level of consistency between the proof and the print.

CHECKING OFFSET PRINTS 13.4

When printing, you should always include a color bar on the print sheet to measure, proof and control the quality of the print. Checking prints is a prerequisite for generating the values that will help you adjust the pre-press work (the production of originals and images, for example) according to the requirements of the print. Factors you should check include dot gain, density, gray balance, trapping, slurring and doubling.

DOT GAIN 13.4.1

When dot gain occurs during the production of the printing plates, it means that the size of the halftone dots change when they are copied onto the printing plate. You will get a dot gain when using a printing plate and negative film, whereas you will get a dot reduction when using a printing plate and positive film. Dot gains in the printing press occur when the ink is transferred from the printing plate to the rubber blanket, and from the rubber blanket to the paper. The ink is pressed out into the actual printing nib and the halftone dots are slightly enlarged, which results in darker tint areas and images. There is also an optical dot gain that is dependent on how light is reflected by the paper stock. The total dot gain of the final print consists of the value of the dot gain/dot reduction during the production of the plate, plus the dot gain from the printing process and the optical dot gain. The dot gain from the printing process has the greatest impact overall.

Dot gain means that the printed result will be darker than the original, and you should therefore compensate for it. In order to compensate accurately, you will need to know the dot gain for the printing process, the paper and the halftone screen that you plan to use. Printers should conduct regular checks of the dot gains and document their values. An image that is not adjusted to compensate for the dot gain will print out considerably darker than intended.

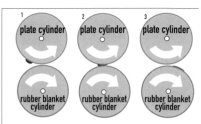
▶ DOT GAIN – PART 2
Halftone dots are compressed, and thereby enlarged, in the printing nip.

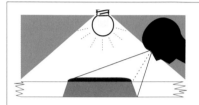
▶ DOT GAIN – PART 3
The dot on the paper creates a shadow of the reflected light that is often larger than the dot itself.

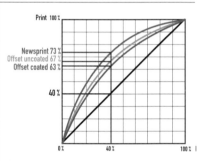
▶ DOT GAIN ON DIFFERENT TYPES OF PAPER

The above diagram shows a comparison of the dot gain on different types of paper.

▶ DOT GAIN

Dot gain is measured with a densitometer and color bars. 40% tones and 80% tones are typical reference values. Dot gain is always measured in absolute percentage units. This means that a 23% dot gain in a 40% tint area will come out as 63% in the printed image. The effect that a 23% dot gain has on the printed result over the entire tonal range can be observed in the curve of the graph.

If you want to know how to define a tint area so it will actually be 40% in the print, draw a horizontal line from 40% on the "Print" axis

until the line meets the curve. From the point of intersection, draw a vertical line down to the "Film" axis, where you can read the correct value. In this case, you need to adjust a 42% tint area to 25%.

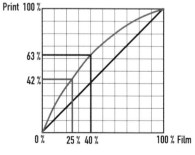

▶ REGISTRATION MARK

This mark is used to check the registration of the different component colors in a print. It is shown here as it is seen on a negative film.

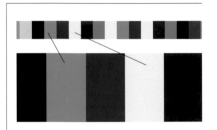

▶ FIELDS WITH SOLID TONES
The density of solid tones is measured against the corresponding fields on the color bar.

▶ NORMAL DENSITY

Common values for the density of full tones when sheet-fed offset printing on coated paper are:

K: 1.9   C: 1.6   M: 1.5   Y: 1.3

▶ GRAY BALANCE
You might get color casts in your print if the gray balance isn't right. For example, here the upper left corner of the image has a cyan cast.

▶ GRAY BALANCE FIELDS
The gray balance can be checked against the gray balance fields of the color bars. Here, CMY-gray is compared to a gray based on only black.

Because the dot gain curve is a continuous curve, it is enough to state the dot gain for one or two tonal values. The dot gain is primarily measured in the 40% tone and sometimes also in the 80% tone. A common value for a dot gain is around 23% in the 40% tone for a print with 150 lpi on a coated paper (negative film). Dot gain is always measured in absolute percentages. This means that a 40% tone in the film or the computer will be 63% in the print (40% + 23%) if you have a 23% dot gain.

Factors that affect the level of dot gain in printing include paper grade, printing process and screen frequency. Uncoated paper stock generally results in a higher dot gain than coated. Newsprint has an even higher dot gain. Paper manufacturers generally provide information about the dot gains of their different paper grades. The type of printing process also affects the level of dot gain. Web-fed offset printing, for example, is characterized by a higher dot gain than sheet-fed offset printing (printing on the same stock). Screen frequency affects the level of dot gain as well. A higher screen frequency always results in a somewhat higher dot gain, assuming the same printing process and paper.

DENSITY 13.4.2
Density is a measurement of how much ink is applied to the paper by the printing press. If the ink layer is not dense enough, the print will look matte and washed out. Too much ink and the halftone dots will bleed and spread, resulting in poor contrast in the print. Excess ink can also cause drying problems that lead to smearing. It is therefore important to use an appropriate amount of ink for the paper you are printing on. The printer should test this. A densitometer is used to measure the solid tones of the color bars, the full-tone density. There is at least one solid tone for each printing ink on the color bars.

GRAY BALANCE 13.4.3
In theory, if you were to print with equal amounts of the three primary colors C, M and Y you would get a neutral gray. However, in practice, you will get what is known as "color cast" [see Chromatics 4.4.2]. This can happen for a number of reasons: the color of the paper, differences in dot gain between the printing inks, the printing inks don't blend completely, or the pigments in the printing inks are not ideal.

▶ GRAY BALANCE VALUES
Examples of gray balance values for a coated, white paper:

C	0	5	10	20	30	40	50	60	70	80	90	95	100
M	0	3	4	11	20	29	38	48	58	68	78	83	88
Y	0	4	5	12	21	30	39	49	59	69	79	84	89

Examples of gray balance values for uncoated newsprint paper:

C	0	5	10	20	30	40	50	60	70	80	90	95	100
M	0	2	4	10	19	28	37	47	57	67	77	82	87
Y	0	1	3	8	17	26	35	45	55	65	75	80	85

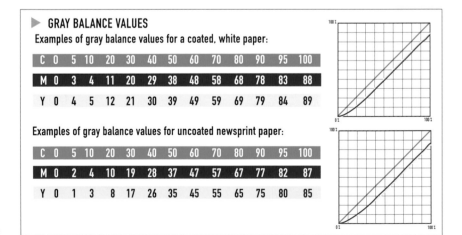

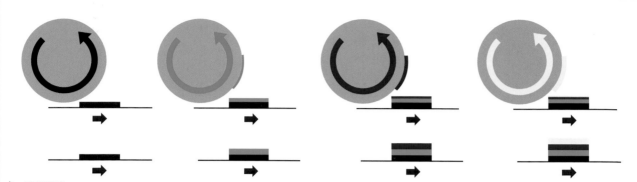

© Fälths & Hässler, Värnamo, 1999

▶ TRAPPING

When printing wet-on-wet, as with four-color prints in offset, the inks don't bond to each other fully. Problems increase with each successive ink printed. In the upper row you can see the actual result of a four-color wet-on-wet printing, while the lower set shows what the result would look like if the inks bonded to each other fully.

Gray balance is important because it helps you determine the right mix of colors. If the colors are not balanced properly, you will get a color cast in your printed product. To achieve the correct balance, you must know how the printing press you are using works with the paper, which printing inks and halftone screens you want to use, and adjust the pre-press work accordingly. In order to check if the gray balance is correct, you have gray balance areas that are printed with predefined CMY-values and reference fields with the corresponding gray tone, printed only with black, to compare the gray balance fields to. If you have the correct gray balance you will visually get a corresponding tonal value in the gray balance fields as in the black reference fields.

TRAPPING 13.4.4

Offset printing inks have more difficulty bonding with other wet inks than to paper. Offset printing is normally done "wet-on-wet," which means that all the necessary ink colors are printed directly on top of each other before they have time to dry. "Trapping" refers to how much ink bonds with, or is "trapped" by, wet ink already laid down on the paper. The level of trapping can be measured using a densitometer. Color bars specify measurements for trapping in which the solid tones of two printing inks have been placed on top of each other. Their combined density is compared with the densities of the corresponding individual solid tones.

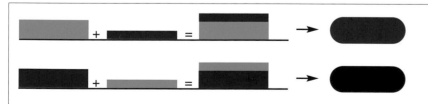

▶ THE PRINTING ORDER AND THE TRAPPING EFFECT

If cyan is printed before magenta, the cyan layer will be thick and result in a cold, bluish, full tone color. If, on the other hand, magenta is printed first, the resulting tone will be more purple-blue.

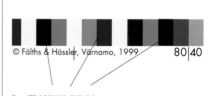

© Fälths & Hässler, Värnamo, 1999   80|40

▶ TRAPPING FIELDS

Trapping can be checked against the trapping fields of the color bars. These fields contain two inks, printed one on top of the other.

▶ TRAPPING

Trapping is measured against the trapping fields as shown in the example above. The formula for calculating the trapping is:

$$\frac{D_{1+2} - D_1}{D_2}$$

D_{1+2} = The density of the area with two inks printed on top of each other, measured with the second ink's filter in the densitometer.

D_1 = The density of the first ink in a solid tone field measured with the second ink's filter in the densitometer.

D_2 = The density the second ink in a solid tone field measured with the second ink's filter in the densitometer.

► MISREGISTRATION

Misregistration causes blurry images and can manifest as discolored edges or gaps in the colored print areas.

► RELATIVE PRINT CONTRAST

Relative print contrast is defined according to the formula:

$$\frac{D_{100} - D_{80}}{D_{100}}$$

D_{100} = Density of a solid tone of a color

D_{80} = Density of an 80% tone of the same color

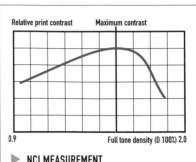

► NCI MEASUREMENT

The full tone density can be found where the curve hits its peak. This is the optimal tone density, which will provide the maximum contrast between the 80% tone and the 100% tone.

► DENSITOMETER

A densitometer measures dot gain and NCI levels in prints.

► PICKOUTS

Pickouts are paper fragments that stick to the printing plate or the rubber blanket and cause white dots in the print. They are particularly visible in dark tint areas. You can reduce the sensitivity of black tint areas to pickouts by making them deep black [see Documents 6.3.2].

MAXIMUM INK COVERAGE 13.4.5

Maximum ink coverage refers to the maximum amount of ink you can apply to a particular paper with a certain printing method. It is expressed as a percentage. For example, if you were to print with 100% coverage of all the four printing inks (CMYK) on top of each other, you will wind up with 400% ink coverage. However, that much ink cannot be used without smearing. Different types of paper can absorb different amounts of ink, so testing the paper you intend to use is important. For example, the maximum ink coverage for a coated, glossy paper is around 340%, whereas the maximum ink coverage for newsprint paper is closer to 240%. You should determine the maximum ink coverage for your materials during pre-press preparations [see Images 5.7].

PRINT CONTRAST/NCI LEVEL 13.4.6

When printing, you want to use as much ink as possible, while maintaining the contrast in the dark areas of the print. In order to calculate the optimal ink coverage, you measure the relative print contrast, which is the difference in density between a 100% tone and an 80% tone, divided by the density of the 100% tone (a 70% tone is usually used for newsprint). Optimal print contrast is reached when the difference in density between the 80% tone and the 100% tone is at its highest, and the density of solid tones is at its highest without a high dot gain. The ink density that provides optimal print contrast also provides optimal ink coverage. A polarization filter should be used when measuring the tones with a densitometer. This procedure is called NCI measurement (Normal Color Intensity).

PRINT PHENOMENA IN OFFSET PRINTING 13.5

In offset printing, a number of undesirable phenomena can occur during the print run. If you are familiar with the different phenomena and why they occur, the problems are easier to correct. Following, we will review some of the most common phenomena: misregistration, picking and pick-outs, smearing, reflection, doubling and slurring (also called mackle).

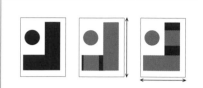

▶ GHOSTING
The phenomenon known as ghosting appears as traces of other printed objects in the printing direction. The image on the left shows the correctly printed image. The two images on the right are printed with different printing directions (indicated by the arrows) to demonstrate the phenomenon of reflection.

MISREGISTRATION 13.5.1

As we mentioned earlier, it is impossible to get a perfect registration of the different printing inks in offset printing; you will always get some misregistration [see 13.3.6]. Misregistration is usually concealed by trapping [see Documents 6.7]. If you have not trapped or if the misregistration is too great, you will see discolored edges or gaps on the colored objects. Misregistration can also cause blurry images. Misregistration differs throughout the printing sheet, and is usually most evident at the outer edges of the printed sheet.

PICKING AND PICK-OUTS 13.5.2

Sometimes small fragments of the paper's surface are pulled off during printing. This is called picking. If these fragments, or "pick-outs" as they are called, land on a printing area on the printing plate, the plate will not absorb ink in those places. This results in small, un-printed white dots on the finished print. The same thing happens when the pick-outs get stuck on the rubber blanket. If you are noticing white spots on your prints, you will have to stop the printing press and wipe any pick-outs off the printing plate and rubber blanket. Picking can occur because of poor surface strength in the paper, viscous ink or a printing speed that is too fast. Because of its especially viscous ink and the fact there is no dampening solution to keep the printing plates clean, water-free offset printing has more problems with picking and pick-outs than wet offset printing.

SMEARING 13.5.3

Printed sheets can smear each other if the ink coverage is too high or if off press processing occurs before they have dried sufficiently. This problem can be solved with drying powder or other drying systems. Cyan ink usually takes the longest to dry, and is therefore the most sensitive to smearing.

REFLECTION 13.5.4

Tint blocks often require a lot of ink, which can cause problems for the rest of the print. Tint areas are also more sensitive to changes caused by other areas of the print. These

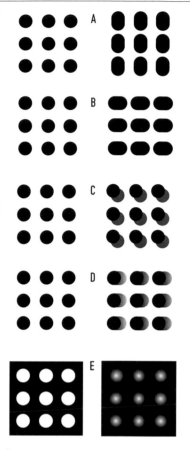

▶ DOT DEFORMATION

A. Slurring in the printing direction can result when the printing pressure is too high, or when the plate cylinder, rubber blanket cylinder and impression cylinder don't rotate at exactly the same speed.

B. Slurring across the printing direction can be caused by the paper or the rubber blanket.

C. Doubling is often the result of a loose rubber blanket.

D. Smearing can occur because the ink coverage is too dense or because the printed sheets are off press processed before they are entirely dry.

E. Choking can be caused by print pressure that is too high, a poorly tightened rubber blanket, ink coverage that is too high, too little dampening solution, or a combination of these factors.

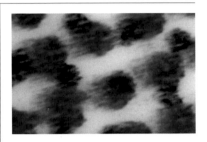

▶ SMEARING
Smearing caused the halftone dots to appear oval in shape.

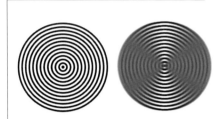

▶ CHECKING FOR SMEARING
Smearing can be checked using a measuring strip. If the halftone dots are smeared an hourglass pattern will appear (see above right).

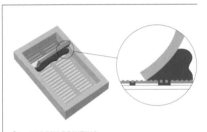

▶ TONING
Toning occurs when non-printing surfaces attract ink and thus become printing surfaces to some extent. This can occur because of hard water in the dampening solution or because the level of water in the ink-water balance is too low.

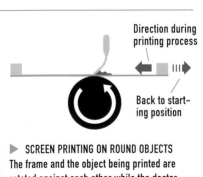

▶ SCREEN PRINTING
Ink is pressed through the cloth with a doctor blade. The cloth is prepared so that ink is only let through the printing areas.

▶ FILM FOR SCREEN PRINTING

The screen printing process requires right-reading, positive film.

Direction during printing process

Back to starting position

▶ SCREEN PRINTING ON ROUND OBJECTS
The frame and the object being printed are rotated against each other while the doctor blade remains static.

two factors can cause a phenomenon known as reflection or ghosting. "Reflections" of other print areas appear in the tint blocks when the plate cylinder does not have enough time to pick up the large quantities of ink needed for the tint blocks. Reflection is most common in the smaller printing press formats [see illustration on page 225].

DOT DEFORMATION—DOUBLING AND SLURRING (MACKLE) 13.5.5

Dot deformation means that the shape of the halftone dots changes, resulting in a dot gain. The deformation might be a result of problems with the periphery speed relationship caused by mechanical or technical errors in the printing process. It can also be a result of shortages in the handling of the print material in the printing press.

One such deformation is known as "slurring," when halftone dots are smeared into oval shapes. Slurring can occur when the pressure between the rubber blanket cylinder and the impression cylinder is too high, or when the plate cylinder and the rubber blanket cylinder do not rotate at exactly the same speed. The latter often happens because the cylinders have different circumferences, and consequently, different periphery speeds. This problem can be solved with a makeready: paper sheets placed between the rubber blanket and the rubber blanket cylinder.

Doubling is a phenomenon that manifests as a double imprint of halftone dots, one stronger and one weaker. This can be due to a loose rubber blanket, which causes the halftone dots to land in different places on the paper with each rotation of the cylinder.

Oval or double halftone dots affect the dot gain and result in higher surface ink coverage than initially intended. As a result, the entire print image will look darker than it should. There are special fields on the measuring strips (color bars) that allow you to check for slurring and doubling.

TONING 13.5.6

As mentioned earlier, too little dampening solution can result in toning of the non-printing surfaces of the paper (called a dry run, or tinting). This means that non-printing areas of the printing plate get colored by the ink and become printing areas. Toning can also occur if the water in the dampening solution is too hard, causing the pigments in the ink to dissolve and color the paper.

SCREEN PRINTING 13.6

The biggest advantage to the screen-printing method is that it allows you to print on almost any material, in any shape or format. The screen-printing method is used to print on porcelain, fabric, metal and cardboard, amongst other things. The diverse range of products printed using this method includes coffee mugs, clothes, cookie tins and signs, to name just a few. Screen printing differs significantly from other printing methods. Instead of a printing form on a cylinder, screen printing uses thin, fine cloth stretched on a frame, with a different frame, or screen, for each printing ink. Ink is pressed through the cloth with a ductor blade and transferred to the material that is being printed (porcelain, fabric, metal, cardboard etc.). The cloth is prepared so that ink only seeps through to the printing areas.

The cloth used is really finely woven net. The net is coated with a screen stencil, which only allows ink to pass through to the printing surfaces. The screen stencil, which consists of a thin film of plastic material, covers the non-printing surfaces of the net while leaving the printing surfaces open. The stencil can be made simply by cutting out the printed areas of the image (of course, this manual method is not used in high production).

Most professional screen stencils are made using film. Regular graphic, right-reading positive film is placed on the screen stencil and exposed. The illuminated, non-printing surfaces harden and the printing areas are washed off during development. There are different methods and materials for producing screen stencils. In some methods, the screen stencil is already mounted on the cloth before it is exposed, in others the screen stencil is mounted on the screen after it has been created.

THE SCREEN CLOTH 13.6.1

Types of screen cloth are usually differentiated by the thickness of the thread used to weave the net, how tightly the net is woven and how large the available printing surface is. Thicker thread and tighter weaving will result in thicker layers of ink on the print. Thick layers of ink require more drying time. The stretching of the cloth on the frame is very important. If the net is not mounted exactly straight, in the direction of the thread and at a right angle to the frame, you can get undesirable moiré effects and interference patterns in the prints [see Output 9.1.6].

Screen cloth can be bought separately but is also sold preinstalled on frames. When the screen stencil is exposed and attached to the tightened cloth, you have to make sure that the non-printing areas do not have any holes. Holes in the screen are common, and are simply patched up with filler.

SCREEN PRINTING INK 13.6.2

Ink that dries due to the evaporation of solvents is a considerable environmental hazard. Today, more environmentally sound inks are being used, including water-based inks and inks dried with ultra-violet light. With screen printing, it is important that the inks dry quickly, because this method does not allow you to print wet-on-wet. Each component color has to dry before the next one can be added.

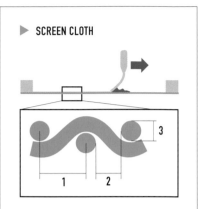

▶ SCREEN CLOTH

Important characteristics of screen printing cloth:

1. Density of the fabric: measured in number of threads per cm (10–200 is normal)

2. Open printing area: the percentage of the cloth surface that is available for printing

3. Thickness of the threads used to weave the fabric: thin, medium, thick and extra thick

▶ SCREEN PRINTING: +/–

Advantages and disadvantages with screen printing:

+ Can be used to print on most materials, including thicker paper and cardboard

+ Low waste

+ Water-based printing inks can be used

– Not appropriate for high screen frequencies

– It is difficult to reproduce the entire tonal range with screen printing technique, and fine tonal transitions cannot always be achieved.

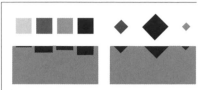

▶ PRINTING FORMS FOR GRAVURE PRINTING

On the left is an etched form used for gravure printing and a print made with it. The figure at the right shows a form for engraving.

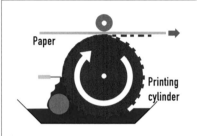

▶ THE PRINCIPLE OF GRAVURE PRINTING

The small halftone wells are filled with ink, and a doctor blade removes any extra ink. The ink is transferred from the printing form to the paper in the printing nip.

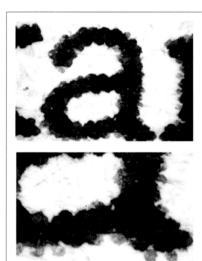

▶ SCREENED TEXT

Because halftone wells are used in gravure printing, any printed text will be screened (converted into halftone screens).

SCREEN PRINTING ON CURVED OBJECTS 13.6.3

When printing on circular objects like bottles or cans, a method different from traditional screen printing is used. In traditional screen printing the print surface and the frame remain fixed and the ductor blade moves across the screen to press ink through the cloth. When screen printing on circular objects, the print surface and the frame move also. The printing surface – a bottle, for example – rotates while the frame moves over it at the same speed [see illustration on page 226]. There are screen-printing presses that use similar methods for printing on flat print surfaces. These presses have an impression cylinder that rotates while the printing surface follows the screen. Other screen-printing presses print on a narrow feed-board.

GRAVURE PRINTING 13.7

Gravure printing is an old printing method with roots in copperplates and etchings. It is an expensive technique, financially feasible only for long print runs. Gravure printing presses are web-fed presses, are often large and print at a very high speed. The gravure technique can be likened to an inverted stamp, where the non-printing areas are higher than the printing areas. Printing plates are not used in gravure printing; the printing form consists of steel cylinders coated with a layer of copper. The printing areas are engraved (a mechanical procedure) or etched (a chemical procedure) in the cylinder. This gives you halftone screens consisting of small wells. In order to produce halftone dots with different sizes on the paper, the wells vary in size, depth or both, depending on the gravure technique. The wells are filled with ink, which is transferred to the print when the paper is pressed against the printing form by a rubber-coated impression cylinder.

THE PRINTING FORM 13.7.1

Before each new etching or engraving, a new copper layer has to be added to the printing form cylinder. The coppering is done using electrolysis with copper sulfate and sulfuric acid.

ETCHING 13.7.2

The first step in creating an etching is reminiscent of producing offset printing plates. A light-sensitive gel coats a pigment film, and hardens when exposed to light, capturing an

---

▶ GRAVURE PRINTING +/−

Advantages and disadvantages with gravure printing:

+ The printing forms last through large-volume runs without getting worn out
+ High volume runs will have low per-unit costs
+ Good image reproduction

− All lines and text are rasterized
− Extensive use of chemicals and solvents in the ink
− High start-up costs (inappropriate for small editions)

image. The gel is not "binary" like the offset plate – whose areas can only be printing or non-printing. The gel becomes more deeply engraved the longer it is exposed. The entire sheet is then transferred to the printing form, and the unexposed gel is washed off.

The actual etching of the copper printing form then takes place. A liquid that has a corrosive effect on the copper and the gel is used. The engraved gel is gradually dissolved by the corrosive solution. Because the gel is dissolved gradually, the underlying copper printing form will also be dissolved to different levels, depending on how thick the engraved gel layer is at any given spot. This process creates "halftone wells" of different sizes and/or depth.

ENGRAVING 13.7.3

Engraving relies on a read-head, which uses a light to read the engraving information from an opalescent film. The film is based on the graphic film originals. The information on the film is transmitted to the diamond-tipped engraving head, which uses physical pressure to create halftone screens (wells) on the printing form. The printing form rotates as it is being engraved, and after each completed rotation, the gravure head inches along the cylinder to engrave the next part of the image. This continues until the entire cylinder is engraved. Gravure cylinders can also be engraved using information directly from a digital source, rather than from film. This is known as direct engraving. Direct engraving requires that the original artwork is in a digital format, which will most likely become the dominant technique in the future.

GRAVURE INK 13.7.4

Gravure ink cannot be viscous, since it must dry very quickly. In gravure printing you can't print wet-on-wet. Gravure ink contains a volatile solvent (toluene) that evaporates rapidly, causing the ink to dry very quickly. The drying time of the ink is further accelerated by hot air drying systems. The evaporated toluene must be recycled.

FLEXOGRAPHIC PRINTING 13.8

As we mentioned earlier, flexographic printing is one of the few modern printing techniques that uses the same principle as the stamp. The printing areas are separated from the non-printing by a difference in elevation. Flexographic printing allows you to print on most materials, including paper, cardboard, plastic and metal. This versatility has caused flexographic printing to become particularly popular with the packaging industry and the hygienic paper industry.

FLEXOGRAPHY 13.8.1

Flexography uses a rubber or plastic printing form and a "direct printing" technique, which means that the printing form transfers the ink directly to the print surface. The printing form is thus a mirror image of the final printed image. Because the printing form is made of an elastic material, the impression cylinder has to be hard. This relationship is the reverse of gravure printing, where the impression cylinder is soft and the printing form hard.

▶ **ETCHED PRINTING FORM**
This figure shows an etched printing form. In the etched form, the halftone wells are identical in size but differ in depth. The difference in depth provides the dots with varying amounts of ink creating different tones in the print.

▶ **DIRECT ENGRAVING**
In direct engraving, the printing form is engraved according to digital information. The engraving is done with a diamond-tipped head whose movement creates halftone wells of differing depth.

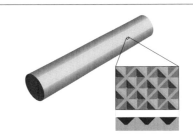

▶ **THE ANILOX ROLLER**
An anilox roller is covered with small wells that enable it to transfer ink to the printing plate evenly and quickly.

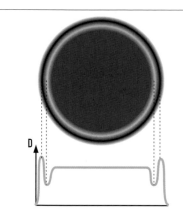

▶ THE FLEXOGRAPHIC PRINT EDGE
Here you can see what a flexographic print
edge looks like (in the dot), as well as a
diagram of the ink density across the dot.
Because the ink used in flexography is so
thin and the printing form is compressible,
an edge is visible in flat color areas. The
edge occurs because the outline of the area
is darker and a small area inside of the outline is brighter than the rest of the area.

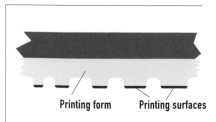

Printing form   Printing surfaces

▶ THE PRINTING FORM FOR FLEXOGRAPHIC PRINTING
The printing form in flexographic printing has elevated
printing surfaces, just like a stamp.

The ink used in flexographic printing has a high liquidity and is often volatile. The ink must be transferred from the ink duct to the paper before it dries. Because the ink dries so fast, you can't use a color roller system like you do in offset printing. Instead, an anilox roller is used to ensure an even transfer of ink to the printing form. The anilox roller is covered with halftone screens consisting of small wells. Ink is transferred directly from the ink duct to the wells of the anilox roller. A doctor blade removes any superfluous ink to further ensure an even transfer of ink from the anilox roller to the print surface.

FLEXOGRAPHIC PLATES 13.8.2

There are two main versions of printing plates used in flexographic printing: flexible rubber plates and photopolymer plates. Photopolymer plates are the most common. The flexible rubber plates consist of a zinc plate which, combined with physical pressure and heat, forms the print-ready plate. The polymer plates are produced by an exposure procedure reminiscent of the production of an offset printing plate. The polymer is photosensitive and the printing surfaces are hardened by exposure to ultra-violet light. Regular graphic film is used for the exposure. The film should be right-reading and negative [see Film and Plates 11.1, 11.1.1 and 11.1.3]. The unexposed non-printing areas are washed off when the plate is developed.

FLEXOGRAPHY INK 13.8.3

Flexography is often used to print on non-absorbent material, so the ink must be able to dry through the evaporation of solvents. The ink is volatile and has to be rapidly transferred from the ink duct to the printing form in order not to dry in the wells of the anilox roller. The ink must have a high liquidity so it can be quickly and evenly transferred to the plate via the anilox roller.

DIGITAL PRINTING 13.9

The words "digital printing" cover a variety of printing methods. These methods have been developed over the last ten years and are most suitable for short print runs. The advantages are speed and low cost for small editions of four-color small prints. Pages are sent directly from the computer to the printing press, and you don't have to develop film or printing plates. It does not require extensive makereadies and you can output proofs with ease. In addition, the ink or toner is dry when it comes out from the printing press, which makes it possible to begin the off-press processing right away without the risk of smearing.

A digital printing press essentially works like a color laser printer with an accompanying RIP. The major differences between a digital printing press and a laser printer are that the machines are much larger, print faster and work with traditional halftone screening techniques. Most systems are based on the xerographic technique.

As mentioned above, digital printing is primarily used for short runs with short delivery times. Digitally printed products can often be delivered within a couple of hours. Digital printing is often used for test runs and pre-editions. If, for example, you are printing a new magazine, it might be a good idea to produce a smaller pre-edition run that can be used for testing with different target groups. As with non-digital printers, there are certain limitations in terms of paper choice, but because of the expanding market for digital printing, there are hundreds of papers to choose from today.

Digital printing is not likely to replace offset printing or other printing methods within the near future, but instead serves to complement them.

COST COMPARISON: DIGITAL VS. OFFSET 13.9.1

If comparing cost graphs for digital and offset printing, digital printing is characterized by low start-up costs and a high cost per unit. With offset printing, the opposite applies: high start-up costs and a low cost per unit. The high per-unit cost of digital prints is due to the fact that digital printing presses are slow in comparison to offset presses. Expensive service agreements for digital printing presses and the high costs of materials (toner, photo conductor, etc.) also contribute to the per-unit cost.

Exactly where the break-even point between digital and traditional offset printing currently lies depends on the type and format of the printed product, though it is usually estimated to be somewhere between 500 and 1,000 units. The future of the break-even

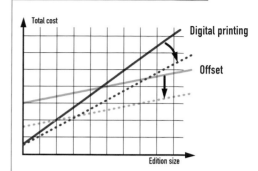

▶ **OFFSET VS. DIGITAL**
Offset printing has a high start-up cost but a low cost per unit. Digital printing has a low start-up cost and a high cost per unit. The financial break-even point occurs where these lines cross.

Because of increasingly tough competition, offset manufacturers are trying to develop printing presses with shorter makereadies in order to lower start-up costs. At the same time, manufacturers of digital printing presses are trying to lower their costs by cutting the prices of supplies, raising the printing speed and accommodating larger formats.

TRADITIONAL	DIGITAL
1 Original	1 Original artwork
2 Output on film	2 Digital imposition
3 Development	3 Rasterizing/printing
4 Proof	4 Off press
5 Manual mounting/	processing
imposition	5 Finished product
6 Plate exposure	
7 Makeready	
8 Printing	
9 Off press processing	
10 Finished product	

▶ **PRODUCTION FLOW**
Digital printing speeds up the production flow by eliminating the film and printing plate steps in the production chain.

▶ DIGITAL PRINTING PRESS
Here is an example of a digital printing press made by Xeikon.

▶ DIGITAL PRINTING CAPABILITIES
- Around 50 A4/letter-pages per minute or more
- Process is completely digital: no film or printing plates needed
- Four-color printing capability
- Changes can be made to the printing form during printing (variable data)

point is difficult to predict, but competition from digital printing has accelerated the technical development of offset presses. Since digital printing was introduced, the make-ready time of new offset presses has been drastically reduced. At the same time, the cost of materials for digital printing is going down and digital printing presses capable of larger print runs have been developed.

When making cost comparisons between digital and offset printing, you should also keep in mind that there are generally additional costs for film and proofs with offset printing, which are avoided entirely in digital printing.

DIGITAL PRINT QUALITY 13.9.2

Because of tough competition among the different manufacturers of digital printing machinery, a lot of time and money has been invested in developing the quality of the finished print – so much so that digital print quality is approaching the standard set by offset printing. The quality of digitally printed products varies considerably between different providers, however. Providers who have succeeded in getting the best out of digital printers are often pre-press service providers and printers with pre-press departments. The main reason for this is that these providers often have the capability to provide a secure and efficient production process, and possess a staff with a lot of experience in digital graphic production as well as evaluating graphic quality.

▶ **THE DIGITAL PRINT/XEROGRAPHY**

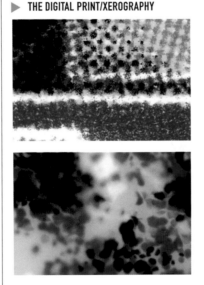

▶ Halftone dots in digital prints are blurrier than those in offset or gravure printing, and the image reproduction of digital printing is of a lesser quality as a result. This is primarily because digital printers print with powder toner instead of liquid ink. Because the halftone dots are divided, the digital prints appear to have a higher screen frequency than they actually do.

▶ Printing with powder toner means that both halftone dots and text become somewhat blurry because the particles don't always end up in the right place. This is the primary reason that text reproduction in digital printing is inferior to offset printing.

THE ANALOG PROOF

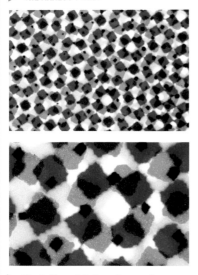

▶ The halftone dots in analog proofs are very precise and sharp. In this image you can see how the imagesetter builds up the halftone dot. You will always get better image reproduction in the proof than in the print.

▶ The text reproduction in analog proofs is very precise and sharp. Here you can see how the imagesetter builds up the text. You will always get better text reproduction in the proof than in the print.

THE OFFSET PRINT

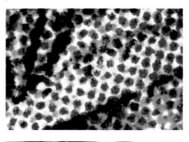

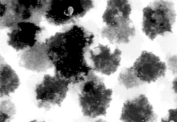

▶ Halftone dots in an offset print are irregular and blurry because of the way they are pressed onto the paper. Offset printing results in a slightly poorer image quality than gravure printing or analog proofs.

▶ Text printed in an offset printer is sharp and has clear outlines. Offset gives you better text reproduction than gravure printing, but slightly poorer than that of the analog proof.

THE GRAVURE PRINT

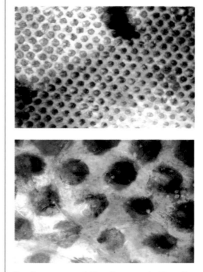

▶ In gravure printing, the reproduction of halftone dots is very precise because they are not pressed onto the paper as they are in offset printing. The image quality is therefore better than that achieved with offset printing.

▶ Everything printed with the gravure technique is built up with halftone screens ("wells"), even solid areas. This means that even the text is rasterised which results in a lesser quality reproduction than offset printing.

▶ THE FLEXOGRAPHIC PRINT

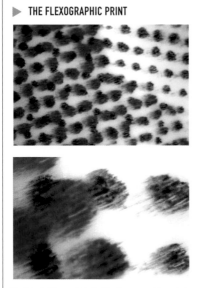

▶ The halftone dots in the flexographic print easily smear because the rubber plate slides against the paper like a stamp.

▶ Text printed with the flexographic technique also smears easily because of the "stamp" principle. This results in text reproduction inferior to that of the offset printing method. Note the flexographic print edge, which is clearly visible inside the contours of the letters.

▶ THE SCREEN PRINT

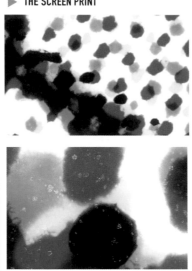

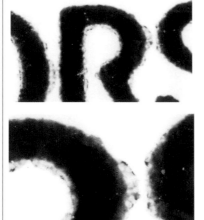

▶ Irregular halftone dots can negatively affect the image quality of screen prints.

▶ Screen-printed text is relatively blurry and of low quality compared to text printed with the offset method.

▶ THE INK-JET PRINT

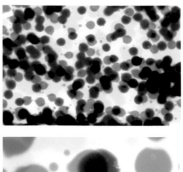

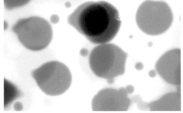

▶ Ink-jet printers generally use a kind of FM screen. The ink is sprayed out on the paper in small drops; each halftone dot consists of several ink drops.

▶ Because of the spraying action of the printer, the outlines of printed text can be blurry. This results in text reproduction inferior to that of the offset method. Note the drops of ink that landed outside of the letters.

▶ VARIABLE DATA

Here is an example of how the principle of variable data is used to change text and image during the print run.

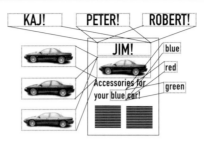

▶ VARIABLE DATA – HOW IT WORKS

By exchanging parts of the rasterized bit-map with smaller, rasterized bit-maps (which describe the objects on the page), the printing press can change the printed image from sheet to sheet.

VARIABLE DATA 13.9.3

When creating a digitally printed product, you have the ability to change information on the prints from sheet to sheet. In the beginning, this was considered the breakthrough function of digital printing and was usually called "variable data." The promise of variable data has not been developed to the extent that was hoped for yet. At present it is primarily used to address mailings and personalize letters with the names of clients, i.e., "Hi Jim! We heard you recently purchased a new car…" The variable data function is generated with information from a database. It is very important that the database is set up correctly and that information is entered into it accurately. Database tasks should be done in close collaboration with the provider of your digital printing services. ■

OFF PRESS PROCESSING

14

STRATEGIC PHASE

CREATIVE PHASE

PRODUCTION OF ORIGINALS

PRODUCTION OF IMAGES

OUTPUT/RASTERIZING

PROOFS

PLATE + PRINTING

▶ POSTPRESS PROCESSING

DISTRIBUTION

CHAPTER 14 OFF PRESS PROCESSING WHEN A PRINTED PRODUCT ROLLS OFF THE PRINTING PRESS, IT IS FAR FROM COMPLETE. OFF PRESS PROCESSING IS THE TERM FOR ALL OF THE FINISHING TREATMENTS APPLIED TO PRINTED SHEETS AFTER THEY COME OFF THE PRESS. TRADITIONALLY, THIS PROCESS IS ALSO KNOWN AS BOOKBINDING.

Though it is the final phase of the graphic production process, off press processing impacts a project from the very beginning, and should be taken into account when the product is being designed. For example, some types of paper are more appropriate for different off press processes than others. The imposition of the pages (how they are arranged on the printed sheets) is also determined partly by the desired off press processing for the product [see Output 9.6]. Therefore, it is important to decide early on in the planning stages what type of off press processing your printed product will need. Despite the importance of off press processing, it is often neglected during the planning process, causing added expense down the line.

In this chapter, we will review basic off press processes such as folding, creasing and cutting, as well as different binding methods, including glue binding and thread stitching. Finally, we will look at the different types of equipment used in off press processing.

WHAT IS OFF PRESS PROCESSING? 14.1

Cropping (cutting), glue binding, creasing, folding, hole punching, enveloping and perforating are examples of common off press processes. When printed sheets intended for books are off press processed, the sheets are bound or glued into blocks, cut to the correct format and then attached to a cover. Products with smaller formats such as brochures, periodicals, etc., are often stapled together with a cover. Printed products with more than two pages are generally folded. If the product has eight or more pages, it is usually also stapled or bound. Generally, all printed products need to be cropped during off press processing.

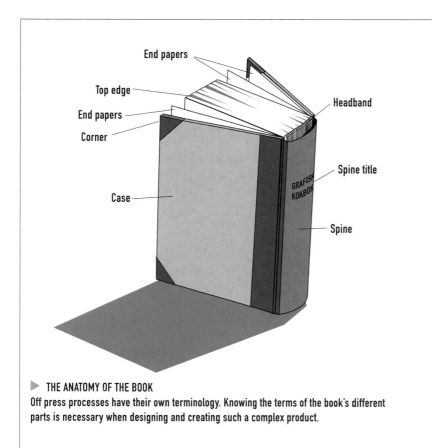

▶ THE ANATOMY OF THE BOOK
Off press processes have their own terminology. Knowing the terms of the book's different parts is necessary when designing and creating such a complex product.

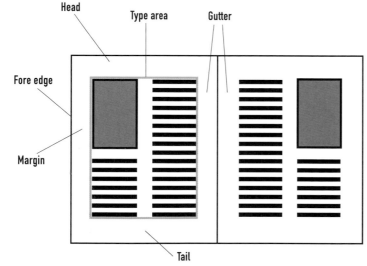

▶ THE ANATOMY OF THE PAGE
The page also has its own anatomy. The terms are intimately connected to the design of the page but play an important role in off press processing.

▶ OFF PRESS PROCESSES
Below is a summary of the most common off press processes.

Cropping (cutting):
The paper is cut to the desired size in order to fit the format of the printing press and off press processing machine. Finally, the printed and bound product is cropped to get the right format and even edges.

Folding:
The paper is folded.

Creasing:
Folds are marked, or "creased," to facilitate folding of heavy and stiff paper.

Binding:
Binding is the joining of several printed sheets into a printed product by using for example metal stitching, glue binding or thread stitching.

Punching:
Printed products are punched so they can be put into binders.

Lamination:
The printed sheet is coated with a protective plastic layer.

Foiling:
A printing form (a stamp) is heated and prints the material using a foil. The result is an depression in the material in the same color as the foil. The color is usually gold or silver although other colors are available, not PMS colors however.

Die-cutting:
If you want your printed product to have a shape other than a rectangle, for example if you need to punch a window in an envelope or cut registers for binders, you can have it die-cut.

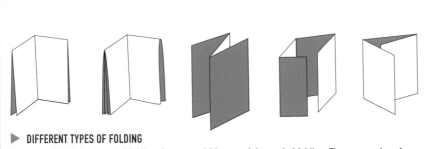

▶ DIFFERENT TYPES OF FOLDING
Two examples of right-angled folding: 8-page and 16-page right-angled folding. Three examples of parallel folding: 6-page Z-folding, tabernacle folding and 6-page roll folding.

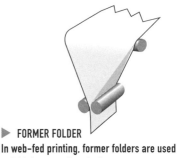

▶ FORMER FOLDER
In web-fed printing, former folders are used to fold the paper lengthwise.

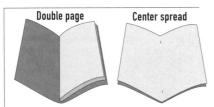

▶ FULL (TWO-PAGE) SPREADS
The left spread consists of two separately printed sheets. The right spread consists of pages from the same sheet (a center spread).

FOLDING 14.2

Folding is a technique used to create smaller individual pages from the large printed sheets. There are two main folding techniques: parallel folding and right-angled folding. Parallel folding, as the name indicates, means that all the folds run parallel to each other. Parallel folding is used when the printed product being processed does not need to be bound. Right-angled folding, on the other hand, means that each new fold is done at a 90-degree angle to the previous one, and is used for products that are going to be bound. There are also combinations of parallel and right-angled folding.

FOLDING METHODS 14.2.1

Buckle folding, a technique generally executed by simpler folding machines, is the most common folding method used in sheet-fed print productions. For slightly more advanced folding techniques like right-angled folding, combination folding machines are generally used. Combination folding machines consist of a buckle folder and one or more knife folders. Web-fed printing presses use, for example former folders, cylinder folders and wing folders.

▶ WARNING—CROSSOVER BLEEDS
You will always get a certain variation in color composition on the printed sheets and even between the left and the right side of a sheet. That's why you should avoid placing objects or images with sensitive colors across a bastard double.

You will never get a 100% registration between two separate pages. That's why you should avoid placing objects or images diagonally across a double-spread.

You should also avoid thin lines that bleed across a double-spread. Thicker lines are less sensitive to misregistration.

▶ RIGHT-ANGLE FOLDER
A right-angle folder can fold the sheet in two directions — both lengthways and sideways.

▶ SIMPLE BUCKLE FOLDER
Buckle folders are used to make simpler folds, for example to fold letters.

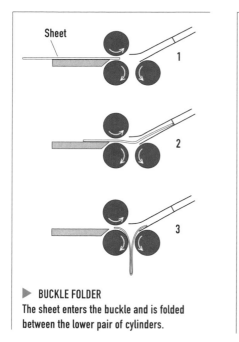

Sheet

1

2

3

▶ BUCKLE FOLDER
The sheet enters the buckle and is folded between the lower pair of cylinders.

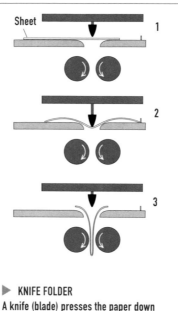

Sheet

1

2

3

▶ KNIFE FOLDER
A knife (blade) presses the paper down between two cylinders.

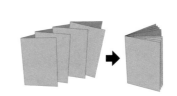

▶ SIGNATURES
The folded sheets (the sections) are inserted into each other. This method is used in saddle stitching, for example.

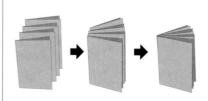

▶ SHEET ORDER
The folded sheets (the sections) are gathered after each other into a bundle. This method is used in glue binding, for example.

FOLDING PROBLEMS 14.3

Certain problems can occur during folding that adversely affect the quality of the printed product. It is particularly important to make adjustments for crossover bleeds and creeps when folding.

CROSSOVER BLEEDS 14.3.1

An 8-page booklet is always made up of two separately folded parts of the large sheet. After the two folded parts of the sheet are inserted into each other, the booklet only has one uninterrupted double-spread that consists of one piece of paper and it is the center spread. The additional two double-spreads consist of pages from both parts of the sheet, two separated pages that need to be carefully registered. Because the text and images, etc., cross over in the double-spreads you are running the risk of easily getting misregistration and crossover bleed. When you are planning your print production, it is best to avoid placing important text or images rich in details across a double-spread (unless it's the center spread) because of the risk of misregistration. Even if a book has more than eight pages, there is still only one double-spread with an uninterrupted print image.

SIGNATURES AND SHEET ORDER 14.3.2

When you plan to bind a printed product with metal stitching, glue binding or thread sewing, you generally use right-angled folding. For metal stitching, right-angle folded sheets, called signatures, are inserted into each other. For glue binding and thread sewing, the folded sheets are placed one after another in sheet order. When you use signatures, you will only have one uninterrupted double-spread without crossover bleeds –

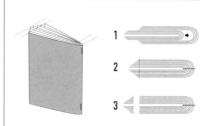

▶ CREEPING
When right-angle folding and especially with signatures, the pages are punched slightly outwards—the closer to the center, the greater displacement. When you crop your printed product in the fore edge, the outer margin will be smaller the closer to the center you get. You can compensate for this problem in the imposition by successively reducing the size of the gutter (the inner margin) as you progress towards the center spread.

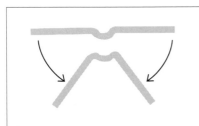

▶ CREASING
The paper is creased in order to reduce the paper's resistance to folding.

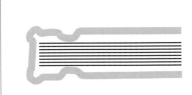

▶ 4-CREASE
Cases are often creased with a 4-crease so the board doesn't crack when it's opened.

▶ ORDER A "DUMMY"
If you are not sure of what type of binding and paper you want, you can order a product dummy from the paper supplier or the bookbinder.

the center spread. When the pages are assembled in sheet order, you will have a double-crossover spread per folded sheet.

CREEPING 14.3.3

When a sheet is right-angle folded, the center spreads are pushed slightly outwards and the middle-pages of the folded booklet are displaced. This phenomenon is called creeping. Creeping becomes even more pronounced when you use signatures because each additional signature pushes the central one further outwards [see illustration]. When you crop your printed product after it's been folded, the type area of the pages "creep" towards the outer margins more and more as you get to the center spread. You can compensate for this problem by successively reducing the size of the gutter (the inner margin) as you progress towards the center spread. This will ensure that the printed image is properly oriented and that the margins are consistent on the page throughout the printed product. Digital imposition programs make adjustments for creeping automatically; these changes must be made by hand when films are manually imposed.

CREASING 14.4

When a paper's weight exceeds 80 lbs, it can be very difficult to fold. To avoid unattractive folds, heavy paper is usually creased before it's folded. Creasing creates a kind of "hinge" that facilitates a clean fold. Paper is often creased with the help of a thin steel "ruler" pressed along the fold lines. The paper's resistance to folding is reduced along the resultant crease. Creasing is frequently used for processing cardboard.

Covers used in glue binding, for example, are usually creased. When glue binding with a thick cover, you will get the best results with a "four-crease" technique. A four-crease is literally a total of four distinct creases in the cover: one on either side of the spine, one a few millimeters from the spine on the front cover, and one a corresponding distance from the spine on the back cover. The creases in the covers prevent damage to the folds and allow the product to be opened with ease.

▶ METAL STITCHING
In the machine the folded sheets are stitched with metal staples.

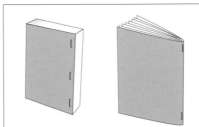

▶ BLOCK STITCHING VS SPINE STITCHING
When using block stitching the sheets are flat whereas in spine stitching the sheets are folded.

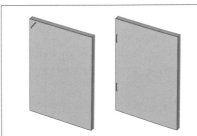

▶ BLOCK STITCHING
Illustrated above is a metal stitching with one staple in the upper left corner (left image) and another two staples along the spine (right image).

BINDING 14.5

Binding is the joining of a number of individual printed sheets into a single entity, be it a book, brochure, etc. The most common binding methods are metal stitching, glue binding, thread stitching and spiral binding. In metal stitching and spiral binding, the cover is attached during the actual binding process. In thread stitching and glue binding there are two ways of attaching, or hanging, the cover. In the first version (for soft covers), the cover is glued to the spine of the bound material. In the second (for hard covers), the first and last pages of the material, called the endpapers, are glued to the insides of the covers. Endpapers are usually colored or patterned papers.

METAL STITCHING 14.6

Stapling papers together with a standard desk stapler is a kind of metal stitching that we've all done. In terms of professional binding, there are two main types of metal stitching. One is block stitching, in which metal stitches (staples) are placed along one edge or on one corner of the pages, much like the desktop stapling we're used to. The second is known as saddle stitching, which places metal stitches in the spine of the material.

BLOCK STITCHING 14.6.1

Block stitching, also called side stitching, is a binding method for simple projects, like internal company publications, for example. Many copy machines and laser printers can even do block stitching, which usually consists of two staples along the left edge, or one at the top left corner of the printed material.

SADDLE STITCHING 14.6.2

Saddle stitching, also called wire stitching, is used with inset sheets. The number of pages you can saddle stitch together is limited – the saddle stitching machine can only handle a limited number of sheets – too many and you will get creeping and have trouble keeping the product closed.

The loop stitch is an example of a modified, regular staple [see illustration]. Loop stitching is used to place the printed product in a binder while being able to easily flip through it.

GLUE BINDING 14.7

When a printed product has too many pages for metal stitching, glue binding is often used instead. This method is relatively inexpensive and uses sheet order imposition. In glue binding, the spine of the insert is glued directly to the cover. The paperback book is an example of a glue-bound product with a full cover, as are most magazines. Case-bound hardcover books also employ glue binding. With hardcover books, the insert is glued to endpapers, which are, in turn, glued to the covers. Most of today's hardcover books are bound using this method.

In glue binding it is important that the fiber direction run parallel to the spine. If the fiber direction is wrong, the glue can cause waviness in the gutter. The product might

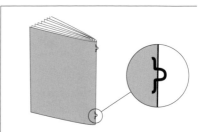

▶ LOOP STITCHES
Loop stitches allow you to put booklets into binders.

▶ COLLATION MARKS
The marks, red in the image, are noted on the imposition. When the signatures are gathered into sheet order, it allows you to check that all folded sheets are included and in the correct order.

▶ GLUE BINDING AND THREAD STITCHING
The upper book is bound using the glue binding method. Because the signatures are gathered in a block, the spine will be slightly wider than the insert. When using thread stitching, the folded part of the sheets is not visible since the spine has been ground down.

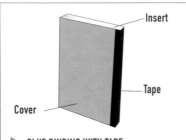

▶ GLUE BINDING WITH TAPE
When glue binding with tape, tape replaces the glue and two separate parts of a sheet are used as a cover.

feel stiff when you try to flip through it, and not want to stay open. Erroneous fiber direction also negatively affects the durability of the binding.

Uncoated papers with a high bulk [see Paper 12.1.5] are preferred to coated, glossy papers or lacquered sheets for glue binding because the glue needs to sink into the paper to a certain extent in order to ensure a strong bond.

After the folded or loose sheets of the printed product have been bundled together in sheet order, the spine is ground down one to three millimeters, creating a coarse surface that provides a good grip for the glue. It is important that images or text that run across the spread are placed with enough of a margin to account for the grinding down of the spine. Glue is then applied, and a spine reinforcement (in the case of a hardcover) or cover is attached.

There are also glue binding methods in which the spine is not ground but perforated. Glue is pressed through the perforations and into the spine. This type of binding is quite strong. In still another similar version binding, tape is used instead of glue. This kind of binding is not particularly durable and is most appropriate for simpler projects that do not require a long lifespan.

THREAD STITCHING 14.8

Thread stitching is the traditional bookbinding method. Folded sheets are placed in sheet order, but instead of being glued the spine is sewn together. As with glue-bound soft cover books (limp-bound), the book block is glued to the cover. However, the spine is not ground – if it was, the thread sewing would disappear. Instead, after the cover is in place along the spine, the book is cropped along the three remaining sides. As with other methods, it is important that the fiber direction run parallel to the spine in order to ensure a strong and aesthetically pleasing product.

▶ HARDCOVERS
Books can be bound in many ways. Glue and thread stitching are common methods.

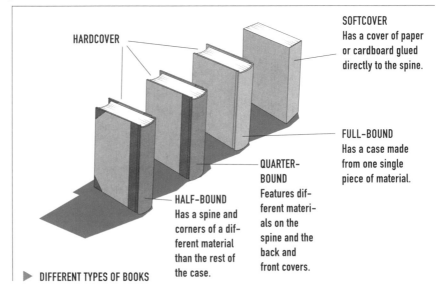

HARDCOVER

SOFTCOVER
Has a cover of paper or cardboard glued directly to the spine.

FULL-BOUND
Has a case made from one single piece of material.

QUARTER-BOUND
Features different materials on the spine and the back and front covers.

HALF-BOUND
Has a spine and corners of a different material than the rest of the case.

▶ DIFFERENT TYPES OF BOOKS

Thread stitched, hardcover (case-bound) books can be made in a number of different ways, depending on how exclusive they need to be. Full-bound, half-bound or quarter-bound are the most common types of thread stitched case-bound books. Full-bound books have a case made from one single piece of material. Half-bound books have a spine and corners of a different material than the rest of the case. For example, half-leather bound books are a version of half-bound which have spines and corners bound in leather. Quarter-bound books feature different materials on the spine and the back and front covers. The case-bound thread stitched book blocks are first glued to the spine and then cut along the other three edges.

SMYTH-SEWN 14.9

The Smyth-sewn stitching technique is a technique combining thread stitching with glue binding, and is used for soft cover books. In terms of expense, this method falls somewhere between glue and thread-stitched binding methods. The actual stitching is performed in a Smyth sewing machine. When the sheets are folded, needles stitch a thread into the back of the sheets. Each sheet is thus stitched separately. When all the sheets are stitched, they are gathered and glued together in a glue binding machine (without grinding the spine). If you were to flip through the final product, it would appear to be thread stitched.

SPIRAL BINDINGS 14.10

Wire-O bindings and spiral bindings are different types of spiral bindings. They are often used for manuals and notebooks. Products like these often need to be kept open flat by the user – as when writing in a notebook or following an instruction manual, for example.

In this binding process, loose sheets (these can be folded sheets in sheet order cut down to loose sheets) are gathered and punched. The spiral binding is then put in place. There are different methods for this, depending on the type of spiral binding you use. Spirals come in a variety of colors and dimensions. One disadvantage of spiral binding is that it is relatively unstable. A spiral bound product often can't stand upright on a bookshelf, for example, neither can it be supplied with a spine title. The method is also relatively expensive.

CROPPING 14.11

Cropping simply means cutting the paper down to the desired size with some kind of blade. This can be done manually with a special cutting machine or simultaneously with another step in the off press processing cycle.

Most printed products are cropped. In sheet-fed print productions, it can be necessary to crop a product up to three different times during the production cycle. First, the paper might require cropping in order to fit the format of the printing press. After they are printed, the sheets may have to be cropped again to fit the format of the off press processing machine(s). Finally, the product must be cropped after it is folded and bound to ensure that its edges are even and smooth.

▶ WIRE-O BINDING
A type of spiral binding that is useful when the book needs be kept open flat.

▶ THE PRICE LADDER OF BINDING
1 Spiral binding
2 Thread stitching
3 Smyth-sewn
4 Glue binding
5 Metal stitching

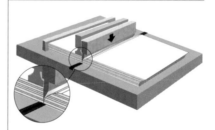

▶ CUTTING MACHINE
In the cutting machine the blade is pressed down into the paper stack with several tons pressure.

▶ THREE-SIDED TRIMMER
In a three-sided trimmer the printed product is cut in head, tail and fore edge.

In the most common binding methods, (metal stitching and glue binding), cropping is usually the last step of the process. Generally, a three-sided trimmer crops the printed product on the head, tail and fore edge. This final cropping is necessary for several reasons. Multiple pages imposed on the same printing sheet are still attached to each other after they've been folded, either at the head or the tail (this applies if you have right-angle folded sheets with eight or more pages). In addition, the creep requires that the bundle be cut along the fore edge.

The blades used in the cropping machines are sensitive and must be sharpened often. Varnished and laminated paper can damage or blunt the blade. A damaged blade can create a striped appearance along the cropped surface of the printed product.

OTHER OFF PRESS PROCEDURES 14.12

Laminating, varnishing, punching and perforating are other procedures performed during off press processing.

LAMINATION 14.12.1

Lamination is the process of coating a printed page with a protective plastic foil. Lamination increases protection against dirt, humidity and wear and tear, and is also done for aesthetic reasons. There are a variety of different types of laminates, including glossy, matte, embossed and textured. Laminates are commonly applied to the covers of printed products.

▶ CUTTING MACHINE
Before it hits the cutting machine, the stack of printed sheets is knocked even. In order to cut, two buttons have to be pressed simultaneously to make sure there are no fingers close to the blade.

▶ EMBOSSING
You can create relief, changes in the surface of the paper, by causing a print to stand out or sink down. The embossing is executed in special embossing printing presses.

▶ FOILING
You can also add a gold or silver surface to the printed product, called a foil.

▶ SEALING
One example of sealing is when you close a roll folded printed product with a sticker.

▶ ENVELOPING
Enveloping can be done both mechanically and manually depending on edition size and complexity. Editions of 2,000 copies or less usually benefit from being stuffed manually.

▶ BLOCKING
Blocking is used to create a pad out of a thick bundle of paper sheets. One of the edges of the block is coated with special glue.

▶ JACKET BAND
A jacket band is a thin strip of paper wrapped around a printed product, for example around a stack of printed products or a poster.

A special laminating machine is required for this process, and coated or glazed paper will give the best quality output. Laminated sheets can be creased and folded.

VARNISHING 14.12.2

Varnishing is a technique used to add a glossy surface to a printed product. Unlike lamination, it does not provide noticeable protection against dirt and wear and tear, and is primarily an aesthetic procedure. Varnish is often applied to the print in the offset press via a regular inking unit or a special unit just for varnish. Coated paper grades will give the best results. UV-varnishing is another common method in which varnish is applied to the print with a special UV-varnishing machine. Because the varnish is cured with ultra-violet (UV) light, it can be applied in a thicker layer, and thus provide a higher quality finish. Varnished sheets should be creased before they are folded to avoid the formation of cracks on the varnish-hard surface.

Varnish can be applied selectively to certain parts of the image – over images and logotypes, for example. This partial-varnishing method is used for aesthetic effect as well as to help prevent areas with dense ink coverage from smearing.

PUNCHING 14.12.3

Paper is punched during off press processing so it can be put into binders. The international standard, known as ISO 838, is the standard outside of North America. Within North America, the holespacing standards are 2 $^3/_4$" cc for 2-hole and 4 $^1/_4$" cc for 3-hole punching ("cc" stands for for center-to-center, and means that the holes are spaced from the center of the hole regardless of its size). Generally, special drills are used to punch paper when this is done during off-press processing, but you may also be able to purchase pre-punched paper from your paper manufacturer.

DIE-CUTTING 14.12.4

If you want your printed product to have a shape other than a rectangle, you can have it die-cut. A punch die is created in the shape you want for your product. The die is then pressed against the printed paper and cuts it to the desired shape. The cost for producing a unique punch die is relatively high for printed products in small editions, but it can be used for reprints.

PERFORATING 14.12.5

Perforations are basically used to create a tearing reference. By punching a dotted line (perforations) in a page, you make it easier to tear off a particular section of that page—a reply card, for example. Perforation is usually done in a letterpress with a special perforation blade, which is pressed into the paper, creating a series of tiny slits. Perforation can also be done in a special punching machine.

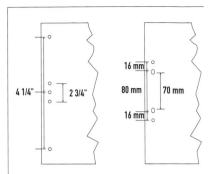

▶ HOLE PUNCHING
U.S. Standard (2 3/4" cc for 2-hole and 4 1/4" for 3-hole punching, left). International standard ISO 838 (two holes, 80 mm apart, right).

▶ DIE-CUTTING
In die-cutting, a punch die cuts through the paper. In the image, a K is punched into the paper. Die-cutting is used to create dividers for binders among other things.

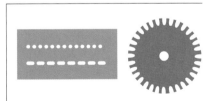

▶ PERFORATION
You perforate printed products to make it easier to tear off a particular section of that page—a reply card, for example. Perforation is usually done in a letterpress with a special perforation blade or, as illustrated here, with the scoring technique.

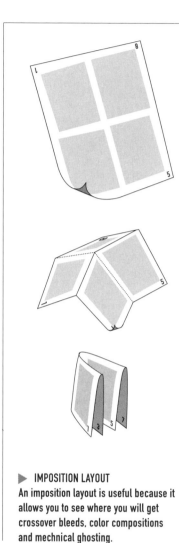

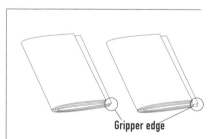

Gripper edge

OFF PRESS PROCESSING FOR SHEET-FED OFFSET PRINTING 14.13

Off press processing for web-fed offset printing is done online, while off press processing for sheet-fed offset printing requires a separate makeready. Below, we will review some important factors affecting off press processing for sheet-fed offset printing.

IMPOSITION LAYOUT 14.13.1

It is important to contact the off press service provider you will be using as early as possible during the production to ask for an imposition layout. This layout lets you see how the pages are arranged on the printed sheet after imposition. Often it is a smaller copy of the printed sheet, folded according to the specifications of their folding machine.

The imposition layout allows you to:
• See where you will get crossover bleeds
• Avoid mechanical ghosting on the printed sheet
• See the color compositions (i.e., the pages on which more than one color can be used, if not all sheets or pages are to be printed in more than one color)

GRIPPER EDGE 14.13.2

The gripper edge is also marked on the imposition layout. The gripper edge, or "lip," is the edge of the printed sheet that a machine "grabs" in order to feed the sheet through the mechanism. The margin between the gripper edge and the print area has to be somewhat wider than the other margins on the sheet. For example, a gripper edge of 7–15 mm is recommended for metal stitching. This edge is necessary when binding because it allows the machine to open the folded sheets. Folding machines don't need an additional gripper edge.

THE GEOMETRY OF THE PAPER 14.13.3

Paper that comes from the manufacturer or that is cropped by the printing house is not perfectly rectangular. The size and shape of the sheets can also vary slightly throughout the paper stack. It is important to be aware of that so the printing and off press processes can be coordinated to produce the best possible results.

When a printing press grabs a sheet of paper, it pushes it against a guide that situates the paper, regardless of size, against the gripper edge and the feed edge. This mechanism, called side guide, ensures that the distance from print area to edge will always be the same throughout the run, regardless of variations in the paper's format or size.

The printer always marks the printer sheets with the corner that the gripper's edge and feed edge of the printing press form. If you continue to use this corner as a guide for off press processing, you can be sure that the print will stay properly oriented on the page, no matter how it is cropped, folded, etc.

OFF PRESS PROCESSING EQUIPMENT 14.14

Printing houses that work with web-fed prints like newspapers have off press processing units "online," i.e., connected directly to the printing press. Sheet-fed offset printing houses, on the other hand, often require that you take the printed sheets to a separate bookbindery for processing, though some may offer a few simple off press services themselves. Bookbinders often specialize, and you might have to look to different bookbinders for different projects depending on the type of off press processing you need.

INDEPENDENT OR ONLINE OFF PRESS PROCESSING 14.14.1

There are thus two basic types of off press processing: independent processing, and online processing, which is connected directly to the printing press. Online processing machines often share a control system with the printing press, and the whole system delivers a finished product at the end of a run. Independent off press processing units require their own makeready, with their own start-up settings that need to be adjusted according to the print run. This means that you will spoil a number of prints before you achieve the desired quality, just as you would with the print makeready.

With an online-system, these settings are done in tandem with the print settings. When processing the sheets, you usually include a certain number specifically for setting the machine. The bookbinder will determine this number based on his/her experience of the equipment.

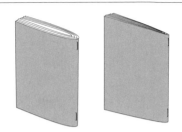

▶ WIRE STITCHED AND FOLDED VS FOLDED AND WIRE STITCHED
If you stitch the sheets into a booklet before they are folded (left image), the pages will be slightly displaced. Compare it to folding each sheet separately and stitching them together (right image).

▶ TO KEEP IN MIND

• It is important that the printed sheets have dried sufficiently before off press processing. If not, the print can smear and ink from one sheet is transferred to another. Tint areas, flat areas with high ink coverage, or images with a lot of color are particularly sensitive. Cyan ink usually takes the longest to dry, and is therefore the most sensitive to smearing.

• To get an attractive and durable printed product you should always fold along the fiber direction [see Paper 12.1.3]. If you fold against the fiber direction, the paper is weakened, the fibers are broken down and an unattractive crack appears in the print crossing the fold. The printed product will also have difficulties remaining closed. When using the glue binding technique, erroneous fiber direction can cause waviness in the paper and decrease the durability of the binding.

• When a paper's substance weight exceeds 80 lbs, it should be creased. If it's not, the surface of the sheet might crack and the product will have difficulties remaining closed.

• When saddle-stitching you should not use sections in order to prevent the printed product from opening itself. The off press processing provider knows what to recommend.

• It is important to have an imposition layout because it allows you to check crossover bleeds and ink settings. You can also avoid printtechnical problems such as ghosting.

• Check with the off press processing provider how much waste, i.e. how many the number of sheets necessary for the off-press makeready, they have estimated. Usually reference copies are included in the estimated waste.

▶ CALCULATING THE WIDTH OF THE SPINE

If you are using the glue binding or thread stitching technique when binding your product, you need to know how thick the insert is in order to get the correct width of the spine.

$$\text{Width of spine in} = \frac{\text{Number of pages}}{\text{ppi of paper used}}$$

Until just a couple of years ago, online off press processing was something only found in web-fed printing presses. However, as the quest for shorter run times and the impact of digital printing methods is felt, online off press processing has become increasingly common. When a print run is small, it can be difficult to justify the expense and time involved in sending the printed product elsewhere for off press processing. Unfortunately, these smaller online off press processing units usually provide a lower quality output than the independent ones.

Recently, combination folding and metal stitching machines intended for the fast and simple production of smaller runs have appeared. These machines can be connected directly to high-volume printers or digital printing presses, or stand independently. They staple the entire bundle before folding all the sheets together. However, you do not get the fine folds on each individual sheet that you would with independent folding and metal stitching machines, and products processed this way often have problems closing. Also, many of the attachable folding and metal stitching machines used with digital printing presses only have one blade, which only cuts the signature along the fore edge. This sets very high registration requirements for the printer and can produce relatively poor results.

Another problem with the off press processing of prints from high-volume printers or digital printing presses is that the print "jumps" on to the sheet, so you do not get a consistent distance from the edge of the paper to the print area. This phenomenon compromises the accuracy of the off press processing, making it difficult to create a fold between two tint areas, etc. ■

THE ENVIRONMENT

15

CHAPTER 15 THE ENVIRONMENT ENVIRONMENTAL ISSUES ARE OF CENTRAL IMPORTANCE TO MANY GRAPHIC COMPANIES. IT IS IMPORTANT TO GET THE GENERAL PICTURE OF THOSE ISSUES AND TO CONSIDER THE ENVIRONMENTAL IMPACT THROUGHOUT THE PRODUCTION CHAIN.

Eva Anderson, Eva Anderson Design

The core concept of environmentally preferable design is self-education and better choices. As you become more familiar with the concept, you will realize that the basis for design by humans is no different than that of design by nature: it is the survival and health of this planet we call home and all its inhabitants. It implies connection: between humans and ecosystems, between present and future, between individual actions and the greater whole.

For designers, these connections are visible in the papers, materials, printing and manufacturing processes we choose, in our creative problem solving, in the ways in which our designs are used and eventually disposed. To be truly aware of our work, we must examine the impacts of every single facet of our design process, constantly monitor the waste we create and resources we use, and commit to developing better habits in our personal as well as professional lives on a daily basis. Energy efficiency, reduction or elimination of materials, re-use and recyclability, as well as the elimination of toxic and non-renewable materials must determine our design decisions.

For graphic designers, this includes knowing how trees and other resources were harvested for the production of paper or other materials. The types of inks that are used – whether they contain harmful metals or if they are vegetable based – and how printers dispose of them. What recycled or recyclable alternatives exist to the plastic chosen for a specific project? Transportation represents another crucial piece of the puzzle. How much of the project was accomplished locally or regionally? Our messages should be scrutinized as well. Do they reinforce ideas of environmental awareness or rampant waste?

Options are increasing, and as more conscientious companies appear in our work and personal lives, we must do our best to support them with our purchases and making our opinions count in the marketplace. This chapter will get you started in your journey, and we encourage you to continue to educate yourself beyond this book, not only relying on the resource list provided, but in your own research as well.

PAPER 15.1

According to the Worldwatch Institute, the use of wood over the last half century has more than doubled, and the consumption of paper has increased nearly six-fold. "The less than one-fifth of the world's population who live in Europe, the U.S., and Japan, consume over one-half of the world's timber, and more than two-thirds of its paper. In the next fifteen years, global demand for paper is expected to grow by half again." This contributes to an expanding economy, but the ecosystem on which it depends is taxed. The signs of stress are evident in shrinking forests, falling water tables, eroding soils, rising CO_2 levels, rising temperatures, and disappearing plant and animal species.[1, 2]

RECYCLED 15.1.1

Just because a paper is recycled doesn't mean that it's the most environmentally preferable. Paper mills have been recycling their own waste and trimmings from envelope converters for many years. This is referred to as *post-industrial waste*.

ALTERNATIVE SOLUTIONS: To truly close the loop, paper must first go to the consumer, be put in the recycling system, and then processed back into pulp for papermaking. This recycled material is *post-consumer waste*.

In addition to relieving solid waste problems, specifying the highest post-consumer recycled paper (or tree-free alternatives) for every job is probably the most significant act a graphic design studio can make in the battle against global warming. Forests "eat" and store carbon dioxide (a greenhouse gas), thus removing it from the atmosphere where it can cause harm.

Today there are so many options that specifying 100% recycled paper with at least 30% post-consumer waste (PCW) should be the minimum standard. Remember that the higher PCW content you use, the more you are helping to build an environmentally based economy.

CHLORINE-FREE 15.1.2

Chlorine bleaching is probably the single most devastating part in the production of paper. Chlorine is used to dissolve wood lignin (the sticky material that holds cellulose fibers together) and to bleach the fibers white. The chemical byproducts that result from the interaction of the chlorine, lignin and cellulose fibers are some of the most toxic substances ever created. Studies have conclusively found a strong link between the production of chlorine-bleached paper products and dioxins, carcinogens capable of causing cancer, reproductive disorders, deformities and developmental problems in children, and impaired immune systems.[3] Because they don't break down, dioxins persist in our air, water and soil, contaminate the food chain, and accumulate in the bodies of wildlife and humans.

▶ LIFE CYCLE ASSESSMENT

One effective tool designers use to analyze the impacts of their design is Life Cycle Assessment (LCA). A review of the entire life span of a product, LCA's weigh all the trade-offs in materials, energy consumption, economic viability, toxicity, processes and disposal. An LCA considers the outputs of "waste" in every stage of the product, including development, useful life and retirement.

For example, one LCA study found that for glass, aluminum, steel, liner board and folding boxboard there was one resounding conclusion: the environmental impact of these materials is significantly reduced when their recycled counterparts are used. Glass was found to have the least environmental impact, followed by paper, steel and recycled aluminum. Plastics and virgin aluminum have the most.[12]

▶ ISO 14,000

ISO 14,000 is a set of management standards set by The International Organization for Standardization (ISO). It is not a set of rules, specific environmental goals or performance standards. Instead, it is intended to encourage organizations to systematically address the environmental impacts of their activities. ISO 14,000 is a series of documents that provide a framework for environmental management systems, environmental auditing, environmental labeling, and product life cycle assessment. When possible, support suppliers who are ISO 14,000 participants.

ALTERNATIVE SOLUTIONS: To fully understand chlorine-free papers in detail, it is important first to define terms.

Totally chlorine free (TCF) is paper made with 100% virgin wood fibers manufactured without adding any chlorine or chlorine derivatives. No harmful dioxins, furans, or other organochlorines result, so collection and disposal of these toxic compounds is unnecessary. If a paper is TCF, it is a virgin grade and contains no post-consumer waste.

Processed chlorine-free recycled (PCF) paper is also made without adding chlorine or chlorine derivatives. Because paper recovered from the solid waste stream and used in making recycled paper may have been chlorine bleached in its first life, the end product cannot be guaranteed totally chlorine-free.

Elemental chlorine free (ECF) paper is manufactured without using elemental chlorine gas as a whitening agent. These papers are typically processed with chlorine dioxide or other chlorine compounds, which some paper makers believe to be less harmful to the environment than elemental chlorine gas. Although lower levels of chlorinated dioxins and furans are found in the mill's effluent and other related chlorinated compounds are reduced, they are not eliminated. Also, chlorine dioxide bleaching methods use 20 times more water and energy than chlorine-free processes.[4]

Non-deinked post consumer waste is recycled waste paper that has not gone through the bleaching process the second time around. Chemicals used in the papermaking process are minimized since the inks are left in the slurry, resulting in a delicate peppered appearance in the final sheet.

Oxygen delignification and ozone bleaching are totally chlorine-free processes used to separate lignin from wood fibers, and to bleach and whiten pulp. Mills using oxygen or ozone bleaching can send the effluent to a recovery system, where the organic material is burned to produce energy and metals and minerals are filtered out, thus closing the loop.

Hydrogen peroxide, which bleaches by oxygenating, is the preferred agent because no harmful byproducts result from its use. This process has been the bleaching agent of choice for newsprint and groundwood. Although stigmatized a decade ago for producing dull paper, the brightness of the pulp needed for fine printing and writing papers has and continues to improve.

ALTERNATIVE (NON-WOOD) FIBERS 15.1.3

While recycled stocks help alleviate solid waste problems, deinking post-consumer paper waste still involves using harsh chemicals and results in by-products of toxic sludge. Although recycled papers contain an increasing percentage of post-consumer content, most are supplemented with virgin wood pulp to enhance tensile strength. The sources: forests (some old growth) and tree farms.

Estimates indicate that as much as half of the 12 billion acres of forests that once covered the earth's surface have already been destroyed. In the last 35 years, wood consumption has doubled, and paper use has more than tripled.[5] Trees do produce consistent fibers, but they take a long time to grow, require a large amount of bleaching and chemical processing, and present industrial harvesting methods that are far from environmentally sustainable.

ALTERNATIVE SOLUTIONS: Recognizing the urgent need to conserve and preserve the world's forests, a new industry is developing around "tree-free" papers. These are made from fast-growing fiber crops such as kenaf and hemp; agricultural wastes, such as vegetables, corn and cereal straw, coffee grounds, and banana stalks; industrial wastes, such as recycled currency, denim scraps, cotton textile rags and factory trimmings; and flax, bagasse, bamboo, and seaweed.

Of these, kenaf is one of the most promising. A member of the hibiscus family, it shoots from seed to 15 feet high in just five months. An acre of kenaf can yield up to 11 tons of usable fiber per year. An acre of forest produces only 4–5 tons of usable fiber in 20-30 years. The kenaf fiber has better strength and performance than that of wood, and because it has a lower lignin content, it requires fewer chemicals and less energy to process. A vigorous plant, kenaf requires a minimum of fertilizers, pesticides and water compared to conventional row crops. Large-scale farming uses chemical fertilizers and pesticides that run off and pollute rivers, lakes, estuaries, oceans and underground water.

Once the backbone of American industry, hemp was "outlawed" in 1935, a move backed by special interest groups such as DuPont and the Hearst Corporations in order to capitalize on their own synthetic and wood-based fiber markets. In spite of its environmental and industrial advantages, the industry still struggles with overcoming hemp's association with marijuana. Like kenaf, hemp (cannabis) is a hardy annual plant requiring minimal water, fertilizer or pesticides. It produces 3 to 6 tons of usable fiber per year.[6] Unlike wood, it requires minimal chemical processing in the treatment of the fibers for papermaking. Because its manufacturing process can be acid-free, hemp paper offers outstanding archival potential (it is said to hold up for 1,500 years).

While many predictions show a diminishing wood supply, an incredible 2.5 billion tons of agricultural wastes around the world are available annually. Converted to 500 million tons of pulp[7], agricultural wastes such as wheat straw could yield enough fiber to supply 1.5 times the world's paper products consumption. The production of pulp from straw can be totally chlorine-free and acid-free, and the solid waste by-product can be safely used as feed or fertilizer.

Although printing on recycled paper was problematic in the 70s, the technology of producing these – and the newer alternative fiber - papers has greatly reduced or even eliminated the issues. Printers now find most recycled stocks print as well as their virgin competitors. Recycled papers, like virgin papers, will take ink differently and range in brightness and price as well, depending on the grade and the finish. Additionally, some recycled and alternative fiber papers come in rolls for web printing. Ask your printer or local paper distributor to help you with specifying the best environmental paper for your project.

The biggest drawback to many of these papers is availability. Because the market is not fully matured and a number of the manufacturers are small mills, distribution is usually limited to minimum quantities or the price is higher than their virgin counterparts. Still, the papers are worth the pursuit – and the additional cost, if any. Remember that when you specify these papers, you help build a market for them, and then it is only a matter of time before demand allows pricing to drop, and availability to become more widespread.

PRINTING INKS 15.2

There are four primary factors to consider when discussing the environmental and human health impacts of printing inks: pigments containing heavy metals, such as barium, copper, and zinc; petroleum based, high volatile organic compound (VOC) solvents used as pigment carriers and for enhanced drying; *hazardous waste* generated in manufacturing and use of the inks; and *coatings*, which are colorless topcoats designed to provide increased gloss, rub resistance and chemical resistance.

The heavy metals in pigments can contaminate soil and groundwater when leached into the environment through landfills, or wreak havoc in wastewater systems which aren't designed to process such industrial waste. Exposure, especially in large quantities, to these compounds through ingestion, inhalation or absorption can cause genetic disorders, lung irritation, spasms, heart problems or cancer. When deinked, the sludge may be classified as hazardous waste if concentrations of heavy metals and other pollutants are present.

Petrochemical *solvents* emit VOCs, polluting gasses which react with sunlight and air to form smog, thus contaminating the air we breathe. When evaporating, they can also be an irritant for printshop workers.

U.S. Environmental Protection Agency (EPA) figures estimate that in the U.S., about 44,000 sheetfed offset printers generate more than 60 million pounds of ink sludge annually. This leftover ink, consisting of oil, pigments, solvents and water, is classified as hazardous waste. In addition, an equivalent amount of waste is generated in the manufacture of printing ink – making an estimated 120 million pounds of *hazardous waste* every year. This waste is often incinerated, releasing more than 300 toxic chemicals and compounds into the air, water and soil.

When considering *coatings*, air pollution is one of the most significant factors. When printing UV coatings, although they emit little or no VOCs, low wavelength UV light reacts with oxygen, and ozone is created. Workers can also be exposed to radiation if working conditions are unsafe or unmonitored. Aqueous coatings do not undergo chemical reactions to dry, but since they are mainly liquid, vapors are vented into the atmosphere, potentially creating high levels of VOCs. However, this challenge has been resolved in recent years, and low- and non-VOC aqueous coatings are available. In terms of recyclablility, aqueous coatings are easier to process than UV coatings. The final answer to the aqueous vs. UV coatings question is a fundamental design issue: is the coating truly needed in the first place?

ALTERNATIVE SOLUTIONS: Avoid colors containing *pigments* with compounds (e.g., barium, copper and zinc) that exceed the threshold levels listed in Section 313 of Title III of the Superfund Amendments and Reauthorization Action[8]. Generally, these would be colors containing warm reds, and certain flourescent and metallic colors. A list of these inks can be found at www.econewsletter.net.

Petrochemical *solvents* in inks can be largely replaced with agri-based oils such as soy, corn, linseed, tung or canola to reduce VOC emissions and create a safer environment for printshop workers. They are also non-toxic, clean up more easily and need less harsh scouring agents, break down more readily in landfills as well as in the deinking and repulping process of paper recycling, and are made of renewable resources (versus petroleum-based, which are finite). Many printers avow that one advantage of using agri-based inks is brighter colors, which can translate into a more efficient print run with less paper waste and post-run disposal volumes. Today, a wide variety of agri-based inks can be found at competitive prices.[9]

Even though the first agri-based ink that may come to mind is soy (due to some very heavy marketing by the American Soybean Association), there are other types of oils that some inkmakers claim to be superior, such as linseed or tung (which, also, are not as controversial as soybean's bio-engineering issues).[10]

Note that an ink may contain as little as 10–20% soy or other alternative oil and still be called agri-based, soy-based or vegetable-based, even thought the remaining component is petroleum-based. Ask your printer to use the highest agri-based ink possible (up to 100% is available).

Printing ink waste at offset printers and ink makers can be completely eliminated from the waste stream and used to formulate quality recycled ink. A patented process, known as Lithographic Ink Recovery Technology (LIRT), recovers 100% of the ink sludge once transported as hazardous waste for incineration. Recovery occurs with no solid, liquid or gaseous emissions to the environment and results in three marketable products: ink, solvent and de-ionized water. It is a completely closed loop process. Rich in pigment, even compared to ink manufactured from virgin raw materials, recycled ink generated by the new process has superior printing qualities and generates less process waste.

With current technology, recycled ink is only available in charcoal black, which is a suitable replacement for black ink. In the future, as source separation becomes feasible and market demand increases, process colors (cyan, yellow, magenta and black) will be available so that four-color reproduction with entirely recycled inks will be possible.

PACKAGING 15.3

Packaging contains, protects, preserves and informs…it also makes up 30% of the U.S. wastestream. The environmental impacts of packaging include pollution and energy consumption from materials manufacture, transportation, disposal and recycling. Most of the impacts occur during manufacture and disposal, where the designer has considerable influence.

ALTERNATIVE SOLUTIONS: Knowing about the various forms of packaging, how they are produced, distributed and disposed of, and having a sense of viable, greener, cost-effective alternatives is essential knowledge that designers cannot afford to overlook. The goals for minimal impact design are:

• Assess the product. Is there a way to re-engineer the product to make it stronger so that the package is eliminated completely?

• Avoid unnecessary packaging and design to make the largest visual impact on the smallest, strongest package possible.

• Keep up with technological developments. For example, one company, Regale (see resource list), has perfected molded pulp technology to replace packaging such as plastic bubble wrap, cardboard shoeboxes, and traditional six-pack beverage carriers. They affirm it is economically, structurally, and environmentally superior to all other mediums.

• Design the package so that it can be refillable or re-usable.

> **IN-HOUSE AUDITING**

1. Create an environmental policy for your workplace. Include criteria such as:

• Use the blank side of a laser printed sheet for fax paper before recycling to reduce paper consumption

• Buy only U.S. EPA Energy Star rated equipment

• Recycle dead batteries at an appropriate facility

• Recharge and buy recycled toner cartridges

• Turn off machines or use a "sleep mode," which can reduce energy consumption by 25–90%

• Purchase recycled disks and other magnetic media

2. Learn what you can about the suppliers you work with. Develop relationships with forward thinking suppliers who can collaborate with new materials and processes, energy- and waste-efficient office equipment and non-toxic supplies. Support local suppliers whenever possible and appropriate.

3. Minimize your waste, then recycle as many materials as possible.

4. Take advantage of electronic communication to send files, rather than relying on courier systems or faxes. When appropriate, make your presentations via email.

- Make the package recyclable or re-usable. To aid the consumer in recycling, clearly mark all packaging with the recycling emblem, and mark plastics according to DIN 6120.
- Design with materials that can be recycled in the target market's community. Use the fewest different kinds of materials possible (e.g., two types of plastics, or plastic and cardboard). If more than one is absolutely necessary, make it easy for the consumer to take them apart for recycling.
- Use sustainably harvested, recycled and/or biodegradable materials with high post-consumer waste content to defray the environmental costs of extracting and processing virgin materials. Look for every opportunity to use renewable resources such as kenaf, agripulp or polylactide (PLA) polymers (from maize) in the primary package and the manual, etc.
- Maximize positive consumer perception.
- Avoid heavy metals, halogenated polymers, and ozone-depleting and other harmful substances.
- The product and package are a team. Make them perform like one.

These goals may conflict. For example, a recycled material could increase the total package weight, while a lightweight material might not be recyclable. Setting environmental priorities in a design brief, along with objectives such as cost, shelf-life, sanitation, tamper-resistance and retail presentation, will help shape the design.[11]

COMPUTERS

Computers are made with more than 700 different compounds, and more than half of these are toxic. If landfilled, a witch's brew of materials including lead, mercury, zinc, arsenic, cadmium, hexavalent chromium, PVC plastic and flame retardants may eventually leak into the soil and contaminate groundwater. Almost 4 pounds of lead resides in one single monitor.

The National Safety Council (NSC) reports that in 1998, approximately 20.6 million personal computers became obsolete in the United States. Only 11% of those computers were recycled. The average life span of a personal computer has decreased from 4–5 years to 2 years. By the year 2004, the NSC estimates that there will be more than 315 million obsolete computers in the U.S. If this is true, there could also be 315 million monitors containing more than 1.2 billion pounds of lead. Currently, almost all are destined for landfills, incinerators or hazardous waste export.[13]

ALTERNATIVE SOLUTIONS:: If recycled, gold, silver, copper, steel, aluminum, wire, cable and other resources can be mined from computers. Until an infrastructure is in place for producers to take back their products (as in Europe), donate old computers to organizations that specialize in their reuse and recycling. ∎

DESIGN PLANNING

1. Balance an environmentally responsible approach with the client's and/or product's needs. Can an innovative material or process be used? Will the client be supportive of this experimentation and accept the risks involved?

2. Understand the product life cycle for the entire project, from the materials used to the disposal, reuse, recyclability, and biodegradability of the product.

MATERIAL SELECTION

1. Minimize the amount of material in your design.

2. Specify high-recycled post-consumer waste (PCW) content.

3. Design for recyclability to avoid disposing of the waste after use.

4. Specify paper made from sustainably harvested timber, or specify kenaf, hemp, straw or other tree-free fibers.

5. Maximize the use of recycled and biodegradable materials. Design so that a material can be recycled into something of greater or equal value first, such as turning cotton scraps into fabric, before converting them into paper.

6. Specify materials that minimize or eliminate the use of hazardous chemicals (such as chlorine) in the production process.

7. Keep a library of "Best Recycled/Tree-Free/Chlorine-free" paper samples. File them from best to good (best being TCF or PCF, then ECF, and with a high PCW content of 50–100%, then 30%+).

PRINT PRODUCTION

1. Ask whether your printer has an environmental policy. Choose printing methods which minimize wastes and conserve water and energy. Can the project be done electronically, from digital to plate, avoiding the need for film negatives and related processing chemicals, etc.?

2. Replace foil stamping or thermography (which are not recyclable) with embossing or debossing. Use a non-toxic color instead of one which contains a heavy metal. Go through your Pantone® book and "X" out all the toxic colors, so you'll be discouraged to spec them.

3. Reserve coatings and laminations for use on long life-cycle projects, where protection, as well as aesthetics, is the intent.

4. Solid ink coverage increases the amount of chemicals required to de-ink reclaimed paper. Use screened areas of a darker color to minimize ink coverage, or choose a paper that has an interesting texture and color for a desired effect.

5. Frequently specify PCW recycled and non-chlorine bleached paper, and encourage your printer to stock it as standard. This simple act has a tremendous ripple effect.

6. Make the most of your press sheets — even if it's to make book marks. Use leftovers of press runs for pro-bono work.

7. Avoid waste by working with your printer to determine sheet size and grain direction before finalizing your design.

FOOTNOTES

1. "Building a New Economy: The Challenge for Our Generation," Press Release, Saturday, January 10,1998; www.worldwatch.org/alerts/pr980110.html

2. "Report Calls for Rapid Scaling Up of Efforts to Preserve Health of Forests and Provide Economic Benefits," www.worldwatch.org/alerts/pr980402.html

3. "The Facts about Chlorine & Dioxin," Seventh Generation; www.seventhgen.com

4. "Choose to Make a World of Difference," CFPA Today, Vol.5 No. 2 Spring 2002, Chlorine Free Products Association

5. "Report Calls for Rapid Scaling Up of Efforts to Preserve Health of Forests and Provide Economic Benefits," WorldWatch Institute; www.worldwatch.org/alerts/pr980402.html

6. "Letters to Earth Journal," paranoia.lycaeum.org/marijuana/hemp/kenaf.vs.hemp.paper

7. "Montana's Straw: Golden Grains, Golden Opportunities A project of the Montana Straw To Paper Working Group," Native Forest Network web site, May 2001 www.nativeforest.org/campaigns/montana_straw/

8. "List of Toxic Inks to Avoid," ECO Newsletter, www.econewsletter.net

9. "Environmentally Preferable Purchasing Guide," Solid Waste Management Coordinating Board, April 2000, www.swmcb.org/EPPG/5_2.htm

10. "Rounding Up Biotech Soybeans," Dan Imhoff, ECO Newsletter, Communication Arts, January/February 1998

11. "Green Packaging — A Guide for the Perplexed," Helen Lewis, Centre for Design at RMIT, Pack Sourcebook 1996–97, www.cfd.rmit.edu.au/outcomes/papers/packaging.html

12. CSG/Tellus Packaging Study, May 1992

13. "Computer Recycling and Waste: A Looming Environmental Crisis," Texas Campaign for the Environment, www.texasenvironment.org/e-waste/e-waste.htm

A STARTER LIST FOR ENVIRONMENTALLY PREFERRABLE MATERIALS, BUSINESS ORGANIZATIONS AND FURTHER RESEARCH

ECO Newsletter (1992-2002), Communication Arts: www.econewsletter.net

Conservatree: www.conservatree.com

Watershed Media: www.watershedmedia.org

Green Seal Choose Green Reports: www.greenseal.org/recommendations

Independent Designers Network : www.indes.net

Chlorine Free Products Association: www.chlorinefreeproducts.org

Printer's National Environmental Assistance Center: www.pneac.org

Great Printers Project: www.pneac.org/greatprinters/gppmore-info.html

GreenDisk: www.greendisk.com

Covenant Recycling Services 619-792-6975

ECOMedia: www.ecomedia.net

O2 (international organization of designers): www.o2.org

U.S. Environmental Protection Agency resources: www.epa.gov/wastewise www.epa.gov/dfe (Design for the Environment)

J. Ottman Consulting, Inc.: www.greenmarketing.com

Business for Social Responsibility: www.bsr.org

The Natural Step: www.naturalstep.org

The Alliance for Environmental Innovation: www.environmentaldefense.org/alliance

The Green Business Letter: www.greenbizletter.com and www.greenbiz.com

WorldWatch Institute: www.worldwatch.com

Institute for Local Self-Reliance: www.ilsr.org

GRAPHIC PRODUCTION

16

- ▶ STRATEGIC PHASE
- ▶ CREATIVE PHASE
- ▶ PRODUCTION OF ORIGINALS
- ▶ PRODUCTION OF IMAGES
- ▶ OUTPUT/RASTERIZING
- ▶ PROOFS
- ▶ PLATE + PRINTING
- ▶ POSTPRESS PROCESSING
- ▶ DISTRIBUTION

CHAPTER 16 GRAPHIC PRODUCTION **MOUNTING A GRAPHIC PRODUCTION GENERALLY INVOLVES NUMEROUS DIFFERENT PARTIES THAT HAVE TO COOPERATE IN ORDER FOR EVERYTHING TO WORK. THE FLOW OF INFORMATION DURING THE GRAPHIC PRODUCTION PROCESS CAN BECOME VERY COMPLEX.**

Before beginning this process, there are a number of questions to consider which will in large part determine the project plan. We will cover those questions in this chapter, including tips for evaluating manufacturers and service providers, how to request an estimate, and how to plan a graphic production. We will also look at the flow of material and information through the process.

BEFORE YOU BEGIN 16.1

There are a number of questions that need to be answered before the production process begins. For example, it is important to consider for whom the printed product is intended, how it will be distributed and used, what the environmental concerns are, etc.

WHY ARE YOU CREATING A PRINTED PRODUCT? 16.1.1

To begin with, you should ask yourself what the purpose of your printed product is – determine what it is you want this product to accomplish, and what it should communicate.
Some possible answers:
• To inform
• To sell
• To entertain
• To package

The answer to this question is often a combination of different purposes. Knowing the reasons behind why you are creating a printed product helps to determine what kind of printed product you should produce and how it should reach the user.

For example:
- If want to sell something you might create an advertisement
- If your intent is to inform the user, you might develop a newsletter or a brochure instead
- To entertain or educate you might create a book

DETERMINING THE USER 16.1.2

It is important to consider the target audience for your product – i.e., who will be using it? Knowing the intended target audience helps to determine what type of printed product should be created and how it should be designed.

Some examples of different groups who might be considered a target audience for a particular product:
- Teenagers
- People of average income
- People with an interest in food
- Senior citizens

REACHING THE USER 16.1.3

You must also consider how you are going to reach your user – i.e., what medium is best suited to reaching your target audience. The choice of media can be crucial in successfully reaching the target group.

Examples of ways in which you might reach your target audience:
- Billboards downtown
- Advertisements in daily or weekly newspapers
- Direct mail

CHOOSING THE TYPE OF PRODUCT 16.1.4

Determining the type of printed product and the number of copies you will need affects the cost and determines which printing method you will need to use.

Some examples:
- Newspaper, 20,000 copies
- Book, 10,000 copies
- Packaging, 100,000 copies
- Poster, 500 copies
- Catalogue, 100,000 copies
- Folder, 5,000 copies
- Advertisement, 200 copies

HOW WILL A PRODUCT BE USED? 16.1.5

It is also important to consider how a product will be used. For example, if it is meant to last a long time, you will need to create a product that is resistant to wear and tear. Some questions to consider:
- How long does this product need to last?
- Will it be archived or thrown away after it is used?
- Will it be handled a great deal?
- Does it need to perform a specific function, such as packaging?

The answers to these questions help determine how a product should be printed, processed, and what materials should be used in its creation.

Some examples:
- A catalogue that will be flipped through a lot should be off press processed so it will last. This might involve lamination of the cover and the use of the glue binding technique.
- A poster that will be hung outside must be resistant to weather, and would fare best if printed with waterproof inks on a durable paper.
- A book intended to last for a long time might require a hard cover with a protective surface treatment and high-quality binding.
- A newspaper can be printed on inexpensive paper and stapled because it need not last very long.

QUALITY REQUIREMENTS 16.1.6

The quality requirements of a particular product affect the cost and delivery time of a production. In addition, quality issues can affect your choice of production partners.

You can divide graphic production into three quality levels: low, medium and high. Typical products requiring only low quality production include product flyers, simple brochures, internal publications, etc. Medium-quality publications include things like newsletters and brochures. Four-color advertisements, annual reports, art books and packaging generally require high-quality production.

Some examples:
- An art book needs the highest image reproduction, printing, paper and off press quality.
- A flyer for the pizzeria around the corner does not need high quality anything, and it is probably more important to keep the printing costs down.

THE BUDGET 16.1.7

When planning your budget, it is important to factor in a margin of safety for problems that might occur during the production.

ENVIRONMENTAL REQUIREMENTS 16.1.8

Are there particular environmental requirements for your product?

Some examples:
- Recyclability.
- Use of agri-based inks and tree-free paper.

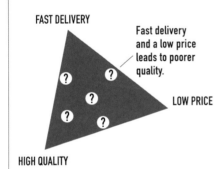

▶ **PRIORITIZE YOUR PRODUCTION.**
It is impossible to combine a low price, fast delivery and high quality. You need to decide where in the triangle you want your printed product based on your priorities.

PRINT PRODUCTION GRAPHIC PRODUCTION

CHOOSING SERVICE PROVIDERS 16.2

Success in graphic production is greatly aided by the formation of good working relationships with a number of graphic service providers. It is important, therefore, to put some thought into your choice of providers.

When comparing different manufacturers and service providers, you should keep the requirements of your project in mind. Think about what steps of the production you would like to do yourself and what you might need or want help with. Undertaking the bulk of the production yourself might be cheaper, but you are taking on more responsibility for the final result.

Keep in mind that some types of productions might be better suited to one provider than another. This especially applies to printers that specialize in certain types of productions, or that use a specific printing process and/or printing press for particular paper formats.

Following are a number of factors that you might find helpful to consider when choosing a service provider.

PRICING 16.2.1

Pricing in the graphic industry is far from standardized. There are a number of ways in which prices are determined. Some printers have standardized price lists while others price jobs individually. It is important to find exactly what services a printer's fees cover. It is also wise to ask about rush charges and under what circumstances they apply.

Prices in the graphic production industry can vary widely from service provider to service provider. For example, scanning a four-color image can cost anywhere between $20 and $100. Factors that affect the price the most are quality and delivery time. If your project does not need the best quality or fastest turn-around time, you can get a relatively reasonable price. On the other hand, if you have high demands on quality and delivery time, you have to be prepared to pay accordingly.

Hiring the right company for the production is also an important factor in keeping costs in line. A vendor who works with the type of production you are requesting on a regular basis will most likely be able to give you a better deal than one that has to make special accommodations for your project. For example, if you want to print a catalog, you will probably get the best price from a printer specializing in that type of production.

QUALITY 16.2.2

In order to ensure that the provider you choose is able to provide competent quality service, you should ask for outside references, as well as review samples of work they have done that are similar to your project.

Find out if the company has a particular specialty. A company that specializes in image editing, for example, should provide better-than-average service in that area, but that extra quality may come at a price. If you don't need top-quality image editing, you might save money by using a provider who does not specialize in that area.

DELIVERY TIME AND DELIVERY SECURITY 16.2.3

How much time does a provider need to complete certain services? The faster the turn-around, the more it tends to cost. Also ask if the company secures their deliveries. Secure deliveries can be crucial in some cases, as with projects like advertisements that are tied to a deadline.

CAPACITY 16.2.4

If you ever need to produce large-volume productions in a short amount of time, it is important to know beforehand if your service provider has the appropriate staff and equipment, as well as the experience, to deal with this type of production.

WORKING WITH YOUR SERVICE PROVIDER 16.2.5

How is the company organized? Is there a specific person with whom you will communicate about your project? Will that contact person always be the same or will they differ depending on the assignment? These questions are important for determining the type of service you can expect and how you will be treated as a client.

VICINITY 16.2.6

Often the biggest advantage of using a service provider in your immediate vicinity is the savings in time – especially if fast turn—around is important. If you can be more flexible with delivery times, there may be significant financial advantages to hiring a provider outside of expensive major metropolitan areas, as their overhead costs will most likely be lower. If you do hire a service provider in another location, you should be aware that it might be difficult to do certain things like be present for the makeready, or make quick decisions when problems occur.

BUSINESS HOURS AND ACCESSIBILITY 16.2.7

What are the business hours of the company? When and for how long are your contact people available? Do they work in shifts? If you need service beyond regular working hours, is that an option? The answers to these questions impact capacity and delivery times. For example, a company that works in shifts can produce higher volumes and can often offer shorter delivery times than a company that does not.

REFERENCES 16.2.8

Ask for references. Ask to see samples of productions the company has done. Do they correspond to the kind of production you are requesting? Ask for names and contact numbers of other clients who have hired the company and ask them about their working relationship.

Successful graphic production is largely about cooperation and communication. Make sure you get to know your service providers well and communicate with them frequently during your production. Choosing partners for graphic production often means starting a relationship that will last for years. Changing service providers may result in unexpected costs at the start and it might take some time to establish a new relationship.

In addition to the above-mentioned factors, there are a number of other points to keep in mind when choosing production partners. For example:

THE COMPANY 16.2.9

Does the company seem stable? Does it have a solid reputation in the industry? What is the ownership structure of the company? Are you planning on having a lengthy relationship with the company?

SIZE AND RESOURCES 16.2.10

How large is the company? Are there several people on staff with overlapping knowledge of the different steps of the process? How vulnerable is the company if someone is on vacation or sick?

COMPANY POLICIES 16.2.11

What policies and agreements have been established between the customer and service provider? What industry policies does the company practice? Are there other agreements or policies that are important to know about when working with the company? A company's policies regarding terms of delivery, quality assurance, and copyright are areas that you should familiarize yourself with.

INVOICING 16.2.12

What invoicing policies does the company have? What are the terms of payment?

QUALITY WORK 16.2.13

How does the company assure a quality product? How do they work to maintain and improve on the quality of their product?

ENVIRONMENTAL CONCERNS 16.2.14

Is the company proactive with regard to the environment? How does it address environmental concerns?

THE FUTURE 16.2.15

What are the company's plans for growth? What services does the company plan to add in the future? How does the company plan to secure its longevity? These questions can be very important because the graphic industry is subject to a lot of changes.

GETTING AN ESTIMATE 16.3

When requesting a price quote from graphic service providers, it is important that all the information about the intended product is included. Otherwise, costs can get out of hand, time delays might occur and the printed product may not turn out as expected. Following are several checklists you can use when requesting estimates for different types of graphic services. The checklists contain examples of information necessary to obtain a good estimate for any one service, and can be combined if you need to request more than one type of service from a provider.

> **CHECKLIST FOR REQUESTING AN ESTIMATE FOR PRE-PRESS SERVICE**

GENERAL INFORMATION

☐ Quality requirements

☐ Programs and computer type (Macintosh/Windows)

☐ The format of the printed product

☐ The volume of the printed product

☐ Which screen frequency should be used?

☐ Should the digital material be archived?

☐ Delivery (messenger, postal mail, digital)

☐ Delivery address

☐ Delivery time

INFORMATION ABOUT ORIGINAL ARTWORK

☐ Type of original work (proof of an existing document, typography in an existing document or language adjustments according to set templates,an original based on a sketch or made entirely from scratch including design)

☐ Type of manuscript

☐ Proof (What type? How many? Distributed how, where and when?)

INFORMATION ABOUT IMAGES

☐ Type of images (black and white, color)

☐ Digital original images, which format?

☐ How many images should be scanned?

☐ The final size of the image

☐ Image edits (selections, retouches or shadows), how many, how complex?

☐ Use of archived images

INFORMATION ABOUT OUTPUTTING

☐ Number of colors the product should be printed with

☐ Print-ready files (file format)

☐ Individual films (page films) or imposed film

☐ Number of film sets

☐ Check-up or adjustment of trapping, knockouts and/or overprinting

☐ Types of halftone screens (stochastic or traditional)

☐ Types of proofs (digital or analog)

PREPRESS SERVICES 16.3.1

Prepress services that you would request an estimate for:
• Producing different types of original artwork
• Image scanning, retouching, color correction
• Print-ready files (i.e PDF or PostScript) or rasterizing, output to film and proof, possible imposition

Below is a brief version of the checklist and the relevant points:

General Information
• *Quality Requirements*
Let them know what the printed product is supposed to be used for and what quality requirements you have. It is important to make this clear so that everyone is in agreement regarding the quality you need in the finished product.

- *Programs and Computer Type (Macintosh/ Windows)*
Specify the programs and program versions you used to create your originals and whether the material you are submitting is in Macintosh or Windows format. The service provider must have compatible hardware and software in order to execute the work.

- *The Format and Volume of the Printed Product*
The number of pages and the format of the product directly affect how much film needs to be used. Often the cost for rasterizing and outputting to film is defined in cost per sheet of film and the makeready of printready files is defined per page. The number of pages also affects the cost of the original artwork. Sometimes printers come up with a flat cost per page, which includes scanning of images, image editing, output to film and proofs.

- *Which screen frequency should be used in the print?*
Screen frequency is an important piece of information that can affect pricing with some service providers. The choice of screen frequency is determined by printing method, type of printing press and paper choice. The choice of paper, in turn, might be determined by which type of off press processing you select.

- *Should the digital material be archived?*
Some companies offer digital archiving of documents and images for future use, but don't take this service for granted – you may have to ask them to do it. Also remember to double-check the copyrights for the text and images used in your project to make sure they can be legally archived.

- *Delivery (messenger, postal mail, digital) and delivery address*
How is the finished product to be delivered? For example, will it be delivered to you as a set of digital images, and if so, should they be high- or low-resolution? If you would like high-resolution, you need to specify whether they should be in RGB or converted to CMYK. You might want complete digital documents with high-resolution images, print-ready files or films. You should also specify how the project should be physically delivered – i.e., via messenger, mail or the Internet – and to whom should it be delivered (if more than one person needs to get it, for example).

- *Delivery Time*
How quickly can the company turn your project around? Keep in mind that there might be additional rush charges.

INFORMATION ABOUT ORIGINAL ARTWORK

- *Type of original artwork*
Specify what original artwork is needed. It might be a proof of an existing document, typography of an existing document or language adjustments according to set templates. Other alternatives may be making an original based on a sketch or entirely from scratch including design.

• *Type of manuscript*

In what format should the manuscript be delivered – digitally or on paper? If it is to be delivered digitally, specify the format.

• *Proof (What type? How many? Distributed how, where and when?)*

In what format should the proof be delivered – i.e., laser printout, color or black and white? Should the proofs be distributed via messenger, mail, Internet, etc.? If they are distributed digitally, what format should they be in? PDF format or some other format? Are there enough proof copies included in the price to send to everyone who needs one?

INFORMATION ABOUT IMAGES

• *Types of images (black and white, color)*

Black and white images and line art are usually cheaper to scan than color images (about half as expensive as color images).

• *Digital images, which format?*

If you are giving the service provider digital images, you should specify the format they are in. RGB images need to be converted into CMYK at an additional cost.

• *The final size of the image and how many should be scanned*

It is important to specify the number of images to be scanned. The final size of the scanned images affects the price, and in some companies the scanning resolution also factors into the price. Although it might be difficult, you should try to estimate the size of the images you will need before production in order to estimate costs.

• *Image edits (selections, retouches or shadows), how many, how complex?*

The cost of selections, retouches and other image edits differ depending on the company. Some offer cost-per-mask or -retouch pricing while others charge an hourly rate. It is a good idea to describe the selections or retouches you will need in order to help the service provider estimate their complexity. For example, it takes more time to create a path around a complicated silhouette like a pine tree than it does around a simple object like a ball.

• *Using [recycling] archived images*

Are there images you want to use in a project that you have already digitally archived with the service provider? If so, specify which ones you wish to reuse as well as how many images will be reused altogether.

INFORMATION ABOUT RASTERIZING, OUTPUT ON FILM AND PROOFS, POSSIBLE IMPOSITION

• *Number of colors the product should be printed with*

The number of colors you are printing with directly affects the number of films that need to be produced.

- *Individual films (page films) or imposed film*
Some pre-press companies offer digital imposition in different formats. They can do the imposition on the computer and expose several pages on one large film. It is generally cheaper than mounting the individual films manually.

- *Number of film sets*
If you are printing a number of identical pages on the same sheet – a 4-up, for example – you will need four identical sets of films.

- *Check-up or adjustment of trapping, knockouts and/or overprinting*
If you try to do the trapping yourself, you run the risk of not having the print accurately trapped. Therefore, it is advisable to have the service provider do any necessary trapping [see Documents 6.7]. If you are not sure if your project requires trapping, knockouts and/or overprinting, you should ask the service provider to look through the documents with you to determine your needs.

- *Types of halftone screens (stochastic or traditional)*
You should let the service provider know if you want to print with a traditional or stochastic halftone screen. Not all pre-press service providers work with stochastic screens. They are somewhat more expensive than traditional screens [see Output 9.1].

- *Types of proofs (digital or analog)*
Proofs are another important issue. Most companies do analog proofs (Chromalin, Agfa-proof, Matchprint, etc.) of the films they deliver. The disadvantage of analog proofs is that you are limited to the paper supplied by the manufacturer. This makes it difficult to simulate the final printing result. Proofs are expensive, but keep in mind that analog proofs are the only way of checking the content of the films. Think about whether proofs are necessary for your project, and also find out if the printer you are planning to use requires you to submit proofs with the films. Sometimes a blue print is enough.

When you work with print-ready files you use digital proofs instead.

Before submitting advertisements, it is common to do what is known as an "advertisement proof." It is a "real" press print printed in an offset press on the run paper, and is, therefore, considerably more expensive than other types of proofs [see Review and Proofing 10.6].

▶ CHECKLIST FOR REQUESTING AN ESTIMATE FOR PRINTED SERVICES
☐ Volume (number of pages)
☐ Edition size
☐ Format
☐ Number of printing inks
☐ Material requirements
☐ Choice of paper
☐ Delivery arrangements
☐ Timeframe for delivery

PRINTING SERVICES 16.3.2
Services provided by the printer include:
- Producing plates
- Printing
- Providing paper

Checklist:
Volume, edition, format and number of printing inks
This information enables you to quickly determine if a printing house is the right one for your production, if the printing press is the correct type and the number of inking units

is adequate. As a principle, the decision on the printing press is determined from a financial point of view.

If your product has more than one, two or four pages, it is wise to select a page number that can be evenly divided with the number of pages that fit on a sheet of paper for a particular printing press, like eight 8 $\frac{1}{2}$" × 11" pages on a 23" × 35"-sheet, for example. Keep in mind that the start-up costs for a print job are often high. Ask how much it costs to print an additional 100 or 1000 copies, for example. Sometimes it is cost-effective to print a larger edition. When choosing a format, staying as close to standard sizes as is practical for your project will help use the paper as efficiently as possible.

Keep in mind that most printing presses have one, two, or four inking units and that productions with a number of colors different from the number of inking units often entail additional costs. Using printing inks other than cyan, magenta, yellow or black – PMS colors, for example – may also raise the costs of your production because they require the press to be cleaned when the inks are changed.

Material requirements
Does the printer require digital files, individual films or film that is already imposed?

Choice of paper
The paper is usually a large expense in the production of a printed product and all paper grades do not fit all printing presses. You should therefore discuss the paper choice with the printer even if you have already decided on the paper stock. It might also be beneficial to ask if the printer has a better price on a similar paper. The printing houses usually have various agreements with the paper supplier and the price can differ significantly among similar paper stock from different companies. Coated paper has a finer surface and can take higher screen frequency but it also costs a bit more [see Paper 12.4.1].

DELIVERY ARRANGEMENTS
Specify whether or not you want delivery costs to be included in the price quote. If not, you will have to arrange for delivery yourself. Most printing houses can assist you with delivery however.

TIMEFRAME FOR DELIVERY
How much time does the manufacturer have to complete the production? Are special rush charges applied if you need the delivery to take place before your agreed-upon deadline?

OFF PRESS PROCESSING SERVICES 16.3.3
Off press processing services include:
• Cropping
• Folding
• Binding

In the following text we will look closer at the checklist and the impact the different factors have.

▶ **CHECKLIST FOR REQUESTING AN ESTIMATE FOR PRINTED SERVICES**

Is the following information included?

☐ Volume (number of pages)

☐ Edition size

☐ Format

☐ Type of off press processing services

☐ Format requirements

☐ Delivery arrangements

☐ Timeframe for delivery

Volume, edition, format and how the material is handed off

The pricing of off press processing services is based on initial costs for makereadies, the makereadies that follow and cost per processed unit. The number of pages and the imposition of the sheets determine how many makereadies you need to do in the off press processing. The fewer pages the sheets have space for and the more pages the printed product has, the more makereadies are necessary. The volume, in turn, affects the cost per unit.

Types of off press processes

The volume and choice of paper stock determine the range of appropriate binding solutions. The different bindings vary in cost [see Off Press Processing, page 245].

Delivery arrangements

Specify if delivery costs should be included in the price quote. If not, you have to arrange for delivery.

Timeframe for delivery

How much time does the company need to complete your order? Are special rush charges applied if you need delivery to take place before your deadline?

> ▶ **EXAMPLES OF PARTNERS**
> - Advertising agencies
> - Media consultants
> - Communication consultants
> - Writing agencies
> - Photographers
> - Translators
> - Production companies
> - Prepress providers
> - Copiers
> - Printers
> - Bookbinders
> - Distributors

PLANNING A GRAPHIC PRODUCTION 16.4

When you have received estimates and selected the service provider, you need to plan the production. Graphic production can be very difficult to plan. Unexpected issues crop up constantly and there are few objective measurements of what is right and wrong. Much of the production is based on proofing rounds until all parties involved are satisfied. Communication and professional skills are crucial for a successful working relationship. It is a great advantage if the parties involved know each other and their requirements and expectations well.

Just because it is difficult to plan graphic production, does not mean you should not do it! That is precisely why you should spend a lot of time preparing and planning. There are a number of important things to consider before creating a plan for a project.

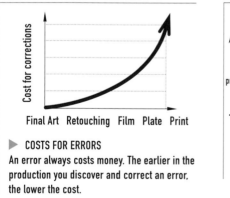

▶ **COSTS FOR ERRORS**
An error always costs money. The earlier in the production you discover and correct an error, the lower the cost.

▶ **PRODUCTION PLAN**
Production plans are helpful tools to keep control of your project.

> ▶ **TOOLS TO HELP YOU PLAN**
> - Timelines
> - To-Do Lists
> - Distribution of responsibilities
> - Database of suppliers
> - Contact persons

PROJECT ORGANIZATION 16.4.1

Before starting, it is important to have a clear picture of who should do what. This is sometimes called project organization or referred to as the project plan. The project plan answers the following questions:

- Who is in charge of the project? Do you yourself have sufficient experience or should somebody else be running things?
- Who are all the people who will be working on the project? Who is responsible for what? Who should proof texts, images, design, content and function?
- Who else should be kept in the loop during the project?
- How can you ensure meeting quality standards and deadlines?
- Which partners are necessary to complete the project?
- How much should you do yourself and what do you need help with? What do you require from your partners?
- Have you already established connections in all relevant areas or do you need to do that first?

Production plans are helpful tools for managing projects. Create the plan backwards, starting with the deadline for the completed project. Find out how long each of the phases in the project takes. Set aside time for delivery, partial deliveries, proof rounds and add some extra time for a safety margin. There will probably be situations in which you will need it.

It is important to set aside a sufficient time for reviews and proofing. The further into the production you are when you discover an error, the more it will cost you to fix it.

MATERIAL AND INFORMATION FLOW 16.5

1. Strategic phase
2. Creative phase
3. Production of originals
4. Production of images
5. Output/rasterizing
6. Proofs
7. Printing plates and printing
8. Off press processing
9. Distribution

The phases are categorized according to their function. They are all unique and it is important to carefully plan each phase before its execution. Each step is related to the execution of the ones that come before and after. As a result, the accurate transfer of material and information from step to step is crucial to achieving the desired outcome. Each detour from the planned information flow compromises quality. A good grasp of the entire production process is necessary, even if you are only involved in a few or just one of the above-mentioned steps.

The flow of information through today's graphic production processes can be very complex. Because each phase in the process is affected by and has an effect on the others the people responsible for each phase need to receive and hand off accurate information in order for everything to work. Different productions have very different requirements,

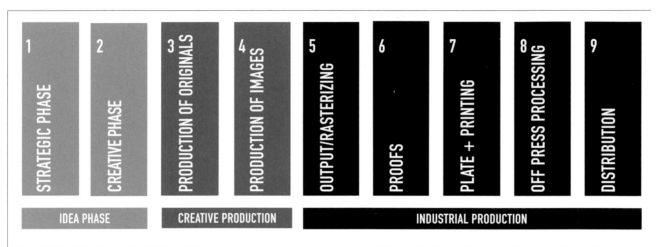

1	2	3	4	5	6	7	8	9
STRATEGIC PHASE	CREATIVE PHASE	PRODUCTION OF ORIGINALS	PRODUCTION OF IMAGES	OUTPUT/RASTERIZING	PROOFS	PLATE + PRINTING	OFF PRESS PROCESSING	DISTRIBUTION

IDEA PHASE	CREATIVE PRODUCTION	INDUSTRIAL PRODUCTION

▶ THE NINE PHASES OF GRAPHIC PRODUCTION
Graphic production can be divided into nine phases. The first two phases involve the development of the creative concept. The next two focus on the implementation and further modification of this concept. The last five steps are more industrial in nature and are determined by decisions made in the preceding phases.

which is why there is such a variety of production plans. For example, participants may not always be involved in the same part of the production chain. Where a particular phase of a production is carried out may change from project to project depending on the type of printed product desired. Because different people and different companies are involved, you can't just assume that "the prepress provider is always responsible for...abc" or " the printing house is always responsible for ...xyz." However, this way of thinking still dominates the graphics industry and constantly causes misunderstandings. One way to sort out the different areas of responsibility is to break down the entire production chain into discrete functions and phases, as we did earlier. Then you can figure out who is responsible for which function(s) in each case.

One company can often handle several phases of production. It does not matter which of the functions it can handle – this might vary from job to job. The most important thing is that you know what responsibilities each phase entails. The responsibilities associated with each production phase are almost always the same, regardless of who performs it.

When we have broken down the production chain according to its functions, we have purposely avoided specifying exactly where the information is coming from because it may vary from case to case. In order for the dissemination of information and the coordination among the different parties involved in a graphic production to work well, someone must manage the process and oversee the whole production. A project manager must be competent in all areas of graphic production in order to successfully coordinate the flow of information and material.

Information and material being transferred from one stage to another should be accurate and organized. It is important to take the time to put things in writing so everybody knows what is going on and misunderstandings are avoided. Aside from information specific to the stage of production, general information about the project should be included. In the following pages, we will review the flow of information and material through the graphic production process, as well as checklists of information for what should be included when handing off material from one phase to the next. ∎

▶ PHASE 1 – STRATEGIC PHASE

INFORMATION IN
Goal/Target Group
Purpose

INFORMATION OUT
How much can the printed
product cost?
What type of printed product
should be produced?
Edition size
Type of delivery
Timeframe for delivery

MATERIAL IN
-

MATERIAL OUT
Mailing list (when products are
distributed)

▶ PHASE 2 – CREATIVE PHASE

INFORMATION IN
How much can the printed
product cost?
What type of printed product
should be produced?
Timeframe for delivery

INFORMATION OUT
Paper
Off press processing
Format
Printing inks (CMYK or PMS)
Typography

MATERIAL IN
-

MATERIAL OUT
Sketches
Original images
Texts

▶ PHASE 3 – PRODUCTION OF ORIGINALS

INFORMATION IN
Printing information (printing
method, screen frequency,
maximum ink coverage, dot gain,
gray balance, UCR/GCR, ICC
profile, etc.)
Printing inks (CMYK or PMS)
Paper
Off press processing
Typography
Format
Crossover bleeds
Ink settings
Trapping values
Size of bleeds
Desired file format
Timeframe for delivery

INFORMATION OUT
Image size in print
Cropping of images
Selection of images (with or
without paths)
Information about trapping
or desired trapping of files
Retouches
Color corrections
Number of pages

MATERIAL IN
Texts
Original images
Sketches
Low-resolution images
Proof of images

MATERIAL OUT
Laser print-out
Files (via Internet or other
storage media)
Original artwork

▶ PHASE 4 – IMAGE PRODUCTION

INFORMATION IN

Printing information (printing method, screen frequency, maximum ink coverage, dot gain, gray balance, UCR/GCR, ICC-profiles, etc.)
Image size in print
Cropping of images
Selection of images
(with or without paths)
Retouches
Color corrections
Printing inks (CMYK or PMS)
Paper
Desired file format
Printing method
Quality requirements
Timeframe for delivery

INFORMATION OUT

-

MATERIAL IN

Original artwork (transparencies, reflectives, etc)

MATERIAL OUT

Low-resolution images
High-resolution images
Proof of images

▶ PHASE 5 – OUTPUT/RASTERIZING

INFORMATION IN

Screen frequency, type and angles
Shape of halftone dots
Film material pos/neg, emulsion up/down
Format and number of pages
Printing inks (CMYK or PMS)
ICC profiles
How many sets of films
Information about trapping
Trapping values
Timeframe for delivery
Printing format (imposition)
Imposition type, imposition scheme (imposition)
Gripper edges – for printing and off press processing (imposition)
Location of measuring strip (color bar)
Paper – compensation for creep (imposition)

INFORMATION OUT

Desired file format
Ink settings (imposition)
Crossover bleeds (imposition)
How many sets of films (imp.)

MATERIAL IN

Laser printout
Files (type of transmission)
Films (manual imposition) or files (digital imposition)
High-resolution images

MATERIAL OUT

Films
Digitally or manually mounted films (imposition)
Imposition dummy (imposition)

▶ PHASE 6 – PROOFS

INFORMATION IN

Printing information (printing method, screen frequency, maximum ink coverage, dot gain, gray balance, UCR/GCR, ICC profiles, etc.)
Printing inks (CMYK or PMS)
Paper
Timeframe for delivery

INFORMATION OUT

-

MATERIAL IN

Films
Files (digital proofs)

MATERIAL OUT

Proofs
Film
Files (digital proofs)

▶ PHASE 7 – PRINTING PLATE AND PRINTING

INFORMATION IN
Paper
Printing inks (CMYK or PMS)
Edition size (final delivery)
Waste (in off press processing)
Timeframe for delivery

INFORMATION OUT
Printing information (printing method, screen frequency, maximum ink coverage, dot gain, gray balance, UCR/GCR, ICC-profile, etc.)
Screen frequency, type and angles
Shape of halftone dots
Trapping values
Film material pos/neg, emulsion up/down
Printing format
Gripper edges (location and size)
Location of measuring strip (color bar)

MATERIAL IN
Proofs
Films
Paper
Imposition dummy

MATERIAL OUT
Printer's sheets
Printer's sheets folded according to imposition dummy

▶ PHASE 8 – OFF PRESS PROCESSING

INFORMATION IN
Format
Number of pages
Edition size
Binding method
Printing method
Timeframe for delivery

INFORMATION OUT
Size of bleeds
Type of imposition (possible imposition scheme)
Gripper edges (location and size)
Waste

MATERIAL IN
Printer's sheets
Printer's sheets folded according to imposition dummy

MATERIAL OUT
Complete printed products

▶ PHASE 9 – DISTRIBUTION

INFORMATION IN
Delivery arrangements
Timeframe for delivery

INFORMATION OUT
-

MATERIAL IN
Mailing list (when distributed)
Complete printed products

MATERIAL OUT
Addressed and packaged printed products

CHECKLISTS

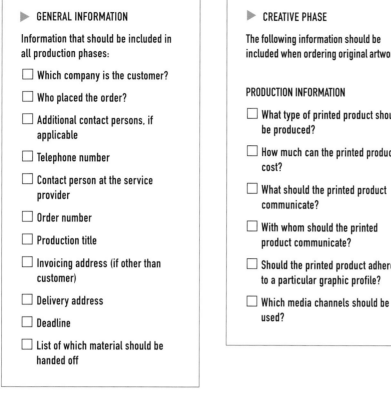

▶ GENERAL INFORMATION

Information that should be included in all production phases:

- ☐ Which company is the customer?
- ☐ Who placed the order?
- ☐ Additional contact persons, if applicable
- ☐ Telephone number
- ☐ Contact person at the service provider
- ☐ Order number
- ☐ Production title
- ☐ Invoicing address (if other than customer)
- ☐ Delivery address
- ☐ Deadline
- ☐ List of which material should be handed off

▶ CREATIVE PHASE

The following information should be included when ordering original artwork:

PRODUCTION INFORMATION

- ☐ What type of printed product should be produced?
- ☐ How much can the printed product cost?
- ☐ What should the printed product communicate?
- ☐ With whom should the printed product communicate?
- ☐ Should the printed product adhere to a particular graphic profile?
- ☐ Which media channels should be used?

▶ PRODUCTION OF ORIGINALS

The following information should be included when ordering original work:

PRODUCTION INFORMATION

- ☐ Printing method
- ☐ Volume
- ☐ Screen frequency
- ☐ Maximum ink coverage
- ☐ Trapping values
- ☐ Number of colors in the printed product
- ☐ Paper
- ☐ Off press processing
- ☐ Typography
- ☐ Format
- ☐ Crossover bleeds
- ☐ Ink settings
- ☐ Size of bleeds
- ☐ Desired file format

CHECKLISTS

▶ PRODUCTION OF IMAGES

The following information should be included when ordering images:

PRODUCTION INFORMATION

- ☐ Number of images
- ☐ Printing method
- ☐ Screen frequency
- ☐ Maximum ink coverage
- ☐ Dot gain or ICC profile
- ☐ Gray balance or ICC profile
- ☐ UCR/GCR
- ☐ Smallest printing dot
- ☐ Image size in print
- ☐ Cropping of images
- ☐ Selection of images (how many, what type, with or without clipping-paths)
- ☐ Retouches
- ☐ Color corrections
- ☐ Paper
- ☐ Desired file format
- ☐ Quality requirements

▶ OUTPUT/RASTERIZING

The following information should be included when ordering output/rasterizing.

PRODUCTION INFORMATION

- ☐ Screen frequency
- ☐ Type of halftone screen
- ☐ Screen angles
- ☐ Shape of halftone dots
- ☐ ICC profile
- ☐ Film material (pos/neg, emulsion up/down)
- ☐ Format
- ☐ Number of pages
- ☐ Number of colors in the printed product
- ☐ Number of film sets
- ☐ Information about trapping or desired trapping of files
- ☐ Trapping values
- ☐ Computer platform (Windows or Macintosh)
- ☐ Software

▶ PROOFS

The following information should be included when ordering proofs:

PRODUCTION INFORMATION

- ☐ Screen frequency (digital proofs)
- ☐ Dot gain or ICC profile
- ☐ Gray balance or ICC profile (digital proof)
- ☐ Optimal density in print (digital proof)
- ☐ Paper

▶ PRINTING PLATE & PRINTING

The following information should be included when ordering printing:

PRODUCTION INFORMATION

- ☐ Paper
- ☐ Number of colors in the printed product
- ☐ Edition size (for final delivery)
- ☐ Waste (for off press processing)

▶ OFF PRESS PROCESSING

The following information should be included when ordering off press processing services:

PRODUCTION INFORMATION

- ☐ Format
- ☐ Number of pages
- ☐ Edition size
- ☐ Binding method
- ☐ Printing method

▶ DISTRIBUTION

The following information should be included when ordering delivery:

PRODUCTION INFORMATION

- ☐ Delivery type
- ☐ Packaging type
- ☐ Addressing

LEGAL

17

CHAPTER 17 LEGAL   DESIGN IS OFTEN VIEWED AS A MYSTERIOUS CRAFT BY OUTSIDERS. IN CONTRAST, DESIGNERS KNOW THEIR WORK AS THE CREATION OF COMMUNICATION VIA THE USE OF VISUAL ORDER AND STRUCTURE. IT IS ONLY AFTER ENTERING THE DESIGN PROFESSION DOES THE DESIGNER LEARN THAT DESIGN IS ALSO A COMPLEX BUSINESS ACTIVITY BALANCING INTERESTS AT THE NEXUS OF ART AND COMMERCE.

Frank J. Martinez, The Martinez Group

The increasing complexity of commerce requires that designers have a basic understanding of how the law influences their work and, in some cases, how they create. Good designers, by necessity, become polymaths, developing the valuable skill of learning how to learn. Unfortunately, knowing the law is an elusive pursuit since it is constantly evolving. Both experienced and beginning designers, face legal challenges almost every day of their working life. These challenges come in many forms and frequently occupy many areas of the law simultaneously.

THE WORKPLACE — THE DESIGNER AS EMPLOYEE [17.1]

Upon entering the workplace, a designer is usually confronted with a choice; whether to become an employee or an independent contractor or, to use the well-known, term, a freelancer. Each of these choices places the designer into a different legal status, creating a different set of rights and obligations for the designer. In fact, each term, is a "term of art," a phrase or word signifying the legal status of the individual under state and, more importantly, federal law as it applies via copyright law. Upon accepting a design position there are many factors to be considered when choosing between working as an employee or as a freelancer. Among them are your experience, the nature of the work to be performed and the requirements of the employer. In many cases, the employer will not provide an option and require the hiring of an employee or freelancer.

As a general rule, most employees are "at-will employees." The at-will employee can choose to leave the job for any reason or no reason. Conversely, the employer may terminate the at-will employee at any time, with or without reason. An employment contract alters the at-will status by the consent of the employer and employee and usually identifies terms related to the length of employment, and other conditions under which the employment could be terminated prior to expiration of the contract. Most employees are not offered employment contracts since they are usually reserved for management level positions or those design positions which require unusually sophisticated skills. Each state has its own body of law regarding employer-employee relations and the negotiation and drafting of any employment agreement should be entrusted to an attorney or other advisor who is familiar with employment law in your state. There are some general terms which will apply wherever you are located and they are discussed later in this chapter. However, legally speaking, copyright law makes no distinction as to the contractual status of employees, since, in the absence of an agreement to the contrary, all employees are considered work-for-hire.

THE DESIGNER AS WORK FOR HIRE [17.1.1]

Copyright law is very specific in identifying the work made for hire status. Title 17 of the United States Code, Section 101 broadly defines a work made for hire as: "1. a work prepared by an employee within the scope of his or her employment; or 2. a work specially ordered or commissioned for use as a contribution to a collective work, as a part of a motion picture or other audiovisual work, as a translation, as a supplementary work, as a compilation, as an instructional text, as a test, as answer material for a test, or as an atlas, if the parties expressly agree in a written instrument signed by them that the work shall be considered a work made for hire…."

As can be seen, Paragraph (1) states that if you are an employee, all of the work you produce is a work made for hire and is, accordingly, the property of your employer. It is important to note that term "property" is a legal term of art which implies that in addition to owning the work itself, an employer also owns any copyright as well as the right to commercially exploit the work. Care should be taken to recognize that the legal definition of the term employer is broader than it first appears. The Supreme Court has found that an employer could also be defined as a hiring party who has "the right to control the manner and means by which the product is accomplished." Therefore, technically, an employer-employee relationship could arise out of a very informal work relationship. While not initially obvious, Paragraph (2) further permits the contractual creation of the work-for-hire status between two parties who may not be in an employment relationship. As you may have guessed, despite the narrowly defined types of work which the statute defines as being eligible as a work for hire, most freelancers fall into this category.

Being a freelancer has many benefits. Among them is the sense of being in control of your career, choosing whom you work for, choosing where and when to work and in many cases, even earning a larger salary. However, as every experienced freelancer knows, the ownership and control of the work created by them normally remains the exclusive property of their employer. Why? Most freelancers, as a condition of their employment, normally enter into an independent contractor's or freelancer's agreement whereby, both parties agree that the work to be created is work made for hire. The use of such contracts is widespread in the design industry and while they come in many different forms, they all share some basic characteristics. In view of the impact that a contract could have on a designer's career, you should seek some knowledge about the terms and conditions that are likely to exist in a work for hire or employment agreement.

CONTRACTS IN DESIGN 17.1.2

There are several myths associated with contracts and their use in design industry. First, there is no such thing as an "ironclad" or "unbreakable" contract. An agreement between two parties is only as good as the intention of the parties. Second, there are no such things as "legal" or "illegal contracts." There are only enforceable or unenforceable contracts. Third, the use of an agreement and negotiating the terms of an agreement with an employer or client is not insulting or adversarial. It's simply a good business practice that clarifies the responsibilities and obligations of the parties. Fourth, a contract that you find in a law book or other self-help guide is nothing more than a good place to start—it is not a substitute for the work of a competent attorney or business professional who understands the needs and circumstances of the designer and the client.

USE OF PRIOR WORK IN PORTFOLIO 17.1.3

Designers rely on their portfolios to demonstrate their skills and experience. On occasion, the terms of an employment or freelance agreement will restrict or eliminate the ability to show the work you've executed for a former employer. Blanket restrictions may not be enforceable as a matter of law. However, when the work or product shown is not known by the consuming public, or when the client has imposed restrictions upon an employer, prohibiting the use of such work in a portfolio could be reasonable. There are no bright line rules regarding the use of work in a portfolio however, one should always exercise common sense when showing work and claiming responsibility for the design in one's portfolio. Exaggerated claims could be interpreted as misrepresentation or even fraud and could lead to the termination of your employment.

COPYRIGHT 17.2

Copyright law is one of the most complex bodies of law in America, surpassed only by the law related to taxation and securities regulation. It has been subject to numerous revisions since it was first enacted into law in 1790. In addition, rarely does a session of Congress pass during which some technical revision or other form of tinkering to copyright law does not occur. Unlike earlier versions of copyright law, registration is not now mandatory for copyright protection since a copyright is deemed to "subsist at the moment of fixation in a tangible medium of expression." In short, when you create a copyrightable work, a copyright arises automatically under federal law. However, registration of a copyright gives the owner of the copyright extra benefits under federal law such as a choice in determining the basis for damages in the event of an infringement and under certain circumstances, even attorney's fees. The rights granted under copyright law are property rights and like other types of property, a copyright can be sold, rented, licensed, or given away. As with any other property right, the ultimate right is the right to exclude and within the context of copyright law, that right is manifested as controlling the right to make copies of the work, hence the term copy-right.

Over the years, the term "writings" has been construed as referring to the expression of original ideas. Now the term encompasses almost any tangible method of expressing a creative idea and has proven to be as varied as the methods of expressing creativity have been. For example, copyright law was enacted prior to the invention of photography. Nonetheless, in 1884 the Supreme Court determined that a photograph of the noted author and playwright Oscar Wilde was protectable under copyright law because the choices made by the photographer and "fixed" in the photograph, evidenced the creative decision-making process. Today, the creative choices expressed in software, web design, multi-media or performance art all comfortably fit within the legal framework developed over 200 years ago.

THE STRUCTURE OF COPYRIGHT LAW 17.2.1

American copyright law has a constitutional basis. Article I, Section 8, Clause 8 of the Constitution, has been interpreted as requiring that Congress create laws to grant, for limited times, exclusive rights to inventors and authors. This is important because the constitutional mandate requires the balancing of competing interests; stimulating the creation of creative works by appealing to the self-interest of authors. The property rights granted to an author are balanced, sometimes even limited by the interests of the people. When these interests come into conflict, the courts tend to place the public's interest before those of the individual author.

Copyright law was not intended to and, in fact, does not protect creative ideas. It protects the methods by which creative ideas are shown. Stated simply, no rights are granted in the ideas, it only protects how the ideas are expressed. In addition, copyright law will not protect facts or other information that may be in the public domain. Others are perfectly free to use the same ideas, facts or information, provided they do not copy the method of expression previously used by another author.

When viewed as a whole, the complexity of copyright law appears overwhelming. Perhaps an easier way to approach understanding copyright is to view it from the perspective of property rights, that is, a group or bundle of rights that you control.

THE BENEFITS OF REGISTRATION 17.2.2

Federal registration confers substantial benefits upon a copyright owner. These benefits include a presumption that the copyright registration is legally valid. Thus, in the event of litigation, an infringer must prove that the work is not entitled to copyright protection. The stakes can be very large since, in the event of a willful infringement, the copyright owner has a choice of actual damages or statutory damages of up to $150,000, plus an award of attorney's fees. Accordingly, federal registration should not be overlooked since it provides a significant financial incentive to police infringement. On more than one occasion, infringement and potential damages have not been pursued because the lack of a properly filed federal registration made it too expensive to police infringement.

REGISTERING A COPYRIGHT 17.2.3

The Copyright Office is located in Washington, D.C. and is part of the Library of Congress. Registration of a copyright requires the use of an official form which can be obtained online www.loc.gov/copyright. In addition to the official forms, the site contains a large amount of information and notices related to copyright. Of special importance are the Circulars and Brochures. These materials contain a significant amount of material and, in them, you can find an answer for most of your copyright questions. Before you begin, there are some basic considerations which should be helpful in getting started.

First, determine the nature of the work and select the proper form. Read the instructions very carefully, since the Copyright Office has strict rules as to how the form is submitted (printed on both sides) and the nature, number and type of specimens of the work that must be submitted with an application. In addition, no application will be processed without payment of the required fees

The Copyright Office defines the nature of a work very broadly. Accordingly, since you may not find contemporary usage or descriptions on the forms, use the next best term which accurately describes the work you wish to register.

Many of the forms listed in the margins are available for downloading with instructions or in a short form version. The examples noted are not a complete listing of the forms available. Unless you are very experienced, you should also download, read and follow the instructions. If you wish to file a group of works, a compilation of works, serial works or have a large project that involves different types of media, you should consider using an experienced attorney since a defective filing could have serious consequences.

THE AUTHOR 17.2.4

Like any other specialized endeavor, copyright law has its own language and some of these terms are so unique that you should take time to become familiar with them. For the purposes of copyright, an author could be either the person or persons (joint authors) who created the work or own the work. It is important to understand this distinction since each term denotes a particular legal status. In the case of the designer who is an employee or a freelancer as work for hire, the author is their employer. These distinctions become quite important when registering a copyright, since the author of the work must be identified with accuracy. In addition, the application must note whether the work was created as a work for hire and whether the work was created anonymously or pseudonymously, such as a stage or professional name. Copyright law abounds with cause and effect. When preparing an application, remember that your choices affect the rights and exclusions derived from a copyright registration. Those rights and your ability to use them cascade from and interlock with each other. Don't let the simplicity of a copyright application deceive you. Do some research before you begin or employ an attorney experienced with the process since correcting a mistake can be extremely time consuming, costly and could limit your rights in the future.

JOINT AUTHORS 17.2.5

A copyrighted work can and is frequently created by more than one person. In addition, since a company or corporation is a legal entity, a person and a company can also be joint authors. Copyright law places special burdens on joint authors, both with respect to the work as well as the relationship between the authors. Under copyright law, joint authors are co-owners of the copyright to a work. Co-ownership under copyright law has been determined as each owner having a divisible ownership right. A co-author can sell or license his or her rights the copyrighted work. When co-creating a work, you may wish to consider a written agreement or other form of contract that defines the rights of each author. In the absence of such an agreement that provides otherwise, each author has a right to license the work, sell their ownership interest in the work, or a right to create derivative works based upon the original copyrighted work. Disputes between co-authors often arise when the authors haven't considered how they wish to control use or dispose of the work after it's registered.

While each author has a right to license the work, such a right is accompanied by a duty of accounting to the other author. Stated simply, if one author licenses the work to a third party, the licensing author has an obligation to pay a share of the licensing fee and any royalty stream to his or her co-author.

EXCLUSIVE RIGHTS UNDER COPYRIGHT LAW 17.2.6

Section 106 of the Copyright Statute only identifies six exclusive rights of the owners of a copyright.

While short, Section 106 has been written so as to be extremely broad in defining the scope of exclusivity and, for all practical purposes, encompasses almost every method of use, display or distribution currently known. Of particular importance, is the emphasis placed on the owner's exclusive right to reproduce, copy, perform a work, or to grant a right to others to do the same.

The exclusive rights of a copyright owner can be divided in many ways. For instance, the owner of the exclusive right in a written work can grant one party the right to create a derivative work in the nature of a screenplay while granting another party the right to translate the work into another language. In another example, the owner of the exclusive rights to publicly perform a work, can authorize a public performance in Chicago, while reserving exclusive performance rights in the rest of the country. This granting of rights is known as "licensing" and the right granted is known as a "license" and the person or company who is authorized to use another's copyright is the "licensee" of the licensor/copyright owner. The extent to which a licensee may use, perform, display, copy the copyrighted work is normally determined by the terms of the license.

NOTIFICATION OF COPYRIGHT 17.2.7

For many years, failure to use the copyright symbol on work of authorship would result in either the loss of a right to register the copyright or the loss of copyright protection. In 1989 however, the requirement and the arcane rules for the use, placement and display of the copyright notice was entirely eliminated. It is still a prudent practice to display a copyright notice whenever possible since it notifies the viewer as to the owner and the rights claimed. Acceptable displays typically include "© 2002 XYZ COMPANY" or

---

CONTINUED

3. Form SR, is used for published and unpublished sound recordings (Sound recordings are works that result from the fixation of a series of musical, spoken, or other sounds, but not including the sounds accompanying a motion picture or other audiovisual work. Common examples include recordings of music, dramatic performances, or lectures. Generally, copyright protection extends to two elements in a sound recording: (a) the performance and (b) the production or engineering of the sound recording. A sound recording is not the same as a phonorecord, which is defined as the physical object in which a work of authorship is embodied. The word "phonorecord" includes cassette tapes, CDs, LPs, 45 r.p.m. disks, as well as other formats.).

4. Form VA, is used for published and unpublished works of visual art. (Visual arts are pictorial, graphic, or sculptural works, including 2-dimensional and 3-dimensional works of fine, graphic, and applied art, or advertisements, commercial prints, labels, artificial flowers and plants, artwork applied to clothing or to other useful articles, bumper stickers, decals and stickers, cartographic works, such as maps, globes and relief models, cartoons and comic strips, collages, dolls, toys, drawings, paintings and murals, enamel works, fabric, floor, and wall covering designs, games, puzzles, greeting cards, postcards, stationery, holograms, computer and laser artwork, jewelry designs, models, mosaics, needlework and craft kits, original prints, such as engravings, etchings, serigraphs, silk screen prints and woodblock prints, patterns for sewing, knitting, crochet and needlework, Photographs and photomontages, posters, record jacket artwork or photo-

graphy, relief and intaglio prints, reproductions, such as lithographs, coll* oty-
pes, sculpture, such as carvings, cera-
mics, figurines, maquettes, molds,
relief sculptures, stained glass designs,
stencils and cut-outs, technical drawings, architectural drawings or plans,
blueprints, diagrams, mechanical drawings, weaving designs, lace designs
and tapestries).

5. Form SE, is used for serial publications (such as, newspapers, magazines,
newsletters, annuals, journals and any
other publication that is issued on a
regular basis.).

6. Form CA, is used to correct or provide additional information given in a
registration.

7. Form CON, is a continuation sheet
and can only be used with Forms CA,
PA, SE, SR, TX and VA.

"COPYRIGHT © 2002 XYZ COMPANY". Non-traditional uses or displays of a copyright notice should be approved by legal counsel since the underlying purpose of the
copyright notice could be compromised by an unorthodox treatment.

ARTIST'S RIGHTS 17.2.8

Section 106 (A) of the Copyright statute defines the rights of certain authors with respect
to "attribution and integrity." These rights are commonly referred to as artist's rights.
The rights defined under the statute are specifically related to preserving the reputation
of the artist as it relates the works of authorship as well as, preserving the work itself. In
particular, an artist has the right to (a) claim authorship of their work, (b) and the right to
prevent the use of his or her name as the author of any work of visual art which they did
not create. The statute further grants an artist the right to prevent the use of their name
as the author of an artwork in the event the work is distorted, mutilated or otherwise
modified in such a way as would be prejudicial to the artist's honor or reputation. Finally
and probably most controversial, the statute grants an artist the right to prevent any destruction of "a work of recognized stature", whether the destruction is intentional or the
result of gross negligence.

As with any law, there are some exceptions. Modifications of a work that occur through
the passage of time or by reason of the nature of the materials used in the work of art, are
not considered a distortion, mutilation or an otherwise prohibited modification. Furthermore, any modification which results from conservation or changes which occur
during a public presentation such as changes in appearance due to lighting or placement
are not considered a prohibited modification of the work of art, unless the modification
is caused by gross negligence.

At the outset, it must be noted that these rights *are only applicable to works of visual art
as defined by the statute* and those rights may not apply to any reproduction, depiction,
portrayal of a work of one work of art in *another work of art*. In addition, written works,
works of graphic design and all *works for hire*, are explicitly excluded under the provisions
of Section 106 (A). Furthermore the rights granted to an artist under Section 106 are
independent and exclusive of the rights granted under a regular copyright. Interestingly,
artist's rights under copyright law cannot be transferred or sold. The statute only allows
the waiver of the artist's rights in a written document signed by the artist. The waiver
must specifically identify the work of art and the uses of the work to which the waiver
applies. By law, any right or use not identified with specificity in the written waiver is not
granted.

As can be seen, the artist's rights protections granted under copyright law are complex
and contain many exceptions and limitations. If you are an artist creating work for instal-
lation or display in public spaces, this section of copyright law will be very important to
you. If you are designer using or incorporating images or details of known works of art,
you should consult with an attorney experienced with these issues since the failure to
acquire a waiver or an improper waiver could result in significant liability for your client.

FAIR USE

Within the creative community, the doctrine of fair use is probably the most cited, most discussed and least understood area of copyright law. When discussing fair use, the underlying principle that the people are the ultimate beneficiaries of all "writings and discoveries" is in full view. Section 107 of the Copyright statute states that:

"the fair use of a copyrighted work, including such use by reproduction in copies or phonorecords or by any other means specified by that section, for purposes such as criticism, comment, news reporting, teaching (including multiple copies for classroom use), scholarship, or research, is not an infringement of copyright."

Stated another way, a fair use of a copyrighted work is a use, by another, that is an exception to the exclusive rights of the copyright owner. From a legal perspective, the doctrine of fair use is a defense to a charge of copyright infringement. If this were not the case, the exclusive rights granted to a copyright owner could inhibit creativity; the very purpose of the statute. The important issue in any fair use analysis is an inquiry into the rights of the copyright owner versus the benefits the public derives from the particular use of the copyrighted work.

When faced with determining whether the infringement of a copyrighted work is, indeed a fair use, a court is required to examine the use with regard to the following four factors.

1. The purpose and character of the use, including whether such use is of a commercial nature or is for nonprofit educational purpose;
2. The nature of the copyrighted work;
3. The amount and substantiality of the portion used in relation to the copyrighted work as a whole; and
4. The effect of the use upon the potential market for or value of the copyrighted work.

Despite the statutory mandate, these four factors do not define what constitutes a fair use and they do not create a "rule" for defining a fair use. Each fair use claim is examined on its own merits, the four factors being merely the beginning point of inquiry which should also include a review of the use as it relates to the six different uses noted in the statue, namely, criticism, comment, news reporting, teaching, scholarship and research. Thus a fair use examination ultimately turns on two basic questions; how is the copyrighted work used by another and what is the effect upon the original work and its author?

It's easy to imagine that a newspaper or design magazine is just as motivated by profit as is any tabloid and both are arguably commercial ventures. In such circumstances, the question of what constitutes a fair use in the nature of news reporting turns not on the publication itself, but upon the nature of the use. Pure news reporting, in the absence of libel, will almost always be considered a fair use. However, use of a copyrighted work, which is then "turned" into news, will not be viewed as benign. Use of a copyrighted work in the absence of a profit motive almost always weighs in favor of fair use. However, as with most rules of law, there are always exceptions and not every commercial use of a copyrighted work will be found automatically to be an unfair use. When a copyrighted work is used in a way where the user adds additional value in the nature of creativity, such as use of a copyrighted work in a work of art, a finding of fair use is much more

---

▶ **EXCLUSIVE RIGHTS AND THE COPYRIGHT STATUTE**

1. to reproduce the copyrighted work in copies or phonorecords;

2. to prepare derivative works based upon the copyrighted work;

3. to distribute copies or phonorecords of the copyrighted work to

the public by sale or other transfer of ownership, or by rental, lease or lending;

4. in the case of literary, musical, dramatic, and choreographic works, pantomimes, and motion pictures and other audiovisual works, to perform the copyrighted work publicly;

5. in the case of literary, musical, dramatic, and choreographic works, pantomimes, and pictorial, graphic, or sculptural works, including the individual images of a motion picture or other audiovisual work, to display the copyrighted work publicly; and

6. in the case of sound recordings, to perform the copyrighted work publicly by means of a digital audio transmission.

likely. Stated simply, a commercial use of another's work never looks good and a court will inquire as to whether the use has resulted in some sort of public benefit as opposed to mere private financial gain.

The conduct of the user can be quite influential in a fair use examination. Seeking permission to use another's work may be an act of good faith, but contrary to perception, being denied permission to use another's work doesn't mean that a subsequent use isn't a fair use. The Supreme Court has specifically ruled that "being denied permission to use a work does not weigh against a finding of fair use." But, judges are human and are not above reviewing the conduct of the parties in a fair use claim. A copyright owner who seeks to unfairly stifle creativity or legitimate criticism or news reporting may actually broaden the boundaries of what is an acceptable fair use.

In every fair use examination, the nature of the original copyrighted work will be considered. Generally speaking, a court is likely to believe that the more creative the original work, the more protection it deserves. Conversely, the more informational or utilitarian an original work is, the greater the opportunity for a finding of fair use. Thus, works which merely recite factual information are not likely to be considered as creative as a novel or even a biography. Unpublished works will generally be afforded more protection since another's use is likely to alter, if not destroy the original author's market for the work.

Whatever the nature of the use, another key issue is the amount and substantially of the original work used in the second work. Thus, the greater portion of an original work used, the less "fair" the second use becomes. Conversely, the less of the original work used, the more "fair" the second use becomes. However, as can be expected, there is no hard and fast rule to be applied here and there may be cases where the portion of the original work used is small but the effect on the market for the original work is substantial. The key issue will be how "fair" the use is with regard to the author and the market for the original work. Accordingly when the second use adversely impacts, usurps, or replaces the market for the original work, the less "fair" the second use becomes. But not every use that harms another work is prohibited. The copying of an original work in a parody, review or critique which happens to be devastating to the original work may, in fact, be a recognizable fair use.

As can be seen, the doctrine of fair use is utterly devoid of rigid rules and relies instead upon an overall all assessment of the extent and purpose of the use, the actions of the parties and the commercial impact upon the original author. An artist engaged in the creation of an artistic work that incorporate works created by another may have reason to believe that their use constitutes a fair use. A graphic artist may reasonably arrive at the same conclusion, but because the use is for a commercial purpose, might be denied a finding of fair use. The bottom line is that there are no safe harbors and no rule of law that you can rely on entirely. Check with an attorney if you are concerned about using another's work especially if your work is in the nature of entertainment. If you are working in film or music, use of another's work is almost always a problem. Unauthorized sampling or copying is universally frowned upon since the legal liability for a record label, music publisher or film studio can be quite significant. Sometimes it takes a little more effort to create a wholly original work, but almost without exception, it's worth the extra effort.

CREATING ORIGINAL WORK 17.4

What is an original work? From a creative perspective, it might be a work that is utterly uninfluenced by another's style or methods. From a legal perspective, original work is work that does not copy a previously created work. Copyright law does not care if a work is "referential" of another's work, it's merely concerned with copying. Works of design that incorporate a preexisting work, if objected to, will always be subject to a traditional fair use analysis. Some designers seem to think that digitizing and manipulating another's work creates a new work. Even transforming another's work by adding new graphic elements, or merging photographic elements from different sources does not create a new work. It simply means that multiple works have been infringed. In addition, it is irrelevant whether the original work is analog or digital. The method of creation and the method of copying are not relevant. An infringement is an infringement.

Almost all works of design are for a commercial purpose. As such, the scope of what may be considered a fair use is likely to be much smaller. That doesn't mean that a work of design can never incorporate another's work, it just makes the fair use analysis more difficult. If you must use another's work, the safest way to proceed is to use the many commercially available resources such as stock photography and other royalty free art.

LICENSING PHOTOGRAPHY 17.5

The use and availability of stock photography has grown significantly with the growth of the internet. Currently, stock photography can be licensed and delivered online. It is important to note that one does not actually buy the work, a use of the work, a license for a particular purpose, is purchased. Therefore, any use outside of the licensed use constitutes an infringement of the work. Occasionally one will hear about "royalty-free" photography or clip art, this is an inaccurate term. When you buy "royalty-free" clip art or photographs, you are actually buying an unrestricted license to use the art.

When commissioning original photography, it is very common for a photographer to retain ownership of the copyright and license the specific use to the client. When commissioning original photography it is important to ensure that your proposed use is properly licensed. Another important task is ensuring that all releases are secured when using locations outside of the photographer's studio and when using live models. If you are using a model who is a minor, ensure that their parent or legal guardians sign the release.

USING PUBLIC DOMAIN WORK 17.6

Any work for which the copyright or patent has expired is now in the public domain. Any work which was dedicated to the public welfare by the author, is in the public domain. Anyone is free to use any public domain work without fear of infringement. There are several ways to determine whether a work is in the public domain. The United States Copyright Office offers a fee based searching service. If you know the title of a work or its last known owner, it's possible to ascertain whether the work is still protected by copyright. In addition, there are commercial search services such as those offered by Thomson & Thomson or CCH Corsearch. These searches can be expensive, but they are

CONTINUED

charts, diagrams, models and technical drawings, including architectural plans and a pseudonymous work is a work in which the author is identified under a fictitious name.

exhaustive and thus represent a valuable resource. Since it can be difficult to ascertain whether a work has fallen into the public domain. The term of copyright has changed many times and the term of protection has been extended several times. If you are working on an important project, and wish to use a work that you believe is now in the public domain, build the cost of a good search into the budget and contact an attorney or someone with good experience with these matters. It is a precaution that is well worth the extra cost and effort.

USING TYPE FONTS ^{17.7}

Thirty years ago, digital type fonts did not exist. Hot type was difficult to obtain and expensive. Therefore, it was difficult to infringe. Digitization has spawned the almost wholesale trading of unauthorized or pirated fonts. With only minor effort, it is possible to find web sites that contain entire libraries of fonts at little or no charge. Surprisingly, protecting fonts is not difficult. They can be protected by copyright. However unlike many other kinds of design, only the software which comprises a digital font is currently protectable by copyright. However, the actual design of the font, its physical appearance, can only be protected by a design patent. In addition, the title of the font can be protected by a trademark registration.

A visit to any type foundry website quickly reveals that many fonts are not actually sold and that many of their names are subject to trademark registrations. Use of the copyrighted software is licensed to the end user. This license is commonly referred to as an end user license agreement or EULA. Most foundries post a copy of their EULA on their website for your review prior to the purchase of license. Most foundries restrict how you can use a font, and they frequently restrict the embedding of their fonts in the .pdf (page description format) format. Therefore using such software might be prohibited or restricted by the EULA since the improper use of the software could actually "embed" and transfer an unauthorized copy of the font software. Documents that contain improperly embedded fonts are easily hacked depriving the font designer of payment for their hard work. In addition, there may be restrictions as to use of the font in a logo or on how many computers the font can be loaded onto at any one time. Many EULAs restrict the number of printers or other output devices used with a font or the EULA might restrict the use of the font software to a single geographic location. It is important to read and understand the end user license agreement. A designer's use of unauthorized or pirated copies of font software creates liability for themselves and for their clients.

The Internet is a rich source of materials and if properly acquired and properly used can be quire helpful. Prior to using any work acquired from the Internet, know your sources. Ensure that your use is licensed and if not ensure that a license is not required. Furthermore, remember that HTML code can and frequently is copyrighted. Copying and using HTML or photographs directly from another website can lead to problems. In addition, using pirated or hacked software raises the specter of both civil and criminal liability under the Digital Millennium Copyright Act.

THE INTERNET AND WEB SITES ^{17.8}

Using the Internet and putting up a website poses many challenges for a designer. From a legal perspective the prohibitions under copyright and trademark law are equally applicable to creating a website. Therefore, ensure that any images or software code are properly licensed. It's one thing to be inspired by the page layout of a competitor's website, it's another matter entirely to copy it. If the site that you are creating will be serving or archiving the work of others, ensure that you have permission to both store and distribute the work of others. If the website is commercial in nature, remember that conducting commercial activities in another state will be viewed as submitting yourself to the jurisdiction of the courts in that state. Displaying or using another's trademarks to further your own commercial purpose, could result in liability under the Lanham Act (trademark law).

Anyone involved in a creative endeavor will encounter situations that test their ethics. We are all influenced by the work of other artists and designers, good designers seem to be constantly aware of the work of their peers and studiously avoid copying or infringing even if it creates personal hardship. Original thinking isn't easy. However, we know it when we see it and the capacity for it grows with exercise. A few minutes spent planning a project can save hours, weeks or months of legal heartache. Large design projects require additional planning. The use of freelance help or third-party vendors almost always requires some form of understanding between the parties. Most attorneys will spend a few minutes answering initial inquires with little or no charge and in many cases, simple readily available legal agreements are sufficient. Take the time to investigate a project thoroughly prior to accepting or actually beginning your work. It is time well spent and in the end, your client will be glad that you did.

One of the most common areas of disputes between designers and clients is determining who is permitted to engage third party vendors and who is responsible for payment. When purchasing printing, color separation or other services, this issue can be quite significant since they are so expensive. As a fundamental matter, it's very important that a designer understands whether or not they are permitted to act on behalf of their client. In legal terms, this is referred to as an "agency" relationship which, if the designer is not careful, can create legal liability for the designer who acts outside of the scope of the agency. Stated simply, if the designer acts outside of the authority granted by the client or against the client's interests, the designer could end up responsible for all of those costs.

As a practical matter, the wise designer will clearly understand what, if any, power they have to enter a contract on behalf of their client. Obviously, these terms should be clearly stated in the agreement between the designer and the client. As a corollary issue, a designer who is authorized to purchase printing should also ensure that the printing contract does not contain terms which are outside the authority granted by the client or contrary to the client's interests. Like many other trades, printers frequently include terms regarding the mandatory purchase of printing overages or no requirement that the printer reprint or refund money for a print run that is short. Even if you're authorized to purchase on behalf of your client, it is always prudent to require that a client provide written authorization for third-party services and that the client reviews and approves the terms of any contract related to such matters. If a client wants you to handle everything, make sure that your agreement grants you the right to act on the client's behalf to the extent the project may require. ■

APPENDIX 18

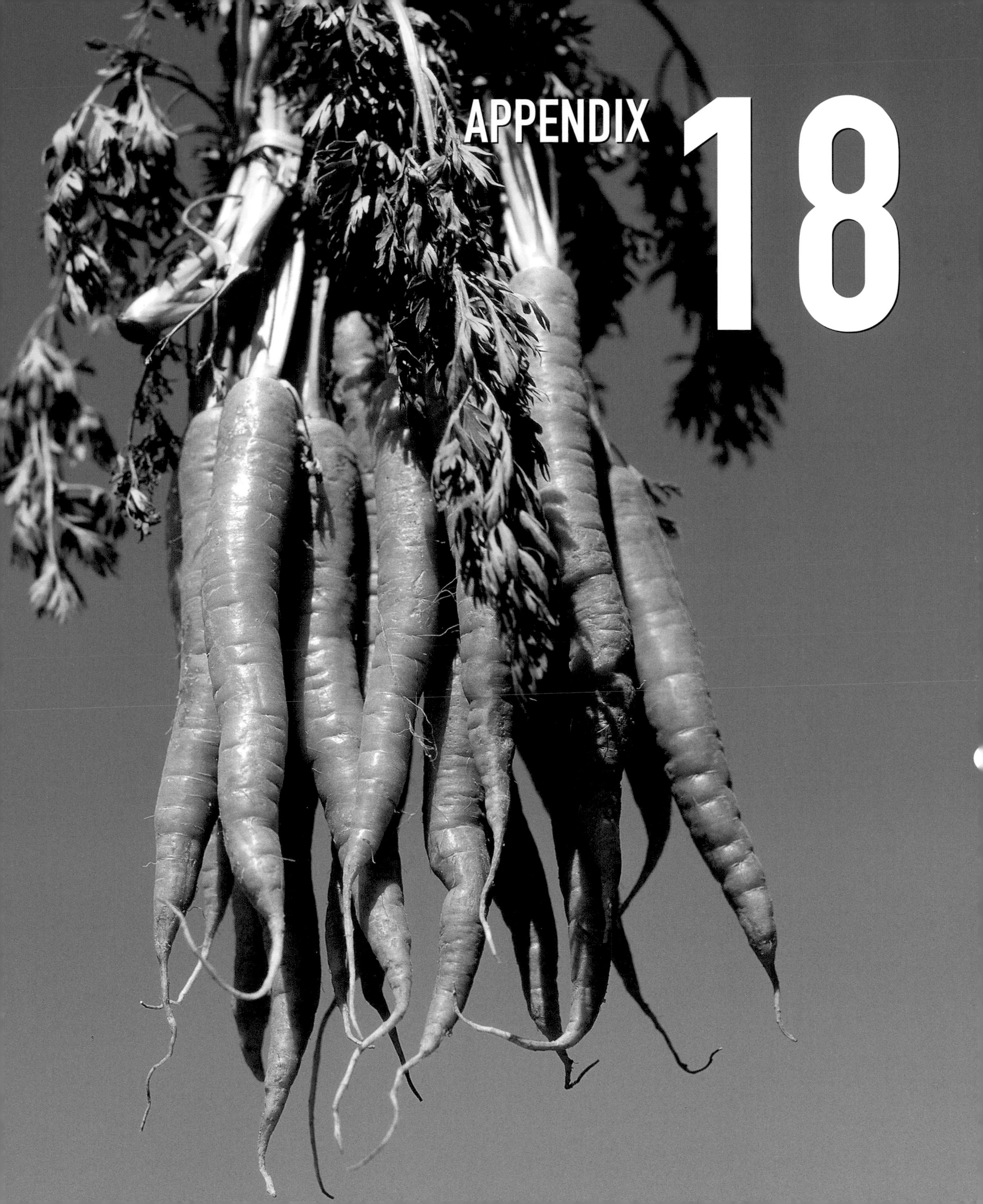

GLOSSARY THIS GLOSSARY SERVES AS A SMALL DICTIONARY OF GRAPHIC TERMS AS WELL AS AN INDEX TO THE BOOK. THE PAGE REFERENCES ARE NOT STATED IN NUMERICAL ORDER BUT IN ORDER OF SIGNIFICANCE. SOME GENERAL TERMS ARE SIMPLY DEFINED WITHOUT REFERING TO A PARTICULAR PAGE.

A

2-set [2-on] 171
Imposition technique for double-sided prints with only one make-ready. After one side has been printed the sheets are turned and, using the opposite gripper's edge, run through the printing press again and printed with the same plate.

3D Studio 14
Illustration program for 3D from Autodesk.

Access levels 133
In a network you can set up access levels and thereby assign different users with different access levels to the network.

Add-in programs 14
Plug-in that expands the functions of a particular program.

Aperture 98
An opening for light, often in an optical system. For example, the value of the aperture determines the size of the opening in a camera that lets in light during exposure.

Assembly film 192
A large film on which you manually mount the individual page films into a complete imposition.

B

Base material 186
Usually paper or paper-like material used for proofs or as a basis for work prints of a photograph.

Bastard double 241, 112, 113
A two-page spread in a printed product that does not consist of one complete sheet, but of pages from two different sheets. Bastard doubles complicate the placement of images across the gutter.

Bernoulli disk
An older type of removable, magnetic storage disk, available in different sizes and holds from 44 to 105 megabytes.

Bezier curve 56, 57, 28
A mathematical description of a curve named after a French Renault engineer, who developed the technique to be able to describe the design of cars. Bezier curves are used for object graphics and to describe typefaces.

Bicubic interpolation 75, 76
See Interpolation.

Binary number system 20
The number system the computer uses, based on the digits 0 and 1. Compare to the decimal system we normally use, based on 0–9.

Binder 214
Printing ink component that encapsulates and binds the pigments.

Bit 20
The smallest memory unit of the computer; can have a value of 0 or 1.

Bit-depth 63, 96
A measurement of the number of colors a pixel in a digital image can assume; states how many bits each pixel is stored with. The more bits per color the higher bit-depth, the more possible colors. A regular RGB-image has 3×8 bits=24 bits.

Bitmap 95, 151–153
The digital information which, using ones and zeros, describes a digital image or page. When halftone screening, the PostScript code is translated into a checkered pattern consisting of ones and zeros—a bitmap.

Blanks   174–175
Preprinted sheets, for example stationary with preprinted logotype and letterhead, on which you can print additional text or images.

Bleed (1)   111–112
Images or objects that are supposed to run all the way to the paper edge has to be printed with bleeds, i.e. be placed a bit outside of the page format, around 5 mm.

Bleed (2)   111–112
Images or objects placed across a two-page spread are called crossover bleeds. Watch out when bleeds cross-over two separate sheets.

Bleeding   175
When two colors bleed into each other, i.e. they mix, it is called bleeding. It is a problem especially pertaining to ink for ink-jet printers. To avoid bleeding, it is necessary that the ink dries fast.

Blocking   246
A type of glue binding for note pads.

Blueline   183, 188
A special kind of analog proof. The printed result is only displayed in one color, blue.

Book block   244, 245
Bound insert for a book that is attached (hung) to the case, for example when glue binding or thread stitching.

Boolean variables   128
A method used to create logical combinations by using boolean variables such as "and," "or" and "not." It is often used when combining search words in archive applications.

Bridge   133, 132
Network unit that connects different parts of a network.

Brightness   77–79
The intensity of colors, also called luminance. How bright or dark an image is.

Buckle folder   240, 241
The most common and simplest method for folding in sheet production.

Bulk   202
Describes how voluminous a paper is, measured in m^3/g or pages per inch.

Byte   20
A measurement of binary memory. One byte consists of 8 bits, the equivalent of 0-255 in the decimal system.

C

Cable connection   137
Direct connection to the Internet, a high-speed connection usually with an upstream transmission speed of 256 to 2,000 kilobits per second.

Cache memory   19
Frequently accessed calculative operations are saved in the computer's cache memory so they can be quickly accessed again.

Calendar finish   205
The paper is pressed to an even thickness and will, as a result, provide good print quality.

Capstan recorder   178
Version of an imagesetter in which the film is successively fed from a roll and exposed in a flat position. The length of the film is not limited by the dimensions of the drum, like in a recorder with an external drum for example.

Card slot   132
The computer has a number of card slots where you can install different types of circuit boards, for example a network interface card or a graphics card.

Cardboard   206
Cardboard is a stiff paper product. Paper manufacturers usually define cardboard as a paper with a weight exceeding 80 lbs.

CCD cell   95
Charge Coupled Device. Cells that

translate the intensity of light into electronic signals. CCD cells are used in scanners and digital cameras.

CCD matrix   97–98
A number of CCD cells organized into a checkered pattern, a "pixel matrix," in which each CCD cell corresponds to a pixel. Generally used in digital cameras.

CD   122–123
Compact Disc, an optical disc for data storage, which can typically store 650-700 megabytes.

CD-DA   122–123
Compact Disc-Digital Audio, CD for storing sound. A regular music CD.

CD-R   122–123
Compact Disc-Recordable. Recordable CD.

CD-ROM   122–123
Compact Disc-Read Only Memory, CD for storing data.

Characterization   44
To measure a process or the characteristics of a machine. You can, for example, characterize the printing process.

Choking   110
When the background is shrunk to avoid misregistration. Also see Trapping.

Chromalin   188, 183
Analog proof from Dupont.

CIE   41, 42
Commission Internationale d'Eclairage (CIE), the International Commission on Illumination, has created this color model based on a standard observer. The human perception of color is described with three sensitivity curves called tristimulus values.

CIELab   41, 42
Version of the CIE model.

CIExyz   41, 42
Version of the CIE model.

Claris Emailer   138
A program for managing electronic mail.

Clipping path   84, 64
A path that cuts out an image in an image editing program.

Cloth density   227
A measurement of how finely woven the screen cloth is.

CMS
See Color Management System.

CMYK   40, 39
Cyan, Magenta, Yellow, Key-color (black), subtractive color model used in four-color printing and four-color printers.

CMYK mode   62
An image saved in CMYK mode technically consists of four separate pixel images in grayscale mode: one that represents cyan, one magenta, one yellow and one black. It also means that a CMYK image uses four times as much memory as an image of the same size and resolution in grayscale mode.

Coated paper   206
Paper whose surface has been treated with a special coating in order to maintain high printing quality. The coating consists of binders (starch or latex) and pigment (fine kaolin clay or calcium carbonate).

Color   36, 214
The human perception of light with a mixture of different wavelengths, for example a blue color when looking at a blue surface in a white light.

Color Art   188, 183
An analog proof from Fuji.

Color bar   169, 193, 220
A special color bar added when imposing and printing. You check the different printing parameters in the different fields of the color bar.

Color cast   86-87, 78, 222
Error in the balance between colors in print and original artwork. Perceived as a general erroneous color tone in the image.

Color composition 52
What composition of wavelengths a light has.

Color correspondence 43
How well the colors of a print correspond to a proof or color guide.

Color filter 94
Light filter that lets through light of a certain color, i.e. of certain wavelengths.

Color gamut (Color space) 39
The color gamut is the range of color that theoretically can be created by a certain color model. The greater color gamut a color model has, the more colors you can create with that particular model.

Color guide 44, 105, 107
A printed guide with color samples and color definitions, necessary when selecting colors.

Color management system 45
Program that takes scanners, monitors, printers, proofs and the color characteristics of the print into consideration.

Color mode 59
Describes color information in a pixel-based image, for example line art, grayscale, index color, RGB or CMYK.

Color model 39
System for creating, defining, or describing colors, for example RGB, CMYK or CIE.

Color reproduction 43
The way in which colors are reproduced, for example on a monitor or in print.

Color sample 105, 107
Samples of color combinations, for example small pieces of paper torn out of color maps such as PMS-guides.

Colorsync 47
Apple's color management system.

Compact Pro 68
File compression software.

Computer platform
Describes the operating system a computer is working with, for example Mac-, NT- or Unix platform.

Coning 219
The printing phenomenon "coning" causes the printed image with the first component color to become wider than the last, which means you can never get 100% registration. The phenomenon occurs because the paper is compressed in each printing unit. Coning occurs both in sheet- as well as web-fed offset.

Continuous tones 143
Tones with even, soft tonal transitions that don't consist of obvious tonal steps, as in the photograph.

Contrast 78
Difference in tone. An image with high contrast has a great difference in tone between dark and bright areas.

Contrast effect 52, 53
A color phenomenon. A color can be perceived in different ways depending on the color it is placed next to. Thus, it can provide two completely separate color impressions if it is placed next to two different colors.

Control program 13
Driver for external units such as printers, scanners, etc.

Coppering 228
Before each etching or engraving in gravure printing, a new copper layer has to be added to the printing cylinder. The coppering is done using electrolysis with copper sulfate and sulfuric acid.

Copy machine 172
A machine used to produce multiple paper originals, utilizes the xerographic method.

Creasing 247
When creasing a folding reference, a crease, in order to facilitate folding of stiff and thick papers for example.

Creeping 241, 170
A folding phenomenon. As a result

of folding the product, the pages are displaced in relation to each other. The problem is bigger when inserting signatures. You compensate for the creep when imposing by adjusting the pages in relation to each other.

Cristalraster 148
AGFA's stochastic screen.

Crop marks (1)
Special marks that show where the printed sheet should be folded.

Crop marks (2) 169
Special marks that state where the printed sheet should be cropped. Also see Registration mark.

Cropping (1)
Used to remove unnecessary parts of an image in order to avoid working with an image larger than needed.

Cropping (2) 245
You crop the paper to desired size in order to adjust to the printing press or off press processing machine and you crop the bound printed product to the right format with even, fine edges.

Cross references 128
Cross referencing in databases is a way of providing a file with many different headings so that you can find the same file under different headings/in different places. Basil, for example, can be filed under both spice and herb.

CRT screen 18
Cathode Ray Tube screens are based on the cathode ray technique: a beam of electrons illuminate the screen. A regular monitor or TV is based on this technique.

CT/LW 65
Continuous Tone/Line Work, a file format from Scitex for pixel images.

CTP 195
Computer To Plate, a technique for setting/outputting printing plates in an imagesetter directly from the computer without using graphic film.

CTP machine 195
An imagesetter used to output printing plates directly from the computer.

CTP plate 195
Special printing plate for CTP equipment.

Cumulus 14
Software from Canto that stores/archives images.

Curing 214
The second drying phase of the offset printing ink in which the alkyd reacts with the oxygen in the air through oxidation. The first drying phase is setting.

D

Dampening distribution roller 218
Roller in the dampening system whose task it is to distribute the dampening solution and to make sure it forms a thin dampening film.

Dampening drop roller 218
Roller in the dampening system that transfers the dampening solution from the duct to the distribution rollers.

Dampening duct roller 218
Roller in the dampening system that takes water from the dampening tub and transfers it to the rollers in the dampening system.

Dampening form roller 218
Roller in the dampening system that transfers the dampening solution from the last distribution rollers to the printing plate.

Dampening rollers 217, 214
Collective term for all types of dampening rollers in a dampening system.

Dampening solution 213
Used in wet offset printing to separate printing- from non-printing surfaces.

Dampening system 218, 217
Term for the entire system of

rollers in an offset printing press that controls the dampening solution supply.

DAT 121, 122
Digital Audio Tape, magnetic tape for storing data, can usually hold 2–8 gigabytes.

Data bus 15
The data bus transports information between the processor and the random access memory in the computer.

Database 126
Registration software. Software that sorts and keeps digital information, such as images and other digital files, in order.

DCS 64, 108
See EPS- DCS/EPSF.

De facto standard 149
A standard that has appeared because a product has reached a dominant position within an industry without having been endorsed by a major standard vehicle, i.e. PostScript from Adobe.

Decimal number system 20
The regular number system we use daily, based on the numbers 0-9.

Decompress 113
When opening compressed files.

Densitometer 222
An instrument used to measure different printing parameters, for example dot gain and full tone density. Available both for measuring film and reflective surfaces.

Density 222
A measurement of the tonal range in a particular base material, for example the tonal range in four-colors on a certain kind of paper or the tonal range in an original slide.

Desktop
The work space on the screen where the icons for waste basket, hard disk, etc. are situated.

Developer 190, 193
Machine that develops exposed film or plate by using chemical developing liquids.

Developing liquid 190, 193
Chemical liquid necessary to develop film or plate.

Diamond Screening 148
Linotype Hell's stochastic screen.

Die-cutting 247
Off press process. Printed products that should have a shape other than a rectangular one are die-cut, for example dividers used for binders.

Digiscript 182
A Preflight program from One Vision that proofs and improves PostScript files.

Digital camera 96, 97, 98
Electronic camera that delivers a digital image instantly.

Digital imposition 163, 164
The imposition of digital files via imposition software.

Digital printing 230
Printing press that prints information directly from the computer in a way similar to a printer.

Digital proof 183, 188
Digital proofs are based on the files used when printing. Made on high-quality printers.

Digital publishing 122
To publish information in a digital format to be read on the screen, for example an encyclopedia on CD or the world wide web.

Dimensional stability 202
A measurement of how resistant a paper is against dimensional changes.

Direct engraving 229
Technique for producing gravure cylinders that engrave the printing cylinder directly from digital information.

Direct printing procedure 191
A printing procedure in which the printing form prints directly on the material, for example flexographic- and gravure printing.

Disk Doubler 68
File compression software.

Disk memory
Another name for the computer's hard disk.

DLT 121
Digital Linear Tape. Magnetic tape for storing data, holds around 40 gigabytes.

Document 20
Files that you have created in the computer are called documents. For example QuarkXPress-, Photoshop- or Excel documents.

Dot gain 194, 220, 91
A measurement of the change in size of the halftone dot from film to print. Measured in percent.

Dot gain adjustment 86
To adjust an image according to the dot gain it will be subject to in the printing process. Is done during four-color separation. Also see Print adjustment.

Dot gain curves 221, 92, 148
Curves that display dot gain over the entire tint area from 0 to 100%. Is generated by measuring color bars with a densitometer.

Dot reduction 194, 220, 91
A measurement of the change in size of the halftone dot from film to print when using positive printing plates. Measured in percent.

Double-sided paper
A paper that has the same surface characteristics on both sides. Compare to single-sided paper.

Doubling 225, 226
Print phenomenon that manifests as dot deformation, a darker print and a double imprint of the halftone dots, one stronger and one weaker. This can be a result of a loose rubber blanket, which causes the halftone dots to land in different places on the paper with each rotation of the cylinder.

Drivers 13
Control programs for external units such as printers, scanners, etc.

Driving roller 218
Roller in the inking pyramid placed against the distribution roller, which absorbs and provides ink to these depending on their location.

Drop roller 218
Roller in the inking pyramid that transfers ink from the duct to a distribution roller by "jumping" between them.

Drum scanner 95
In this type of scanner, the original is attached to a rotating glass drum.

Dry offset 215
See Water-free offset.

Dry run 218
Occurs when the dampening solution is set too low in the ink-dampening balance. As a result, non-printing surfaces attract ink and become printing. Also called tinting.

Drying (1) 214
The process in which the printing ink dries on the paper.

Drying (2) 204
When the paper dries in the dryer section, it is determined what level of dryness the paper should have. Levels of dryness depends on what the paper will be used for.

Drying powder 214
Powder sprayed between the printed sheets in the stream feeder to prevent the printing ink from smearing on the sheet above it. Also called spraying powder.

Duct roller 218
The duct roller in the ink pyramid takes ink from the ink duct and transfers it to the other rollers in the ink pyramid.

Ductor knife 217
The ductor knife is located in the ink duct and determines the ink supply in the printing press. It's controlled by the ink screws of the printing press, which are adjusted manually or digitally.

Dummy 242
A test sample of an imposition, a binding or a complete printed product. It is usually hand made.

Duotones   60, 61
A grayscale image printed with two printing inks instead of one. If you want to reproduce fine details in a black and white image, make it softer or tint it a color other than pure black, you use duotones. You usually print with black plus one spot color of your choice.

DVD   123–124
Digital Versatile Disc, an optical disc for storing data, holds up to 17 gigabytes.

Dye sublimation printer   176, 188
[Thermo-transfer printer] Printer based on the sublimation technique, i.e. color layers are transferred to the paper by heating a "color ribbon."

E

Editable
Possible to change.

Electrolysis   228
Electro-chemical treatment used to treat the surface of the gravure printing cylinder.

Elliptical raster dot   147
Raster dot with an elliptical shape rather than circular. The shape of the raster dot provides the screen with different characteristics.

Email, electronic mail   138
Electronic letters consisting of small text files that are sent between computers.

Emulsion layer   190, 191, 177
A layer on the film that consists of photographic emulsion and is exposed in the imagesetter.

Emulsion side   191
The side of a graphic film with a light-sensitive emulsion layer.

Endpapers   242, 239
The pages glued to the cover of case-bound books in order to attach the insert, are called endpapers. Sometimes consist of a colored or printed paper which are then called separate endpapers.

Engraving   229
Technique for producing gravure prints using physical pressure and a diamond-tipped head to create halftone wells.

EPS-DCS/EPSF   64, 108, 103
Encapsulated PostScript-Desktop Color Separation. A file format for four-color converted digital images. The image file consists of five component files: a low-resolution image for screen display and a high-resolution file for each of the four component colors.

EPS   64, 108, 103
Encapsulated Postscript. A file format for digital images and illustrations. Manages both object- and pixel based graphics.

Etching   228
Technique for producing gravure printing forms by using a chemical treatment.

Ethernet   136, 132, 134
One of the most common network solutions.

Ethertalk   132, 136
Apple's network protocol used in Ethernet networks.

Eudora   139
A program for managing electronic mail.

European color scale   186
A standard in Europe for defining color characteristics in printing inks. Corresponds to the American standard SWOP.

Exabyte   120, 121
Magnetic tape for storing data, holds around 4 to 8 gigabyte.

Excel   103
Program from Microsoft used for calculations and statistics.

Expose   190, 177, 192, 193
To illuminate a light-sensitive layer on a film or printing plate with light in order to transfer an image.

Exposure dot   143, 144
The dot that an imagesetter or printer's laser beam exposes. Builds the halftone dot.

Exposure frame   193
Device necessary for exposing a printing plate. Comes with vacuum equipment and an exposure timer.

Exposure time   193
The time it takes to expose a printing plate or piece of film, and get the correct result.

Extensions   14
Plug-ins that expand a particular program's functions.

External drum   177
Version of imagesetter in which film is exposed on the outside of a rotating drum.

F

"Fake" duotones   61
A grayscale image printed on a tinted area is called a "fake" duotone. The white parts of the grayscale image get the color of the tinted area.

Feedboard   216
The stream feeder in a sheet-fed printing press sets the sheets on the feedboard which transports them to the registration. The feedboard assures the stream feeder only feeds one sheet at a time.

Fetch   138
Program for transmitting files on the Internet via FTP.

Fiber direction   201
The direction along which the paper fibers are oriented. The same direction as the paper has been produced in.

Fiber-optical networks/FDDI   136
Fiber Distributed Data Interchange. Networks based on an optical transmission technique via fiber cables.

File head   150
The beginning of a digital file where particular information is stored, for example information about which program has created the file.

File structure   118, 126
A predetermined order based on which you organize and sort files.

Files   21
Digital blocks of data are called files. A file can be a program, a system file or a driver.

Fill   57
Curves and closed objects can be filled with colors, tonal transitions and patterns. Used in object graphics.

Fillers   203
Different agents mixed into the pulp stock. The most common fillers are ground marble or limestone ($CaCO_3$) and clay. These ingredients improve the opacity and the color of the print on the paper. The fillers also provide the paper with softness and elasticity. By adding calcium carbonate the paper is better protected from aging.

Film   190
Graphic film is used as original artwork for producing the printing form.

Film assembly   192
Film that is mounted into a complete print assembly and used for producing plates.

Film development   190
After exposure, the image on the film is developed and fixated by chemical liquids.

Film set   192
A set of film of the same page, one for each printing ink, for example four films for a four-color page.

Final proof   180
The absolutely last proof before starting to print.

Firewall   139
A system that protects a local network from external intervention via network connection, for example via the Internet.

First Class   139
A program for managing electronic mail and file transfers.

Five-cylinder unit 217
A special type of printing unit consisting of two plate cylinders, two rubber blanket cylinders and an impression cylinder.

Flatbed scanner 95
In this type of scanner, the original is placed and scanned flat on a glass plate.

Flexographic print edge 230
A print phenomenon in flexography that is visible as a dark outline around printed areas.

Flexography 229
A direct printing technique. The printing areas are elevated compared to the non-printing ones. Primarily used in the packaging industry. The printing form is made of rubber or a plastic material.

Flight Pro 182
A Preflight program.

Flightcheck 182
A Preflight program.

Floppy disc 120
A magnetic storage medium for data 3.5 inches in diameter. Standard in all computers. Holds 0.7 or 1.4 megabytes.

FM screen 148
Frequency modulated screen. Also called stochastic screen.

Foiling 239
Placing a foil on a printed product. The foil is heated; it elevates and forms a relief.

Folder
A printed product that only consists of a folded sheet, no binding.

Folding 240
When folding sheets of paper. Is usually done in folding machines.

Font 24, 25, 27
A collection of type in a particular typeface stored in a file. File types for fonts are, for example, Truetype and PostScript Type 1.

Font file 24, 25, 27
See Font.

Font ID 29
A unique ID number assigned to all font files.

Font size
Size of font – stated in points.

Font software 26
Software that can edit fonts, such as Macromedia Fontographer.

Fore edge 239
The outer margin of a page, as opposed to the inner margin, the gutter.

Format 201
States the size of a surface, for example a printed product's final size. Common standard formats are 8 $^1/_2$ × 11 and A4.

Formation 204
How evenly a paper is built up. If you hold up a piece of paper to a light source and it's even, i.e. without "clouds", it has a good formation.

Former folder 240
A special type of folding machine usually used in web-fed offset printing.

Four-color printing
Printing with the four primary colors, CMYK.

Four-color separation 40, 85, 62, 155
(CMYK conversion)
To convert a digital image from the additive color system, RGB, into the subtractive color system, CMYK. When the image is four-color separated it's adjusted according to applicable printing characteristics.

Four-color set 192
A set of four films, one for each printing ink, of the same page that forms the basis of a printed four-colored page.

Four-up
See Many-up.

Freehand 58, 14
Illustration application from Macromedia.

Framemaker
Page layout application from Adobe, particularly suitable for productions with larger formats, such as catalogue productions.

Frequency 36
How often something occurs, for example light waves per second, measured in Hz.

FTP 138
File Transfer Protocol. Protocol for transmitting files on the Internet.

Full-tone area 222
A printed surface 100% covered with printing ink.

Full-tone density 222, 223, 224
The density of a full-tone area, used among other things to measure the ink coverage in the printing press, measured with a densitometer. Also see Density.

Gamma value 70, 71
A value describing a curve used when compressing tones or setting screens.

Gang-up 171
A type of imposition in which a page is placed multiple times on the same printing sheet, for example a 2-up that will provide you with two copies of the same page out of each sheet.

GB, Gbyte
Gigabyte, i.e. 1,073,741,824 bytes, see Byte.

GCR 86, 87, 88, 89
Gray Component Replacement. A special method for separation; you reduce the ink amount in the parts of the image that contain all the three primary colors CMY by fully or partially substituting the common component with black.

GIF 65
Graphic Interchange Format. A file format in index mode mainly used for the web. Can contain up to 256 colors.

Giga
10^9=1,000,000,000.

Gigabyte
1,073,741,824 bytes, see Byte.

Glazing 204
A post-treatment in the paper production process that gives the paper a higher gloss. The glazing provides a higher image quality but reduced opacity and stiffness.

Glossy paper 206
Paper that has been treated to get a glossy surface.

Grammage substance 201
A measurement of the paper's weight per surface unit, measured in g/m².

Gravure head 229
Used to engrave the printing forms for gravure printing, are supplied with a diamond-tipped head.

Gray balance 87, 79, 222
Describes the state when a certain combination of the primary colors, CMY, gives a neutral, gray tone, for example 40% cyan, 30% magenta and 30% yellow.

Graphics card 16
A circuit board installed in the computer that enables the computer to control the monitor.

Grey test marks 220
Special fields for measurement based on a theoretically neutral combination of CMY. If it is not neutrally grey in print, you have a color cast.

Gripper's edge 216, 248
The part of the paper that the printing press or off press processing machine grabs when the paper is fed into the machine.

Gutter 239
The inner margin of a bound, printed product.

H

Halftone cells   143, 144

Each halftone dot consists of exposure points within its own halftone cell. The exposure points are placed in the halftone cell so that they form the halftone dot. The size of the halftone cell is, in turn, determined by the screen frequency.

Halftone dot   143, 144

The smallest unit that a screen consists of. All tones in print, both photographs and illustrations, are based on halftone dots.

Halftone matrix

See Halftone cells.

Halftone screen matrix

See Halftone cells.

Halftone screen rosettes   147, 186

Halftone screen phenomenon. Many halftone dots form a circular pattern in the print which might be perceived as distracting.

Halftone screening   143

Used to simulate gray tones in print, usually dots of different sizes.

Halftone wells   228

Small wells in the printing form used for gravure printing that form the printing surfaces. Can be generated using etching or engraving.

Hard disk   16, 120

Magnetic storage medium. All computers have an internal hard disk where all types of files are stored, for example programs, documents, operating systems etc. There are also external hard disks that can be attached to the computer.

Harden (Cure)   228

When etching the printing form for gravure printing, you use a light-sensitive gel that is hardened by exposing it to light.

Hardware RIP

See RIP.

Hexachrome-separation   91,

A version of HiFi color separation separated into six printing inks.

Hierarchical structure   126

A way of storing and sorting files according to a "heading" model; files are sorted under main- and sub headings.

HiFi Color   40, 91

Subtractive color model that lets you add two to four colors in addition to CMYK in order to obtain a wider color range in print.

High-resolution image   109, 163, 164

Image with a sufficiently high resolution for the print; requires a lot of storage space.

Hinted fonts   29

A set of suggestions stored in the font about how the printer should print the font.

Histogram   76

Graphic representation of tone administration in a digital image.

Hole punching   247

In order to be able to enter the printed product into binders.

Hub   134

Network unit that connects different parts of a network.

Huffman compression   66

Lossless compression method. Mainly used for line art.

Hydrophilic   213

Attracts water.

Hydrophobic   213

Repels water.

I

ICC   46

International Color Consortium, a group of soft- and hardware manufacturers in the graphic industry working to find a common color management standard.

ICC-profile   46

A standard for describing color characteristics of scanners, monitors, printers, proofs and prints. Is used by most color management

systems. Created by using a spectrophotometer.

Icon

A symbol used in computer context, for example the icon for a PDF file.

Illustration software   103, 14

Used to make illustrations. Usually object-based.

Illustrator   58, 14

Illustration software from Adobe.

Image editing   75, 145

To create, edit, change or retouch images in the computer.

Image editing software   103, 14

Software necessary to create, edit, change or retouch images in the computer.

Image link   109

See Link.

Image resolution   59, 74

Information density of a digital, pixel-based image, measured in ppi (pixels per inch).

Imposed film   164, 193

Film that is output in the format of the printing sheet, containing a number of pages on each. Makes an assembly.

Imposition   14

Imposition program from Quark.

Imposition program   164

Program that performs digital impositions based on files, for example Preps from Scenicsoft and Presswise from Imation.

Impression cylinder   214

Cylinder in the printing press that presses the paper against the cylinder that transfers the ink to the paper.

Index color mode   62, 59

An image in index color mode holds up to 256 different colors, defined in a palette in which each box contains a color and has a number. This means that all the pixels of the image will have a value between 1 and 256 depending on the palette color it has. Thus, the image only contains a pixel image with the same memory

size as a grayscale image, as well as a palette.

Indirect printing procedure   191

A printing procedure in which the ink of the printing form is tranferred via a rubber blanket cylinder to the paper, i.e. offset.

Infrared light   37, 36

Radiant heat. The invisible light, closest to the red hues in the spectrum, i.e. wavelengths around 705 nm.

Ink   36, 214

The physical substance of color, for example printing ink. Also see Color.

Ink coverage   217, 223, 87

The amount of ink added in the printing process. Also describes the maximum allowed amount of each component color on a certain paper in a certain printing process. Expressed as a percent.

Ink dampening balance   220

To achieve good print quality in an offset print, there has to be a balance between the dampening solution and the printing ink.

Ink duct   217, 218, 219

The space in the printing press that supplies the ink.

Ink form roller   218

Roller in the ink pyramid that transfers printing ink from the last distribution rollers to the printing plate.

Ink pyramid   217, 218

Term for the entire system in a printing system that manages four-color supply.

Ink rollers   217

Collective term for all types of rollers in an ink pyramid.

Ink screws   217, 218, 219, 220

Controls the ink doctor and thereby the supply of ink to different parts and zones along the ink duct/printing press. Can either be controlled manually or digitally depending on the printing press.

Ink zones 217
The ink supply is controlled in a number of zones across the printed sheet, which makes it possible to adjust the ink amount within each zone.

Ink-jet printer 175, 188
A printer based on a technique that "squirts" liquid ink on the paper.

Insert 241
Type of imposition for binding. The folded sheets are inserted into each other, often used when saddle stitching.

Integrated circuits 16
The "chip" of the computer, for example processors or memory circuits.

Internal drum 178
Special construction of imagesetters. The exposure of film takes place inside a stationary drum.

Internet 138
Worldwide computer network.

Internet Explorer 138
Web browser from Microsoft.

Interpolation 75, 76
Technique for re-calculating information in a digital image, for example when changing the resolution or rotating an image.

Iris 188
Digital proof system from Scitex.

ISDN 137
Integrated Services Digital Network. Hard- and software for digital transmissions via the telephone network.

Isopropyl alcohol 213
Alcohol added to the dampening solution in order to reduce surface tensions in the dampening solution.

J

Jacket band 246
A thin strip of paper wrapped around a printed product, for example around a stack of printed products or a poster.

Jaz 120
A removable magnetic disk for data storage. Holds 1 or 2 gigabytes.

JPEG 67, 65
Joint Photographic Experts Group. A lossy compression method for images. Also operates as an image format. Compatible with most computer platforms.

K

Knockout (1) 110
When a graphic object is placed over another, for example a text over a tint area, and you don't want the colors of the text and the background to mix, you should knock out space for the text. A hole the same shape as the text in the tint area is knocked out and the text is printed on an un-printed, paper white surface.

Knockout (2) 58
To make a hole in an object-based image so that the object behind it becomes visible.

L

Layer 83, 64
A technique in image editing applications for separating different parts of an image until it's finished. Useful when creating manipulations and collage or graphics consisting of several parts, for example an image and a text, or a motif and a shadow.

Life Cycle Analysis
A method for analyzing a product's environmental impact from when it's produced until it's recycled. It is the only way to get detailed information about the negative environmental impact.

Light intensity 94, 96
The intensity of light, also called brightness or luminance.

Line arrangement 150, 103, 31
The way in which the right margin of a text column is broken off. May rearrange when changing rip or font.

Line art 60
Line art are images that only consist of surfaces in full color or no color at all. The pixels in the image are either black or white.

Line rearrangement 150, 103, 32
When the line arrangement in a document changes, for example when changing fonts.

Line screen 147
A screen based on thin lines of varying thickness, instead of halftone dots.

Linear 37
A mathematical relationship dependent on a constant factor.

Link 109
Reference, for example from a low-resolution image to the corresponding high-resolution one. When printing a document, the program finds the high-resolution image by using the link and replaces the low-resolution one. The link keeps track of the name and location of the high-resolution image in the computer's file structure.

Lithographic principle 213
Works with printing surfaces that attract grease (ink) and repel water and non-prining surfaces that attract and are covered with water that repels the greasy ink.

Live Picture 14
Image editing application from Live Picture.

Localtalk 136
Apple's network solution for connecting Apple Macintosh computers.

Logarithmic 37
A mathematical, non-linear relationship. The eye's perception of light is logarithmic. We can perceive tonal transitions easier in light than in dark areas.

Loop stitch 243
A version of an ordinary staple, used when metal stitching. It's used to facilitate putting the printed product in a binder and being able to easily flip through it.

Low-resolution image 109, 163, 164
Image with low resolution, usually 72 ppi. Requires little storage space. Is usually used as mounting image and is then exchanged, manually or automatically, for a high-resolution image when outputting film.

Lowercase letter 25
Small letters, as opposed to uppercase letters.

Luminance
See Brightness.

LZW 67
Lossless compression method named after the researchers Lempel, Ziv and Welch who developed it. LZW can be used when images are saved in the TIFF-format.

M

Mac OS 13
Apple's operating system used in Macintosh-based computers.

Machine finish
See Calendar finish.

Machine point 152
See Exposure point.

Magnetic direction 125
Direction in a magnetic field between a magnetic north- and south pole. Used in magnetic read- and write techniques on magnetic media for data storage.

Magnetic disk 120
Medium for data storage based on magnetic read- and write techniques, for example hard disks, Zip disks or floppy disks.

Magnetic field 122, 125
An area with a magnetic direction originated between a magnetic north- and south pole.

Magnetic tape 121
Medium for data storage based on magnetic read- and write techniques, for example DAT- or DLT tape.

Makeready 218, 170
Term for all settings and preparations you need to do in the printing press before the first approved printed sheet has been produced.

Manual mounting 192, 164, 194
Films that are manually mounted into complete film assemblies.

Many-up 171
Type of imposition. One page is placed multiple times on the same printer sheet, for example two-up gives two copies of the same page from each printed sheet.

Matchprint 188
Analog proof system from 3M.

Maximum ink coverage 86, 223
States the maximum amount of ink of the component colors in percent on a certain paper in a certain printing process. The value is mainly determined by the possibility of smearing and is usually between 240 and 340% for a four-color print (the theoretical value is 400%, 100% for each color). The value is used for print adjustment when four-color separating.

Mbyte
Megabyte, i.e. 1,048,576 bytes, see Byte.

Mechanical pulp 203
When producing mechanical pulp, cellulose fibers are extracted from the wood by grinding.

Metamerism 52
When two colors that look identical in a particular light look completely different in another.

Mirror hard drives 133
A backup function based on a set of hard disks. A program makes sure that all changes made on one hard disk are also made on the other. That way you will always have two identical sets of files.

Misregistration 224, 105, 110
Print phenomenon: the component colors don't print directly on top of each other, i.e. in register.

MO-disks 124
Magneto-optical disks, a removable optical disk for data storage available in differnt sizes. Hold between 128 and 1,300 megabytes.

Modem 137
Communication equipment that enables a computer to call up and transfer files to or from another computer via the analog telephone network.

Modem port 137
A connection in the computer–parallel port–where you connect the modem.

Moire 146, 186
A screen phenomenon visible as distracting interference patterns in images and tint areas. A similar phenomenon occurs on TV, for example when someone is wearing a checkered suit.

Monotype 25
Typeface manufacturer.

Mounting
See Manual mounting.

Multiple Master 30
File type for fonts that can assume different widths and boldness creating a large variety of styles from a single font. Version of PostScript Type 1.

Nanometer (nm)
A measurement of length (1 nanometer=0.000001 millimeter). Used to, among other things, state the wavelength of light.

NCS 42
Natural Color System, a Swedish color system. It is based on the coordinates of brightness, color and saturation and can be visualized as a double-cone. Is mostly used within the textile- and painting industries.

Negative film 190
Graphic film which has black non-printing surfaces and transparent printing surfaces.

Netscape Navigator 138
Web browser from Netscape.

Network 130
Net connection enabling exchange of information between computers, printers, scanners, servers, and other networked devices.

Network cable 131
The physical cable that connects the network.

Network Interface Card 16, 132
A circuit board installed in the computer enabling it to communicate on a specific network.

Network protocol 132
A collection of rules for how communication on a particular network should work.

Network server 133
A computer that manages the network, controls and supervises its traffic and authorizations.

Network traffic load 135
States the level of traffic, i.e. how much information is sent on a network at a given moment.

Network unit 133
Unit used to build a network, for example switches, bridges and hubs.

O

Off press processing 238
All the procedures performed on the printed paper sheets until you have a complete printed product. Procedures include cropping, folding and binding.

One-sided paper
A paper with different surface characteristics on the front- and back sides, for example postcards (coated side with image and uncoated side for writing).

Original image
For example a slide, paper copy of a photograph or a drawing.

OST 137
A type of ISDN communication card.

Output device 142
For example a printer or imagesetter.

Output resolution 144
The resolution a certain output device, such as a printer or imagesetter, has. Measured in dpi.

Overprint 110
When, for example, a text is printed on a tint area and the colors of the two objects mix. The opposite phenomenon, in which the colors of the objects are not mixed, is called knockout.

Oxidation 214
The second drying process of the offset printing inks. The alkyd undergoes a chemical reaction with the oxygen in the air, a process called oxidation.

P

Packet 134, 135
Describes an amount of data sent on a network. The information sent on a network is divided into a number of packets.

Page description language 149
A code language that describes the design of a page. See PostScript.

Page film 196, 164
Graphic film containing one page of the printed product. Page films are mounted into complete impositions. As opposed to imposed film, which corresponds to the format of the printed sheet and contains multiple pages.

Page-independent 152, 154
In a document saved in PDF-format, the pages are stored independent of each other. All the information about a page is stored with a description of the page. As a result you can choose to print whichever page without having to print the others—the format is "page-independent." If you saved the same document in the page-

dependent PostScript-format, you would have to print none or all of the pages, simply because the pages are dependent on each other.

PageMaker 103, 14
Widely used page layout program from Adobe.

Palette 62
A set of colors in the computer. Also see Index color mode.

Parallel folding 240
A type of folding in which the folds are parallel to each other, as opposed to right-angle folding.

Parallel port 16
A connection in the computer where you connect printers or modems for example.

PDF (1) 156
Portable Document Format. A file format from Adobe created with the program Acrobat Distiller.

PDF (2) 151, 152
Printer Description File, a printer description necessary when outputting from QuarkXPress. Contains information about a particular output device and is necessary in order to be able to output on it.

Perfector printing unit 217
A type of printing unit that does not have an impression cylinder. Both sides of the sheet are printed simultaneously with two rubber blanket cylinders which use each other as impression cylinders.

Photo multiplier 96, 95
Unit that translates intensity of light into electronic signals.

Photographic conductor 172
Material whose electrical charge can be modified by light, used in laser printers, see the xerographic process.

Photosensitive polymer 192, 190
A light-sensitive layer on the surface of a printing plate.

Pick-outs 225
Paper fragments are torn off the paper by the ink, so called picking, land on the rubber blanket or the

printing plate and cause white dots in the print.

Picking 225
When the printing ink tears off paper fibers from the paper.

Picture element 59, 18
Also called a pixel. A digital image or the smallest visual component of a monitor. The number of pixels per inch or centimeter is a measurement of image- and monitor resolution.

Pixel graphics 59
Image based on pixels, as opposed to an object image based on geometric objects and mathematical curves. A pixel-based image should not be enlarged more than 15-20%, in order to maintain optimal resolution.

Planet card 137
A type of ISDN-communication card.

Plate 193
See Printing plate.

Plate cylinder 214, 216
The printing cylinder to which you attach the printing plate. In offset printing, the plate cylinder transfers the ink/image to the rubber blanket cylinder which, in turn, transfers it to the paper.

Plate development 193
After exposing, the printing plate is developed using chemical liquids.

Plate exposure 193
The process of exposing the printing plate using ultra-violet light that shines through a graphic film.

Plate makeready 218, 219
To mount and adjust the printing plate in the printing press.

Plate scanner 217
A scanner that scans the already exposed printing plates so that you can adjust the basic ink settings in advance.

Plug-ins 14
Small programs that enhance the computer's functions.

PMS colors 41, 106, 107
Pantone Matching System, based on combinations of nine different colors. Is primarily used for spot colors.

Polycarbonate 123
The plastic material of a CD.

Polymer layer 190, 193
A light-sensitive layer of plastic, polymer, covering the surface of an offset printing plate.

Portfolio 14
Archive software from Extensis.

Positive film 191
Graphic film with transparent non-printing surfaces and black printing surfaces.

Post-treatment 204
When paper is post-treated in different ways depending on which quality and surface characteristics it should have.

PostScript 153
A page description language from Adobe, standard for graphic outputs.

PostScript 3 153
The third version of the page description language PostScript. "Level" has been removed from the name. Compare to PostScript Level 1 and 2.

PostScript Code 149
Program code that describes a PostScript file.

PostScript Extreme 156
A PostScript 3-rip technique that can rip several pages of a document at the same time using different processors.

PostScript interpreter 152
Software that interprets PostScript code and transfers it to a bitmap with exposure points or screen points.

PostScript Level 1 153
The first version of the page description language PostScript. Is the basis for PostScript Level 2 and PostScript 3. Level 1 is, in comparison to the other two versions, a relatively simple page

description language, i.e. it does not, for example, support color management.

PostScript Level 2 153
The second version of the page description language PostScript. Supports, among other things, color management (something PostScript Level 1 does not do).

PostScript printer
A printer based on the page description language PostScript.

PostScript rip 152
A rip based on the page description language PostScript. See RIP.

PostScript Type 1 30, 103
File type for fonts, is based on PostScript.

PostScript-head 150
The first information in a PostScript-file, for example information about which program has created the file.

Powerpoint 103
Presentation software from Microsoft. Used for presentation graphics.

PPD 151, 152
PostScript Printer Description. Contains information about a particular output unit and is necessary in order to output to the unit.

ppi 59
Pixels per inch. States the resolution of images, monitors and scanners.

Preflight 182
To, using special software, review, proof and adjust documents and their components before outputting on film or printing plate.

Prepress provider 9, 10
Company that supplies reproductive services, for example scanning of images and output of film.

Preps 164, 14
An imposition program from ScenicSoft.

Press proof 185
A proof run on the printing press before the actual edition is printed.

PressWise 164, 14
An imposition program from ScenicSoft.

Preview 59
An EPS-image contains a preview image in the PICT file format. The preview image can be in black and white or color and always has a resolution of 72 ppi because that is the standard resolution of monitors. It's used when placing EPS-images in documents.

Primary colors 39
The primary colors of a color system, for example CMY and RGB.

Primary colors
Three primary colors from the spectrum: cyan, magenta and yellow in print and red, green and blue on the screen and in a scanner.

Print adjustment 85
The digital image is adjusted according to the prerequisites and characteristics of the print and the paper. Is done when color-separating.

Print carrier
Material you print on, usually paper.

Print contrast 224
The relative contrast in print is defined as the difference in density between a 100%-tone and an 80%-tone divided by the density of the 100%-tone. The optimal ink coverage and relative contrast in a printing process is called NCI-level.

Print curves 221
Different curves concerning the character of a printing press on a certain paper, for example dot gain curves and optimal ink coverage.

Print cylinder 214
See Plate cylinder.

Printability 207
A measurement of the printing capability of the paper.

Printed image 194
Image created by the ink. In offset it is transferred from plate to rubber blanket to paper.

Printer driver 149, 151
Control program for printers.

Printer font 25, 27, 30
Font file used when outputting or for monitor display. Used for large fonts and only works if you have ATM installed.

Printing form 190
To produce the printing form; for example to expose and develop an offset plate.

Printing method 212
Term for a certain printing method, such as offset-, screen- or gravure printing.

Printing plate 193
Printing form used in offset printing.

Printing unit 216
A set of printing cylinders, for example plate cylinder, rubber blanket cylinder and impression cylinder, in an offset printing press.

Process colors 104
The colors you print with, usually CMYK.

Processor 15
The computer's "brain." It performs all calculations. The speed of the processor is fundamental when determining the capacity of the computer. It is determined by its clock frequency, the number of possible calculations per second.

Profiles 45, 46
Each apparatus in the production process has its strong and weak sides. Those characteristics can be measured and stored in profiles by using a color management program.

Proof print 183
A proof of what the complete printed product will look like. Is either done digitally or from the films that are the basis for printing.

Proof system 183
An analog or digital system for producing proofs. See Proof print.

Proscript 182, 183
A preflight program from Cutting Edge Technology that proofs PostScript files.

Pulp stock 203
The pulp stock is the complete mixture of ingredients for a particular paper quality.

Pulp stock preparation 203
When preparing the pulp stock the cellulose fibers are beaten; you add fillers, sizers and, if desired, color. See Pulp stock.

Punching 194
To make a hole. You punch a hole in film and plate in order to mount them correctly using the registration pins.

Quadtone image 61
A grayscale image printed with four printing inks instead of one. If you want to reproduce fine details in a black and white image, make it softer or tint it a color other than pure black, you use quadtones. You usually print with black plus three spot colors of your choice.

QuarkXPress 103, 14
Widely used page layout program from Quark.

R

Rag paper 205
Paper that, aside from wood fibers, also consists of cotton fibers.

Rainbow from 3M 188
Digital proof system from 3M.

RAM 16
Random Access Memory, the computer's high-speed, temporary working memory.

Read device 121
Device necessary to read certain types of media for data storage, for example a Jaz-reader for Jaz-disks.

Read head 95, 120
Part of a scanner or reader of data storage media, for example a CD-reader, that reads the information in the image or on the disk.

Read speed 119
The speed with which data can be read and transferred from a data storage medium. Stated in kilobytes per second.

Recto 171
The front side of the print sheet, i.e. the side printed first.

Recto-Verso 171
Type of imposition for double-sided prints. You impose one time for the recto-side and another for the verso one.

Reference color 220
A well-known color with a natural tone. Common reference colors are skin, grass or sky.

Reference values 92
Standard values for different printing parameters, for example dot gain, full-tone density, etc.

Reflection 225, 169
Print phenomenon caused by the ink pyramid's inability to supply enough ink to certain areas of the plate. Is visible as traces of objects in tint areas in the printing direction.

Reflective images 68
Photographic images on paper.

Reflectivity 37, 39
The extent to which in-coming light is reflected on a certain material dependent on its texture and surface treatment.

Registration (1)
When all printing inks are situated correctly in relation to each other, for example component colors in a four-color print run or the inks on the recto and verso.

Registration (2) 216
When the sheets in the sheet transportation of a printing press are adjusted in order to assure that they run through the press in a synchronized manner. If the sheets

are not registered, the print might end up in different places on the different sheets.

Registration box　126
You enter information and descriptions about the object that is being archived in registration boxes in an archive software.

Registration edge　216
The edges of a sheet that are registered in the printing press.

Registration mark　1: 219, 169, 2: 155
1. A special registration mark on the print necessary to print the component colors of a multi-color print on top of each other as precisely as possible.
2. Term for all registration marks and crop marks in the QuarkXPress dialogue box for printout.

Registration pins　194, 219
A registration system consisting of small pins. Is partly used when mounting films and exposing plates, and partly at the makeready of the printing process in order to obtain the best possible registration between component colors.

Relative print contrast　224
 A measurement of the relative contrast in print. Is defined as the difference in density between a 100%-tone and an 80%-tone divided by the density of the 100%-tone. The optimal ink coverage and relative contrast in a printing process is called NCI-level.

Repeater　133
Network unit that connects different parts of a network and improves its signals.

Reprinting (Rerun)　195
When printing additional copies of the same printed product without making major changes.

Resolution　59
Describes the density of information in a digital image. Can also describe the smallest printing- or reading point in, for example, imagesetters or scanners. Measured in dpi and ppi.

Recycled paper　205
Paper that consists of recycled fibers. The most common ones consist of either 50, 75 or 100% recycled fibers.

Reversed film　191
A film whose printed image is a mirror image if looking at it with the emulsion side up. Used in offset productions for example.

Rewritable media　123
Rewritable media for data storage, i.e. information stored on the disk, can be erased and rewritten.

RGB　40, 39
Red, Green, Blue. Additive color system used in screen displays and scanners for example.

RGB-mode　62, 59
An image in RGB-mode technically consists of three separate pixel images in grayscale mode that each represents red, green and blue. This means that an RGB-image uses three times as much memory as a grayscale image of the same size and resolution.

Rich black　106
When pairing black ink with additional ink/inks in order to achieve a darker and deeper black color.

Right-angled folder　240
A type of folding in which the folds are placed at a 90-degree angle in relation to each other, as opposed to parallel folding.

Right-reading film　191
A film with a right-reading printed image if looking at it emulsion side up, for example a film used for screen printing.

RIP　143, 152
Raster Image Processor. Hard- or software that calculates and rasterizes pages before they are output on an imagesetter or printer.

RIP time　152, 153
The time it takes the RIP to interpret the PostScript code for one page, that is to create the bitmap with exposure points.

ROM　16
Read Only Memory, pre-programmed memory circuit which stores the computer's most basic functions.

Rotation　76, 108
A change in angle of objects in the computer. Images should not be rotated in the page layout program.

Round halftone dot　147
The normal shape of a halftone dot. The shape of the halftone dot determines the characteristics of the screen.

Router　134, 135
Network unit that connects different parts of a network and divides it into zones. Common when connecting several LAN's into a WAN.

Runability　207
The paper's ability to run through the printing press.

Sampling factor　70
The relationship between the resolution of the image and the screen frequency of the print is called the sampling factor. Tests have shown that the optimal sampling factor is 2, i.e. the resolution of the image should be twice as high as the screen frequency.

Sans Serif　29, 105
Typeface family without serifs, for example DIN and Helvetica.

Satellite unit　217
A printing unit with one large impression cylinder around which there are a number of printing units, one for each printing color.

Scaling　73
The change in size of images and other digital objects.

Scaling factor　74
The relation in size between original image and printed image. If, for example, you are printing an image three times the size of the original, the scaling factor is 3.

Scanner　94
Device used to read, "scan," original artwork into the computer.

Scanner program　85
Program that controls the scanning of images. Here you adjust resolution, colors, sharpness, four-color separation, etc.

Scanner-camera　98
Digital camera that operates based on the scanning technique, i.e. the read head "sweeps" across the image.

Scanning resolution　73, 74, 94, 97
The resolution you select when scanning images. Determined by screen frequency, sampling factor and scaling factor. Determines how many scanning points per inch the scanning should have. Measured in ppi.

Screen angles　146, 147
A halftone screen is placed so that the lines formed by the dots are at a certain angle. When printing with four-colors, the screens of the four colors have to be placed at certain predetermined angles.

Screen cloth　227
A finely woven cloth that lets through printing ink. Is tightened on a screen frame and coated with a photosensitive layer.

Screen fonts　25, 27, 30
Font file used for screen display. Consists of small bitmap-images.

Screen frame　227
A frame around which the screen cloth is tightened.

Screen frequency　19
States how often the image is updated in a monitor display. Measured in Hertz or Hz.

Screen frequency   143, 144, 70
Describes how "fine" a halftone screen is by stating the number of screen lines per inch. Measured in lines per inch, lpi.

Screen percent value
Tonal value between 0 and 100%.

Screen phenomena   186, 145
Different screen phenomena that may occur when rasterizing. Often results in undesired patterns, such as moire.

Screen printing   226, 194
A printing method used for large formats, such as advertisement billboards and hard print carriers, for example steel signs. The printing form consists of a finely woven cloth that lets through printing ink and is tightened to a frame. The non-printing surfaces are covered so that the ink cannot get through the cloth.

Screen ruling meter   192
Measures screen frequency and screen angles in a halftone screen.

Screen stencil   227
Plastic layer that covers the non-printing surfaces on the screen cloth.

SCSI   17
Small Computer Standard Interface, a standard for transferring information within the computer and between external units such as hard disks, scanners, printers, etc.

SCSI-cable   16
A special cable for SCSI-transmission between computer and external units.

SCSI-port   16
You can connect different external units such as hard disks, Jaz-readers and scanners via the computer's SCSI-port.

Search box   128
The box in which you specify a search in archive software.

Secondary colors   39
If you mix the primary colors (CMYK) two and two, the result is secondary colors: red, green and blue-violet (RGB).

Sector storage   123
Data storage technique based on information being stored in different sectors. Is often used as storage technique on magnetic disks.

Segmentation   135
A network can be divided into different network segments in order to reduce network traffic in different parts of the network.

Selection   85
To cut an image along its contours in the computer. Also called vignette.

Self-extracting   113
For self-extracting, compressed files, you don't need a decompression program. They are decompressed by themselves when double-clicking on the file.

Separation
See Four-color separation.

Separation settings   92
The settings that control the print adjustment in the four-color separation process, for example dot gain, maximum ink coverage, etc. See Four-color separation.

Sequential coding   122
Lossless compression method. Mainly used for line art.

Sequential storage   122
Data storage technique based on information being stored consecutively. Often used as a storage technique on magnetic tape.

Serial port   16
You connect, for example, keyboards and mice to the serial port.

Server   133, 119
Powerful computer for special applications, for example file management and outputs in a network.

Plate set   194
A set of plates for the same print sheet, for example four plates for a four-color sheet.

Setting   214
First step in the drying process of offset inks. The oil component is absorbed by the paper and the pigment, alkyd and resin form a gel on the surface of the paper. Curing, or oxidation, is the second phase.

Sharpness   80, 81
If an image appears "soft" it is generally due to a lack of sharp transitions between the dark and light hues in an outline. Instead of a sharp transition, the outline consists of a soft, tonal transition. To sharpen the image, you need to find the soft, tonal transitions that make the image appear blurry and make them sharper.

Shielded   131
To provide a cable with protection against noise, it can be shielded. The shield consists of a protective foil sheath wrapped around the wire.

Shutter speed   98
The time the shutter in the camera is open and lets in light exposing the film.

Sign
A letter, digit or symbol.

Signal bandwidth   132
How far a signal maintains its strength. Is affected by the cable type.

Simulate   45, 44
To try to make something look like something else, for example a print to look like the proof.

Single-pass   96
Technique for scanning all three colors (RGB) in an original artwork in one sweep.

Slurring   225
Print phenomenon that causes dot deformation and a darker print. Slurring means that the halftone dots are smeared, causing oval dots. The phenomenon can occur when the pressure between the rubber blanket cylinder and the impression cylinder is too high or when the plate cylinder and rubber

blanket cylinder are not rotating at exactly the same speed.

Smearing   222, 214, 86
The sheets smear ink on each other. Print phenomenon that occurs when using too much printing ink on the sheet or when the ink has not had time to dry.

Smyth-sewn   245
A technique combining thread stitching with glue binding used for soft-bound books.

Soft proof   181
Reviewing and proofing of a document on the screen.

Soft proof (Screen proof)   181
A review and evaluation of a printed product on the screen, for example a file in PDF-format.

Software   12
A term for all types of programs, from operating system to application.

Software RIP   152
See RIP.

Spectrophotometer   47
Instrument used to measure the spectral composition of colors. Also used, among other things, to generate ICC-profiles.

Spectrum   36
The visible part of light ranges from red tones (705nm) to blue-violet tones (385nm).

Spot colors   106, 107, 104
Printing inks of special colors, for example from the PMS system. Are generally used as a complement to black or to achieve an exact color four-color inks cannot provide. Are mixed according to a recipe.

Square halftone dots   147
A screen can consist of square halftone dots instead of the more common round ones. The shape of the halftone dot provides the screen with its varying characteristics.

Stabilize   44
To assure that one or a system of units provide the same results con-

sistantly. Instability can be a result of mechanical or environmental errors, for example if the temperature and humidity requirements are not met.

Start-up cost
The cost for starting a process, for example the cost for a makeready in a printing press or an off press processing machine.

Stochastic screen 147
A screening method with varying distance between the halftone dots instead of size. Also called FM-screening.

Storage capacity 126
Describes how much memory is available on a particular storage medium, measured in megabytes.

Storage durability 119, 120
Describes how safe a media for data storage is and for how long it holds the information.

Storage media 119
Used to store digital files, storage media includes hard drives, floppy disks, CD's, etc.

Storage space
See Storage capacity.

Strata Studio 14
3D illustration program for from Strata.

Stream feeder 216
The part of the printing press that draws the paper into the printing press.

Stream feeder edge 216, 248
The edge of the paper that is first drawn into the printing press.

StuffIt 68
File compression program from Aladdin Systems.

Subtractive color system 38, 105
Color system that mixes colors by using a number of primary colors. The primary colors are generated because the wavelengths of white light are filtered: some are let through and some aren't. CMYK is a subtractive color system.

Suffix 312
Word- or file ending. Used for abbreviations at the end of the file name in order to determine different file types, for example xxx.pdf.

Suitcase 31
A common utility for typeface management. Allows you to activate fonts that you don't need while working without having to restart programs or keep them in the system folder. You can group fonts, something which allows you to, in one sweep, activate and deactivate all fonts belonging to a particular production or customer.

Surface bonding strength 207
A measurement of the paper surface strength. Important because the printing inks can cause the surface of the paper to flake off while printing.

SWOP 105, 186
Specifications for Web Offset Publications. Standard for defining printing inks in the United States. Compare to the European standard, the European Color Scale.

Symbol font 25
A font consisting of different symbols instead of letters, for example Zapf Dingbats.

Syquest 121
A removable, magnetic data storage disk which used to be very common in graphic production but is no longer produced.

System folder 27
This folder contains the computer's operating system. Without the operating system the computer cannot start.

T

Tail 239
The bottom part of a page, or the foot of the page, as opposed to the head of the page.

Tailor 182
A preflight program

TCP/IP 132
Transmission Control Protocol/Internet Protocol, network protocol used on the Internet and in local networks. The most standardized and commonly used network protocol.

Telecommunication 137
Data communication via the analog telecommunications network.

Terabyte
1,099,511,627,776 bytes.

Tertiary colors 39
If you mix secondary colors derived from primary colors, the result is tertiary colors, i.e. colors consisting of all three primary colors.

Test bar 172, 193, 220
See Color bar.

Test run 231
A small edition of a printed product printed before the full run.

Textile stitching
See Thread stitching.

Theoretical transmission speed 139
The theoretical transmission speed is a measurement of how fast you can (theoretically) transport data on a network.

Thread stitching 244
The traditional bookbinding method. You use folded sheets placed in sheet order but the backs of the sheets are not glued (as in glue binding) but stitched instead. Also called thread sewing.

Three-cylinder unit 216
The most common printing unit found in sheet-fed offset today. Consists of an impression cylinder, a rubber blanket cylinder and a plate cylinder.

Three-pass 96
Scanning technique that scans original artworks three times, i.e. one for each of the colors RGB.

Three-shot camera
Digital camera technique for exposing in three rounds, i.e. each component color is read one at a time. See Three-pass.

Three-up 171
See Many-up.

Thumbnail image 127
Small, low-resolution images created to facilitate identifying an image.

TIFF 65, 108
Tagged Image File Format, a common file format for digital images.

Tint area 105, 112, 169
An even color tone across a designated surface. For example a red, halftone-screened rectangle.

Tinting 226
When non-printing surfaces on the plate attract ink and become printing. For example, it may occur when the dampening solution is too hard and the pigments are dissolved in the water or when there is too little dampening solution in the ink-humidity balance.

Tonal range 43, 68, 145
The same thing as density range. The magnitude of tones that can be created in a certain type of medium, for example in a scanner, in an original image or in a print. Also see Color range.

Tonal space 37, 70
Part of the tonal range.

Tonal step 37, 145
The difference between two tones.

Tonal transitions 143, 80, 186
Tonal transitions consist of transitions between a number of colors on certain distances. Tonal transitions can be linear or circular.

Tonal value
Describes the amount of a primary color, given as a percent.

Tone scale 76
All tones from 0 to 100% of a particular color.

Transmission speed 134
The speed at which data is transmitted, for example to or from a storage medium or over a network.

Trapping 223
A print phenomenon. Describes how well printing inks bond to each other. Printing inks printed on top of each other wet-on-wet don't bond 100%.

Trapping program
Program that executes traps in a documet, for example Trapwise from ScenicSoft.

Trapwise 110
Program from ScenicSoft that performs trapping on documents.

Tristimulus value
See CIE.

TrueType 30, 103
File type for fonts, is not based on PostScript.

Twin wire 204
The main drainage of the pulp stock in the paper machine takes place on the twin wire where the water is absorbed by two straining cloths.

Twisted-pair cable 131
A type of network cable.

Two-up 171
See Many-up.

Type area 239
The area inside the margins of a page where you normally would place the content.

Type Reunion 33
A utility from Adobe. Groups all fonts by family.

Typebook 27
A program that prints samples of fonts.

Typeface
The distinctive design of a set of type, distinguished from its weight, posture and type size.

Typeface samples
Printed samples of typefaces.

Typeface suitcase 27
A special folder in which all screen fonts of different versions and sizes are stored.

Typestyle 24
The weight or posture of a font, distinguished from a font's typeface design and type size.

Typography
To set and design text.

UCA 87
Under Color Addition. Special separation method. The black is added to areas of the images that should be really dark.

UCR 87
Under Color Removal.

UGRA/FOGRA bar 169, 193, 220
A utility consisting of different color fields; used to check the quality of the print and printing plate.

Ultraviolet light 37
For us humans, an invisible light situated closest to the violet colors of the spectrum, less than 385 nm. Has so much energy that the skin protects itself from it by getting tanned.

Unix 13
An operating system mainly used in powerful computers for special applications, for example image editing applications and servers.

Uppercase letters 25
Capital letters, as opposed to lowercase letters.

Variable data 232
Technique that enables you to change the content of each printed page at full printing speed. Is also called personalized printing.

Varnishing 247, 107
A technique used to add a glossy surface to a printed product. It does not provide noticeable protection against dirt and wear and tear, and is primarily an aesthetic procedure. The varnish is applied

by a regular inking unit or a special varnishing unit in an offset printing press.

Vector graphics 56
Images based on contours of short, straight lines. Was previously used for fonts. The term is sometimes erroneously used for object graphics or bezier curves.

Vector images 56
See Vector graphics.

Verso 171
The back side of the printed sheet. Compare to Recto.

Video board 17
A circuit board installed in the computer for enabling display of moving images on the screen.

Video data 123
Digital information about a moving image.

Viewing light 52
The light you view a photograph or printed product in. Affects color perception. A normal, neutral lighting has a color temperature of 5000K. It approximately corresponds to regular daylight and is therefore used as a reference light for images, proofs and prints.

Viscosity 214
A measurement of how viscous a liquid is.

VOC
Volatile organic compounds.

Volatile ink 229
Printing ink that dries quickly, used for gravure printing.

VRAM 19
In order to be able to work with moving or large images, the screen has to have a lot of video RAM, also called VRAM.

Water-free offset 215
Also called dry offset. A version of regular offset printing in which you use ink-repellent silicone instead of water for the non-printing surfaces. A special silicone-coated printing plate is used.

Wavelength 36
A physical measurement of the length of the light waves, measured in nanometer (nm). Visible light has wavelengths between 385 and 705 nm.

Web-fed offset 90
Offset method that feeds the paper from a roll as opposed to the paper sheets used in sheet-fed offset.

Wet offset 213
See Offset printing.

Wet-on-wet 223
To print the inks directly on top of each other before they have had time to dry, used in offset printing.

White point 77
The brightest tone in an image. Together with the black point, the white point controls the contrast of the image.

White-printing printer 172
A laser printer is white-printing if the laser beam describes the areas of the sheet that should not be coated with colors.

Windows 2000 13
An operating system from Microsoft.

Wire-o-binding 245
A type of spiral binding usually used for manuals and notepads.

Wood-free paper 203
Paper consisting of less than 10% mechanical pulp and more than 90% chemical pulp.

Wood-pulp paper 203
Paper consisting of more than 10% mechanical pulp and less than 90% chemical pulp.

Word 103, 14
A widely used word processing program from Microsoft.

WAN 131
Wide Area Network. Large network that connects various local networks.

WordPerfect   103, 14
Word processing program from
Corel.

Write head   120
Writing unit in a reader/printer
for data storage media, for
example CD-burners.

Write speed   119
The speed at which data is transferred and written to a data storage
medium.

WWW   138
World Wide Web. A way of
publishing pages utilizing multi-
media and hypertext links on the
Internet.

Xerographic process   169
A dry printing process that uses
the attracive forces of electric
charges to transfer toner to paper.
Is used in copy machines and laser
printers.

Z

Z-folder   240
A type of parallel folder.

Zip (1)   120
A removable, magnetic disk for
data storage, holds 100 megabyte.

Zip (2)   68
File compression program.

Zones/Zone-divided networks   135
A network can be divided into
zones in order to reduce network
traffic in various parts of the network. ■

SUFFIX LIST

▶ **SUFFIX**

Below is a list of frequently occurring file-name endings, so called suffix.
The suffix states what kind of file you're dealing with and you'll find them on all Windows-files and on some Macintosh-files.

Filename.ai	Adobe Illustrator format	Filename.pict	Pict-image (Mac-format)
Filename.art	Bezier file from Adobe Streamline (Illustrator format)	Filename.ppd	PostScript Printer Description-file
Filename.att	Email attachment (has lost its actual file suffix)	Filename.pm6	Adobe Pagemaker 6.X-file from PC-environment
Filename.bmp	Standard Windows pixel graphic	Filename.prn	PostScript-file from PC-environment
Filename.c	Cyan-file in a five-file EPS	Filename.ps	PostScript file
Filename.cdm	Corel metafile	Filename.psd	Photoshop format
Filename.cdr	Corel Draw-file	Filename.pub	Ventura-file
Filename.cgm	Computer Graphics Metafile (Unix)	Filename.qxp	QuarkXPress-file from PC-environment
Filename.dcs	A five-file EPS (DCS-file)	Filename.rtf	Rich Text Format--formatted text file in standard format
Filename.doc	Microsoft Word-file	Filename.sct	Scitex CT
Filename.eps	EPS-file from PC-environment	Filename.sea	Self-extracting compressed file from the compression program Stuffit.
Filename.exe	Program-file in PC-environment		
Filename.fh7	Freehand 7.X-file	Filename.sgm	SGML-coded text file
Filename.fon	Font-file	Filename.sgml	SGML-coded text file (Mac-format)
Filename.gif	Pixel graphic in Graphic Interchange Format	Filename.sit	Non-selfextracting compressed file from the compression program Stuffit.
Filename.htm	HTML-file		
Filename.html	HTML-file (Mac-environment)	Filename.skv	Text-file defined by semicolon
Filename.hqx	BinHex-compressed file	Filename.smp	Low-resolution OPI-image
Filename.jpe	JPEG-image from PC-environment	Filename.tga	Truevision Targa, 24 bits image-format
Filename.jpg	JPEG-image from PC-environment	Filename.tif	TIFF-image from PC-environment
Filename.jpeg	JPEG-image from Mac-environment	Filename.ttf	TrueType-font in PC-environment
Filename.k	Black file in a five-file EPS	Filename.txt	Raw text-file from PC-environment
Filename.lay	Low-resolution OPI-image	Filename.wmf	Windows Meta File-image
Filename.lzw	LZW-compressed image	Filename.wp	Word Perfect-file
Filename.m	Magenta file in a five-file EPS	Filename.wpg	Word Perfect graphic-format
Filename.pdf	PDF-file	Filename.xls	Microsoft Excel-file from PC-environment
Filename.pcd	Kodak PhotoCD	Filename.y	Yellow file in a five-file EPS
Filename.pct	Pict-image (PC-format)	Filename.z	Compressed Unix-file
Filename.pcx	Paint Brush-file	Filename.zip	Compressed file from the compression program ZIP
Filename.pfm	PostScript Type 1-font (PC-environment)		

THANKS!

Milou Allerholm
Magnus Almgren
Eva Anderson
Ida Andersson
Mats Andersson
Mattias Andersson
Lotta Bjurman
Mr Björn Carlsson
Ragnar Dybeck
Tomas Ek
Anders Ekberg
Johanna Ekberg
Peter Freund
Maria Gunnarsson
Jim Harper
Eva Henriksson
Joanna Hornatowska
Albert Håkansson
Erik Jarl
Morten Johansson
Roger »Ro-Jah« Johansson
Clas-Göran Jönsson
Andreas Karperyd
Petter Kolseth
Jaromir Korostenski
Göran Lindholm
Frank J Martinez
Helena Modéer
Johan Möller
Josef Obiols
Sandra Praun
Martin Sandolf
Lennart Stenius
Ulf Sunnberg
Erling Torfasson
Helena Wahlman

The students on KTH Grafisk Teknik -98

IGP AB
Bromma-Tryck AB
Colorcraft AB
Crossmedia AB
Magazine AB
Fälth & Hässler
Ciao Ciao

THE EDITORIAL ADVISORY BOARD

An essential part has been to provide the book with relevant and correct content. The book has been created in dialogue with an editorial advisory board consisting of representatives from universities, printers, advertising agencies, paper suppliers and publishers.

Björn Blanck
Sven Dolling
Nils Enlund
Patrick Geuder
Lotta Gill
Leif Handberg
Rebecka Lindberg
Fredrik Sjögren
Marika Taillefer

PRINT PRODUCTION

As a supplement to "A Guide to Graphic Print Production" there is a package of digital slides available on CD.

The CD is packed with 472 pages, with the most important illustrations, check lists and tables from the book in PDF-format.

This gives you the perfect tool for teaching based on the book.

Please visit www.kapero.com for more information.

http://www.kapero.com